MINITAB HANDBOOK
FOR BUSINESS
AND ECONOMICS

THE DUXBURY SERIES IN STATISTICS AND DECISION SCIENCES

MINITAB HANDBOOK FOR BUSINESS AND ECONOMICS

REVISED PRINTING

Robert B. Miller
University of Wisconsin—Madison

PWS-KENT Publishing Company
Boston

PWS–KENT
Publishing Company

20 Park Plaza
Boston, Massachusetts 02116

PWS-Kent Publishing Company is a division of Wadsworth, Inc.

Portions of this book previously appeared in *Minitab Handbook*, Second Edition, by Ryan/Joiner/Ryan, copyright © 1985 by PWS Publishers.

ISBN 0-534-92478-6
(previously ISBN 0-87150-092-2)

Minitab is a registered trademark of Minitab, Inc.

Printed in the United States of America.
2 3 4 5 6 7 8 9—93 92 91

Sponsoring Editor: *Michael Payne*
Production Coordinator: *Elise Kaiser*
Production: *Technical Texts, Inc.*
Composition: *Polyglot Pte. Ltd.*
Cover Printer: *New England Book Components*
Text Printer/Binder: *Halliday Lithograph*
Cover art copyright © 1987 by Julie Gecha.

PREFACE

This *Handbook* is designed to help you learn how to use Minitab to solve statistical problems in business and economics. Minitab is a general purpose statistical system that can be run in either interactive or batch mode, and on mainframe computers, minicomputers, or microcomputers. Minitab has evolved over the years from a classroom aid to a system that permits an analyst not only to do routine statistical tasks, but also to make creative use of plots, simulations, transformations, as well as exploratory analysis. Many companies, universities, and government agencies around the world make Minitab available to analysts, and even more will do so with the advent of personal computers. Minitab is easy to learn and easy to use. It is an ideal companion for the student or the worker faced with the need to analyze data and to formulate problems involving random variation.

Version 5 of Minitab is used in this book. Version 5 is a substantial revision of earlier versions. Some of the old commands have been dropped, and new ones have been added. If you have an older version of Minitab, you will be able to use this *Handbook*, but you will find some incompatibilities.

This *Handbook* is a close relative of the book *Minitab Handbook*, Second Edition, by Barbara F. Ryan, Brian L. Joiner, and Thomas A. Ryan, Jr. These authors approached me about the possibility of writing a handbook slanted toward business and economics applications. My reaction has been to retain, quite literally, the best features of their book, to try to improve on it where I thought I could, and to add discussion of topics that I thought would make the book appealing to people interested in statistical applications in business and economics. The biggest single addition is the material on time series analysis; the second biggest is an expansion of the material on simulation. Discussions with a number of people who teach statistics in business schools led me to believe that these topics deserved special attention. I was also encouraged to de-emphasize nonparametric statistics, and I have done so.

Another contribution I feel I have made is the inclusion of data sets with a business and economics flavor. Most of these data sets came to me through consulting or executive education experiences. I solicited the RESTAURANT data set in Chapter 4 from my colleague Bill Strang and received his permission to include it in both this book and the one by Ryan,

Joiner, and Ryan. Two or three of the data sets are artificial but are based on true stories. I hope their pedagogical value outweighs any drawbacks due to the artificiality. The fields of business and economics are rich in sources of data. I recommend that users of Minitab, or any other statistical system, not limit themselves to the data sets in this *Handbook* or any other instructional manual. Opportunity for the collection and analysis of primary data is plentiful, and the benefits of working with primary data are immense.

In this *Handbook* you will find two chapters devoted to simulation (Chapters 6 and 7) and two devoted to regression (Chapters 10 and 11). The first of each pair of chapters covers the basics, while the second of each pair covers more advanced topics. I have used this arrangement to try to make the book easy to use in the classroom. Another device with the same purpose is the presentation of elementary time series material in early chapters, where it can be worked into a unit on descriptive statistics. Chapter 12 covers identification, fitting, checking, and forecasting using ARIMA models. It illustrates how to do these things with Minitab, but it is not intended to teach these topics to a novice. The reader should have some training in these topics before tackling Chapter 12.

I would like to acknowledge the help of a number of people. My special thanks must go to Brian Joiner, Barbara Ryan, and Tom Ryan for inviting me to work on this book and for granting me permission to insert many sections of their book into mine. I am grateful to my editor, Michael Payne, for his encouragement, for gentle and gentlemanly prodding, and for not giving up. Those who have reviewed the manuscript have been helpful, particularly in making me aware of what the market is likely to bear. They are Richard Brock, California State University, Sacramento; Jonathan Cryer, University of Iowa; John McKenzie, Babson College; Richard Madsen, University of Missouri; David Pentico, Virginia Commonwealth University; James Scott, Creighton University; Lawrence Sher, University of Kansas; Bert Steece, University of Southern California; William Stewart, College of William and Mary; and Andrew Welki, John Carroll University. I offer a grateful word of thanks to Elise Kaiser and Betty O'Bryant, who have so cheerfully and competently seen to the all-important details of the editing and production.

Finally, my thanks go to my wife and children who helped with the reading of the proofs and proved to be very understanding of the eccentricities of an author.

For further information about the Minitab system contact:

Minitab, Inc.
3081 Enterprise Drive
State College, PA 16801
Telephone: 814/238-3280 #Telex: 881612

CONTENTS

MINITAB HANDBOOK
FOR BUSINESS
AND ECONOMICS

1/INTRODUCTION TO MINITAB

Minitab is an easy-to-use, general-purpose statistical computing system. It is flexible, powerful, and designed especially for people who have no previous experience with computers. In this chapter we discuss how Minitab works; and in the chapters that follow, we will show how Minitab can be used to solve various types of statistical problems. We begin with an example, then follow with an overview of what you need to know to use Minitab.

1.1/ A SIMPLE EXAMPLE

Table 1.1 lists the unemployment rates of Blacks and Whites in the United States for the 12 months of 1984. Our goals are to

1. calculate the ratio of Black to White unemployment rates for each month;
2. find the mean and standard deviation of the ratios for the 12 months;
3. make a histogram of the 12 ratios.

Minitab commands that perform these operations are shown in Exhibit 1.1. Notice that these commands are given in English, just about the same way you would tell someone to do the calculations by hand. Minitab stores the data in a worksheet that it maintains in the computer. The first command

```
READ THE FOLLOWING DATA INTO COLUMNS C1 AND C2
```

tells the computer to take the data from the lines that follow the READ command and put them into columns C1 and C2 of the worksheet. The command

```
END
```

1

TABLE 1.1   Unemployment Rates for
            U.S. Blacks and Whites,
            1984

	Unemployment Rates (seasonally adjusted)	
Month	Whites	Blacks
January	6.9	16.7
February	6.7	16.2
March	6.7	16.6
April	6.7	16.8
May	6.5	16.0
June	6.3	15.2
July	6.3	16.6
August	6.4	15.8
September	6.3	15.1
October	6.3	15.3
November	6.1	15.1
December	6.2	15.0

Source: U.S. Department of Commerce,
Survey of Current Business, Dec. 1984,
pp. 5–10.

EXHIBIT 1.1   Minitab Program for Unemployment Data

```
READ THE FOLLOWING DATA INTO COLUMNS C1 AND C2
6.9    16.7
6.7    16.2
6.7    16.6
6.7    16.8
6.5    16.0
6.3    15.2
6.3    16.6
6.4    15.8
6.3    15.1
6.3    15.3
6.1    15.1
6.2    15.0
END
LET C3 = C2/C1
PRINT C1, C2, C3
DESCRIBE C3
HISTOGRAM C3
```

signals the end of the data. Exhibit 1.2 shows the worksheet after the data are read.

The next command

```
LET C3 = C2/C1
```

says to divide column C2 of the worksheet by the corresponding entries in column C1 and store the ratios in column C3. Exhibit 1.3 shows the worksheet at this point. Column C3 now contains the ratios of the

---

EXHIBIT 1.2 Minitab's Worksheet after Reading the Data

C1	C2
6.9	16.7
6.7	16.2
6.7	16.6
6.7	16.8
6.5	16.0
6.3	15.2
6.3	16.6
6.4	15.8
6.3	15.1
6.3	15.3
6.1	15.1
6.2	15.0

EXHIBIT 1.3 Worksheet after LET Command

C1	C2	C3
6.9	16.7	2.42029
6.7	16.2	2.41791
6.7	16.6	2.47761
6.7	16.8	2.50746
6.5	16.0	2.46154
6.3	15.2	2.41270
6.3	16.6	2.63492
6.4	15.8	2.46875
6.3	15.1	2.39683
6.3	15.3	2.42857
6.1	15.1	2.47541
6.2	15.0	2.41935

unemployment rates for each month. The next three commands give printed output.

    PRINT C1-C3

says to print the contents of these three columns.

    DESCRIBE C3

says to calculate and print various descriptive statistics, including the average (or mean), of the numbers in C3.

    HISTOGRAM C3

says to print out a histogram of the numbers in C3. Output from these three commands is shown in Exhibit 1.4.

GETTING STARTED

To use Minitab, you must first learn a little bit about your computer system. Each one is different, so we cannot give you the exact details, but we can give you some general guidance.

Most people use Minitab on a computer terminal that consists of a screen and a keyboard. The screen is often called a CRT (for cathode-ray tube). Some people use typewriterlike terminals. These use paper in place of a screen. In both cases, you give the computer directions by typing them on the keyboard. Always check each line you've typed before you push the carriage return key. On most computers, you can correct errors by simply backspacing and retyping. Once the carriage return is pushed, however, it is usually more difficult to make corrections.

There is a third way to use a computer: with a keypunch machine and computer cards. This used to be the only way to use computers. Now most keypunches have been replaced by terminals, which are both friendlier and cheaper to use. If you are using Minitab with a keypunch, see your local computer experts for help.

Finally, you can use Minitab on a microcomputer. If you do, you may have to learn about floppy disks (they look like flexible records) and disk drives. However, you will still have a keyboard and a screen.

Thus, the first step is to learn about the equipment you will use: where it is located, how to turn it on, how the keyboard works, and so forth. You may have to connect the terminal to the computer with a telephone and a device called a modem. Then you must learn the correct telephone number. These are all minor details that are fairly easy to learn, although they can cause a lot of frustration at times.

There are two basic ways to use Minitab: in interactive mode and batch mode. Most people use interactive mode, which we will discuss in this chapter. If you are using Minitab in batch mode, see your local computer experts for help. Almost all Minitab commands work the same way in both modes.

EXHIBIT 1.4   Output from the Commands PRINT, DESCRIBE, and
HISTOGRAM

```
PRINT C1, C2, C3
  ROW      C1      C2        C3

    1     6.9    16.7    2.42029
    2     6.7    16.2    2.41791
    3     6.7    16.6    2.47761
    4     6.7    16.8    2.50746
    5     6.5    16.0    2.46154
    6     6.3    15.2    2.41270
    7     6.3    16.6    2.63492
    8     6.4    15.8    2.46875
    9     6.3    15.1    2.39683
   10     6.3    15.3    2.42857
   11     6.1    15.1    2.47541
   12     6.2    15.0    2.41935

DESCRIBE C3

                  N      MEAN    MEDIAN    TRMEAN    STDEV    SEMEAN
   C3            12    2.4601    2.4451    2.4490   0.0645    0.0186

                MIN       MAX        Q1        Q3
   C3         2.3968    2.6349    2.4183    2.4771

HISTOGRAM C3

Histogram of C3   N = 12

Midpoint    Count
    2.40       4    ****
    2.44       2    **
    2.48       4    ****
    2.52       1    *
    2.56       0
    2.60       0
    2.64       1    *
```

The second step is to get on (often called logon or login) to your computer. You may need an account number, an identification number, and a password. You will have to learn exactly what to type, and you may have to type everything very carefully and in what seems to be a strange form. Once you have logged-on, you are in what's usually called the computer's operating system.

The third step is to ask to use Minitab. This may involve nothing more than typing the word Minitab. In any case, it should be very simple. At this point, you are in Minitab. You can now type the commands in this book.

USING MINITAB YOURSELF

In Exhibit 1.5 you see a complete Minitab session conducted on an IBM AT computer at the University of Wisconsin School of Business. To help you see what is going on, all commands typed by the user are highlighted. In the actual run the output in Exhibit 1.5 appeared on the monitor screen. It was then printed to make the exhibit and step numbers were added to make the discussion below easier to follow.

In this example the computer has already been turned on. The operating system issues the prompt C: \> and waits for the user's response. The user types MINITAB (step 1 in Exhibit 1.5). This activates a batch program that has been stored in the computer's memory. The steps numbered 2, 3, 4, and 5 in the exhibit are automatically issued from this batch program. They change the directory to\MINITAB MYDATA and then activate Minitab. This results in an introductory message from Minitab, step 6, and then a prompt MTB >. This says that Minitab expects a command. The command READ C1 C2 is issued by the user. After typing the command, checking for mistakes, and correcting mistakes, if any, the user pushes the return key. Now Minitab expects data and prompts with DATA>. The user types the first line of data, checks for errors, and pushes the return key. Two other lines of data are entered in this way. The END command (step 11) tells Minitab that data entry is complete, so Minitab issues an MTB > prompt.

In step 12, two columns are added together by using the LET command. In step 13 the LET is misspelled, and since LTT is not a Minitab command, Minitab issues an error message. The command is typed correctly in step 14. These steps illustrate an advantage of interactive computing: a mistake can be corrected immediately. In batch computing, a job must be submitted and the output retrieved before error reports can be read. Then the errors must be corrected and the job resubmitted.

In step 15 the user issues a PRINT command, and in step 16 Minitab prints the output on the monitor screen. The user ends the run with the command STOP in step 17, and Minitab sends a sign-off message in step 18. At this point the operating system of the computer takes control.

At times you will want output on paper. Just type the word PAPER. Output from all the commands that you type after the PAPER command will be put into a computer file to be printed later. You can stop this process at any time by typing the word NOPAPER, and you can restart it by typing PAPER again. At the end of your session, after you type STOP, everything that you put into your file will be printed on paper, provided that your computer is connected with a printer.

An alternative that is often more convenient when using a microcomputer is the OUTFILE command. Suppose you want to send output

EXHIBIT 1.5   Example of a Minitab Session

```
C:\> MINITAB      (1)

C:\> PROMPT $P $G      (2)

C:\> PATH = C:\MINITAB      (3)

C:\> CD\MINITAB\MYDATA      (4)

C:\MINITAB\MYDATA >MINITAB      (5)
MINITAB RELEASE 5.1.1 *** COPYRIGHT - MINITAB, INC. 1986      (6)
U.S. FEDERAL GOVERNMENT USERS SEE HELP FGU
DEC. 26, 1986 *** Minitab for MS-DOS micros
STORAGE AVAILABLE 16279

MTB > READ  C1  C2      (7)
DATA> 8 3      (8)
DATA> 10 2      (9)
DATA> 5 6      (10)
DATA> END      (11)
      3 ROWS READ
MTB > LET C3=C1+C2      (12)
MTB > LTT C4=C1-C2      (13)
* ERROR * NAME NOT FOUND IN DICTIONARY

MTB > LET C4=C1-C2      (14)
MTB > PRINT C1 C2 C3 C4      (15)
  ROW     C1     C2     C3     C4  ⎫
                                   ⎪
    1      8      3     11      5  ⎬  (16)
    2     10      2     12      8  ⎪
    3      5      6     11     -1  ⎭

MTB > STOP      (17)
*** Minitab Release 5.1.1 *** Minitab, Inc. ***      (18)
Storage available 16279
```

from Minitab to a file named BANK. LIS on a floppy disk in disk drive A:.
In response to a Minitab prompt, just type OUTFILE 'A: BANK. LIS' and
push the return key. The output from all subsequent commands will go to
the file as well as show up on the monitor. To stop this process, just type
NOOUTFILE. You can restart it by typing OUTFILE 'A: BANK. LIS'.
Subsequent output will be added to the file until another NOOUTFILE
command is issued. Later, after you STOP the Minitab run, you may

access the file A: BANK. LIS with your word processor, edit it, and then print it out.

1.2 / A BRIEF OVERVIEW OF MINITAB

Minitab consists of a worksheet where data are stored and about 150 commands. In the worksheet, you can store columns of data and single-number constants. The columns are denoted by C1, C2, C3, ... and may have names. The stored constants are denoted by K1, K2, K3, ... The total worksheet area and the number of columns and stored constants available to you depend on your particular computer. On some computers the worksheet is enormous; on others it is quite restricted. The total area that you have is printed when you use Minitab.

When you want Minitab to analyze data, you type the appropriate commands. There are commands to read, edit, and print data, to do plots and histograms, to do arithmetic and transformations, and to do various statistical analyses such as *t*-tests, regression, and analysis of variance. A brief summary of all Minitab commands is given in Appendix C.

SOME RULES

1.   Every command starts with a command name, such as READ or HISTOGRAM. On most commands, this is followed by arguments. An argument is either a column number (such as C10), a column name (such as 'HEIGHT'), a constant (such as 75.34), a stored constant (such as K15), or the name of a computer file.

2.   Only the first four letters of the command name and the arguments, which must be in the proper order, are used by Minitab. Other text may be added for annotation, if you wish. However, we recommend that you use only letters and commas for this extra text. Never use numbers or symbols such as ; : – * & or +, since these are used in special ways by Minitab. Using these rules, the command

READ FOLLOWING DATA INTO COLUMNS C1 AND C2

could be written as

READ DATA INTO C1 AND C2

or simply as

READ C1 C2

We could not have written

READ 1ST SCORE INTO C1 AND 2ND INTO C2

since the extra text contains a 1 in 1ST and 2 in 2ND. Minitab would try to use these as arguments.

3. A list of consecutive columns or stored constants may be abbreviated by using a dash. For example, you could use

    READ C2-C5

    instead of

    READ C2, C3, C4, C5

4. Columns and stored constants may be reused any number of times. If you store new data in a column or stored constant, the previous contents are automatically erased.

5. If you type a number, do not use commas within the number. Thus, type 1041 instead of 1,041.

6. Each command must start on a new line. You need not start in the first space, however. If the entire command will not fit on one line, end the first line with the ampersand symbol (&) and continue the command onto the next line. For example,

    PRINT C2, C4-C20, C25, C26, C30, C33 &
    C35-C40, C42, C50

Minitab commands are described throughout this *Handbook* in a box like this one. In these descriptions, the symbol C can be replaced by any column name or number, K by any constant, and E by either a column or a constant. Arguments in square brackets are optional. Any extra text used to help explain the commands is written in lower-case. Here are some examples.

PRINT the data in C

You could replace C by C18, omit the extra text, and get

    PRINT C18

PRINT E, ..., E

This says you may print any list of columns and constants. For example,

    PRINT C1 C4 C2 K1-K4

Sum C [put into K]

Here storage in K is optional. If you use the form

    SUM C10

then Minitab calculates and prints the sum of all the numbers in C10. If you type

    SUM C10 store in K1

then Minitab stores the sum in K1 but does not print it.

1.3 / SOME BASIC MINITAB CAPABILITIES

This section introduces the basic capabilities of Minitab and makes it possible for you to write simple Minitab programs of your own. More information on basic capabilities is given in Appendices B and C.

INPUT AND OUTPUT OF DATA

Both the commands READ and SET let you type data into Minitab's worksheet. The difference between them is how you type the data: READ expects data one row at a time, whereas SET expects it one column at a time.

Exhibit 1.1 (p. 2) showed how to use READ to enter data into columns C1 and C2. Here is how to use SET.

```
SET into C1
6.9 6.7 6.7 6.7 6.5 6.3
6.3 6.4 6.3 6.3 6.1 6.2
END
SET into C2
16.7 16.2 16.6 16.8 16.0 15.2
16.6 15.8 15.1 15.3 15.1 15.0
END
```

The first SET puts the 12 numbers that follow it into C1. The second SET puts the 12 numbers that follow it into C2. After these two SETs, the worksheet looks exactly the same as it did in Exhibit 1.2. When you enter data, use whichever command you prefer. Sometimes SET will be easier, and sometimes READ will be.

As you type the data, check each line before pushing the carriage return on your terminal. If you notice an error, you can probably backspace and correct it. When you finish typing all your data, we suggest that you print out a copy with the PRINT command. Again, check for errors. If you find an error, say in C2, then you could use SET to reenter all the data in C2, or you could use the special commands described on pages 13–14 to correct the data.

READ the following data into C, ..., C

This command is followed by lines of data. Each line of data is put into one row of the worksheet.

EXAMPLE

```
READ C2 C3 C5
   1   3   980
   3   0  1430
   2   4  2190
END
```

Following this, the worksheet contains

C1	C2	C3	C4	C5
	1.0	3.0		980
	3.0	0.0		1430
	2.0	4.0		2190

Numbers can be put anywhere on a line as long as they are in the correct order. Numbers must be separated by blanks or commas. (More details are on p. 293.)

SET the following data into C

This command is followed by lines of data. You may put as many numbers as you want on one line, and you may use as many lines as you want. All the numbers will go into the same column.

EXAMPLE

```
SET C3
   1.5  2     6.3 2 1
   6.23 5.01
END
```

Following this, C3 will contain the seven numbers: 1.5, 2.0, 6.3, 2.0, 1.0, 6.23, and 5.01.

Numbers can be put anywhere on a line as long as they are in the correct order. Numbers must be separated by blanks or commas. No numbers may be put on the SET line itself. (More details are on p. 294.)

END of data

Type this command after typing the data for READ or SET.

PRINT E, ..., E

EXAMPLES

```
PRINT C1-C4 C10
PRINT K2 K4 K6
PRINT C20
```

This command may be used to print columns or constants that have been stored in the worksheet.

STORED CONSTANTS

Any operation that results in a single-number answer can put that number into a stored constant. The stored constant may then be used in place of a number on any command. SUM is a command that results in a one-number answer. If C1 contains the numbers 5, 3, 6, and 2, then SUM C1 calculates $5 + 3 + 6 + 2 = 16$. Since the answer is one number, we can store it in a constant. Here is an example:

```
SET   C1
   5, 3, 6, 2
END
SUM C1, PUT IN K1
LET K2 = 4
LET K3 = K1+K2-8
PRINT K1-K3
```

DOING ARITHMETIC WITH LET

The LET command makes it easy to do very complicated calculations. In most data analysis, however, you will use just simple forms of this command. Here, we give a brief introduction to LET.

LET uses the following symbols:

+ for add
− for subtract
* for multiply
/ for divide
** for raise to a power (exponentiation)

EXAMPLE

```
LET K1 = 3
LET K2 = 5*13
LET K3 = K1+K2+4
SET C1
   4 6 5 2
END
LET C2 = 2*C1
LET C3 = K1*C1
LET C4 = C2+1
LET C5 = C3+C4
LET C6 = C1**2
```

After these commands, K1 = 3, K2 = 65, and K3 = 72. The following table shows what C1-C6 contain.

C1	C2	C3	C4	C5	C6
4	8	12	9	21	16
6	12	18	13	31	36
5	10	15	11	26	25
2	4	6	5	11	4

Parentheses may be used for grouping. For example,

```
READ C1 C2
    8   1
    6   3
    4   4
END
LET C3 = 10*(C1+C2)
LET C4 = 10*C1+C2
LET C5 = C1/C2+1
LET C6 = C1/(C2+1)
```

At this point the worksheet contains

C1	C2	C3	C4	C5	C6
8	1	90	81	9	4.0
6	3	90	63	3	1.5
4	4	80	44	2	.8

Note that the expressions for C3 and C4 look similar, as do those for C5 and C6; but the results are not the same. LET follows the usual precedence rules of arithmetic; that is, operations within parentheses are always performed first, then **, then * and /, and finally + and −. If you are not sure of the sequence of a calculation, you can always use parentheses to make sure it is done right.

LET E = arithmetic expression

An arithmetic expression may be made up of columns and constants and arithmetic symbols (+ − */**) and parentheses. Unlike other Minitab commands, no extra text may be used on a LET line (except as discussed on p. 306). LET can be used to correct numbers (see below). LET can be used to evaluate very complicated expressions (see p. 40 and Section B.3).

CORRECTING DATA IN THE WORKSHEET

Three commands are useful for correcting numbers that you have already entered in the worksheet: LET, DELETE, and INSERT. Exhibit 1.6 shows a worksheet that contains two errors: one number is wrong and one line is omitted. The number in row 3 of C1 should be 1.3, not 3.1. To correct it, we use a special feature of the LET command:

```
LET C1(3) = 1.3
```

To change one number in C1, just type C1, then the row number enclosed in parentheses. Exhibit 1.6 shows the worksheet after LET was used.

EXHIBIT 1.6   Correcting Data in the Worksheet

Worksheet Should Be		But It Was Typed As		After LET		After INSERT	
C1	*C2*	*C1*	*C2*	*C1*	*C2*	*C1*	*C2*
1.5	102	1.5	102	1.5	102	1.5	102
1.7	106	1.7	106	1.7	106	1.7	106
1.3	120	3.1	120	1.3	120	1.3	102
1.4	118	1.4	118	1.4	118	1.4	118
1.5	101	1.5	102	1.5	102	1.5	101
2.1	130	1.1	124	1.1	124	2.1	130
1.1	124					1.1	124

The line containing 2.1, 130 was left out. It should be put between rows 5 and 6. To insert this line, we use

```
INSERT BETWEEN ROWS 5 AND 6 OF C1, C2
   2.1, 130
END
```

INSERT between rows K and K of C, ..., C

This command inserts rows of data into the worksheet. The data are typed following the INSERT line. The row numbers K and K must be consecutive integers. (The second K is redundant but helps avoid errors.)

To put rows of data at the tops of columns, use

```
INSERT between rows 0 and 1 of C,...,C
```

To add rows of data to the end of columns, omit the two row numbers and use

```
INSERT into C,...,C
```

If you insert data into just one column, then you may string the data across the data lines, as in SET.

DELETE rows K, ..., K of C, ..., C

Deletes the indicated data and closes up the worksheet. You may abbreviate a list of consecutive rows by using a colon. For example,

```
DELETE 1:10, 25:30 C1
```

would delete rows 1 through 10 and 25 through 30 from C1.

HOW TO NAME COLUMNS

Any column may be given a name. The name serves two purposes:

1. The column may be referenced by its name. It is often easier to remember the name of a variable than the number of a column.

2. All output is labeled with the name.

Many users find that naming columns takes a little extra time but pays off in the long run by making output easier to read.

NAME C = 'name', C = 'name', ..., C = 'name'

A name may be from one to eight characters long. Any characters may be used, with two exceptions—a name may not begin or end with a blank and a name may not contain the symbol ' (called an apostrophe or single quote). Either the column number or its name may be used in any succeeding command. When column names are used, they must be enclosed in single quotes (apostrophes). The name of a column can be changed by using another NAME command.

EXAMPLE

```
NAME C1 = 'HEIGHT', C2 = 'L+W'
PRINT 'HEIGHT' C2
```

ENDING A SESSION

STOP

If you use Minitab in interactive mode, type STOP when you are finished using Minitab. After typing STOP you will be in your computer's operating system.

If you use Minitab in batch mode, STOP should be the last Minitab command in your program.

1.4 / ANOTHER EXAMPLE: PAID VACATION

Mean numbers of paid vacation days for professional and administrative employees in medium-sized and large firms in 1982 are given in Exhibit 1.7. We want to see how the mean number of paid vacation days changes with number of years of service.

EXHIBIT 1.7   Paid Vacation Days for Professional and Administrative
              Employees in Medium-Sized and Large Firms, 1982

After	*Mean Number of Paid Vacation Days*
1 year	10.3
3 years	11.0
5 years	13.2
10 years	16.3
15 years	18.7
20 years	21.0
25 years	22.7

Source: Bureau of the Census, *Statistical Abstract of the United States*, Washington, D.C.: U.S. Department of Commerce, 1984, p. 437.

EXHIBIT 1.8   Minitab Commands to Analyze Paid Vacation Data

```
READ INTO C1 AND C2
  1 10.3
  3 11.0
  5 13.2
 10 16.3
 15 18.7
 20 21.0
 25 22.7
END
NAME C1 'YROFSERV' C2 'VACA.DAY'
PRINT C1 AND C2
PLOT C2 VS C1
SET INTO C3
2 2 5 5 5 5
END
NAME C3 'INC.YR'
LET C4 = C2
DELETE ROW 1 OF C2
DELETE ROW 7 OF C4
LET C5 = C2-C4
NAME C5 'INC.DAY'
PRINT C1-C5
LET C6 = C5/C3
NAME C6 'DAY/YR'
DELETE ROW 1 OF C1
PLOT C6 VS C1
```

Exhibit 1.8 shows Minitab commands to do this analysis. The first command puts the data into columns of the worksheet. Next we give names to the columns containing the data. The next two commands print and plot the data. The output is in Exhibit 1.9. We see from the plot that while the mean number of vacation days increases with years of service, the rate of increase slows slightly for the longer service times.

We can quantify the rate of increase by calculating the ratio of the increase in paid vacation days to the increase in years of service. The

---

EXHIBIT 1.9   Paid Vacation Data: Output from PRINT and
                 PLOT Commands

```
PRINT C1-C5
  ROW   YROFSERV   VACA. DAY   INC. YR     C4    INC. DAY

   1        1        11. 0        2       10. 3      0. 7
   2        3        13. 2        2       11. 0      2. 2
   3        5        16. 3        5       13. 2      3. 1
   4       10        18. 7        5       16. 3      2. 4
   5       15        21. 0        5       18. 7      2. 3
   6       20        22. 7        5       21. 0      1. 7
   7       25

PLOT C6 C1

  DAY/YR   -
           -        *
           -
   1. 00+
           -
           -
           -
           -
   0. 75+
           -
           -             *
           -
   0. 50+
           -                  *
           -                       *
           -    *
           -                                     *
   0. 25+
         +---------+---------+---------+---------+------YROFSERV
         0. 0      10. 0     15. 0     20. 0     25. 0
```

increases in years of service are most easily calculated by inspection and
SET into column C3 with commands

```
SET INTO C3
2 2 5 5 5 5
END
NAME C3 'INC.YR'
```

EXHIBIT 1.10   Calculation and Plot of Increase in Paid Vacation Days
and Increase in Years of Service

```
PRINT C1-C5
 ROW   YROFSERV   VACA.DAY   INC.YR    C4   INC.DAY

   1        1       11.0        2     10.3    0.7
   2        3       13.2        2     11.0    2.2
   3        5       16.3        5     13.2    3.1
   4       10       18.7        5     16.3    2.4
   5       15       21.0        5     18.7    2.3
   6       20       22.7        5     21.0    1.7
   7       25

PLOT C6 C1

DAY/YR  -
        -          *
        -
  1.00+
        -
        -
        -
        -
  0.75+
        -
        -
        -          *
        -
  0.50+                         *
        -                            *
        -
        -   *                               *
        -
  0.25+
          +---------+---------+---------+---------+------YROFSERV
         0.0       5.0      10.0      15.0      20.0
```

We calculate the increases in paid vacation days with the commands

```
LET C4 = C2
DELETE ROW 1 OF C2
DELETE ROW 7 OF C4
LET C5 = C2-C4
NAME C5 'INC.DAY'
PRINT C1-C5
```

Columns C1–C5 are printed out to show the results of the calculations. The output is in Exhibit 1.10. Column C4 is simply C2 "shifted down" to allow the calculation of the increase in paid vacation days in C5. The calculation of the required ratios is accomplished with the commands

```
LET C6 = C5/C3
NAME C6 'DAY/YR'
```

Finally, to plot the rates of increase versus years of service, we issue the commands

```
DELETE ROW 1 OF C1
PLOT C6 VS C1
```

The plot is shown in Exhibit 1.10. We see that the largest rate of increase occurs between 3 and 5 years of service, the lowest between 20 and 25 years of service.

1.5 / MORE INFORMATION ON MINITAB

HELP ON MINITAB COMMANDS

Information about Minitab is stored in the computer. If you forget how to use a command, you can ask Minitab for help. For example, to find out about the command SET, type

```
HELP SET
```

Minitab will respond with a brief explanation of SET.

In general, to get help on a command, type HELP followed by the command name. To find out about other help you can get from Minitab, type

```
HELP HELP
```

SAVED WORKSHEETS

Saved worksheets are a very convenient way to store data in a computer file for use in Minitab. The following example creates a file called VACATION, containing the data in Exhibit 1.7.

```
READ C1 AND C2
     1   10.3
     3   11.0
     5   13.2
    10   16.3
    15   18.7
    20   21.0
    25   22.7
END
NAME C1 'YROFSERV' C2 'VACA.DAY'
SAVE 'VACATION'
```

Before we typed SAVE, we gave names to two columns. These names are also stored in the file VACATION. Any time later, either in the same session or in another session, we can put these data and names back into Minitab's worksheet by typing

```
RETRIEVE 'VACATION'
```

After RETRIEVE, Minitab's worksheet is exactly the same as it was when SAVE was typed. After you RETRIEVE a worksheet, you can find out what is in it by typing the command INFO.

SAVE the worksheet in 'filename'

Puts the entire Minitab worksheet into a computer file. The file will contain all columns, stored constants, and column names. This file can be input by Minitab's RETRIEVE command. The filename must be enclosed in single quotes (apostrophes).

One drawback with Minitab saved worksheets is that only Minitab can read them. You cannot use your computer's editor to print them or modify them. You cannot use them with other programs. However, saved worksheets are a very convenient way to store data for further Minitab analyses.

Caution: File usage and naming conventions vary enormously from computer to computer. You should check with someone who knows your local computer system if you have any difficulty using SAVE and RETRIEVE.

RETRIEVE the worksheet stored in 'filename'

Inputs data from a saved worksheet. After using RETRIEVE, the worksheet will contain the same columns, stored constants, and column names it had when SAVE was used to create the file.

Note: Anything you might have in the worksheet when you type RETRIEVE is erased before the saved worksheet is brought in.

EXHIBIT 1.11   Example of INFO Command Using VACATION Data on
Page 16

```
RETRIEVE 'VACATION'
INFO

COLUMN        NAME          COUNT
C1            YROFSERV        7
C2            VACA. DAY       7


CONSTANTS USED:   NONE
```

MANAGING THE WORKSHEET

Occasionally, you may forget what you have in the worksheet. The INFO
command can help you. See Exhibit 1.11.

INFORMATION on status of the worksheet

Prints a list of all columns used, the number of values in each, the name of
each (if they have been named), and a list of all stored constants used.

You may erase columns and constants that you no longer need.
Sometimes you may need to do this because you run out of space. On other
occasions, you will want to do it to reduce unnecessary clutter.

ERASE E, ..., E

You may erase any combination of columns and stored constants. For
example

```
ERASE C2 C5-C9 K1-K7 C20
```

SUBCOMMANDS

Some Minitab commands have subcommands. These allow more control
over the way the command works. For example, the HISTOGRAM
command will automatically choose a scale for the display, but if you want
a different scale, you can specify your own by using the subcommands
INCREMENT and START. An example follows.

```
HISTOGRAM C1;
   INCREMENT 10;
   START 0.
```

The specific details of these two subcommands will be described on page 30. Here we are interested in describing the syntax. To use a subcommand, end the main command line with a semicolon. The semicolon tells Minitab that there will be a subcommand on the next line. End each subcommand line with a semicolon until you are finished typing subcommands. Then end the last subcommand line with a period. Minitab waits until it sees the period to start doing the calculations.

If you accidentally forget to end the last subcommand with a period, you can put the period on the next line. For example,

```
HISTOGRAM C1;
   INCREMENT 10;
   START 0;
   .
```

Always begin each subcommand on a new line. You may type the subcommand anywhere on the line. We often indent subcommands for clarity.

Occasionally, you will discover an error after entering a subcommand in interactive mode. In this case, type ABORT as the next subcommand. This will cancel the whole command. You can then start over again with the main command.

MISSING DATA CODE

Many data sets are missing one or more observations. When you enter these data with READ, SET, or INSERT, type the asterisk symbol (*) in place of the missing value. For example,

```
READ C1 C2
   28   5.6
   24   5.2
   25   *
   24   51
END
```

All Minitab commands automatically take the * into account when they do an analysis.

Sometimes you enter data into the worksheet, discover that a value is wrong, and have no way to find out the correct value. You could change this value to *, using a special feature of LET. For example, if the wrong value is the fifth number in C18, use

```
LET C18(5) = '*'
```

Notice: You must enclose the asterisk in single quotes (apostrophes) when using it with LET. The missing data code is explained more fully in Appendix B.

EXERCISES

1–1   The following program calculates the average improvement in reading scores for the eight students in a reading improvement class. Each data line corresponds to one student; the first number is the "before" score and the second number the "after" score.

```
READ INTO C1, C2
   10      12
   10      14
    8      11
    6      15
    8      10
   11      12
    8      12
   12      15
LET C3 = C2-C1
DESCRIBE C3
PRINT C1, C2, C3
STOP
```

    (a)   Pretend that you are Minitab and carry out all the steps of the program. Keep a worksheet as you go along. What does the worksheet contain at the end of the program? What is printed out?

    (b)   Run this program on the computer.

1–2 *(a)*   Write a Minitab program to print out a table of squares and square roots of the integers from 1 to 20.

    (b)   Run the program.

1–3 *(a)*   Suppose you have the following data for the students in a small class.

Student Identification Number	Grade on Exam 1	Grade on Exam 2	Grade on Exam 3
23651	92	82	96
23658	84	84	80
23690	75	79	83
22100	98	60	72
23101	62	55	40
23400	79	72	81
23121	81	70	78

    A student's grade in this course is simply the average of the three exam grades. Write a Minitab program that (1) prints out a list containing each student's identification number followed by the course grade and (2) finds the class average for each exam and for the course grades (Why can the DESCRIBE command be used in part 2 but not in part 1?)

(b)   Run the program.

1–4   What is wrong with each of the following commands?
(a)   READ 1ST SCORE INTO C1, 2ND SCORE INTO C2
(b)   LET C10 = C5*2,431
(c)   SET DATA INTO COLUMNS C1 AND C2
(d)   READ DATA INTO COLUMNS 1 AND 2

1–5   Write and run a program to find the area of a circle of radius 15, using stored constants.

1–6   Pretend that you are the computer and work through the following program:

```
NAME C1 = 'RATES'
SET INTEREST RATES INTO 'RATES'
0.05  0.06  0.04
LET C2 = C1+1.0
LET C3 = 1.0/C2
NOTE DISCOUNT FACTORS IN C3
LET K1 = C3(1)
LET K2 = C3(2)
LET K3 = C3(3)
LET K4 = K1*K2*K3
PRINT K4
NOTE   PRESENT VALUE OF 1 DUE
NOTE   THREE YEARS HENCE WHEN
NOTE   ANNUAL INTEREST RATES
NOTE   ARE 0.05, 0.06, AND 0.04.
STOP
```

1–7   *(a)*   Pretend that you are Minitab and carry out the steps of the following program. What does the worksheet contain at the end of the program? What is printed out? What have you calculated?

```
SET INTO C1
5  3  4  1  6  2  1  2
SUM C1, PUT IN C2
LET C3 = C2/8.0
PRINT C3
STOP
```

(b)   Run the program.

1–8   *(a)*   The United States may soon convert to the metric system. Write a Minitab program that converts feet to meters. In particular, print a table that gives the distance in feet and the corresponding distance in meters for 1, 2, . . . , 50 feet. (Multiply the number of feet by 0.3048 to get the number of meters.)

(b) Run the program.

1-9 (a) Write a Minitab program that produces a table giving the temperature in degrees Fahrenheit (from 20° to 80°F) and the equivalent temperature in degrees Celsius. To convert from degrees Fahrenheit to degrees Celsius, first subtract 32. Then multiply this result by 5, then divide by 9. This is given by the formula $C = (F - 32)(5/9)$.

(b) Run the program.

1-10 Data on mean number of paid vacation days for technical and clerical employees and for production employees are given below. Repeat the analysis of Section 1.4 for these employees. Compare the characteristics of the different groups.

	Type of Employee	
After	Technical and Clerical	Production
1 year	9.5	7.6
3 years	10.4	10.1
5 years	12.8	11.9
10 years	15.8	15.3
15 years	18.5	17.7
20 years	20.6	20.2
25 years	22.5	21.9

Source: Bureau of the Census, *Statistical Abstract of the United States*, Washington, D.C.: U.S. Department of Commerce, 1984, p. 437.

2/ONE-VARIABLE DISPLAYS AND SUMMARIES

Much can be learned from data by looking at appropriate plots and tables. Sometimes such displays are all we need to answer our questions. In other, more borderline, cases they will help guide us to appropriate follow-up procedures. In fact, one great advantage of computers is their ability to make a variety of data displays quickly and easily. In this chapter we introduce some of the most useful displays and some simple summary measures, such as the mean and median.

We begin with a description of three basic types of data because the type of analysis you should use depends on the type of data you have.

2.1/THREE BASIC TYPES OF DATA

Not all numbers are created equal. Categorical data act merely as names; they tell us nothing about order or size. Ordinal data tell us about order but not about size. Interval data give information about size as well as order.

CATEGORICAL DATA. Simple examples of categorical variables are sex, which has two values (male and female), and state in the United States, which has fifty values (Alabama, Alaska, ..., Wyoming). When such data are stored in the computer, they often are converted to numbers. This is usually just for the convenience of the computer. Sex might be coded 1 = male and 2 = female, or as 1 = female and 2 = male, or even as 1410 = male and 2063 = female. State might be coded in alphabetical order, going from 1 = Alabama to 50 = Wyoming.

One problem with computers is that they will do what you ask—even if it is nonsense. For example, a computer will average categorical data, even though that average probably does not have any meaning. Suppose, for exmple, you have a data set of 30 men (coded 1) and 70 women (coded

2). A computer will calculate the average sex as 1.7. With computers, as with other tools, it is up to you to see that they are used properly. One of the goals of this book is to help you do this.

Categorical data are also called nominal data, classification data, or enumerate data.

ORDINAL DATA. One example is army rank: private, corporal, sergeant, lieutenant, major, colonel, and general. We know that a general is one rank higher than a colonel and a corporal is one rank higher than a private. But is the distance from private to corporal the same as the distance from colonel to general? Does distance between army ranks really have any meaning? Probably not.

Perhaps the most common occurrence of ordinal data is in surveys and questionnaires. For example,

"The President is doing a good job." Check one:

Strongly   Strongly
Disagree   Disagree   Indifferent   Agree   Agree

When entered into the computer, ordinal data usually are converted to numbers. For example, 1 = strongly disagree, 2 = disagree, ..., 5 = strongly agree. Here we would know that a 4 was more favorable toward the President than a 3, but we would not have any clear idea how much more favorable.

INTERVAL DATA. These usually are based on measurements such as length, weight, or time. On an interval scale, 4 is halfway between 3 and 5. For example, the difference between a 4-centimeter rod and a 3-centimeter rod is the same as the difference between a 5-centimeter rod and a 4-centimeter rod. Unlike categorical and ordinal data, interval data occur naturally as numbers.

EXERCISE

2-1 For each of the following, indicate whether the data are best considered as nominal, ordinal, or interval, and justify your choice.

(a) The response of a patient to treatment: none, some improvement, complete recovery.

(b) The style of a house: split-level, one-story, two-story, other.

(c) Income in dollars.

(d) Temperature of a liquid.

(e) Area of a parcel of land.

(f) Highest political office held by a candidate.

(g) Grade of meat: prime, choice, good, or utility.

(h) Political party.

2.2 / HISTOGRAMS

Exhibit 2.1 lists data on 50 orders placed with a manufacturing firm. The data are times (in days) elapsed from receiving to filling the orders. Exhibit 2.2 gives the output from Minitab's HISTOGRAM command. Minitab grouped the times into 11 intervals, each of width 10. The first interval has a midpoint of 30, goes from 25.5 to 35.5, and contains one observation. The second interval has a midpoint of 40, goes from 35.5 to 45.5, and contains three observations.

A histogram gives a graphical summary of the data. In Exhibit 2.2, we

---

EXHIBIT 2.1   Times Elapsed from Receiving to Filling Orders

28	68	78	91	107
42	71	80	91	108
43	71	81	94	108
44	71	83	94	116
47	72	84	94	120
48	73	85	95	120
50	74	85	96	122
54	74	86	97	124
58	76	87	104	127
65	76	88	106	127

EXHIBIT 2.2   Histogram of Order Times

```
HIST C4

Histogram of TIMES   N = 50

Midpoint     Count
      30         1   *
      40         3   ***
      50         4   ****
      60         1   *
      70         9   *********
      80         7   *******
      90        10   **********
     100         4   ****
     110         4   ****
     120         5   *****
     130         2   **
```

can see that the lowest time is around 30, the highest is around 130, and the most popular interval is the one at 90—one fifth of the times are in this interval.

When we talk about the scale of a histogram, we mean the intervals: how many, how wide, and where they start. Minitab automatically chooses a scale. If you want a different scale, you can specify it with subcommands. For example, suppose you wanted the intervals to be 27.5 to 42.5, 42.5 to 57.5, 57.5 to 72.5, ..., 117.5 to 132.5. Here the width, or increment, of each interval is 15, and the starting midpoint is 35. The following instructions can be used:

```
HISTOGRAM 'TIMES';
  INCREMENT = 15;
  START = 35.
```

Exhibit 2.3 shows the output from this command.

Any time that a data point falls on a boundary between two intervals, it is put in the higher interval. The histogram is designed primarily for interval data, although it can be used with ordinal and even categorical data as well.

EXHIBIT 2.3   Histogram of Order Times —Different Scale

```
HISTOGRAM 'TIMES';
INCREMENT = 15;
START = 35.

Histogram of TIMES    N = 50

Midpoint    Count
    35.0        2   **
    50.0        6   ******
    65.0        7   *******
    80.0       14   **************
    95.0        9   *********
   110.0        6   ******
   125.0        6   ******
```

HISTOGRAM C, ..., C

Prints a histogram for each column. Observations on the boundary between two intervals are put in the interval with higher values. You may specify your own scale with the subcommands INCREMENT and START.

INCREMENT = K

Specifies the distance between midpoints or, equivalently, the width of each interval.

START with midpoint at K [end with midpoint at K]

Specifies the midpoint for the first and, optionally, the last interval. Any observations beyond these intervals are omitted from the display.

BY C
SAMESCALE

The BY and SAMESCALE subcommands are useful when you want to produce several histograms. They are described in Section 5.1.

EXERCISES

2-2   (a)   Make a histogram of the following numbers:

36, 43, 84, 81, 84, 45, 64, 71, 81, 78, 79, 43, 79

   (b)   Make histograms for numbers that are 10 times the numbers in part (a). The LET command may be useful. Compare this display to the one in part (a). Is the overall impression the same?

   (c)   Repeat part (b) with numbers 5 times those in part (a). Compare this display to those in parts (a) and (b).

   (d)   Make a histogram of the numbers in part (a), using the subcommand START 37.5. The intervals will be 4 units wide, as they are in part (a), but will have different midpoints. The first interval will contain values from 35 through 39, the second interval will contain values from 40 through 44, the next 45 through 49, and so on. Compare the overall shape of this display to the one in part (a).

2-3   (a)   Write and run a Minitab program to get a histogram for the following data:

21, 43, 92, 86, 81, 85, 45, 60, 64, 71, 89, 78, 79, 43, 79

   (b)   What are the boundaries for each of the intervals (the class boundaries)? In what interval class did the number 86 fall? The number 45?

2-4   Get histograms of the A/S ratios in the Woodruff Sale data set (p. 271), using the following scales:
   (a)   first midpoint at 0.0, interval width of 0.025
   (b)   first midpoint at 0.0, interval width of 0.050
   (c)   first midpoint at 0.0, interval width of 0.200
   (d)   first midpoint at 0.0, interval width of 0.350
   (e)   first midpoint at 0.0, interval width of 0.500

Compare these five histograms with respect to their shapes. Do some histograms give a better picture of the data than others? Are some of the histograms more useful for certain purposes? Explain.

2–5   Make a histogram of the ratios of Black to White unemployment rates listed in Exhibit 1.3. How would you characterize this distribution? Can you think of reasons why the July ratio is so high?

2–6   The following numbers are *percents* of year-round housing units with air conditioning in the United States as of April 1, 1980. The data are listed by state and read down the column; that is, Alabama = 70.7 and Wyoming = 19.8. (The District of Columbia is included after Delaware.) The source of the data is the 1984 *Statistical Abstract of the United States*.

70.7	66.0	70.1	64.7	68.0	19.8
0.9	18.1	36.9	69.0	58.1	
71.1	32.1	34.3	41.1	74.0	
71.3	66.3	48.7	59.6	83.2	
40.1	58.6	69.9	40.2	48.8	
30.7	66.0	70.1	47.4	9.6	
46.5	78.4	19.7	81.5	64.8	
64.6	61.7	77.0	18.8	14.8	
67.1	82.2	69.9	41.1	38.5	
84.0	10.6	24.3	31.6	37.4	

Construct a histogram of these numbers.

2–7   This exercise uses the stock market data listed on p. 278.
   (a)   Make a histogram of the rates of return on IBM's stock.
   (b)   Make a histogram of the rates of return on Xerox's stock.
   (c)   Make a histogram of the rates of return for IBM, Xerox, and the market, all having the same scales.
   (d)   Which stock shows the greatest return? The greatest risk?

2.3 / DOTPLOTS

The Woodruff sales data (p. 271) provide A/S ratios of 61 parcels of residential property sold in 1975. A/S ratios are nothing more than the ratios of assessed values to sales values of the listed parcels. Exhibit 2.4 contains a dot plot of these A/S ratios. This display is very similar to a histogram with many small intervals that has been turned on its side. In Exhibit 2.4, there are over 40 spaces (or intervals) in the display, each space representing 0.03. This is a much finer scale than HISTOGRAM would use. The numbers that label the axis give the middle of each space. Thus the space labeled 0.30 goes from .285 to .315, the next space goes from .315 to .345, and so on. An observation that falls on the boundary between two spaces goes in the lower interval. This convention is the

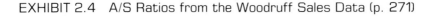

EXHIBIT 2.4   A/S Ratios from the Woodruff Sales Data (p. 271)

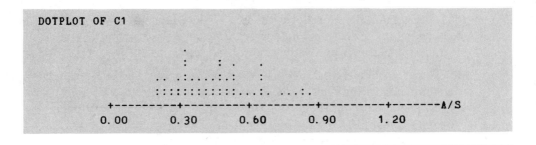

opposite of the one we used for HISTOGRAM. However, it seems to be the more natural one for DOTPLOT. Thus a ratio of .315 would be put in the interval labeled 0.30.

A histogram groups the data into just a few intervals (for the 61 A/S ratios, HISTOGRAM would use 14 intervals). A dotplot, on the other hand, groups the data as little as possible. Ideally (if we had wider paper or a printer with higher resolution), we would not group the data at all. Histograms are used when we want just an overall indication of what the observations are. Dotplots are used when we want to see what each observations is. Histograms tend to be more useful with large data sets, dotplots with small data sets. Histograms show the shape of a sample (we will discuss shape in Section 2.8); dotplots do not. Dotplots are useful if you want to compare two or more sets of data. We will do that in Chapter 5.

DOTPLOT C, ..., C

Makes a dotplot for each column. Observations on a boundary are put in the lower (smaller values) interval. WIDTH (p. 53) controls the width of DOTPLOTS. You may specify your own scale on DOTPLOT with the following subcommands.

INCREMENT = K

Specifies the distance between tick marks (the + signs) on the axis. Since there are ten spaces between tick marks, the width of each space will be K/10.

START at K [go to K]

Specifies the first and, optionally, the last tick mark on the axis. Any points outside are omitted from the display.

> BY C
> SAMESCALE
>
> These two subcommands are useful when you want to compare several dotplots. They are described in Section 5.1.

EXERCISES

2–8   Make a dotplot of the ratios of Black to White unemployment rates listed in Exhibit 1.3. How does it differ from the histogram you got in Exercise 2–5?

2–9   *(a)*   Make a dotplot of the numbers in Exercise 2–6.

    (b)   Label the lowest five and highest five dots with the names of the corresponding states. What do you conclude?

2–10   Make dotplots of the rates of return mentioned in Exercise 2–7. Compare them to the corresponding histograms. What is the effect of the grouping done by the HISTOGRAM command?

2.4 / STEM-AND-LEAF DISPLAYS

A stem-and-leaf display is similar to a histogram but uses the actual data to create the display, whereas HISTOGRAM uses the symbol *. The display is a relatively new technique introduced by statistician John Tukey in the late 1960s. It is designed primarily for interval data, although it can be used with any set of numbers.

    Exhibit 2.1 gave the filling times for 50 orders. Suppose we make a stem-and-leaf display of these data. Exhibit 2.5 shows the display after we have entered the first four times: 28, 43, 42, and 44. The digits to the left of the vertical line are called the stems. The digits to the right are called the leaves. To create the display, we split each fill time into 2 parts; the 10s digit became the stem, and the 1s digit became the leaf. For example, 64 was split into 6 = stem and 4 = leaf. The 28 was split into 2 = stem and 8 = leaf, and so on. The stems for the entire data set were listed to the left of the vertical line. Each leaf was put on the same line as its stem. At this point, the line with stem = 2 has just one leaf, an 8. This represents the time 28. The line with stem = 4 has three leaves: 3, 2, and 4. These represent the three fill times 43, 42, and 44.

    Exhibit 2.6 gives the stem-and-leaf display for all 50 orders. Reading from the top of the display, we see that the times are 28, 43, 42, 44, 47, 48, 50, 54, 58, ..., 124, 127, 127. This display contains the same information as the original list of numbers but presents it in a more compact and usable

---

EXHIBIT 2.5   Stem-and-Leaf Display of First Four Times

2	8
3	
4	324
5	
6	
7	
8	
9	
10	
11	
12	

EXHIBIT 2.6   Stem-and-Leaf Display of 50 Times

2	8
3	
4	32478
5	048
6	58
7	1112344668
8	013455678
9	11454467
10	46788
11	6
12	002477

---

form. We can easily see the range of the data—from a low of 28 to a high of 127—and the most popular categories—the 70s, followed by the 80s and 90s. The general shape of the picture is nearly symmetric. There are no gaps (stems with no observations) and no outliers (observations that are much smaller or much larger than the bulk of the data).

Exhibit 2.7 gives the display produced by Minitab's STEM-AND-LEAF command. This differs from our hand-drawn display in several ways. First, an extra column, called depths, was added to the left of the display. In addition, the message LEAF DIGIT = 1.0 was added. We will discuss both of these next.

FURTHER DETAILS

The depth of a line tells how many leaves lie on that line or "beyond." For example, the 11 on the fifth line from the top says that there are 11 leaves

EXHIBIT 2.7   Stem-and-Leaf Display Produced by Minitab

```
STEM C4

 Stem-and-leaf of TIMES      N = 50
 Leaf Unit = 1.0


      1       2 8
      1       3
      6       4 23478
      9       5 048
     11       6 58
     21       7 1112344668
    ( 9)      8 013455678
     20       9 11444567
     12      10 46788
      7      11 6
      6      12 002477
     └┘      └┘└──────────┘

   depths  stems    leaves
```

on that line and above it; the 12 on the third line from the bottom says that there are 12 leaves on that line and below it. The line with the parentheses contains the middle observation if the total number of observations, N, is odd. It contains the middle two observations if N is even, as it is here. The parentheses enclose a count of the number of leaves on this line. Note that if N is even and the two middle observations fall on different lines, then no parentheses are used in the depth column.

In this example, Minitab listed each stem on one line. In some cases, Minitab will use two lines or five lines for each stem (an example is given in Exercise 2–13). The number of lines per stem is always 1, 2, or 5 and is determined by the range of the data and the number of values present. In our example, all times contained two or three digits, so it was easy to split each number into a stem and a leaf. When numbers contain more than two digits, the STEM-AND-LEAF command drops digits that do not fit. For example, the number 927 might be split as a stem = 9, leaf = 2, and 7 dropped.

Decimal points are not used in a STEM-AND-LEAF display. Therefore the numbers 260, 26, 2.6, and .26 would all be split into stem = 2 and leaf = 6. The heading LEAF UNIT tells where the decimal point belongs. For the number 260, LEAF UNIT = 10; for 26, LEAF UNIT = 1; for 2.6, LEAF UNIT = .1; and for .26, LEAF UNIT = .01.

STEM-AND-LEAF has a subcommand, INCREMENT, which allows you to control the scale of a stem-and-leaf display. For example, suppose we wanted Minitab to produce the display of the order fill times with two lines per stem. The first line contains all numbers between 40 and 44, the second line contains all numbers between 45 and 49, and so on. Therefore the distance of increment from one stem to the next is 5. To specify this scale, use

```
STEM-AND-LEAF 'TIMES';
   INCREMENT = 5.
```

STEM-AND-LEAF OF C, ..., C

Prints a stem-and-leaf display for each column.

INCREMENT = K

Specifies the distance from one stem to the next. The increment must be of the form 10ρ or $2 \times 10\rho$ or $5 \times 10\rho$, where ρ is any integer—positive, negative, or zero. Thus examples of allowable increments are 1, 20, 1000, 0.5, and .001.

BY C
SAMESCALE

These two subcommands are useful when you want to produce several stem-and-leaf displays. They are described in Section 5.1.

EXERCISES

2–11 *(a)* Do a stem-and-leaf display of the following numbers by hand:

36, 43, 84, 81, 84, 45, 64, 71, 78, 79, 43, 79

(b) Use Minitab to do a stem-and-leaf display of the numbers in part (a). Compare it to your hand-drawn display.

(c) Multiply the numbers in part (a) by 10. Then use Minitab to get a stem-and-leaf display. Explain the differences between the displays in parts (b) and (c).

(d) Multiply the numbers in part (a) by 2. Use Minitab to get a display of these numbers. How does this display compare to the one in part (b)?

(e) Multiply the numbers in part (a) by 5 and get a stem-and-leaf display. Compare this display to the one in part (a).

2–12 Make a stem-and-leaf display of the ratios of Black to White unemployment rates in Exhibit 1.3. Compare your display with the histogram and dotplot in Exercises 2–5 and 2–8.

2–13 Make stem-and-leaf displays of the rates of return mentioned in Exercise 2–7. How do they compare to the histograms and dotplots you got in Exercises 2–7 and 2–10?

2–14 Redo Exercises 2–3 and 2–4, using stem-and-leaf displays.

2.5 / ONE-NUMBER STATISTICS

We often want to summarize an important feature of a set of data by using just one number. For example, we might use the mean to indicate the center or typical level of the data. We could use the range, the largest value minus the smallest value, to indicate how spread out the data are. In this section we first discuss DESCRIBE, a command that prints a table of summary numbers. Then we show how these summaries can be computed singly, first for columns of data and then across rows.

THE DESCRIBE COMMAND

Exhibit 2.1 contains fill times for 50 orders, and Exhibit 2.7 shows a stem-and-leaf display of these times. Exhibit 2.8 gives the output from the DESCRIBE command for the fill times data. The statistics printed by DESCRIBE are as follows:

N = 50. This says that there were 50 orders.

MEAN = 83.66. This is the average of all 50 times. The mean, often written as $\bar{x}$, is the most frequently used measure of the center of a batch of numbers.

MEDIAN = 84.5. To find the median, first order the numbers. If N, the number of values, is odd, the median is the middle value. If N is even, the median is the average of the two middle values. Here $N = 50$, so the median is the average of the 25th and 26th values. These are 84 and 85, so their average is 84.5. The median is another

---

EXHIBIT 2.8 Output from DESCRIBE

```
DESCRIBE C4
```

	N	MEAN	MEDIAN	TRMEAN	STDEV	SEMEAN
TIMES	50	83.66	84.50	83.91	24.39	3.45

	MIN	MAX	Q1	Q3
TIMES	28.00	127.00	71.00	98.75

value used to indicate where the center of the data is. (In a stem-and-leaf display, the line with parentheses contains the median.)

TRMEAN = 83.91. A 5% trimmed mean. The smallest 5% (rounded to the nearest integer) and the largest 5% of the values are trimmed; the remaining 90% are averaged. Here $N = 50$, so $.05 \times 50 = 2.5$. This is rounded to 2. Thus the two smallest values, 28 and 42, and the two largest values, 127 and 127, are trimmed. The remaining 46 values are averaged to give the trimmed mean.

STDEV = 24.39. Standard deviation. This is the most frequently used measure of how spread out the data are. The general formula is

$$S = \sqrt{\Sigma(x - \bar{x})^2/(N - 1)}$$

Here is a simple example: For the data 1, 3, 6, 4, 6, we have $N = 5$, mean $= 4$, and

$$\text{STDEV} = \sqrt{\frac{(1 - 4)^2 + (3 - 4)^2 + (6 - 4)^2 + (4 - 4)^2 + (6 - 4)^2}{5 - 1}}$$

$$= \sqrt{4.5} = 2.122$$

SEMEAN = 3.45. Standard error of the mean. This is a more advanced concept and is discussed on page 127. The formula is $\text{STDEV}/\sqrt{N}$. For the times data,

$$\text{SEMEAN} = \text{STDEV}/\sqrt{N} = 24.4/\sqrt{50} = 3.45$$

MAX = 127.00. The maximum or largest value.

MIN = 28.00. The minimum or smallest value.

Q3 = 98.75. The third or upper quartile.

Q1 = 71.0. The first or lower quartile.

The median is the second quartile, Q2. The three numbers Q1, Q2, Q3 split the data into four essentially equal parts as follows: First, order the observations from smallest to largest. The Q1 is at position $(N + 1)/4$ and Q3 is at position $3(N + 1)/4$. If the position is not an integer, interpolation is used. For example, suppose $N = 10$. The $(10 + 1)/4 = 2.75$, and Q1 is between the second and third observations (call them x_2 and x_3), three fourths of the way up. Thus $Q1 = x_2 + .75 (x_3 - x_2)$. Since $3(10 + 1)/4 = 8.25$, $Q3 = x_8 + .25 (x_9 - x_8)$, where x_8 and x_9 are the eighth and ninth observations. In the example, $N = 50$, so $(N + 1)$ $(N + 1)/4 = 12.75$ and Q1 is between the 12th and 13th observations. These are both 71, so $Q1 = 71$. Q3 is between the 38th and 40th observtion and is equal to 98.75. *Note*: There are several other definitions for quartile. All, however, give essentially the same answer.

NMISS. When some values are recorded as "missing," a count is given. Here no times were missing, so the NMISS line was not printed by DESCRIBE.

DESCRIBE C, ..., C

Prints the following statistics for each column.

N	Number of nonmissing values in the column
NMISS	Number of missing values. This is omitted if there are no missing values.
MEAN	
MEDIAN	
TRMEAN	5% trimmed mean
STDEV	Standard deviation
SEMEAN	Standard error of the mean
MAX	Maximum value
MIN	Minimum value
Q3	Third quartile
Q1	First quartile

ONE-NUMBER STATISTICS FOR COLUMNS

DESCRIBE prints a collection of summary statistics. Minitab also has commands that calculate and store such statistics, one at a time.

N C [put in K]

NMISS C [put in K]

MEAN C [put in K]

MEDIAN C [put in K]

STDEV C [put in K]

MAX C [put in K]

MIN C [put in K]

SUM C [put in K]

SSQ C [put in K]

COUNT C [put in K]

The answer is printed if it is not stored.

Three of these statistics are not printed by DESCRIBE: SUM, SSQ, and COUNT. The command SUM just adds all the values in the column. SSQ is the sum of the squares of the values. For example, for the data 1, 3, 5, 4, $SSQ = 1^2 + 3^2 + 5^2 + 4^2 = 51$. The command COUNT gives the total number of entries in a column. Thus COUNT = N + NMISS.

COLUMN STATISTICS WITH LET

All of the statistics for columns can also be used in a LET statement. Here are some examples:

```
LET K1 = MEAN(C1)
LET C2 = C1-MEAN(C1)
LET K2 = SUM(C1)/N(C1)
LET K3 = MEDIAN('HEIGHT.F')
```

Notice that you must enclose the column in parentheses when you use a column statistic such as MEAN, SUM, or MEDIAN in a LET command. Using LET, you can easily calculate many statistics that are not built into Minitab. For example, another measure of the center of a set of numbers is the midrange. This is the average of the smallest and largest values. It can be calculated by

```
LET K1 = (MAX(C1)+MIN(C1))/2
```

Another measure of the spread of a set of numbers is the median of the absolute deviations from the median. This can be calculated by

```
LET K1 = MEDIAN(ABSO(C1-MEDIAN(C1)))
```

ONE-NUMBER STATISTICS FOR ROWS

The statistics we have just described for columns are also available for rows. The command names are the same except that an R (for row) has been added.

```
RN C, ..., C put in C
RNMISS C, ..., C put in C
RMEAN C, ..., C put in C
RMEDIAN C, ..., C put in C
RSTDEV C, ..., C put in C
RMAX C, ..., C put in C
RMIN C, ..., C put in C
RSUM C, ..., C put in C
RSSQ C, ..., C put in C
RCOUNT C, ..., C put in C
```

These commands compute summaries across rows rather than down columns. The answers are always stored in a column.

EXAMPLE

```
RSUM C1-C3 PUT IN C4
RMAX C1-C3 PUT INTO C5
```

C1	C2	C3		C4	C5
1	7	3		11	7
4	2	3		9	4
1	3	2		6	3

EXERCISES

2-15 Consider the output in Exhibit 2.1.

(a) How many times are equal to 94 days? Over 94 days?

(b) The mean length is 83.7 days. How many fill times are less than the mean?

(c) The range of a set of numbers is defined as

$$\text{maximum value} - \text{minimum value}$$

Find the range for the fill time data.

(d) There is a connection between the range and the standard deviation of a data set: In many data sets the range is approximately four times the standard deviation. Is this true for the fill time data?

(e) Calculate the two values (MEAN − STDEV) and (MEAN + STDEV). In many data sets, approximately two thirds of the observations fall between these two values. Is this true for the fill time data?

2-16 Consider the following 11 observations:

$$5, 3, 3, 8, 9, 6, 9, 9, 10, 5, 10$$

(a) By hand, calculate each of the statistics printed by DESCRIBE.

(b) Use DESCRIBE to check your answers.

2-17 The median is said to be "resistant" to the effects of a few outlying points in a data set. That is, the median will not be very different even if there are a few unusually large values or unusually small values in the data set. The mean, however, is not resistant to outliers.

Enter the 11 observations in Exercise 2–16 into C1. Use DESCRIBE to find the mean and the median. Now use the command

    LET C1(1) = 25

to change the 5 in row 1 to a 25. Again use DESCRIBE to find the mean and median. How have they changed? Now use the command

    LET C1(1) = 100

to change the first observation to a 100. Find the mean and median. How have they changed?

2-18 (a) Use Minitab to compute the standard deviation of the numbers

$$6, 8, 4, 10, 12, 3, 4, 10$$

(b) Add 29 to each number. Now compute the standard deviation. How does your answer compare with that in part (a)?

(c) Multiply the data in part (a) by 29 and compute the standard deviation. How does your answer compare with that in part (a)? If you are not sure, divide the standard deviation in part (c) by the one in part (a).

2–19 Suppose that the final exam scores for one section of a statistics course were as follows,

97, 80, 31, 100, 91, 86, 72, 68, 74, 19, 98, 82, 85, 88, 93, 78, 79

(a) Find the sample mean and median by hand, and check your results by using Minitab.

(b) Use Minitab to make a histogram of the scores.

(c) What does this picture tell you about why there is a difference between the mean and the median?

2.6 / SUMMARIZING CATEGORICAL AND ORDINAL DATA

The preceding sections described techniques that are designed primarily for interval data. This section introduces TALLY, a command that is designed especially for categorical and ordinal data.

The Woodruff study data described on page 272 contains two categorical variables. They indicate whether the parcel is vacant or improved and whether the parcel has water frontage or not. Exhibit 2.9 is a TALLY of these two variables. The first table shows that 20 parcels were vacant (type 0) and 30 parcels were improved (type 1), for a total of 50 parcels. The second table shows there were 36 parcels without water frontage (type 0) and 14 parcels with water frontage (type 1).

Exhibit 2.10 shows a table that has all four statistics calculated by TALLY for the variable IMPROVE. CUMCNT gives the cumulative

---

EXHIBIT 2.9   TALLY of Improvement and Water Frontage

```
TALLY 'IMPROVE' 'WATER'

IMPROVE  COUNT     WATER  COUNT
      0     20         0     36
      1     30         1     14
     N=     50        N=     50
```

EXHIBIT 2.10   Example of the TALLY Command

```
TALLY 'IMPROVE';
ALL.


  IMPROVE   COUNT  CUMCNT  PERCENT   CUMPCT
        0      20      20    40.00    40.00
        1      30      50    60.00   100.00
       N=      50
```

---

counts. There were 20 parcels of type 0 (vacant) and 20 + 30 = 50 of types 0 and 1 (vacant and improved). PERCENT is (COUNT/N) × 100. Thus 40.00% = (20/50) × 100 and 60.00% = (30/50) × 100.

CUMPCT gives the cumulative percent. This is CUMCNT/N. You can use subcommands to ask for each of these statistics individually or use the subcommand ALL to get all four, as we did in Exhibit 2.10. Note in the Woodruff example that CUMCNT and CUMPCT are not very useful, since there is no intrinsic order to the variable IMPROVE. These two statistics are most often used with ordinal data.

TALLY C, ..., C

Prints a separate frequency table for each column. The columns must contain integers from −10000 and +10000. Any one or more of the following subcommands may be used. They specify what to print in the table. If no subcommands are given, just COUNTS are printed.

COUNTS
PERCENTS
CUMCOUNTS   Cumulative counts
CUMPERCENTS   Cumulative percents
ALL   Same as using all four preceding subcommands

2.7 / BOXPLOTS

A boxplot is a display that summarizes the main features of a batch of data: the center, the middle half, the extent of the data, and possible outliers.

We again use the Woodruff sales data (p 271). Exhibit 2.11 contains a boxplot of the A/S ratios. It also contains the ordered data to facilitate

EXHIBIT 2.11   BOXPLOT of A/S

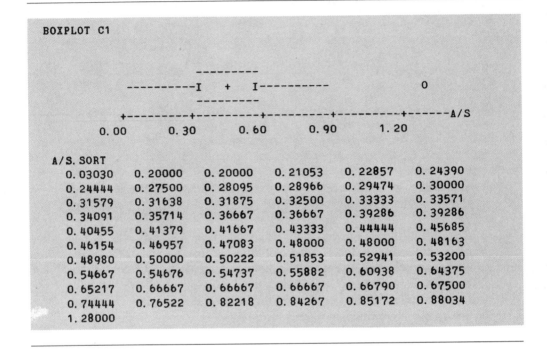

```
BOXPLOT C1

                                 ---------
                      ----------I    +    I----------                    O
                                 ---------
              +----------+----------+----------+----------+------A/S
            0.00       0.30       0.60       0.90       1.20


A/S. SORT
    0.03030    0.20000    0.20000    0.21053    0.22857    0.24390
    0.24444    0.27500    0.28095    0.28966    0.29474    0.30000
    0.31579    0.31638    0.31875    0.32500    0.33333    0.33571
    0.34091    0.35714    0.36667    0.36667    0.39286    0.39286
    0.40455    0.41379    0.41667    0.43333    0.44444    0.45685
    0.46154    0.46957    0.47083    0.48000    0.48000    0.48163
    0.48980    0.50000    0.50222    0.51853    0.52941    0.53200
    0.54667    0.54676    0.54737    0.55882    0.60938    0.64375
    0.65217    0.66667    0.66667    0.66667    0.66790    0.67500
    0.74444    0.76522    0.82218    0.84267    0.85172    0.88034
    1.28000
```

calculations. The boxplot uses a + (here it is at 0.462) to indicate the median of the data. The box, drawn by the computer with the letter I at each end and dashes on the top and bottom, shows the middle half of the data. The smallest quarter (except for rounding problems) of the observations is to the left of the box, and the largest quarter of the observations is to the right of the box. Observations outside the box are indicated by dashes (for ordinary observations), by asterisks (for unusual observations), and by the letter O (for very unusual observations).

To explain what "unusual" means, we need a few definitions. Hinges are a minor variation of quartiles. In many cases they are exactly equal to the quartiles; in all cases they are very close. To find the hinges if N is odd, first calculate $(N + 1)/4$. This gives the position of the hinges. Suppose $N = 29$. Then $(N + 1)/4 = 7.5$. Then for the lower hinge, H1 = $(x_7 + x_8)/2$, where x_7 is the seventh observation from the bottom and x_8 is the eighth. The upper hinge, H2, is the average of the seventh and eighth observations, counting down from the top. In the Woodruff sales data, $(N + 1)/4 = 15.5$. Thus H1 is the average of the 15th and 16th observations from the bottom, which gives H1 = 0.322, and H2 is the average of the 15th and 16th observations from the top, which gives H2 = 0.584. The hinges form the edges of the box in the boxplot. Thus the lower I is placed at 0.322 and the upper I at 0.584.

We define the hinge spread as H2 − H1. The hinge spread is approximately the interquartile range and is the width of the box. Next we define the inner fences as

$$F1 = H1 - 1.5(\text{hinge spread}) \qquad \text{and} \qquad F2 = H2 + 1.5(\text{hinge spread})$$

In the Woodruff sales data, the inner fences are F1 = 0.322 − 1.5(0.256) = −0.062 and F2 = 0.584 + 1.5(0.256) = 0.968. The two most extreme observations that are still within the inner fences are called adjacent values. Dashed lines are drawn from each hinge out to the corresponding adjacent value. In the Woodruff sales data, the two adjacent values are the first observation, 0.0303, and the next to last observation, 0.880.

The outer fences are defined as

$$G1 = H1 - 3(\text{hinge spread}) \qquad \text{and} \qquad G2 = H2 + 3(\text{hinge spread})$$

Observations between G1 and F1 and observations between F2 and G2 are considered unusual and plotted with an asterisk. There are no such values in the Woodruff sales data. Observations beyond the outer fences are considered very unusual and plotted with the letter O, which is symbolic of "outlier." There is one outlier in Exhibit 2.11: 1.28.

BOXPLOT C, ..., C

Prints a boxplot for each column. You may specify your own scale with the subcommands INCREMENT and START.

INCREMENT = K

Specifies the distance between tick marks (the + signs) on the axis. Since there are ten spaces between tick marks, the width of each space will be K/10.

START at K [go to K]

Specifies the first and optionally the last tick mark on the axis. Any points outside are omitted from the display

BY C
SAMESCALE

These two subcommands are useful when you want to compare several boxplots. They are described in Section 5.1.

The command WIDTH (p. 53) controls the width of the display. If you have wide paper for output and want a wide boxplot, use WIDTH.

EXERCISE

2–20 Write and run a program to draw boxplots of the data in the following exercises.

   (a) Exercise 2–2.
   (b) Exercise 2–5.
   (c) Exercise 2–7.
   (d) Exercise 2–11.
   (e) Exercise 2–16.
   (f) Exercise 2–18.

2.8 / TRANSFORMATIONS TO SYMMETRY

When analyzing data, it is not always clear what units should be used for a given variable. For example:

> Should gasoline consumption be measured in miles per gallon or in gallons per mile?
>
> Should a price increase be measured in dollars or in percent change?
>
> Should the acidity of rain be measured in terms of the proportion of hydrogen ions or in terms of pH?

Choosing the appropriate units for a variable can often make its analysis much easier.

SYMMETRY

A histogram is symmetric if the distribution of the high values is the mirror image of the distribution of the low values. For example, histogram (c) of Exhibit 2.13 is fairly symmetric. Histogram (a), however, is skewed toward high values—that is, the high values are stretched out in comparison to the low values. Histogram (d) is skewed toward low values. Since it is usually easier to analyze symmetric data, we often transform skewed data to make it more nearly symmetric. When we transform a variable, we are simply changing the unit of measurement. Transformations are widely used by experienced data analysts.

Of all the transformations made on data in business practice, the three most popular are the square root, logarithm, and negative reciprocal.* These are listed in Exhibit 2.12.

---

*Recall that if $y = \log_e x$, then $e^y = x$. For example, $\log_e 20.086 = 3$ because $e^3 = 20.086$; $\log_e 1.649 = 0.5$ because $e^{0.5} = \sqrt{e} = 1.649$. We use the negative reciprocal, $-1/x$, rather than just the reciprocal, $1/x$, to preserve the *order* of the observations. Thus if 42 is the smallest observation in our data set, then $-1/42$ will be the smallest observation in the transformed data set. If we used the reciprocal, $1/42$, the transformed observation would be the largest in the transformed data set, and everything would be turned around.

EXHIBIT 2.12   Three Transformations

Transformation	Strength	Formula	Minitab Example
Square root	Moderate	$\sqrt{x}$	LET C2 = SQRT(C1)
Logarithm	Strong	$\log_e(x)$	LET C2 = LOGE(C1)
Negative reciprocal	Stronger	$-1/x$	LET C2 = −1/C1

Exhibit 2.13 illustrates the effect of each transformation. Part (a) shows the consumption of newsprint for 90 U.S. cities in 1960. (This data set is described on p. 279.) This distribution is clearly "skewed" toward high values. Part (b) shows what happened when we took the square root of each observation and then made a histogram. It is not as skewed as the original data, but it still has a tendency toward a long tail in the high values. In part (c) the logarithmic transformation produced a fairly symmetric distribution. The (negative) reciprocal transformation in part (d) went much too far. Now the lower values are stretched out, and the high values are clumped together.

These three transformations all have the same general function: They compress the upper end of the distribution of values relative to the lower end. Thus they reduce asymmetry when the data are skewed toward high values. These transformations are also ordered, square root being the weakest. That is, it will symmetrize a histogram that is just slightly skewed. This is followed, in strength, by log and then negative reciprocal. The middle transformation, log (x), symmetrized the newsprint data fairly well.

EXHIBIT 2.13   Newsprint Consumption of 90 U.S. Cities

(a)

```
Histogram of CONSUME    N = 90
Each * represents 2 obs.

Midpoint    Count
       0      84   ***********************************************
   50000       4   **
  100000       0
  150000       0
  200000       0
  250000       0
  300000       1   *
  350000       1   *
```

(continues)

EXHIBIT 2.13 *Continued*

(b)

```
Histogram of SQRTCON   N = 90
Each * represents 2 obs.

Midpoint   Count
     0      13    ******
    50      56    ****************************
   100      14    *******
   150       2    *
   200       2    *
   250       1    *
   300       0
   350       0
   400       0
   450       0
   500       0
   550       1    *
   600       1    *
```

(c)

```
Histogram of LOGECON   N = 90

Midpoint   Count
     5       2    **
     6      14    **************
     7      28    ****************************
     8      25    *************************
     9      10    **********
    10       8    ********
    11       1    *
    12       0
    13       2    **
```

(d)

```
Histogram of -1/CON   N = 90

Midpoint    Count
-0.0045       2    **
-0.0040       1    *
-0.0035       1    *
-0.0030       1    *
-0.0025       0
-0.0020       5    *****
-0.0015      10    **********
-0.0010      17    *****************
-0.0005      29    *****************************
-0.0000      24    ************************
```

EXERCISES

2-21 We mentioned before that the mean and median are approximately equal if the data are symmetric. Compute the mean and median for each of the following transformations of the newsprint consumption data on page 279: the raw data, the square root of consumption, the base 10 logarithm of consumption, the natural logarithm of consumption, and the negative reciprocal of consumption. In each case, divide the median by the mean. If the mean and median are relatively close, this ratio will be near 1. How do these ratios compare with the appearance of symmetry in Exhibit 2.13?

2-22 Obtain stem-and-leaf diagrams, boxplots, and dotplots for each of the transformations of the newsprint consumption data on page 279. Describe the effects of the transformation on each of these displays.

3/PLOTTING DATA

The displays we have used thus far have involved only one variable at a time. Often we are interested in the relationships between two or more variables, such as the relationship between height and weight, between smoking and lung cancer, or between advertising expenditures and sales.

3.1/SCATTERPLOTS

If both variables are interval or ordinal, the most useful display is a scatterplot. As an example, consider the data in Exhibit 3.1, which are assets, total deposits (demand and time), and numbers of banks in selected Midwest and Sun Belt states in 1982. Assets and deposits are in billions of dollars. Exhibit 3.2 gives a scatterplot of the total deposits versus assets. With the region data in column C1, assets in C2, deposits in C3, and number of banks in C4, this plot was produced with the commands

```
NAME C2 'ASSETS' C3 'TOT.DEP'
PLOT C3 VS C2
```

From the plot we see that the total deposits increase more or less linearly as assets vary from $13.6 billion to $216.4 billion. The 2s and 3s on the plot mean that two or three points are plotted at the same plotting position. For example, there were two states with bank deposits totaling about $36 billion and assets totaling about $29 billion. Reviewing the data, we see that these states are Indiana and Minnesota.

A useful descriptive statistic that can be employed in conjunction with a scatterplot is the (product moment) correlation coefficient. The correlation coefficient measures the extent to which the points in the scatterplot tend to cluster about a straight line.

CORRELATION coefficient between data in C and C

Computes the (linear) correlation coefficient between the two columns of data. The usual Pearson product moment correlation coefficient is used.

$$r = \frac{\Sigma(x - \bar{x})(y - \bar{y})}{\sqrt{\Sigma(x - \bar{x})^2 \Sigma(y - \bar{y})^2}}$$

CORRELATION coefficients for data in C, ..., C

If more than two columns are specified, Minitab prints a table giving the correlations between all pairs of columns.

EXAMPLE

CORRELATION C1, C2, C3

Three correlations are given: the correlations between C1 and C2, between C1 and C3, and between C2 and C3.

The correlation coefficient assumes values between -1 and 1. Values close to -1 indicate clustering along a negatively sloping line, values close to 1 indicate clustering along a positively sloping line, and values close to 0 indicate either no relationship or a nonlinear relationship. To compute the correlation coefficient between assets and total deposits in Exhibit 3.1, all

---

EXHIBIT 3.1   Bank Data

State	Region*	Assets	Total Deposits	Number of Banks
Alabama	1	20.3	16.5	294
Arizona	1	16.6	13.4	30
California	1	216.4	165.3	361
Florida	1	59.4	49.2	477
Georgia	1	30.0	23.1	416
Illinois	0	130.2	91.8	1250
Indiana	0	36.3	29.8	400
Iowa	0	25.5	21.5	643
Kansas	0	19.6	16.5	620
Louisiana	1	30.8	25.9	278
Michigan	0	56.6	46.0	374
Minnesota	0	36.8	28.0	759
Mississippi	1	13.6	11.5	167
Nebraska	0	14.0	11.4	461
Ohio	0	62.4	47.6	355
Tennessee	1	28.1	22.9	346
Texas	1	152.8	120.3	1598
Wisconsin	0	30.0	24.3	624

*1 denotes Sun Belt, 0 denotes Midwest.

Source: Statistical Abstract of the United States, 1984, p. 511.

EXHIBIT 3.2   Scatterplot of Total Deposits versus Assets

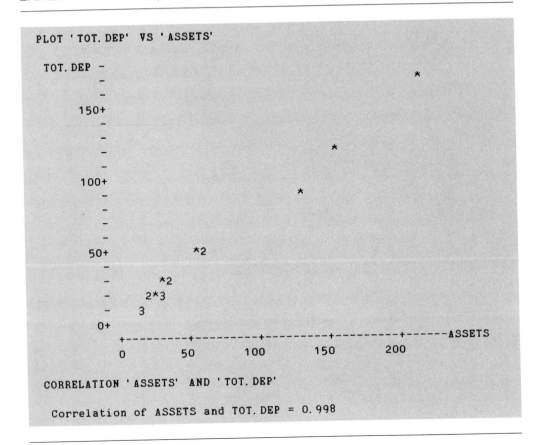

```
PLOT 'TOT.DEP' VS 'ASSETS'

TOT. DEP -
         -                                                        *
         -
         -
   150+
         -
         -
         -                                       *
         -
   100+
         -                                 *
         -
         -
         -
    50+                      *2
         -
         -            *2
         -          2*3
         -          3
     0+
         +----------+----------+----------+----------+------ASSETS
         0          50        100        150        200

CORRELATION 'ASSETS' AND 'TOT. DEP'

Correlation of ASSETS and TOT. DEP = 0.998
```

we have to do is type

    CORRELATION BETWEEN 'ASSETS' AND 'TOT.DEP'

The computer prints out the value 0.998 in this case. This correlation indicates strong linearity with a positive slope in the scatterplot, an impression confirmed by inspecting the plot in Exhibit 3.2.

PLOT C versus C

Gives a scatterplot of the data. The first column is put on the vertical (or y) axis and the second column on the horizontal (or x) axis. Ordinarily, each point is plotted with the symbol*. When more than one point falls on the same plotting position, a count is given. When the count is over 9, the symbol + is used. Minitab will automatically choose "nice"' scales, or you may specify your own scales with the following subcommands:

XINCREMENT = K
XSTART at K [end at K]
YINCREMENT = K
YSTART at K [end at K]

XINCREMENT is the distance between tick marks (the + symbols) on the x axis. XSTART specifies the first and, optionally, the last point plotted on the x axis. Any points outside are omitted from the plot. YINCREMENT and YSTART are for the y axis. The commands WIDTH and HEIGHT control the size of plots.

HEIGHT of plots = K lines
WIDTH of plots = K spaces

On almost all computers, PLOT prints a plot that is 19 lines tall (plus two lines for labels) and 57 spaces wide (plus 18 spaces for labels). The commands HEIGHT and WIDTH allow you to change this size. If your output is on wide paper, you might want to make some plots very large to get better resolution. If you have many small data sets, you might want small plots.

HEIGHT and WIDTH apply to all PLOT, LPLOT, MPLOT, and DOTPLOT commands that follow them. For example, suppose you type WIDTH = 30. If, later in your session, you type PLOT C2 VS C1, this plot will be 30 spaces wide (plus 18 spaces for labels, giving a total of 48 spaces). If later still you type LPLOT C2 C1 C3, this plot, too, will be 30 spaces wide. If you want to return to 57 spaces wide, use another WIDTH command.

The command HEIGHT also applies to TSPLOT, but WIDTH does not.

EXERCISES

3–1   (a)   Plot standardized weight versus standardized height for all the female students in the Class experiment (p. 281). Use the CENTER command to standardize height and weight. Use the CORRELATION command to compute the correlation coefficient between height and weight. Are the results as you expected?

      (b)   Repeat part (a) for male students.

      (c)   Are there noticeable differences between males and females? Explain.

3–2   For the data in Exhibit 3.1 plot assets versus number of banks. Does there appear to be much of a relationship between these variables? Compute the correlation coefficient.

3–3   For the data in Exhibit 3.1, plot total deposits versus number of banks. Does there appear to be much of a relationship between these variables? Compute the correlation coefficient.

3.2 / PLOTS WITH SYMBOLS

A LETTER PLOT: LPLOT

A scatterplot shows the relationship between two variables. We can add information about a third variable by using different symbols for different points. For an example, let's take a close look at the bank data in Exhibit 3.1 (p. 51). The "Region" column indicates whether the state is in the Midwest (denoted by 0) or in the Sun Belt (denoted by 1).

Exhibit 3.3 uses Minitab's LPLOT command to plot the asset and deposit data with labels. Each observation with a 0 in C1 was plotted with

---

EXHIBIT 3.3   LPLOT of Deposits versus Assets

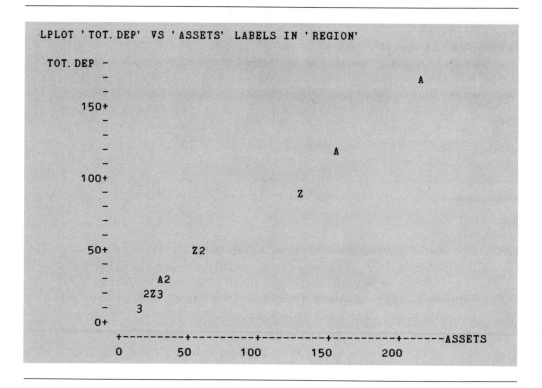

the letter Z, and each observation with a 1 in C1 was plotted with the first letter of the alphabet, A.

One problem with the plot in Exhibit 3.3 is that the points where two or more states are plotted have numerical, rather than alphabetical, plotting symbols. The three large states—California, Illinois, and Texas—squeeze the smaller states toward the origin. One way to inspect the smaller states in more detail is to produce a plot without the three large states. This is easily accomplished with the commands

```
COPY C1-C3 INTO C11-C13;
  USE C2 = 0:100.
NAME C11 'REG' C12 'A.L.E.100' C13 'DEPOSITS'
LPLOT C13 VS C12 WITH CODES IN C11
```

The output is in Exhibit 3.4. The COPY command (p. 298) allows us to choose states with bank assets less than or equal to $100 billion.

EXHIBIT 3.4   LPLOT of Deposits versus Assets for Assets Less Than
$100 Billion

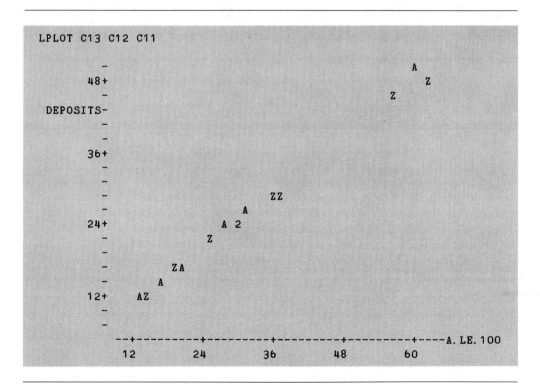

LPLOT C vs C, using labels as coded in C

XINCREMENT = K
XSTART at K [go to K]
YINCREMENT = K
YSTART at K [go to K]

LPLOT (the L is for labels or letters) plots data with labels given by

$$\ldots -2 \; -1 \; 0 \; 1 \; 2 \; 3 \ldots 24 \; 25 \; 26 \; 27 \; 28 \ldots$$
$$\ldots \; X \quad Y \; Z \; A \; B \; C \ldots X \; Y \; Z \; A \; B \; \ldots$$

The subcommands specify scales as they do in PLOT (see p. 52). WIDTH and HEIGHT (p. 53) control the size of LPLOTS.

ANOTHER PLOT WITH SYMBOLS: MPLOT

The data set on page 273 gives square feet of living area, assessed value, and market value for 60 residential parcels. We expect the assessed and market values to be positively correlated with area. We may compare the two sets of values by plotting them against area on the same set of axes. If the columns containing assessed values, market values, and square feet of living area are named ASSESSED, MARKET, and SFLA, then we can use the following commands:

```
MPLOT 'ASSESSED' VS 'SFLA' AND 'MARKET' VS 'SFLA'
CORRELATION OF 'ASSESSED' 'MARKET' AND 'SFLA'
```

The resulting output is in Exhibit 3.5. The letter A identifies the assessed values. B identifies the market values. Occasionally, two values fall on the same position, and the number 2 is plotted. In this plot we see that, with only two exceptions, the market values are higher than the assessed values. The clustering of the Bs at the top of the plot and As at the bottom shows a substantial difference between market and assessed values for all sizes of dwellings. The plot shows much greater variability in the assessed values than in the market values. This suggests a need to train and more closely supervise the assessors, since their values show less relation both to trends in and levels of market values than we would have hoped.

MPLOT C vs C, C vs C, ..., C vs C

XINCREMENT = K
XSTART at K [go to K]
YINCREMENT = K
YSTART at K [go to K]

MPLOT (the M is for multiple plot) puts several plots all on the same axes. The first pair of columns are plotted with the symbol A, the second pair with the symbol B, and so on. If several points fall on the same spot, a count is given.

The subcommands specify scales as they do in PLOT (p. 52). WIDTH and HEIGHT (p. 53) control the size of MPLOTS.

DIFFERENCE BETWEEN LPLOT AND MPLOT

These two commands both put data for several groups or variables on the same plot. Essentially, the only difference between them is how the data

EXHIBIT 3.5   Assessed Values (A) and Market Values (B) Plotted against Square Feet of Living Area for 60 Residential Parcels

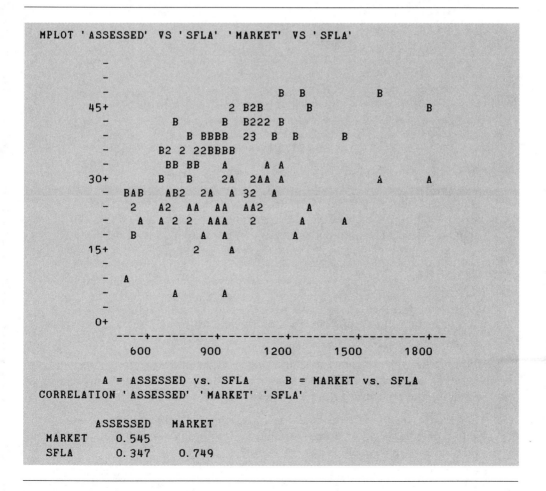

```
MPLOT 'ASSESSED' VS 'SFLA' 'MARKET' VS 'SFLA'

       -
       -
       -                           B  B           B
   45+                      2  B2B      B                    B
       -         B          B  B222 B
       -           B  BBBB   23  B  B       B
       -       B2 2 22BBBB
       -       BB  BB    A        A  A
   30+         B    B     2A   2AA  A               A        A
       -  BAB     AB2  2A   A  32   A
       -   2    A2  AA   AA   AA2        A
       -    A   A 2 2   AAA    2        A    A
       -   B         A   A        A
   15+             2     A
       -
       -  A
       -         A       A
       -
    0+
        ----+----------+----------+----------+----------+--
           600        900       1200       1500       1800

         A = ASSESSED vs. SFLA     B = MARKET vs. SFLA
 CORRELATION 'ASSESSED' 'MARKET' 'SFLA'

           ASSESSED    MARKET
 MARKET     0.545
 SFLA       0.347       0.749
```

are organized. Any plot that can be done by LPLOT can also be done by MPLOT and vice versa if you reorganize the data appropriately. For example, the plot in Exhibit 3.3 can be done with MPLOT as follows:

```
NAME C1 'ASSET.SB' C2 'DEP.SB' C3 'ASSET.MW' C4 'DEP.MW'
READ 'ASSET.SB' 'DEP.SB'
           20.3      16.5
           16.6      13.4
          216.4     165.3
           59.4      49.2
           30.0      23.1
           30.8      25.9
           13.6      11.5
          152.8     120.3
           28.1      22.9
END
READ 'ASSET.MW' 'DEP.MW'
          130.2      91.8
           36.3      29.8
           25.5      21.1
           19.6      16.5
           56.6      46.0
           36.8      28.0
           14.0      11.4
           62.4      47.6
           30.0      24.3
END
MPLOT DEP.SB' VS 'ASSET.SB' AND 'DEP.MW' VS 'ASSET.MW'
```

In this case the Midwest states will be denoted by Bs.

In general, LPLOT requires all data for the horizontal axis to be stacked in one column, all data for the vertical axis to be stacked in a second column, and codes for group membership to be stacked in a third column. MPLOT requires a separate pair of columns for each group.

EXERCISES

3-4   Produce an LPLOT of height versus weight by sex for the Class data (p. 281).

3-5   Plot market values against style and against grade in the Property data set (p. 273). Do any MPLOTs you think might be useful. (This could involve recoding the style and/or grade values to integers and using LPLOT.)

3-6   For the life insurance data on the next page, plot benefit payments versus value of insurance in force by state. How would you describe the relationship between these two variables?

3-7   For the life insurance data on the next page, plot benefit payments versus

policies by state. How would you describe the relationship between these
two variables?

3-8   For the life insurance data below, produce an LPLOT of benefit payments
versus value of insurance in force by state, using "region" to generate
labels.

Life Insurance — Insurance in Force and Benefit Payments
by State: 1982 (applies to policyholders and payments in
the U.S.)

Division and State	Policies (1,000)	Insurance in Force Value (bil. dol.)	Avg. per Family (dol.)	Benefit Payments[1] (mil. dol.)
U.S.	**389,560**	**4,476.7**	**49,300**	**47,993.6**
Regions:				
Northeast	79,856	984.4	50,900	12,458.1
No. Central	103,072	1,197.6	52,400	13,232.1
South	148,844	1,461.5	48,600	13,601.2
West	57,788	833.2	44,900	8,702.2
N. Eng.	**20,279**	**250.6**	**50,200**	**3,179.3**
Maine	1,762	16.8	37,000	205.8
N.H.	1,601	18.1	47,200	184.7
Vt.	766	8.5	40,000	100.2
Mass.	8,472	110.0	47,000	1,298.1
R.I.	1,938	19.2	49,800	240.5
Conn.	5,740	78.0	64,400	1,150.0
Mid. Atl.	**59,577**	**733.8**	**51,200**	**9,278.8**
N.Y.	25,197	341.7	49,200	4,412.6
N.J.	11,712	168.1	60,000	2,067.7
Pa.	22,668	224.0	48,800	2,798.5
E. No. Cent.	**73,942**	**840.6**	**52,700**	**9,625.6**
Ohio	19,069	214.8	52,300	2,560.6
Ind.	9,776	104.4	49,100	1,175.9
Ill.	21,114	246.7	55,800	2,834.2
Mich.	16,291	187.7	54,200	2,030.8
Wis.	7,692	87.0	47,500	1,024.1
W. No. Cent.	**29,130**	**357.0**	**51,800**	**3,606.5**
Minn.	6,596	89.5	55,300	859.3
Iowa	4,855	59.6	51,400	685.3
Mo.	8,698	95.6	48,600	947.3
N. Dak.	1,058	14.5	54,500	117.2
S. Dak.	996	12.7	46,500	128.9
Nebr.	2,768	34.9	54,900	377.8
Kans.	4,159	50.2	51,800	490.7

(continues)

Life Insurance *Continued*

Division and State	Insurance in Force		Avg. per Family (*dol.*)	Benefit Payments[1] (*mil. dol.*)
	Policies (*1,000*)	Value (*bil. dol.*)		
So. Atl.	**74,465**	**719.3**	**47,800**	**7,176.3**
Del.	1,442	16.3	69,700	149.1
Md.	7,795	88.6	54,200	921.7
D.C.	2,549	33.3	106,700	195.9
Va.	10,532	111.2	53,700	994.9
W. Va.	3,249	28.7	39,200	291.6
N.C.	12,491	105.1	45,100	1,010.2
S.C.	7,659	54.6	46,100	463.1
Ga.	12,410	112.1	53,100	911.4
Fla.	16,338	169.4	38,300	2,238.4
E. So. Cent.	**31,183**	**248.7**	**45,400**	**2,249.6**
Ky.	6,119	55.3	40,200	531.2
Tenn.	9,318	86.3	49,400	815.3
Ala.	11,855	70.5	48,700	611.5
Miss.	3,891	36.6	40,100	291.6
W. So. Cent.	**43,196**	**493.5**	**51,500**	**4,175.3**
Ark.	2,849	33.2	38,000	299.6
La.	10,068	84.7	53,100	689.0
Okla.	5,109	60.8	47,800	529.6
Tex.	25,170	314.8	53,900	2,657.1
Mt.	**17,380**	**223.3**	**47,300**	**2,211.4**
Mont.	1,130	13.2	40,600	136.8
Idaho.	1,371	15.9	44,000	174.4
Wyo.	672	9.5	48,100	87.6
Colo.	4,838	70.0	54,600	628.9
N. Mex.	1,750	22.5	44,000	209.0
Ariz.	3,972	48.5	43,100	577.6
Utah	2,148	26.4	49,000	237.1
Nev.	1,499	17.3	45,100	160.0
Pac.	**40,408**	**609.8**	**44,100**	**6,490.8**
Wash.	5,328	75.1	41,900	810.4
Oreg.	3,138	45.4	40,100	529.3
Calif.	29,439	455.6	43,900	4,846.3
Alaska	670	10.0	56,400	62.4
Hawaii	1,833	23.7	63,700	242.4

[1]Comprises death payments, matured endowments, disability and annuity payments, surrender values, and policy dividends.
Source: American Council of Life Insurance, Washington, D.C., *Life Insurance Fact Book*, annual.

3.3 / PLOTTING TIME SERIES

A time series is a collection of observations whose values are associated with epochs of time. Examples are the records of monthly sales of a product, of daily closing prices of your favorite stock, and of the annual rainfall in your hometown. Graphical techniques are extremely useful in the study of time series. The most basic time series plot results from plotting the observed values versus their corresponding time periods.

TSPLOT C

Plots the data in C versus the integers 1, 2, 3, etc. This type of plot is often used for time series data. You may specify the scale for the data axis by the following subcommands:

INCREMENT = K
START at K [go to K]

These subcommands have the same meaning as they do in PLOT (p. 52). Time series data often have an associated period. For example, they may be collected monthly (period = 12) or hourly (period = 24). Plotting symbols that reflect this period are used, if you specify a period:

    TSPLOT period = K [starting at K] C

You should specify the starting point if the first observation in C does not correspond to the first period. For example, if C1 contains monthly data starting in March, use

    TSPLOT 12 3 C1

If the time series is too long to fit across the page, the plot is automatically broken into several pieces. The width of a page is controlled by the command OW (p. 306). The command HEIGHT (p. 53) controls the height of a TSPLOT. (The command WIDTH does not apply to TSPLOT.)

Exhibit 3.6 is a program that reads in and plots two time series. The first series is annual U.S. gross national product (GNP) in billions of dollars for the years 1947–1982. The phrase "current dollars" means that

EXHIBIT 3.6   Current and Constant Dollar GNP, 1947 —1982

```
READ C1 C2
232.8 468.3
259.1 487.7
258.0 490.7
286.2 533.5
330.2 576.5
347.2 598.5
366.1 621.8
366.3 613.7
399.3 654.8
420.7 668.8
442.8 680.9
448.9 679.5
486.5 720.4
506.0 736.8
563.3 755.3
563.8 799.1
594.7 830.7
635.7 874.4
688.1 925.9
753.0 981.0
796.3 1007.7
868.5 1051.8
935.5 1078.8
982.4 1075.3
1063.4 1107.5
1171.1 1171.1
1306.6 1235.0
1412.9 1217.8
1528.8 1202.1
1706.5 1274.7
1899.5 1340.5
2127.6 1399.2
2368.8 1431.6
2626.1 1480.7
2937.7 1502.6
3059.3 1476.9
END OF DATA
NAME C1 'GNPCUR'
NAME C2 'GNPCON'
TSPLOT 10 7 'GNPCUR'
TSPLOT 10 7 'GNPCON'
```

GNP is reported in dollars valued as of the reporting year. These figures do not take into account the erosion of the value of the dollar due to inflation. The second series is GNP in billions of 1972 dollars or "constant dollars." The effects of inflation have been removed from the second series by attributing to each dollar the value it would have had if it had been spent in 1972.

The output from the program is shown in Exhibit 3.7. The horizontal axis is the time axis. A few years have been entered by hand to show how to read the scale. The vertical axis is in units of GNP. Notice that the plotting symbols have been arranged to agree with the final digits of the years they represent. Thus the symbol representing 1947 is a 7, 1948 an 8, and so forth. The commands to do this are

```
TSPLOT 10 7 'GNPCUR'
TSPLOT 10 7 'GNPCON'
```

Both plots in Exhibit 3.7 show the rise in GNP over the 36-year period,

---

EXHIBIT 3.7   Time Series Plots of Annual GNP

(a) Current Dollars

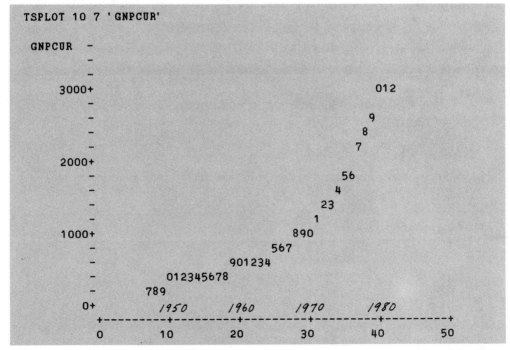

(continues)

EXHIBIT 3.7   *Continued*

(b) Constant Dollars

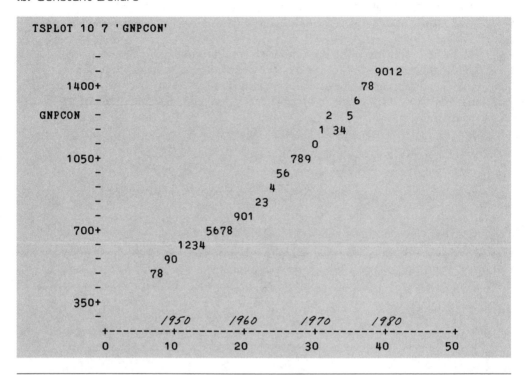

but remember that the rate of increase in part (a) is exaggerated by inflation. Part (b) gives a clearer picture of the rate of increase. The picture would be even clearer if both series were plotted on the same scale.

MULTIPLE TIME SERIES PLOTS

There are two ways to display two series on the same plot. One uses the MPLOT command, the other the MTSPLOT command.

To use the MPLOT command, we issue

```
SET INTO C3
(47:82)
END
NAME C3 'YEAR'
HEIGHT 30
MPLOT C1 VS C3 AND C2 VS C3
```

The HEIGHT command (see p. 53) has been used to improve the resolution of the plot. The output is in Exhibit 3.8, where current dollar GNP is denoted by As and constant dollar GNP is denoted by Bs. While

---

EXHIBIT 3.8   Multiple Time Series Plot of Current and Constant Dollar GNP

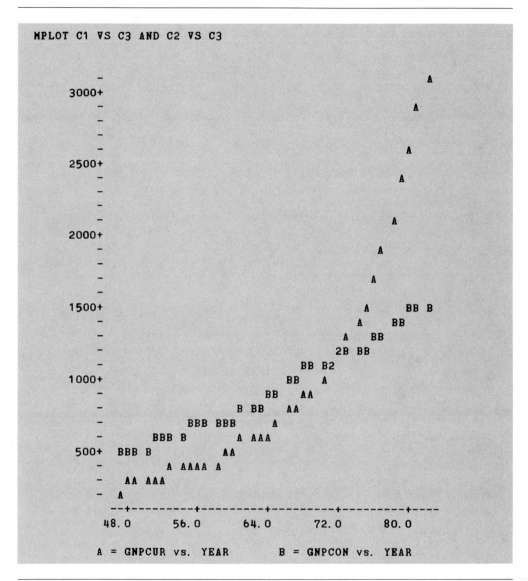

some of the rapid rise in current dollar GNP between 1972 and 1982 is due to increased production, much of it is due to inflation.

To use the MTSPLOT command, we simply issue

```
MTSPLOT C1 AND C2
```

Exhibit 3.9 shows the output.

EXHIBIT 3.9   Output from MTSPLOT

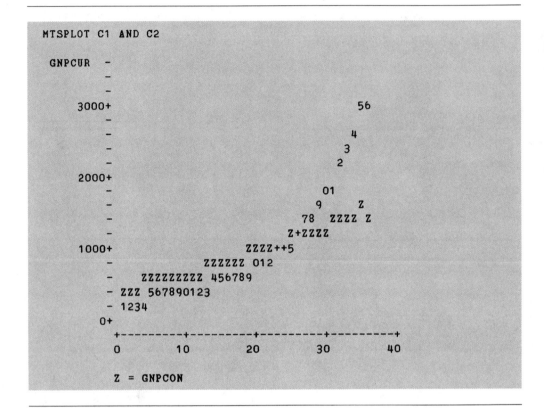

```
MTSPLOT C1 AND C2

GNPCUR  -
        -
        -
        -
  3000+                                              56
        -
        -                                            4
        -                                            3
        -                                            2
  2000+
        -                                        01
        -                                     9     Z
        -                                   78  ZZZZ Z
        -                                 Z+ZZZZ
  1000+                              ZZZZ++5
        -                        ZZZZZZ 012
        -              ZZZZZZZZ 456789
        -  ZZZ 567890123
        -  1234
     0+
        +----------+----------+----------+----------+
        0         10         20         30         40

        Z = GNPCON
```

EXERCISES

3–9   For the quarterly GNP data on page 274, issue the following commands

```
TSPLOT 4 'GNP.CUR'
TSPLOT 4 'GNP.CON'
LET C10 = 'GNP.CUR'/'GNP.CON'
TSPLOT C10
```

Interpret the variable in the time series plot.

3–10 For the monthly money supply data on page 275, issue the commands

```
TSPLOT 12 'SA.M1'
TSPLOT 12 'NSA.M1'
LET C10 = 'GNP.CUR'/'GNP.CON'
TSPLOT 12 C10
```

Interpret the seasonal pattern in the plot of C10.

3–11 For the monthly rate of return data on page 278, create a multiple time series plot with the command

```
MTSPLOT 'IBM' 'XEROX' 'MARKET'
```

Connect the plotting symbols of the three series. What do you conclude?

3–12 For the seasonally adjusted U.S. unemployment rate, January 1970 through December 1979, produce a periodic time series plot. (See pp. 283–285 for a description of these data. Use the COPY command to create the appropriate column for plotting.) How would you describe the behavior of this series over this decade?

3.4 / LAGS, CHANGES, AND PERCENTAGE CHANGES

In time series analysis it is frequently necessary to consider lags of a series. A lag is simply a previous time epoch. For example, if you are considering annual data, one lag from 1985 is 1984, two lags is 1983, and so on. One can consider lags from any starting time. To make the discussion concrete, let's use a few of the current GNP values shown in Exhibit 3.6. If we execute the following commands, with years in column C3,

```
COPY C1 C3 INTO C11 C13;
  USE ROWS 1:5.
NAME C11 'CUR' C13 'YR'
PRINT C13 C11
```

we get the output in part (a) of Exhibit 3.10.

For the year 1948 the lag 1 value of GNP is 232.8, for 1949 the lag 1 value is 259.1, and so forth. We cannot calculate the lag 1 value for 1947 because we do not have in our data set a GNP figure for 1946. You may wish to write the lag 1 values in the exhibit. If you do that and subtract the lag 1 values from the current GNP values, row by row, you will compute the *annual changes* in GNP. Note that the changes for 1948, 1950, and 1951 are positive, but the change for 1949 is negative.

The percentage changes in GNP are calculated by dividing the changes by the lag 1 values and then multiplying by 100. You may wish to add the percentage changes to the table in part (a) of Exhibit 3.10. The Minitab commands to compute the lags, changes, and percentage changes are

```
LAG C11 PUT IN C14
LET C15 = C11-C14
LET C16 = 100*C15/C14
NAME C14 'LAG1.CUR' C15 'CHANGE' C16 '%CHANGE'
PRINT C13 C11 C14-C16
```

The output is in part (b) of Exhibit 3.10. The asterisks in row 1 of the

---

EXHIBIT 3.10   Computation of Annual Lags, Changes, and Percentage
                Changes in Current GNP, 1947–1951

(a)

```
PRINT C13 C11
    ROW    YR    CUR

     1     47    232. 8
     2     48    259. 1
     3     49    258. 0
     4     50    286. 2
     5     51    330. 2
```

(b)

```
PRINT C13 C11 C14-C16

    ROW    YR     CUR   LAG1. CUR    CHANGE    %CHANGE

     1     47   232. 8        *          *          *
     2     48   259. 1     232. 8    26. 3000    11. 2973
     3     49   258. 0     259. 1    -1. 1000    -0. 4245
     4     50   286. 2     258. 0    28. 2000    10. 9302
     5     51   330. 2     286. 2    44. 0000    15. 3739
```

---

output denote "missing data," that is, the values that cannot be calculated
because a 1946 GNP value was not provided.

To put the concepts in this section into action, issue the following
commands (with GNPCUR in C1, GNPCON in C2, and YEAR in C3):

```
LAG C1  C14
LET C4 = C1-C14
LET C5 = 100*C4/C14
LAG C2  C15
LET C6 = C2-C15
LET C7 = 100*C6/C15
NAME C4 'CHNG.CUR' C5 '%CH.CUR' C6 'CHNG.CON' &
    C7 '%CH.CON'
PRINT C3 C1 C4 C5 C6 C7
```

Compare the percentage changes in current and constant GNP is as many
ways as you can think of.

LAG [K] data in C, put in C

Puts the Kth lags of the first column into the second column. K asterisks are entered at the top of the second column. If K is omitted, K = 1 is used.

EXAMPLE

    LAG 3 IN C1, PUT IN C2

C1	C2
5	*
3	*
8	*
7	5
10	3
2	8

EXERCISES

3–13 For the data in Exhibit 3.6, compute the second lags, changes, and percentage changes in GNP by issuing the commands

```
LAG 2 C1 C21
LET C22 = C1-C21
LET C23 = 100*C22/C21
PRINT C3 C1 C21-C23
```

Is it true that the sum of the lag 1 changes for 1949 and 1950 is equal to the lag 2 change for 1950? Why or why not? What is the relationship between the lag 1 and lag 2 percentage changes?

3–14 Issue the commands listed on page 68. Make TSPLOTS of the resulting time series. Comment on the behavior of the series.

3–15 For the GNP data in Exhibit 3.6, find the ratio of current to constant GNP with the command

```
LET C10 = C1/C2
```

This ratio is a measure of inflation. Compute and analyze its annual percentage changes.

3–16 For the quarterly money supply data on page 274, issue the following commands

```
LAG 'SA.M1' PUT IN C7
LET C8 = 'SA.M1'-C7
LAG 4 'SA.M1' PUT IN C9
LET C10 = 'SA.M1'-C9
LAG C10 C11
LET C12 = C10-C11
PRINT 'SA.M1' C7-C11
```

Interpret each column of figures. Produce TSPLOTS of these series and interpret them. SA.M1 stands for seasonally adjusted M1.

4 / TABLES

Minitab's TABLE command provides two general types of capabilities. The first type, considered in Section 4.1, makes tables of counts and percents. It is a generalization of the TALLY command (see Section 2.6). The second type, considered in Section 4.2, provides summary statistics, such as means and standard deviations, for related variables.

AN EXAMPLE: THE WISCONSIN RESTAURANT SURVEY

Because tables arise naturally in survey work, we will illustrate the TABLE command using data from an actual survey, the 1980 Wisconsin Restaurant Survey, conducted by the University of Wisconsin Small Business Development Center. This survey was done primarily to "allow educators, researchers, and public policy makers to evaluate the status of Wisconsin's restaurant sector and to identify particular problems that it is encountering." A second purpose was to develop data that would "be useful to small business counselors in advising managers as to how to effectively plan and operate their small restaurants."

Nineteen of Wisconsin's counties were selected for study. Lists of restaurants were drawn up from telephone directories, and these were sampled in proportion to the population of the county. A sample of 1000 restaurants yielded 279 usable responses.

In a full analysis of these data we would be concerned about possible biases from the sampling method and from the 28% response rate. Here, however, we are interested only in providing summaries of the returned questionnaires—not in making inferences to all restaurants.

The data base thus consists of 279 cases, one for each restaurant with usable data. In this book we will use only a few of the many variables in the survey. The data set is listed on page 286 and is saved in the worksheet called RESTRNT. The first 12 variables were taken from the questionnaires, while the other four were calculated from the 12 basic variables. Each of the 279 respondents failed to answer at least one question. Thus there are a number of missing values, which are coded by * (see p. 22 and p. 304 about missing data).

4.1/ TABLES OF COUNTS AND PERCENTS

We begin by describing the basic TABLE command. Then, as needed, we will introduce other features.

As a first example, we will classify the restaurants by type of ownership and size. The variable OWNER takes on three values: 1 = sole proprietorship; 2 = partnership; and 3 = corporation. SIZE also takes on three values: 1 = under 10 employees; 2 = from 10 to 20 employees; and 3 = over 20 employees. Exhibit 4.1 uses the TABLE command to print the appropriate table.

EXHIBIT 4.1   Number of Restaurants Classified by Type of Ownership and Size

```
TABLE 'OWNER' 'SIZE'

 ROWS: OWNER      COLUMNS: SIZE

                 1          2          3         ALL

    1           83         18          2         103
    2           16          6          4          26
    3           40         42         50         132
   ALL         139         66         56         261

   CELL CONTENTS --
                  COUNT
```

The first column of this table gives counts for restaurants with SIZE = 1. There were 83 restaurants with OWNER = 1 and SIZE = 1; that is, there were 83 sole proprietorships with under ten employees. Similarly, there were 16 partnerships and 40 corporations with under ten employees. Altogether, there were 139 restaurants with under ten employees.

The grand total, 261, is the total number of restaurants in this table. This is less than the 279 restaurants that are in the data base. Therefore, only 261 restaurants had usable data for both OWNER and SIZE. The other 18 had missing data on either OWNER or SIZE or both.

The last row and last column are called the margins of the table, and the counts there are called marginal statistics. The other nine counts form the main body of the table.

> ## TABLE the data classified by C, ..., C
>
> Prints one-way, two-way, and multi-way tables of counts. The classification variables must contain integer values between − 10000 and 10000.

PERCENTS

It often is easier to interpret a table if we convert counts to percents. TABLE has three subcommands to do this: ROWPERCENT calculates row percents, COLPERCENT calculates column percents, and TOTPERCENT calculates total percents.

Exhibit 4.2 contains an example using total percents. To calculate the total percent in a cell, Minitab divides the count in that cell by the grand total, 261 in this case, then multiplies by 100. For example, (83/261) × 100 = 31.80% of the restaurants were sole proprietorships with fewer than ten employees. Thus almost one third of the restaurants in the study were small: one owner and under ten employees. Over half the restaurants, 53.26%, have under ten employees, and just over half, 50.57%, are owned by corporations.

Exhibit 4.3 contains an example using both row and column percents. To calculate row percents. Minitab divides the count in each cell by the row total, then multiplies by 100. For example, there are 103 restaurants in row one; therefore, (83/103) × 100 = 80.58% of the sole proprietorships had under 10 employees. Only 1.94% of the sole proprietorships had more than 20 employees. The remaining 17.48% had between 10 and 20

EXHIBIT 4.2   Percents for Restaurants

```
TABLE 'OWNER' 'SIZE';
TOTPERCENT.

ROWS: OWNER     COLUMNS: SIZE

                1         2         3       ALL

    1       31.80      6.90      0.77     39.46
    2        6.13      2.30      1.53      9.96
    3       15.33     16.09     19.16     50.57
  ALL       53.26     25.29     21.46    100.00

  CELL CONTENTS --
              % OF TBL
```

EXHIBIT 4.3   Row and Column Percents for Restaurants

```
TABLE 'OWNER' 'SIZE';
ROWPERCENT;
COLPERCENT.

 ROWS: OWNER      COLUMNS: SIZE

               1        2        3      ALL

    1      80.58    17.48     1.94   100.00
           59.71    27.27     3.57    39.46

    2      61.54    23.08    15.38   100.00
           11.51     9.09     7.14     9.96

    3      30.30    31.82    37.88   100.00
           28.78    63.64    89.29    50.57

  ALL      53.26    25.29    21.46   100.00
          100.00   100.00   100.00   100.00

   CELL CONTENTS --
                    % OF ROW
                    % OF COL
```

---

employees. On the other hand, the corporations were split fairly evenly among the three sizes: 30.30% had under ten employees; 31.82% had from 10 to 20 employees; and 37.88% had over 20 employees.

To calculate column percents, Minitab divides the count of each cell by the column total, then multiplies by 100. Notice that among restaurants with under ten employees, the majority, 59.71%, were sole proprietorships, whereas among restaurants with over 20 employees, the overwhelming majority, 89.29%, were corporations.

TABLE C, ..., C

Subcommands for counts and percents

COUNTS

Prints a count of the number of observations in each cell. If no subcommands for statistics are given, then counts are printed by default.

ROWPERCENT

Prints row percents in each cell. The row percent for a cell is

$$\frac{\text{(number of observations in the cell)}}{\text{(number of observations in the row)}} \times 100$$

COLPERCENTS

Prints column percent in each cell. The column percent for a cell is

$$\frac{\text{(number of observations in the cell)}}{\text{(number of observations in the column)}} \times 100$$

TOTPERCENT

Prints total percents in each cell. The total percent for a cell is

$$\frac{\text{(number of observations in the cell)}}{\text{(number of observations in the table)}} \times 100$$

EXERCISES

4–1 The following refer to Exhibit 4.1.
  (a) How many restaurants had corporate ownership? How many were partnerships?
  (b) How many were partnerships with 10 to 20 employees? How many were partnerships with over 20 employees?
  (c) How many restaurants had ten or more employees? Twenty or fewer employees?
  (d) How many had ten or more employees and were owned by a corporation? How many had ten or more and were not owned by a corporation?

4–2 Refer to Exhibits 4.2 and 4.3.
  (a) What percent had fewer than ten employees? More than 20 employees? Ten or more employees?
  (b) What percent were partnerships with fewer than ten employees? Corporations with ten to 20 employees?
  (c) Of the partnerships, what percent had 10 to 20 employees? More than 20 employees?
  (d) Of the restaurants having fewer than ten employees, what percent were partnerships?
  (e) Of the partnerships, what percent had ten or more employees?

4.2 / TABLES FOR RELATED VARIABLES

So far, we have discussed frequency tables—tables whose cells contain counts and percents. We can also create tables whose cells contain summary statistics on related variables.

Exhibit 4.4 contains a table of means. This table has the same two classification variables (also called factors), OWNER and SIZE, that we used in Exhibit 4.1. Now, however, each cell contains the mean sales of all restaurants in the cell. For example, sole proprietorships with under ten employees had average sales of $115,550; all restaurants with under ten employees had average sales of $146,300; all restaurants in the study (with usable data on OWNER, SIZE, and SALES) had average sales of $339,000.

Any number of summary statistics on any number of variables can be put in a table. Exhibit 4.5 has three statistics in each cell: MIN gives the minimum sales in each cell, MEDIAN gives the median, and MAX gives the maximum. (Notice that medians do not appear in the margins of the table. Minitab did this to save computing time. Median is the only statistic that does not appear in the margins.)

Exhibit 4.5 merits careful study. First, look at the cell with OWNER = 1, SIZE = 1. The minimum sales is 0. Thus, one restaurant reported no sales for 1979. Suppose we go back to the data listing on page 286. This sales figure is on line 203. This restaurant also has market value listed as 0. All other responses, however, seem reasonable. Perhaps the restaurant owner forgot to answer these two questions, or gave unreadable answers, or the person who entered the data into a computer file

---

EXHIBIT 4.4   Mean Sales for Restaurants (in thousands of dollars)

```
TABLE 'OWNER' 'SIZE';
  MEAN 'SALES'.

  ROWS: OWNER      COLUMNS: SIZE

             1         2         3       ALL

    1    115. 55   237. 94   579. 00   148. 49
    2     88. 12   321. 25   695. 00   228. 12
    3    231. 50   313. 84   887. 96   507. 78
  ALL    146. 30   291. 57   861. 74   339. 00

  CELL CONTENTS --
        SALES: MEAN
```

EXHIBIT 4.5   Sales for Restaurants (in thousands of dollars)

```
TABLE 'OWNER' 'SIZE';
  MIN 'SALES';
  MEDIAN 'SALES';
  MAX 'SALES'.

  ROWS: OWNER      COLUMNS: SIZE

                1         2         3      ALL

    1      0.00     39.00    425.00      0.00
          98.00    220.00    579.00      --
         435.00    507.00    733.00    733.00


    2      2.00    200.00    480.00      2.00
          76.00    267.50    750.00      --
         250.00    550.00    800.00    800.00


    3      2.00    100.00    225.00      2.00
         133.50    274.00    565.00      --
        3450.00    720.00   8064.00   8064.00


  ALL      0.00     39.00    225.00      0.00
           --        --        --        --
        3450.00    720.00   8064.00   8064.00


  CELL CONTENTS --
          SALES: MINIMUM
                 MEDIAN
                 MAXIMUM
```

---

mistakenly typed a zero instead of an *. Or, perhaps the owner answered 0 when he meant to answer, "I don't know." Unfortunately, the original questionnaire had been destroyed by the time these problems were discovered, so the best we can do now is replace the two 0s by *, the missing data code. The appropriate commands are

```
LET 'SALES'(203) = '*'
LET 'VALUE'(203) = '*'
```

The problem of a 0 for SALES was very easy to find. If we carefully look at the patterns in the table, we can find another unusual value. Within each OWNER category, minimum sales increase as the number of employees increases. The medians follow the same pattern. Now look at the maximums. In the first two OWNER categories, maximum sales increase as we go across the row. In the last OWNER category, however, this pattern does not hold: Corporations with under ten employees have a much larger maximum than corporations with 10 to 20 employees. In fact, the sales figure of $3,450,000 is suspiciously large.

Again, we go back to the data listing on page 286. This sales figure is on line 111. Look at the other information for this restaurant. The owners said that they were very pessimistic about the future, had made only $10,000 in capital improvements, and valued the business at just $100,000. These responses do not make much sense for a restaurant that had gross sales of $3,450,000. This sales figure is almost certainly in error. Again, we will replace it by an *.

The simple table in Exhibit 4.5 brought two errors to our attention. There are probably many more still in the data set. Most data sets initially contain many errors, and one of the first steps in any analysis is to try to find them. The simple displays and summaries of Chapters 2 and 3, and the TABLE command, can help. Use the TALLY command on each categorical variable to discover values out of range. Use DESCRIBE and perhaps STEM-AND-LEAF on all interval variables to find values out of range and unusual patterns. Both DESCRIBE and STEM-AND-LEAF would have uncovered the zero on SALES. Neither, however, would have revealed the restaurant with $3,450,000 of SALES. In itself, $3,450,000 is not unusual, but in the context of OWNER and SIZE it is. This value is called a multivariate outlier; it is unusual in the context of several variables. The plotting commands of Chapter 3 and the TABLE command display several variables at once and can help find multivariate outliers.

TABLE C, ..., C

Subcommands for summary statistics on related variables

MEANS for C, ..., C
MEDIANS for C, ..., C
STDEVS for C, ..., C
MINIMUMS for C, ..., C
MAXIMUMS for C, ..., C
N for C, ..., C
NMISS for C, ..., C
STATS for C, ..., C
DATA for C, ..., C

The first seven subcommands calculate one summary statistic for each related variable, for each cell of the table.

N gives the number of observations in a cell that have a value for the related variable. NMISS gives the number of observations that have an *

(missing value) for the related variable. (Thus COUNT = N + NMISS.)
STATS is the same as typing N, MEAN, and STDEV.
DATA prints all values of the related variable, in each cell.

EXERCISES

4–3　Refer to Exhibits 4.4 and 4.5. If the desired results are not available from these exhibits, please say so.

　(*a*)　What was the median sales volume of partnerships with under ten employees? Of all partnerships? Of all restaurants?

　(*b*)　Which type of restaurant had the highest mean sales volume? The lowest?

4–4　Exhibit 4.4 contains mean SALES classified by OWNER and SIZE. Use the TABLE command to determine the total number of restaurants in the table in Exhibit 4.4. Compare this to the total number of restaurants in Exhibit 4.1. Why is there a difference?

4–5　Use the restaurant data (p. 286) to answer the following:

　(*a*)　Find the mean and median number of seats for each TYPEFOOD. Discuss the results.

　(*b*)　Find the mean and median amount of sales per seat for each different TYPEFOOD. Discuss the results.

　(*c*)　Find the mean and median amount of sales per employee for each of the three sizes of restaurants. Discuss the results.

4.3 / ADVANCED FEATURES OF TABLE

In Sections 4.1 and 4.2. we introduced some of the basic features of TABLE. These are all you will need to read the rest of the book. The TABLE command, however, can produce more sophisticated displays — tables with three or more classification variables printed in a variety of layouts. In this section, we will present several examples, each illustrating a feature of TABLE.

THE LAYOUT SUBCOMMAND

The output in Exhibit 4.6 uses the LAYOUT subcommand. This table is similar to the one in Exhibit 4.5; it has the same two classification variables, and it has three statistics per cell. Now, however, the two classification variables are both used on the rows, and no classification

EXHIBIT 4.6   Sales Volume by Type of Ownership and Size (in thousands
              of dollars)

```
TABLE 'OWNER' 'SIZE';
STATS 'SALES';
LAYOUT 2, 0.

ROWS: OWNER / SIZE
                SALES    SALES    SALES
                  N      MEAN    STD DEV
   1
          1       75    115.55     76.58
          2       18    237.94    135.76
          3        2    579.00    217.79
   2
          1       16     88.12     64.65
          2        4    321.25    157.06
          3        4    695.00    145.26
   3
          1       38    231.50    544.47
          2       38    313.84    138.90
          3       47    887.96   1261.47
  ALL
        ALL      242    339.00    663.40
```

variables are used on the columns. This is what the LAYOUT subcommand says to do: Put the first two classification variables on the rows, with OWNER first and SIZE nested within OWNER, and put the next 0 classification variables on the columns. Since there are no classification variables on the columns, Minitab printed the three statistics across the page to save space. For some purposes, this layout is more useful than the LAYOUT 1,1 shown in Exhibit 4.5.

THREE OR MORE CLASSIFICATION VARIABLES

The output in Exhibit 4.7 contains three two-way tables, one for each value of TYPEFOOD. The first table gives a breakdown of the 108 fast food restaurants (TYPEFOOD = 1 is fast food) by OWNER and SIZE; the second table gives a breakdown of the 71 supper clubs (TYPEFOOD = 2), and the third table gives a breakdown of the 73 remaining restaurants (TYPEFOOD = 3).

In general, if there are three or more classification variables, the first is used for the rows, the second is used for the columns, and the remaining are used to determine the separate tables. This arrangement can be

EXHIBIT 4.7   Example of a Table with Three Classification Variables

```
TABLE 'OWNER' 'SIZE' 'TYPEFOOD'

  CONTROL: TYPEFOOD =  1
  ROWS: OWNER       COLUMNS: SIZE

               1          2          3        ALL

     1        32          9          1         42
     2         6          2          0          8
     3        20         19         19         58
   ALL        58         30         20        108

  CONTROL: TYPEFOOD =  2
  ROWS: OWNER       COLUMNS: SIZE

               1          2          3        ALL

     1        23          7          0         30
     2         2          4          2          8
     3         9         13         11         33
   ALL        34         24         13         71

  CONTROL: TYPEFOOD =  3
  ROWS: OWNER       COLUMNS: SIZE

               1          2          3        ALL

     1        26          2          1         29
     2         5          0          2          7
     3        10          9         18         37
   ALL        41         11         21         73

  CELL CONTENTS --
                COUNT
```

changed with the LAYOUT subcommand. For example,

```
TABLE 'OWNER' 'SIZE' 'TYPEFOOD';
  LAYOUT 2, 1.
```

puts the first two variables on the rows and the next one variable on the columns. No variables are left over, so there is just one table. Output is in Exhibit 4.8.

In Exhibit 4.8, the last row contains marginal counts summed over both OWNER and SIZE. In general, the marginal statistics used in a table

---

EXHIBIT 4.8   Illustration of How the LAYOUT Subcommand Changes the
              Appearance of a Table

```
TABLE 'OWNER' 'SIZE' 'TYPEFOOD';
LAYOUT 2,1.

 ROWS: OWNER / SIZE        COLUMNS: TYPEFOOD
                    1         2         3        ALL
  1
           1       32        23        26        81
           2        9         7         2        18
           3        1         0         1         2
  2
           1        6         2         5        13
           2        2         4         0         6
           3        0         2         2         4
  3
           1       20         9        10        39
           2       19        13         9        41
           3       19        11        18        48
 ALL
          ALL     108        71        73       252

 CELL CONTENTS --
                  COUNT
```

---

are for the rows and columns printed in the table. Therefore, marginal
statistics and percents (row, column, and total) will change when you
change layouts.

Sometimes the marginal statistics are not needed and just clutter up a
table. This is often true when there are three or more classification
variables. The subcommand NOALL can be used to suppress them. For
example,

```
TABLE 'OWNER' 'SIZE' 'TYPEFOOD';
  LAYOUT 2, 1;
  MEAN 'SALES';
  NOALL.
```

TABLE C, ..., C

Subcommands to control the output.

LAYOUT K, K

The first K says how many classification variables to use for the rows of the table, and the second K says how many classification variables to use for the columns. For example,

```
TABLE C4 C5 C8-C12;
   LAYOUT 3, 2.
```

says to use the first three variables, C4, C5, and C8, for the rows and the next two variables, C9 and C10, for the columns. There are two variables left over, C11 and C12. A separate table is produced for each combination of entries in C11 and C12.

If no LAYOUT subcommand is given, LAYOUT 1.0 is used for tables with one classification variable, and LAYOUT 1,1 is used for tables with two or more classification variables.

The first K of LAYOUT may be 0,1 . . . ,10. The second K may be 0, 1, or 2.

NOALL

suppresses the printing of all marginal statistics.

4.4 / TABLING TIME SERIES

Data collected periodically (monthly, quarterly, etc.) are usefully displayed in two-way tables. As an example, let's display monthly values of money supply M1 (coins, currency, and demand deposits), 1970–1984, by year and by month. (See p. 275 for the data. We are using the not seasonally adjusted (NSA) data here). We need two qualitative variables, one for year and one for month. The data we need to enter are laid out schematically below.

Year	Month
1970	1
1970	2
*	*
*	*
*	*
1970	12
1971	1
*	*
*	*
*	*
1971	12
*	*
*	*
*	*
1984	12

Each column contains 180 numbers, but with lots of repetitions. These numbers will be troublesome to enter directly, but fortunately the SET command permits us to enter "patterned" data very efficiently.

A list of numbers that is to be repeated may be enclosed in parentheses and the number of repetitions placed immediately before or after the parentheses. For example, the commands

```
SET INTO Cl
3(1,2,3,4)
END
```

will set the numbers

```
1 2 3 4 1 2 3 4 1 2 3 4
```

into column C1. The commands

```
SET INTO C2
(1,2,3,4)3
END
```

will set the numbers

```
1 1 1 2 2 2 3 3 3 4 4 4
```

into column C2. The number before the parentheses says to repeat the list that number of times; the number after the parentheses says to repeat each item in the list that number of times.

Let's see if we can use this technique to solve our time series data entry problem. To simplify the output, let's forget about the "19" part of the year designations and denote 1970 by 70, 1971 by 71, and so on. We want to repeat each item in the list (70, 71, . . . , 84) twelve times. Minitab lets us write the list as (70:84). In other words, consecutive numbers can be denoted by the first and last numbers in the list separated by a colon. We now enter the year designations with the commands

```
SET YEAR INTO C4
(70:84)12
END
```

The entry of the month designations is much simpler. We write

```
SET MONTH INTO C5
15(1:12)
END
```

This repeats the list (1, . . . , 12) fifteen times. We complete our table by reading in the money supply, naming columns, and using TABLE.

The complete set of commands is

```
SET YEAR INTO C4
(70:84)12
END
```

```
SET MONTH INTO C5
15(1:12)
END
SET MONEY SUPPLY INTO C3
```

(money supply data entered here)

```
NAME C4 'YEAR' C5 'MONTH' C3 'M1.NSA'
OUTPUTWIDTH 132
TABLE 'YEAR' BY 'MONTH';
  MEANS OF 'M1.NSA'.
```

The resulting table is in Exhibit 4.9. The OUTPUTWIDTH command allows us to print out a wide table on paper without breaking it into panels (even though it would not be displayed this way on a terminal screen). The MEANS subcommand places the observations in the body of the table and the yearly and monthly means in the margins. The means are especially useful in searching for trends and seasonal patterns. For example, average monthly M1 rose from $211.15 billion in 1970 to $544.98 billion in 1984. On the average, the month with the smallest M1 is February, while the month with the largest M1 is December.

If you want the table in Exhibit 4.9 without marginal means, use the DATA subcommand instead of MEANS.

EXERCISES

4–6   Write commands to enter the qualitative variables to table quarterly gross national product for the years 1965–1972. Be sure to name the variables.

4–7   This exercise uses the unemployment data on page 283.

    (a)   Read the number of unemployed persons into C1 and the number in the labor force into C2. Divide C1 by C2 and store in C3. Now C3 contains the unemployment rate *not seasonally adjusted*. Produce a TSPLOT of this series.

    (b)   Produce a periodic table of unemployment rates for the years 1960–1969. The data for these years can be obtained with the COPY command with the USE subcommand (see p. 300). Describe the behavior of the yearly and monthly means. Do you detect a "seasonal effect" in the monthly means?

    (c)   Repeat part (b) for the decades 1950–1959 and 1970–1979.

    (d)   Over the three decades you have studied, do you find a month that consistently has the highest average unemployment?

    (e)   Enter the monthly means from the three decades into three different columns. SET 1, 2, ..., 12 into a fourth column and do an MPLOT of the three sets of monthly means against the fourth column. Describe what you see.

EXHIBIT 4.9　Table of Money Supply by Month and Year with Monthly and Yearly Averages, 1970–1984

```
OUTPUTWIDTH 132
TABLE 'YEAR' BY 'MONTH';
MEANS 'M1.NSA'.
```

ROWS: YEAR　　COLUMNS: MONTH

	1	2	3	4	5	6	7	8	9	10	11	12	ALL
70	212.90	204.00	205.50	210.10	206.20	208.90	210.10	210.00	212.80	214.40	216.70	222.20	211.15
71	222.60	216.60	218.60	223.70	221.10	225.20	227.50	225.90	227.70	229.10	231.20	236.90	225.51
72	237.50	231.40	234.20	239.50	234.70	238.80	241.80	241.30	244.50	247.00	250.50	258.90	241.68
73	259.40	251.20	251.60	257.00	253.60	259.30	261.20	258.60	259.50	261.40	265.70	273.30	259.32
74	271.80	264.10	266.50	271.60	266.30	271.50	273.50	271.00	272.60	274.80	278.80	285.20	272.31
75	281.80	273.30	276.40	281.40	278.10	286.00	288.00	286.30	287.80	288.50	293.50	299.00	285.01
76	296.80	289.00	291.40	299.90	295.10	299.40	302.30	301.00	302.50	307.00	309.70	318.60	301.06
77	317.70	309.00	312.20	322.70	315.60	321.70	326.30	324.30	327.70	332.00	335.40	344.10	324.06
78	343.40	332.00	334.90	347.50	342.40	349.40	353.90	351.70	357.00	359.40	362.90	372.50	350.58
79	367.80	356.40	360.80	376.20	367.10	376.70	383.30	381.90	385.60	387.70	389.80	398.60	377.66
80	396.10	386.30	387.80	392.60	383.30	393.10	400.50	404.30	411.10	417.30	421.30	424.80	401.54
81	421.80	410.60	417.30	436.30	423.50	427.80	432.80	430.90	432.30	435.10	440.40	452.20	430.08
82	454.30	437.90	440.90	456.30	446.10	451.30	454.80	454.90	461.40	471.30	479.90	491.80	458.41
83	489.60	480.50	489.20	505.30	500.70	510.00	517.40	514.70	517.80	524.00	528.50	539.70	509.78
84	536.80	523.90	530.40	545.60	537.30	547.90	549.90	545.00	548.50	548.20	555.90	570.40	544.98
ALL	340.69	331.08	334.51	344.38	338.07	344.47	348.22	346.79	349.92	353.15	357.35	365.88	346.21

```
CELL CONTENTS --
      M1.NSA: MEAN
```

(*f*) Enter the two qualitative variables needed to classify the unemployment rates for 1950–1979 (in C3) by year and month. Print out the periodic table and compare it with the tables that you created for the three separate decades.

4–8   Select any time series that interests you, enter it into the computer, and display it graphically and in a table or tables.

5/COMPARING TWO OR MORE SETS OF DATA

Comparisons based on data from two or more groups require attention to

1. the way the data are related;
2. the way the data are entered into the worksheet.

5.1/PAIRED DATA

As an example, consider the White and Black unemployment rates in Exhibit 1.1. These data are *paired* because each row of data contains a pair of rates generated in the same month. The data are in unstacked form because the White and Black rates are in different columns. Exhibit 5.1 shows how the unemployment rates might have been entered in stacked form. The commands

```
SET INTO C4
 6.9   6.7   6.7  6.7  6.5  6.3
 6.3   6.4   6.3  6.3  6.1  6.2
16.7  16.2  16.6 16.8 16.0 15.2
16.6  15.8  15.1 15.3 15.1 15.0
END
```

put the White and Black rates in column C4. The commands

```
SET INTO C5
2(1:12)
END
SET INTO C6
12(1)  12(2)
END
```

EXHIBIT 5.1   Entry of Unemployment Rates in Stacked Form

```
SET INTO C4
 6.9  6.7  6.7  6.7  6.5  6.3
 6.3  6.4  6.3  6.1  6.2  6.2
16.7 16.2 16.6 16.8 16.0 15.2
16.6 15.8 15.1 15.3 15.1 15.0
END
SET INTO C5
2(1:12)
END
SET INTO C6
12(1) 12(2)
END
NAME C4 'UNEM.RT' C5 'MONTH' C6 'RACE'
PRINT C1-C6
```

ROW	C1	C2	C3	UNEM.RT	MONTH	RACE
1	6.9	16.7	2.42029	6.9	1	1
2	6.7	16.2	2.41791	6.7	2	1
3	6.7	16.6	2.47761	6.7	3	1
4	6.7	16.8	2.50746	6.7	4	1
5	6.5	16.0	2.46154	6.5	5	1
6	6.3	15.2	2.41270	6.3	6	1
7	6.3	16.6	2.63492	6.3	7	1
8	6.4	15.8	2.46875	6.4	8	1
9	6.3	15.1	2.39683	6.3	9	1
10	6.1	15.3	2.50820	6.1	10	1
11	6.2	15.1	2.43548	6.2	11	1
12	6.2	15.0	2.41935	6.2	12	1
13				16.7	1	2
14				16.2	2	2
15				16.6	3	2
16				16.8	4	2
17				16.0	5	2
18				15.2	6	2
19				16.6	7	2
20				15.8	8	2
21				15.1	9	2
22				15.3	10	2
23				15.1	11	2
24				15.0	12	2

put month codes in column C5 and race codes in column C6. Remember that the SET command reads the command 2(1:12) as two copies of the sequence 1, 2, . . . , 12. It reads the command 12(1) 12(2) as 12 copies of 1 followed by 12 copies of 2. The commands

```
NAME C4 'UNEM.RT' C5 'MONTH' C6 'RACE'
PRINT C1-C6
```

name columns C4–C6 and print out the worksheet. (We assume that columns C1–C3 as displayed in Exhibit 1.3 are present.) The data are printed out in unstacked and stacked form.

The unstacked form is most useful if we want to compute comparative statistics such as ratios of Black to White unemployment rates by month, as we did in Exhibit 1.3. The stacked form is useful if we want to apply commands such as TABLE or BOXPLOT. It is convenient to be able to move easily between unstacked and stacked forms. The Minitab commands for doing this are STACK and UNSTACK.

STACK (E, ..., E), ..., (E, ..., E) store in (C, ..., C)

This command stacks blocks of columns and constants on top of each other. In general, each block must be enclosed in parentheses. However, if each block contains just one argument, the parentheses may be omitted. If you want to create a column of subscripts, use the subcommand

SUBSCRIPTS into C

In this case, all rows in the first block will be given subscripts of 1, all rows in the second block subscripts of 2, and so on.

UNSTACK (C, ..., C) into (E, ..., E), ..., (E, ..., E)

SUBSCRIPTS are in C

This command separates one block of columns into several blocks of columns and/or stored constants. In general, each block must be enclosed in parentheses. However, if each block contains just one argument, the parentheses may be omitted.

For most applications, the subcommand SUBSCRIPTS will be needed. The rows with the smallest subscript are stored in the first block, the rows with the second smallest subscript are stored in the second block, and so on. If you do not use SUBSCRIPTS, each row is stored in a separate block. The numbers in the subscript column must be integers between $-10,000$ and $10,000$. They need not be in order; nor do they need to be consecutive integers.

Suppose the data are read in as in Exhibit 1.1, which is in unstacked form. To stack, the command is

```
STACK C1 ON C2 PUT IN C4
```

The race codes can be automatically stored by using the SUBSCRIPTS subcommand. The command is

```
STACK C1 ON C2 PUT IN C4;
    SUBSCRIPTS IN C6.
```

The month codes must still be entered with the commands

```
SET INTO C5
2(1:12)
END
```

To unstack the data in column C4, issue the command

```
UNSTACK C4 PUT IN C1 AND C2;
    SUBSCRIPTS IN C6.
```

THE SAME AND BY SUBCOMMANDS

When data are stored in several columns, we may nevertheless wish to display the data in histograms, stem-and-leaf diagrams, or dotplots that all use the same scale. This facilitates comparison of the different variables or the same variable measured at different times, for example. The SAME subcommand allows us to do this.

SAME

This subcommand can be used with the commands STEM-AND-LEAF, HISTOGRAM, and DOTPLOT. It is useful when you want to compare several columns of data. If you use SAME with STEM-AND-LEAF or HISTOGRAM, then the same scale will be used for all columns you list on the main command. If you use SAME with DOTPLOT, then not only are all plots given the same scale, but they are also put in the same display. If you do not use SAME, then each column listed on the main command line is scaled separately.

To illustrate, consider the bank data in Exhibit 3.1. If the region codes are in column C1, assets in column C2, and deposits in column C3, then the command

```
HISTOGRAM C2 AND C3;
    SAME.
```

produces the output in Exhibit 5.2. The two histograms use exactly the same classes. If the SAME subcommand is omitted, the two histograms are

EXHIBIT 5.2   Histograms of Assets and Total Deposits on a
              Common Scale

```
HISTOGRAM C2 AND C3;
  SAME.

Histogram of ASSETS    N = 18

Midpoint    Count
      20        7   *******
      40        5   *****
      60        3   ***
      80        0
     100        0
     120        0
     140        1   *
     160        1   *
     180        0
     200        0
     220        1   *


Histogram of TOT. DEP    N = 18

Midpoint    Count
      20       12   ************
      40        3   ***
      60        0
      80        0
     100        1   *
     120        1   *
     140        0
     160        1   *
     180        0
     200        0
     220        0
```

scaled separately. As another illustration, suppose that deposits of Midwest banks are stored in column C4 and the deposits of Sun Belt banks in C2, as shown on page 58. Then the command

```
DOTPLOT C2 C4;
   SAME.
```

produces dotplots of the two sets of deposits on a *common scale*. When data are stored in one column, we may wish to produce histograms, stem-and-leaf diagrams, or dotplots of the data broken down by groups coded in another column. The BY subcommand allows us to do this.

BY C

This subcommand can be used with the commands STEM-AND-LEAF, HISTOGRAM, DOTPLOT, and DESCRIBE. A separate display is produced for each different value in C. All are put on the same scale. The column C must contain integers from -10000 to $+10000$.

To illustrate, let's return to the bank data in Exhibit 3.1, again with region codes on column C1 and assets in column C2. To get histograms of the assets of Midwest and Suń Belt states, on a common scale, we issue the command

```
HISTOGRAM C2;
  BY C1.
```

The output is in Exhibit 5.3 on page 94.

EXERCISES

5–1   The table below shows U.S. balances in millions of dollars on international transactions, by areas and selected countries for 1980 and 1982. Minus signs (-1) denote debits.

Area or Country	1980 Balances on		1982 Balances on	
	Merchandise	*Goods and Services*	*Merchandise*	*Goods and Services*
United Kingdom	2,970	5,313	2,352	−1,217
Belgium-Luxembourg	4,761	5,517	2,766	3,054
France	2,277	2,768	1,662	1,754
Germany	−243	−3,795	−2,688	−7,032
Italy	1,297	1,678	−649	−672
Netherlands	5,559	4,240	4,979	4,547
Other Western Europe	2,699	1,885	2,237	1,300
Eastern Europe	2,699	3,097	2,682	3,087
Canada	−1,277	7,515	−9,198	203
Latin America and other Western Hemisphere	1,320	13,551	−5,397	8,947
Japan	−10,411	−8,849	−16,991	−15,680
Australia and South Africa	584	3,603	2,623	4,232
Other Asia and Africa	−37,520	−28,830	−16,878	−6,979
Int'l and unallocated	−1,287	−1,780	−23	129

Source: Bureau of the Census, *Statistical Abstract of the United States*, U.S. Department of Commerce, Washington, D.C.: 1984, p. 820, Table 1453.

EXHIBIT 5.3   Histograms of Bank Assets on a Common Scale for
Midwestern and Sun Belt States

```
HISTOGRAM C2;
  BY C1.

Histogram of ASSETS   REGION = O   N = 9

Midpoint    Count
      20       3  ***
      40       3  ***
      60       2  **
      80       0
     100       0
     120       0
     140       1  *
     160       0
     180       0
     200       0
     220       0

Histogram of ASSETS   REGION = 1   N = 9

Midpoint    Count
      20       4  ****
      40       2  **
      60       1  *
      80       0
     100       0
     120       0
     140       0
     160       1  *
     180       0
     200       0
     220       1  *
```

(a) Read these data into the worksheet in unstacked form with the 1980
balances on merchandise in column C1, the 1980 balances on goods
and services in column C2, the 1982 balances on merchandise in
column C3, and the 1982 balances on goods and services in column
C4.

(b) Use the commands

```
LET K1 = SUM(C1)
LET K2 = SUM(C2)
LET K3 = SUM(C3)
LET K4 = SUM(C4)
PRINT K1, K2, K3, K4
```

to get the total balances of payments of merchandise and on goods and services for the years 1980 and 1982. How did the balances change between 1980 and 1982? Compute the changes and percentage changes in the total balances.

(c) Use the command

```
LET C5 = C3-C1
LET C6 = 100*C5/C1
LET C7 = C4-C2
LET C8 = 100*C7/C2
```

to compute changes and percentage changes by areas and selected countries. Compare the areas and countries by these two measures.

(d) Use the STACK command to stack the 1980 balances on merchandise on the 1982 balances on merchandise. Put the results in column C10.

(e) Use the commands

```
SET INTO C11
2(1:14)
END
SET INTO C12
14(1) 14(2)
END
PRINT C10-C12
```

to put area and country codes into column C11, to put year codes into column C12, and to print columns C10–C12. What area or country does the code 5 denote? The code 10?

(f) Use the command

```
TABLE BY C11 AND C12;
   DATA IN C10.
```

to get balances on merchandise by area and country and by year. What would you get from the following commands?

```
STACK C5 ON C7 PUT IN C13;
SUBSCRIPTS IN C15.
SET INTO C14
2(1:14)
END
TABLE C14 C15;
   MEAN C13.
```

Issue the commands and see whether you answered correctly.

(g) Issue the commands

```
STACK C1 ON C2 ON C3 ON C4 PUT IN C20
SET INTO C21
4(1:14)
END
```

```
SET INTO C22
(1:2)28
END
SET INTO C23
2(1:2)14
END
TABLE C21 C22 C33;
    DATA C20.
```

Explain the output from these commands. How would you name the columns to make the table more self-explanatory?

(h)   Issue the commands

```
HISTOGRAM C1 AND C2;
    SAME.
HISTOGRAM C10;
    BY C12.
```

Explain the output.

5–2   For the data in Exhibit 3.1 with deposits of Midwest banks in column C4 and deposits of Sun Belt banks in column C2, issue the commands

```
DOTPLOT C2 C4;
    SAME.
DOTPLOT C2 C4
```

Compare the results.

5–3   Sometimes it is useful to split data into groups based on an interval scale variable. In this exercise we look at the bank data in Exhibit 3.1. Let's create a new variable that has three values:

  1 if assets are between 0 and 50 billion dollars;
  2 if assets are between 50.0001 and 100 billion dollars;
  3 if assets are between 100.0001 and 300 billion dollars.

To create this variable, first suppose that the bank data have been entered into C1–C4. Then use CODE (see p. 302 for a full description of CODE) as follows:

```
CODE (0:50) TO 1 (50.0001:100) TO 2 (100.0001:300) TO &
3 IN C2 PUT IN C5
```

(a)   Use DOTPLOT and DESCRIBE to compare the deposits of the states in each of these three groups.

(b)   Compare the numbers of banks in the three groups.

(c)   Issue the command

```
TABLE BY C1 AND C5;
    STATS OF C3.
```

Interpret your results.

5.2 / SEPARATE GROUPS

UNSTACKED DATA

As a project for a sample survey course, in the spring of 1985 a student selected food stores randomly from the three major geographical divisions of Madison, Wisconsin: Eastside, Isthmus (central city and university campus area), and Westside. For each of the selected stores she determined the price of a two-liter, nonreturnable bottle of a leading soft drink. A program to input the data in unstacked form and to do some descriptive analysis is shown in Exhibit 5.4.

We see that the Eastside has the lowest mean price. The Isthmus has both the highest mean and the smallest standard deviation of the three regions. People who shop in the Isthmus appear to be paying a premium for this soft drink.

STACKED DATA

Exhibit 5.5 shows how the food store survey data could be entered and analyzed in stacked form. In the exhibit we have issued the TABLE

EXHIBIT 5.4   Entry of Food Store Survey Data in Unstacked Form

---

```
SET EASTSIDE INTO C1
1.19 1.59 1.89 1.19 1.99 1.09 0.98
END
SET ISTHMUS INTO C2
1.39 2.05 1.89 1.59 1.69 1.79
END
SET WESTSIDE INTO C3
0.99 1.99 2.09 1.19 1.59 1.49 1.09
END
NAME C1 'EASTSIDE' C2 'ISTHMUS' C3 'WESTSIDE'
DESCRIBE C1-C3
```

	N	MEAN	MEDIAN	TRMEAN	STDEV	SEMEAN
EASTSIDE	7	1.417	1.190	1.417	0.405	0.153
ISTHMUS	6	1.7333	1.7400	1.7333	0.2317	0.0946
WESTSIDE	7	1.490	1.490	1.490	0.432	0.163

	MIN	MAX	Q1	Q3
EASTSIDE	0.980	1.990	1.090	1.890
ISTHMUS	1.3900	2.0500	1.5400	1.9300
WESTSIDE	0.990	2.090	1.090	1.990

EXHIBIT 5.5   Entry of Food Store Survey Data in Stacked Form

---

```
SET INTO C11
1.19 1.59 1.89 1.19 1.99 1.09 0.98
1.39 2.05 1.89 1.59 1.69 1.79
0.99 1.99 2.09 1.19 1.59 1.49 1.09
END
SET C12
7(1) 6(2) 7(3)
END
NAME C11 'PRICE' C12 'LOCATION'
TABLE C12;
  STATS C11.

  ROWS: LOCATION

            PRICE      PRICE      PRICE
              N         MEAN     STD DEV

       1       7       1.4171     0.4048
       2       6       1.7333     0.2317
       3       7       1.4900     0.4320
     ALL      20       1.5375     0.3783
```

---

command to get descriptive statistics. The output in Exhibit 5.4 would have resulted from the command

```
        DESCRIBE C11;
          BY C12.
```

The BY subcommand can also be used with HISTOGRAM, STEM-AND-LEAF, and BOXPLOT.

EXERCISE

5–4   A questionnaire was distributed to a group of employees at an insurance company to determine awareness of fringe benefits. One of the items in the questionnaire asked for a mark on a scale from 1 to 5 that expressed the degree to which the respondent was aware of the details of the retirement plan. (A 1 indicated strong lack of awareness; a 5 indicated strong awareness.) Seventy-three of the respondents had children; 56 did not. The responses are summarized below.

Response	Frequency of Respondents with Children	Without Children
1	10	11
2	13	10
3	15	24
4	20	7
5	15	4

(a) Enter the data into columns C1 and C2 in unstacked form. Hint: Use the command

```
SET INTO C1
10(1) 13(2) 15(3) 20(4) 15(5)
END
```

to enter the column C1 data. What commands do you use to enter the column C2 data?

(b) Issue the commands

```
DOTPLOT C1 C2;
    SAME.
HISTOGRAM C1 C2;
    SAME.
STEM C1 C2;
    SAME.
DESCRIBE C1 C2
```

Which graphical display do you prefer?

(c) Stack column C1 on column C2 and put the result in C3. Set codes for with and without children into C4. Issue the commands

```
DOTPLOT C3;
    BY C4.
HISTOGRAM C3;
    BY C4.
STEM C3;
    BY C4.
DESCRIBE C3;
    BY C4.
```

Compare the output with what you got in part (b).

5.3 / COMPARING SEVERAL RELATED GROUPS

In Section 5.1 we considered comparisons of paired data. Here we show how LPLOT and MPLOT can be used to compare more than two *related* groups.

USING LPLOT WITH STACKED DATA

As part of an effort to evaluate four different brands of microcomputer keyboards, an office manager selected five typists at random from a pool of typists. Each of the five typists typed a passage on each of the four keyboards. The order in which the keyboards were presented to the typists was determined randomly. The number of words per minute was recorded for each typist-keyboard combination. The data are reported in Exhibit 5.6. The following program was used to enter these data in stacked form. (You could also use the patterned data feature on SET to enter the data for TYPIST and BRAND. See p. 295.)

```
NAME C31 'RATE' C32 'TYPIST' C33 'TBRAND'
SET 'RATE'
70 68 68 60
57 67 68 65
72 75 72 70
63 68 72 52
62 72 78 67
END
SET 'TYPIST'
1 1 1 1 2 2 2 2 3 3 3 3 4 4 4 4 5 5 5 5
END
SET 'TBRAND'
1 2 3 4 1 2 3 4 1 2 3 4 1 2 3 4 1 2 3 4
END
```

In this form we can make two plots:

```
LPLOT 'RATE' VS 'TYPIST' SYMBOLS 'TBRAND'
LPLOT 'RATE' VS 'TBRAND' SYMBOLS 'TYPIST'
```

The output is shown in Exhibit 5.7.

The two plots give slightly different insights into the structure of the data. The plot in part (a) shows that typists 3 and 5 had, on the average, the best rates, though they were not the best on every keyboard. No one brand

---

EXHIBIT 5.6   Words per Minute on Keyboard

Typist	Keyboard Brand			
	1	2	3	4
1	70	68	68	60
2	57	67	68	65
3	72	75	72	70
4	63	68	72	52
5	62	72	78	67

EXHIBIT 5.7   Two LPLOTS of Typist Data

(a)

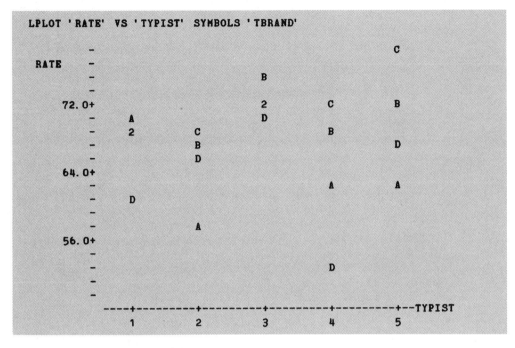

(b)

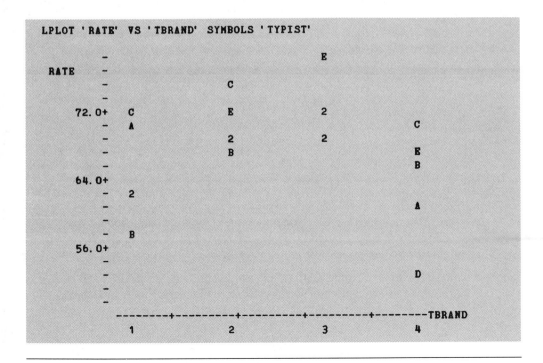

of keyboard had the highest yield for each typist. Brand 3 (symbol C) was the best for typists 2, 4, and 5. Brand 1 (symbol A) was best for typist 1, brand 2 for typist 3.

The plot in part (b) shows how the five typists did on each brand. Brands 2 and 3 are superior to brands 1 and 4, on the average. The choice between brands 2 and 3 is not clear-cut. Other factors need to be taken into account. In Exhibit 5.7 the Minitab output has been edited by directing it to a word processor and changing the symbols printed by Minitab on the horizontal axes. The purpose of the editing is to show the typist and brand indicators as whole numbers and directly under the plotted data.

USING MPLOT WITH UNSTACKED DATA

Part (b) of Exhibit 5.7 could be produced from unstacked data by issuing the commands

```
READ INTO C41—C45
70 57 72 63 62
68 67 75 68 72
68 68 72 72 78
60 65 70 52 67
END
SET INTO C46
1 2 3 4
END
NAME C41 'RATE'
NAME C46 'TBRAND'
MPLOT C41 VS C46, C42 VS C46, C43 VS C46, C44 VS C46, &
      C45 VS C46
```

To produce part (a) of Exhibit 5.7 with MPLOT, the data must be entered in a different order (see Exercise 5–5). The stacked form thus appears to be more convenient for plotting purposes.

EXERCISES

5–5   How do you enter the data in Exhibit 5.6 in order to make part (a) of Exhibit 5.7 using MPLOT?

5–6   Assume that the White and Black unemployment rates are in stacked form as in Exhibit 5.1. What command do you use to plot both White and Black unemployment rates by month on the same graph?

5–7   Assume that the White and Black unemployment rates are in unstacked form as in Exhibit 1.1. What commands do you use to plot both White and Black unemployment rates by month on the same graph?

6/BINOMIAL
AND NORMAL
DISTRIBUTIONS
AND ELEMENTARY
SIMULATIONS

Uncertainty is a daily companion, and unforeseen events can change our lives. Statistical models help us to think about uncertainty and to formulate predictions about events that are beyond our control. In this chapter you will learn four Minitab commands that allow you to do calculations for a variety of important models. They are RANDOM, PDF, CDF, and INVCDF.

6.1/BERNOULLI TRIALS

EXAMPLE

Suppose one of the machines in your plant makes window envelopes that are used in billing customers. When the machine is operating normally, about ½% of the envelopes it produces are unusable because the windows do not meet alignment specifications. Each batch of 300 envelopes is expected to contain one or two unusable envelopes because ½% of 300 is 1.5. The number of bad envelopes in any given batch of 300 is subject to chance, however, and you need to know the chances of observing any specified number of bad envelopes. Then when a batch is inspected, you will know whether the number of bad envelopes actually observed is unlikely and therefore cause for corrective action.

One way to approach this problem is to observe many batches of 300 envelopes produced by your machine while it is operating normally. This can be done by setting up a sampling inspection study in your plant, which can be designed to yield information about your machine, such as amounts of down time and convenience of location, in addition to the percentage of bad envelopes produced.

Another approach, which can supplement the empirical approach outlined above, is to use a statistical model to generate hypothetical data that might come from your empirical study. This is the approach illustrated in this chapter.

A BERNOULLI MODEL

A very simple model for the envelope process is the Bernoulli model. It says that each envelope is the result of an independent replication of the production process, which is stable under normal operating conditions. This means that the envelopes are produced independently and each has a ½% chance of being bad. Minitab's RANDOM command will simulate a sequence of Bernoulli trials.

RANDOM K observations into each of C, ..., C

Bernoulli p = K [success = K failure = K]

Simulates observations from K Bernoulli trials into each column. The value *p* is the probability of a success on each trial. Each success is assigned the value 1, and each failure is assigned the value 0.

Exhibit 6.1 uses the RANDOM command to simulate 300 envelopes. Each 0 represents a good envelope, and each 1 a bad one. We see that there was one bad envelope in this batch, the 137th envelope. A second execution of the RANDOM command (not shown) also yielded one bad envelope, the 128th one.

It would be interesting to repeat the RANDOM command a large number of times and keep a record of the numbers of bad envelopes in the batches of 300. This would appear to require us to type the command many times. Fortunately, though, Minitab will save us this trouble because it allows us to store a sequence of commands and execute them as many times as we desire. (See Appendix B, Section B.11 for a detailed description of the command storage capability.)

To do the envelope simulation 30 times, the commands are

```
STORE 'ENVELOPE'
RANDOM 300 OBSERVATIONS INTO C1;
  BERNOULLI TRIALS WITH p = 0.005.
LET K1 = SUM(C1)
PRINT K1
END
EXECUTE 'ENVELOPE' 30 TIMES
```

The commands listed between the STORE and END commands are stored in a program file called ENVELOPE. These commands are not

---

EXHIBIT 6.1 Simulation of 300 Envelopes Using RANDOM

```
RANDOM 300 C1;
 BERNOULLI P = 0.005.
PRINT C1
 C1
     0    0    0    0    0    0    0    0    0    0    0    0    0    0    0
     0    0    0    0    0    0    0    0    0    0    0    0    0    0    0
     0    0    0    0    0    0    0    0    0    0    0    0    0    0    0
     0    0    0    0    0    0    0    0    0    0    0    0    0    0    0
     0    0    0    0    0    0    0    0    0    0    0    0    0    0    0
     0    0    0    0    0    0    0    0    0    0    0    0    0    0    0
     0    0    0    0    0    0    0    0    0    0    0    0    0    0    0
     0    0    0    0    0    0    0    0    0    0    0    0    0    0    0
     0    0    0    0    0    0    0    0    0    0    0    0    0    0    0
     0   [1]   0    0    0    0    0    0    0    0    0    0    0    0    0
     0    0    0    0    0    0    0    0    0    0    0    0    0    0    0
     0    0    0    0    0    0    0    0    0    0    0    0    0    0    0
     0    0    0    0    0    0    0    0    0    0    0    0    0    0    0
     0    0    0    0    0    0    0    0    0    0    0    0    0    0    0
     0    0    0    0    0    0    0    0    0    0    0    0    0    0    0
     0    0    0    0    0    0    0    0    0    0    0    0    0    0    0
     0    0    0    0    0    0    0    0    0    0    0    0    0    0    0
     0    0    0    0    0    0    0    0    0    0    0    0    0    0    0
     0    0    0    0    0    0    0    0    0    0    0    0    0    0    0

TALLY C1

       C1   COUNT
        0    299
        1      1
       N=    300
```

---

executed until the EXECUTE command is issued. In this example the commands are executed 30 times, thus simulating 30 batches of 300 envelopes. The results of the simulation are summarized in Table 6.1.

TABLE 6.1 Summary of 30 Simulations of Envelope Process

Number of Bad Envelopes	Number of Batches with This Number	Percent of Total
0	4	13.3
1	11	36.7
2	7	23.4
3	6	20.0
4	1	3.3
5	1	3.3
Total	30	100.0

About 37% of the batches had one bad envelope, while about 23% had two bad envelopes; 13% of the batches had no bad envelopes. The largest number of bad envelopes observed was five, but only one batch had this many bad ones.

THE GENERAL BERNOULLI MODEL

Bernoulli trials have been used to model coin flips, the sex of children, deaths of insured lives, and a host of other phenomena. Each trial must result in one of two outcomes called success and failure, and on each trial the probabilities of success and failure are p and $q = 1 - p$. The trials are statistically independent. In most applications a success is coded with 1 and failure with 0, but other codings can be used. The higher the probability of

---

EXHIBIT 6.2   Simulation of Nine Bernoulli Sequences with Different
Probabilities of Success

```
RANDOM 20 C1-C3;
   BERNOULLI .2.
RANDOM 20 C4-C6;
   BERNOULLI .5.
RANDOM 20 C7-C9;
   BERNOULLI .8.
PRINT C1-C9
```

ROW	C1	C2	C3	C4	C5	C6	C7	C8	C9
1	0	0	0	1	1	0	1	1	0
2	0	1	0	0	1	1	1	1	1
3	1	0	0	1	1	1	1	1	1
4	0	0	0	1	0	0	1	1	1
5	0	0	0	1	1	1	1	1	1
6	0	0	1	0	0	1	1	1	1
7	0	0	0	1	0	0	1	1	1
8	1	0	1	0	0	1	1	1	1
9	0	1	0	0	0	0	0	1	1
10	0	0	0	1	0	1	1	0	1
11	0	0	1	0	0	0	0	0	0
12	0	0	1	1	0	0	0	1	0
13	1	0	0	1	1	1	1	1	1
14	0	0	0	0	1	0	1	1	1
15	0	0	1	1	1	0	1	1	1
16	0	0	0	0	1	1	0	1	1
17	0	1	0	0	1	0	1	1	1
18	0	0	0	1	0	1	0	1	0
19	0	0	0	1	0	0	0	1	1
20	0	0	0	0	1	1	1	0	1

success, the greater the number of successes expected in a sequence of trials. Exhibit 6.2 illustrates this by giving nine sequences of 20 trials with different values of p. In C1–C3, $p = 0.2$ was used; in C4–C6, $p = 0.5$ was used; and in C7–C9, $p = 0.8$ was used. In all nine sequences, the zeros and ones have the appearance of randomness. No clear patterns are evident. The sequences in C7–C9 have more ones than the sequences in C1–C3. This is because the value of p was larger for C7–C9 than it was for C1–C3. The value of p determines how many ones you are likely to get. It does not, however, have anything to do with "how random" the sequence is.

EXERCISES

6–1   Enter the commands on page 104 and then make a table like Table 6.1. Do your results differ from those shown there? Why?

6–2   Repeat Exercise 6–1. You now have results for 90 batches of envelopes. Combine them and construct a table like Table 6.1. Summarize in a short paragraph the implications of the "Percent of Total" column.

6–3   Modify the commands on page 104 to generate 30 replications of 100 trials from a Bernoulli process with $p = 0.5$. Can you think of a physical situation for which this Bernoulli process might be a model? Execute the commands and summarize the results in a table.

6.2 / THE BINOMIAL DISTRIBUTION

The binomial distribution is a model for the number of successes observed in a sequence of Bernoulli trials of fixed length. For example, in Section 6.1 we looked at the number of bad envelopes in batches of 300 envelopes. There a bad envelope was a success, and the sequences were of length 300. In traditional notation the sequence length is denoted by n and the probability of success by p. The probabilities in the binomial distribution give the likelihoods of observing various numbers of successes. The PDF command can be used to compute these probabilities.

PDF for values in E [put results into E]

BINOMIAL with n = K and p = K

Calculates probabilities for the binomial distribution with the specified parameters n and p. If you do not store the results, they will be printed. If you use no arguments on the PDF line, a table of all probabilities is printed. For example,

```
PDF;
    BINOMIAL n = 10, p = .4.
```

prints a table with probabilities for 0, 1, 2, ..., 10 successes. If any probabilities at the beginning or end of the list are very small (less than .00005), they are not printed.

Exhibit 6.3 shows the binomial probabilities for batches of 300 envelopes. These probabilities imply that about 22% of all batches have no bad envelopes, 34% have one bad envelope, 25% have two bad envelopes, and so forth. There is about 1 chance in 10,000 that a batch has eight bad envelopes. In other words, if you examined 10,000 batches of 300 envelopes, you would expect to find one batch that had eight bad envelopes. You may compare these percentages with the "Percent of Total" column in Table 6.1. The binomial probabilities are the "Percent of Total" column you would get if you repeated the commands on page 104 an extremely large number of times.

EXHIBIT 6.3   Binomial Probabilities for Batches of 300 Envelopes

---

```
PDF;
  BINOMIAL N = 300 AND P = 0.005.

      BINOMIAL WITH N = 300   P = 0.005000
          K                P( X = K)
          0                 0.2223
          1                 0.3351
          2                 0.2518
          3                 0.1257
          4                 0.0469
          5                 0.0139
          6                 0.0034
          7                 0.0007
          8                 0.0001
          9                 0.0000
```

The RANDOM command can be used to simulate data from binomial distributions. To illustrate, Exhibit 6.4 shows 100 simulations of batches of 300 envelopes. This is clearly a much easier way to simulate the envelope process than the way we did it in Section 6.1!

EXHIBIT 6.4   One Hundred Simulations of Batches of 300 Envelopes

---

```
RANDOM 100 C1;
  BINOMIAL N = 300 AND P = 0.005.
HISTOGRAM C1

  Histogram of C1   N = 100

  Midpoint    Count
        0       18   *********************
        1       31   *******************************
        2       32   ********************************
        3       14   **************
        4        3   ***
        5        2   **
```

As another illustration, Exhibit 6.5 on page 110 shows 600 simulations of sequences of $n = 16$ Bernoulli trials with $p = 0.5$, and the corresponding binomial distribution.

RANDOM K observations [into each of C, ..., C]

BINOMIAL with n = K and p = K

Simulates random observations from a binomial distribution. The BASE command (p. 111) also applies.

EXERCISES

6-4   This exercise has you compute and plot some binomial probabilities so that you will have a better idea what they look like.
   (a)   First, let's fix n at 8 and vary p. Use $p = .01, .1, .2, .5, .8$, and .9. For each value of p, compute the binomial probabilities and plot those probabilities versus the corresponding values of the variable.
      (i)   How does the shape of the plot change as p increases?
      (ii)   Compare the two plots in which $p = .1$ and $p = .9$. Do you see any relationship? What about the two plots in which $p = .2$ and $p = .8$?
   (b)   Next, let's fix p at 0.2 and vary n. Use $n = 2, 5, 10, 20$, and 40. For each value of n, compute the binomial probabilities and get a plot as

---

EXHIBIT 6.5   Six Hundred Simulations of Sequences of $n = 16$ Bernoulli
Trials with $p = 0.5$

```
RANDOM 600 C1;
  BINOMIAL N = 16 AND P = 0.5.
TALLY C1

        C1   COUNT
         2     2
         3     4
         4    24
         5    44
         6    64
         7   101
         8   109
         9   103
        10    82
        11    45
        12    16
        13     4
        14     1
        15     1
        N=   600


PDF;
  BINOMIAL 16 0.5.

      BINOMIAL WITH N =   16   P = 0.500000
        K              P( X = K)
        0               0.0000
        1               0.0002
        2               0.0018
        3               0.0085
        4               0.0278
        5               0.0667
        6               0.1222
        7               0.1746
        8               0.1964
        9               0.1746
       10               0.1222
       11               0.0667
       12               0.0278
       13               0.0085
       14               0.0018
       15               0.0002
       16               0.0000
```

in part (a). How does the plot change as n increases? How about the spread? The shape? Does the "middle" move when n increases?

6-5 Two instruments are used to measure the amount of pollution in Lake Erie. They sit side by side, but they never agree exactly. Sometimes instrument A gets a higher reading than instrument B, and sometimes it is the other way around. Suppose the instruments are identical and each one has a 50–50 chance of giving the higher reading on any given occasion. Also suppose the readings are independent.
(a) What are the chances that instrument A gives the higher reading 15 or more times out of 20?
(b) What would you think if you measured the water quality 20 times with each instrument and the reading from instrument A was bigger 15 times out of 20? What are some of the possible causes of such an event?

6-6 Suppose X is a binomial random variable with $n = 16$ and $p = .75$.
(a) Write a Minitab program to calculate the mean of X using the formula $\mu = \Sigma x P(X = x)$. Does the answer agree with the answer you get when you use the formula $\mu = np$?
(b) Write a Minitab program to calculate the variance of X using the formula $\sigma^2 = \Sigma(x - \mu)^2 P(X = x)$. Use the value of μ from part (a). Does the answer agree with the formula $\sigma^2 = npq$?
(c) Simulate 1000 binomial observations with $n = 16$ and $p = .75$. Use DESCRIBE to estimate μ and σ. Do these results agree reasonably with those in parts (a) and (b)?

6.3 / RANDOM NUMBER GENERATION AND THE BASE COMMAND

Minitab's random number generator uses an algorithm that generates a long sequence of numbers that appear to be random. Each time you use the RANDOM command, Minitab haphazardly chooses a different place to start, and therefore you get a different set of simulated data. Occasionally, you may want to generate the same set of "random" data several times. To do this, type the BASE command with the same value of K each time, before using the RANDOM command.

BASE = K

The value of K tells Minitab where to start reading its list of random numbers. (Note: K determines where in the list to start. It is not the first random number Minitab gives you.) If you type two RANDOM commands in the same program, the second RANDOM will continue reading the list of random numbers where the first RANDOM stopped.

K should be a positive integer. The BASE command applies to all distributions used with RANDOM.

6.4 / THE NORMAL DISTRIBUTION

The normal (or Gaussian) distribution is fundamental to statistical theory and practice. It is frequently used to approximate other distributions and as a model for data. We will give an example of each of these applications.

APPROXIMATING THE BINOMIAL DISTRIBUTION

The binomial distribution with $n = 16$ and $p = 0.5$ is presented in Exhibit 6.5 in Section 6.3. The probabilities are symmetrically distributed about the mean value of $np = 16(0.5) = 8$. Moreover, as values farther away from the mean are considered, their probabilities decrease. Let us compare these probabilities with the values of the probability density function (pdf) of the normal distribution with the same mean $\mu = 8$ and the same standard deviation $\sigma = \sqrt{npq} = \sqrt{(16)(0.5)(0.5)} = 2$. The PDF command will allow us to do this.

PDF for values in E [put results into E]

NORMAL with mu = K, sigma = K

Calculates probability density function. The subcommand NORMAL states that you want the pdf for a normal distribution with the specified mean and standard deviation. If you do not use any subcommand, PDF calculates values for the "standard" normal distribution with $\mu = 0$ and $\sigma = 1$. If you do not store the results, they are printed. If you do store them, they will not be printed.

See Exhibit 6.6. Recall that MPLOT plots the first pair of columns with the letter A and the second pair with the letter B. When two points overlap, it plots a 2. In this MPLOT there are many overlaps. The binomial probabilities are converted, by hand, to a bar chart. The area of the bar at a given value is equal to the probability of that value. To get the normal curve, a smooth curve was drawn through the A points on the plot. (The formula for the normal curve appears on p. 132.) Note the quality of the normal approximation.

EXHIBIT 6.6   Binomial and Approximating Normal Curve (A = binomial;
B = normal)

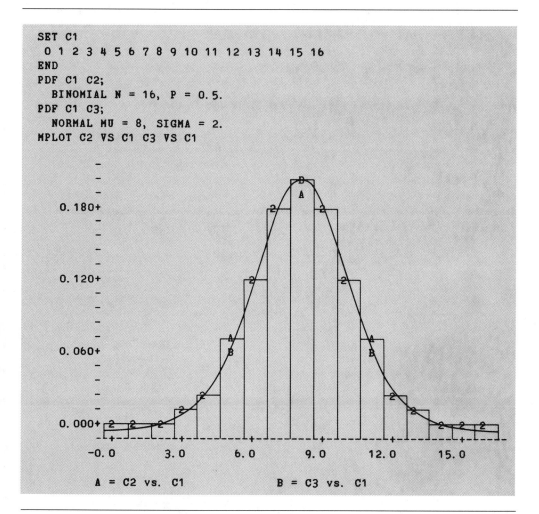

```
SET C1
 0 1 2 3 4 5 6 7 8 9 10 11 12 13 14 15 16
END
PDF C1 C2;
  BINOMIAL N = 16, P = 0.5.
PDF C1 C3;
  NORMAL MU = 8, SIGMA = 2.
MPLOT C2 VS C1 C3 VS C1
```

A = C2 vs. C1   B = C3 vs. C1

If we were to use a normal approximation for a binomial with $p = \frac{1}{2}$ and $n = 30$, the approximation would look even better. In general, for any fixed value of p, the larger n is, the closer the binomial distribution is to a normal. Here we used $p = 0.5$. In the exercises we will look at other values of p.

APPROXIMATING RATES OF RETURN

The Return data set on page 278 includes 60 monthly rates of return on the common stock of Xerox Corporation. We shall investigate a normal approximation to the distribution of these rates of return. To reduce the problem to essentials, we shall standardize the rates (that is, subtract the mean and divide by the standard deviation) and print out the standardized rates in ascending order. Commands for doing this are (with the rates in a column named 'XEROX')

```
LET K1 = AVER('XEROX')
LET K2 = STAN('XEROX')
LET C12 = ('XEROX'-K1)/K2
LET C13 = SORT(C12)
NAME C12 'Z' C13 'ORDER.Z'
PRINT C13
```

Exhibit 6.7 shows the ordered, standardized rates of return. The marks in this exhibit divide the values into five classes with boundaries listed in Table 6.2.

EXHIBIT 6.7   Ordered Standardized Monthly Rates of Return for Xerox Corporation

ORDER. Z

-2.4804	-0.7775	-0.4601	-0.0752	0.3875	0.8339
-1.9609	-0.7679	-0.4408	-0.0271	0.4250	0.9638
-1.5472	-0.7294	-0.3927	0.0113	0.4924	1.0600
-1.4991	-0.7198	-0.3831	0.0594	0.5376	1.2139
-1.2778	-0.6717	-0.3254	0.0594	0.6078	1.2620
-1.1527	-0.6140	-0.2869	0.1364	0.7233	1.7526
-1.1143	-0.5467	-0.2292	0.1556	0.8002	1.7719
-1.0854	-0.5467	-0.1522	0.3481	0.8195	2.0028
-1.0854	-0.5370	-0.1137	0.3769	0.8291	2.1952
-0.8641	-0.5178	-0.1137	0.3769	0.8291	2.4646

TABLE 6.2   Classification of Standardized Rates of Return (Xerox)

Class	Class Boundaries	Number in Class	Proportion in Class	Cumulative Proportion in Class
1	−2.5 to −1.5	3	0.0500	0.0500
2	−1.5 to −0.5	17	0.2833	0.3333
3	−0.5 to 0.5	23	0.3833	0.7166
4	0.5 to 1.5	12	0.2000	0.9166
5	1.5 to 2.5	5	0.0833	0.9999
	Total	60	0.9999	

Exhibit 6.8 contains a bar chart of the standardized rates of return. The *area of each bar is equal to the proportion* of values in the class. For example, the bar over the third class has a base of length 1 and a height of 0.3833. This gives an area of base × height = 1 × 0.3833 = 0.3833, which is the proportion of values in the third class. In Exhibit 6.8 a standard normal curve has been drawn through the bar chart. The PDF command was used to help construct this exhibit. The commands used were

```
SET C1
-2.5:2.5/0.5 #Generate -2.5, -2.0, ..., 2.0, 2.5.
END
SET C2
0 2(.05) 2(.2833) 2(.3833) 2(.2) 2(.0833)
END
PDF C1 PUT IN C3;
  NORMAL 0,1.
NAME C1 'VALUE' C2 'PROP' C3 'NORM.PDF'
MPLOT C2 VS C1 AND C3 VS C1
```

EXHIBIT 6.8   Bar Chart of Standardized Rates of Return and
                Approximating Normal Curve

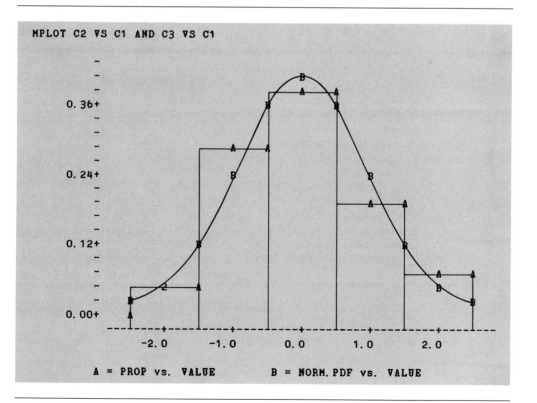

The distribution of standardized rates of return appears to be approximated rather well by the standard normal curve.

SIMULATING DATA FROM A NORMAL DISTRIBUTION

Suppose the monthly rates of return on your favorite stock are normally distributed with a mean of 0.04 and a standard deviation of 0.10. Over the next 24 months, would you expect any of your rates of return to be greater than 0.15? Greater than 0.25? Less than 0? Would you expect the mean of the sample of 24 rates to be close to the population mean? How close? What do you think a histogram of the 24 observations might look like?

Exhibit 6.9 simulates 24 observations. In this sample, three of the rates are greater than 0.15, none is greater than 0.25, and six are negative. The largest rate is 0.217, and the smallest is −0.203. The sample mean is 0.046, which is close to the population mean of 0.04. Of course, if we were to take a second sample of 24 rates, we would get different results. Properties such as mean rates of return vary from sample to sample, even though the population mean remains fixed. In Chapter 7 we will study how much such properties can vary.

The output from the PRINT command in Exhibit 6.9 has been edited for clarity. You need to read down the columns to find the numbers in increasing order.

EXHIBIT 6.9   Simulation of 24 Observations from a Normal Population with Mean 0.04 and Standard Deviation 0.10

```
RANDOM 24 C1;
  NORMAL MU = 0.04 SIGMA = 0.10.
SORT C1 C2
PRINT C2
 C2

     -0.20333  -0.04878   0.01217   0.07579   0.08970   0.13565
     -0.11007  -0.04784   0.03206   0.07942   0.09488   0.19956
     -0.09396   0.00451   0.05206   0.08202   0.12178   0.21559
     -0.08239   0.00994   0.05364   0.08682   0.12212   0.21685

DESC C2
```

	N	MEAN	MEDIAN	TRMEAN	STDEV	SEMEAN
C2	24	0.0458	0.0647	0.0493	0.1053	0.0215

	MIN	MAX	Q1	Q3
C2	-0.2033	0.2168	-0.0347	0.1151

RANDOM K observations into each of C, ..., C

NORMAL mu = K, sigma = K

Puts a random sample of K observations into each column. If no subcommand is given, random data are simulated from a "standard" normal distribution with $\mu = 0$ and $\sigma = 1$.

The BASE command (p. 111) can be used to get the same sequence again.

A USEFUL TRICK FOR SIMULATING DATA

Suppose we wanted 50 random samples, each containing 20 observations. We could use

```
RANDOM 20 observations into C1-C50
```

or we could use

```
RANDOM 50 observations into C1-C20
```

With the first command, each sample is in a separate column. With the second command, each sample is in a separate row. Sometimes it is better to have samples in rows, and sometimes it is better to have them in columns. It all depends on what we want to do with the samples.

As an example, suppose we wanted to simulate 100 samples, each of size 20, from a normal distribution with $\mu = 35$ and $\sigma = 2$ and then determine how many of these samples have at least one observation over 40. We could use the following program:

```
RANDOM 100 C1-C20;
   NORMAL 35, 2.
RMAX C1-C20 into C21
PRINT C21
STEM-AND-LEAF C21
```

In this case, putting the 100 samples into rows, rather than columns, saved us a great deal of work.

EXERCISES

6–7 Standardize and order the rates of return on IBM common stock listed in the Return data set on page 278. Organize the observations into a table like Table 6.2. Produce a plot like the one in Exhibit 6.8. Does the normal curve appear to provide a reasonable description of the IBM rates of return?

6–8 *(a)* Make a histogram of the heights for the Class data on page 281. Does the histogram appear bell-shaped?

(b) Make a histogram of the weights for the Class data on page 281. Does the histogram appear bell-shaped?

(c) Why might height and weight behave differently?

(d) Construct bar chart/normal curve plots like Exhibit 6.8 for the heights and the weights.

6-9 In samples from a normal distribution, about 68% of the observations should fall between $\bar{x} - s$ and $\bar{x} + s$. About 95% of the observations should fall between $\bar{x} - 2s$ and $\bar{x} + 2s$. Simulate a random sample of size 100 from a normal distribution (you choose μ and σ). What percentages do you find in these two regions?

6-10 Repeat Exercise 6-9, using real data. For example, use the heights in the Class data set on page 281. Or use the rates of return on IBM common stock in the Return data set on page 278.

6-11 In this exercise we look at the distribution of a linear combination of normal random variables. Simulate 200 observations from a normal distribution with $\mu = 0.02$ and $\sigma = 0.05$ in C1. Simulate another 200 with $\mu = 0.04$ and $\sigma = 0.01$ into C2. Then compute the following:

```
LET C3 = 0.6*C1
LET C4 = 0.4*C2
LET C5 = C3+C4
LET C6 = 0.6*C1+0.4*C2
LET C7 = 0.4*C2+0.6*0.04
LET C8 = C1+C2
```

Now use DESCRIBE C1–C8 and HISTOGRAM C1–C8. Try to give formulas indicating how the means and standard deviations of the various columns are related. What sorts of distributions do the various columns seem to have? If you interpret C1 and C2 as rates of return on two stocks, can you give interpretations of C3–C8?

6.5 / CUMULATIVE DISTRIBUTIONS

A cumulative distribution function (cdf) gives the percentage of observations falling to the left of any specified value. In Table 6.2 the last column is labeled "Cumulative Proportion in Class." From this column you can learn that 5% of the standardized rates of return were less than or equal to -1.5, 33.33% were less than or equal to -0.5, 71.66% were less than or equal to 0.5, 91.66% were less than or equal to 1.5, and 100% were less than or equal to 2.5. Minitab's CDF command allows us to do similar calculations for many distributions. We shall illustrate the binomial and normal distribution calculations.

CDF for values in E [put results into E]

BINOMIAL with n = K and p = K

Calculates the cumulative distribution function (cumulative probabilities) for the binomial. If you do not store the results, they will be printed. If you use no arguments on the CDF line, a table of all cumulative probabilities is printed. Values that are essentially 0 (less than .00005) and values that are essentially 1 (over .99995) are omitted from the table.

CDF for values in E [put results into E]

NORMAL with mu = K, sigma = K

Calculates the cumulative distribution function. Answers are printed if they are not stored.

Exhibit 6.10 (which is a repeat of Exhibit 6.6) shows a bar chart of the binomial distribution with $n = 16$ and $p = 0.5$. The area of the shaded bars is equal to the probability that seven or fewer successes will be obtained in the 16 Bernoulli trials. This area is obtained by issuing the command

```
CDF for value 7;
    BINOMIAL n = 16, p = 0.5.
```

The area is 0.4018. The normal curve with mean 8 and standard deviation 2, which is also sketched in Exhibit 6.10, can be used to approximate the shaded area. We find the left-tail area below 7.5 with the command

```
CDF for 7.5;
    NORMAL mu = 8, sigma = 2.
```

The area is 0.4013, very close to the exact value of 0.4018.

Any area under a normal curve may be computed by using the CDF command. For example, suppose you want to compute probabilities for rates of return that are normally distributed with mean 0.04 and standard deviation 0.1. The probability that a rate of return is negative is found by issuing

```
CDF 0;
    NORMAL 0.04, 0.1.
```

The area is 0.3446. The probability that the rate of return is between 0.1 and 0.25 is pictured in Exhibit 6.11. The required area is the difference between the cumulative areas to the left of 0.25 and 0.1, respectively. We use the following commands to compute the two cumulative areas and to

EXHIBIT 6.10   Binomial and Approximating Normal Curve (A = binomial;
B = normal)

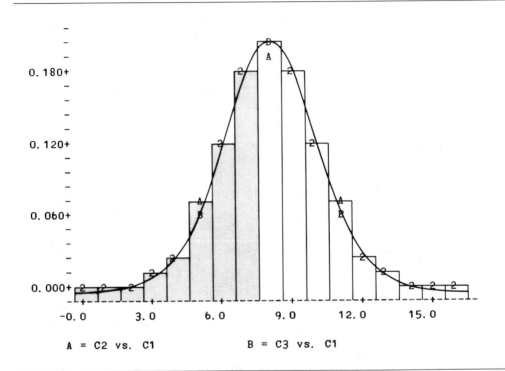

A = C2 vs. C1   B = C3 vs. C1

find the difference:

```
SET C1
0.25 0.1
END
CDF values in C1 put results in C2;
   NORMAL mu = 0.04, sigma = 0.1.
LET K1 = C1(1)-C1(2)
PRINT K1.
```

These commands are also shown in Exhibit 6.11. We see that the required area is 0.2563. In other words, about 26% of our rates of return will be between 0.1 and 0.25.

EXERCISES

6-12   (a)   Use the CDF command to compute the probability that an observation from a binomial distribution with $n = 16$ and $p = 0.5$ will be equal to 7, 8, or 9.

EXHIBIT 6.11   Normal Curve with $\mu = 0.04$ and $\sigma = 0.10$

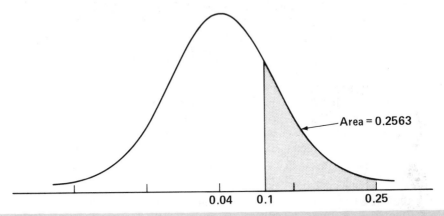

```
SET C1
0.25 0.1
END
CDF values in C1 put results in C2;
  NORMAL mu = 0.04, sigma = 0.1.
LET K1 = C2(1)-C2(2)
PRINT K1
K1 = 0.2563
```

(b) Approximate the probability in part (a) using the appropriate normal distribution.

6–13 (a) For a binomial distribution with $n = 25$ and $p = 0.8$, compute the probability that the number of successes will be equal to 21, less than or equal to 21, greater than or equal to 24, and between 21 and 24 inclusive.

(b) Compute the normal approximations of the probabilities in part (a).

(c) For which of the probabilities is the normal approximation the most accurate? The least accurate?

6–14 Suppose a normal distribution has mean 100 and standard deviation 10. Use the CDF command to find each of the following.

(a) The area below 90.
(b) The area above 110.
(c) The area below 80.
(d) The area above 120.
(e) The area between 90 and 110.
(f) The area between 80 and 120.
(g) The area between 80 and 110.

6–15 In this exercise you will compute and plot the pdf and cdf of a normal distribution with mean $\mu = 100$ and standard deviation $\sigma = 10$. The normal pdf is essentially zero for values smaller than -3σ and for values larger than $+3\sigma$, so we will use the values 70, 72, 74, ..., 130. Run the following program.

```
SET C1
70:130/2 #Generate 70 to 130 in steps of 2.
END
PDF C1, PUT IN C2;
    NORMAL 100,10.
CDF C1, PUT IN C3;
    NORMAL 100,10.
NAME C1 'X' C2 'PDF(X)' C3 'CDF(X)'
PLOT C2 VS C1
PLOT C3 VS C1
```

Sketch the two curves and comment on their shape.

6.6 / INVERSES OF CUMULATIVE DISTRIBUTIONS

The command CDF calculates the area associated with a value. The command INVCDF does the opposite—it calculates the value associated with an area. Exhibit 6.12 gives an example using a normal curve with $\mu = 100$ and $\sigma = 10$. We want to find the value x that has area of 0.25

EXHIBIT 6.12   Normal Curve with $\mu = 100$ and $\sigma = 10$

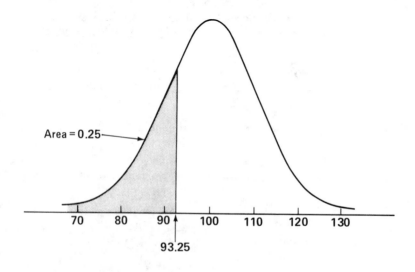

below it. The command

```
INVCDF 0.25;
    NORMAL 100,10.
```

prints the answer 93.25. Thus one quarter of the area under this normal curve lies below 93.25.

INVCDF for values in E [put results into E]

NORMAL with mu = K, sigma = K

Calculates the inverse cumulative distribution function. Note that the values given to INVCDF are probabilities and thus must be between 0 and 1. Answers are printed if they are not stored.

The INVCDF command can also be used with the binomial distribution. For example, with $n = 5$ and $p = 0.40$ the cumulative probability for 3 is 0.913 (see the top half of Exhibit 6.13). Therefore

```
INVCDF .913;
    BINOMIAL 5, .40.
```

gives the value 3.

EXHIBIT 6.13   Cumulative and Inverse Probabilities for Binomial with
$n = 5, p = 0.40$

```
CDF;
  BINOMIAL N = 5 P = 0.40.

    BINOMIAL WITH N =   5  P = 0.400000
       K   P( X LESS OR = K)
       0            0.0778
       1            0.3370
       2            0.6826
       3            0.9130
       4            0.9898
       5            1.0000


INVCDF 0.8;
  BINOMIAL 5 0.4.

       K   P( X LESS OR = K)      K   P( X LESS OR = K)
       2            0.6826        3            0.9130
```

Notice that Exhibit 6.13 contains six probabilities, one corresponding to each possible number of successes. These are the only probabilities for which INVCDF can give an exact answer. Exhibit 6.13 also shows what happens when there is no exact answer. The value below and the value above the requested probability are both printed. If you put storage on the CDF command, then the larger value (here it is 3) is stored.

INVCDF for probabilities in E [put results into E]

BINOMIAL with n = K and p = K

Calculates the inverse cumulative distribution function. Answers are printed if they are not stored.

If there is no exact answer for a probability you specify, both the value below and the value above are printed. If you request storage, the value above is stored.

EXERCISES

6–16 Use the INVCDF command to find the quartiles of the standard normal distribution; that is, find three values that divide the distribution into four equal areas. (The standard normal distribution has $\mu = 0$ and $\sigma = 1$.)

6–17 Use the INVCDF command to find the quintiles of the standard normal distribution; that is, find four values that divide the distribution into five equal areas.

6–18 Put the standardized rates of return in Exhibit 6.7 into the five classes defined by the quintiles you got in Exercise 6–17. Are there about 12 values in each class? Compute proportions and cumulative proportions.

6–19 Repeat Exercise 6–18 for the IBM rates of return in the Return data set on page 278.

6–20 (a) Use the INVCDF command to find the deciles of the standard normal distribution; that is, find nine values that divide the distribution into ten equal areas.

(b) Standardize and order the heights in the Class data set on page 281. Put the resulting values into the ten classes defined by the deciles of part (a). Are there about ten values per class?

7/OTHER DISTRIBUTIONS AND MORE ADVANCED SIMULATIONS

In the last chapter we saw how to perform various calculations for the binomial and normal distributions and how to simulate drawing random data from these distributions. Simulation of data from models is a powerful tool for studying complex processes found in practice. In this chapter we will see that Minitab enables us to study some rather sophisticated models. The first example that we will look at illustrates the celebrated central limit theorem.

7.1/HOW SAMPLE MEANS VARY AND NORMAL PROBABILITY PLOTS

The central limit theorem states that, under fairly general conditions, the distribution of means of random samples is approximately normal. This statement is the basis for the confidence intervals for means discussed in Chapter 8. To illustrate it, let's simulate a number of samples from a population of integers. We will think of drawing chips from a bowl. The bowl contains ten chips numbered 0, 1, ..., 9. A random drawing from the bowl produces a random digit. A sequence of drawings, with replacement, is a sample of random digits. Using the trick described on page 117, we can simulate 200 samples of size 10 with the command

```
RANDOM 200 C1-C10;
  INTEGERS BETWEEN 0 AND 9.
```

EXHIBIT 7.1   Histogram of 200 Random Integers

```
Histogram of C1    N = 200

Midpoint    Count
   0.00       19   ********************
   1.00       17   *****************
   2.00       14   **************
   3.00       26   ***************************
   4.00       21   *********************
   5.00       19   *******************
   6.00       19   *******************
   7.00       17   *****************
   8.00       23   ***********************
   9.00       25   *************************
```

Exhibit 7.1 shows the output from the command

```
HISTOGRAM OF C1;
   INCREMENT = 1.0;
   START WITH MIDPOINT AT 0.
```

The 200 integers in C1 are indeed distributed about equally among 0 through 9. Of course, we do not expect exactly 20 of each of the integers to appear, because of random variation, but we do not expect very large departures from such a distribution either. The solid line in Exhibit 7.1 marks the frequency of 20. The dashed line marks the actual frequencies in C1.

The distribution with 20 of each of the integers 0 through 9 has mean 4.5 and standard deviation $\sqrt{8.25} \approx 2.87$. Exhibit 7.2 shows the means and standard deviations of the numbers in columns C1–C10. Again, the differences between the actual means and standard deviations and the theoretical ones of 4.5 and 2.87 are due to random variation.

We can compute the means of the 200 samples and store them in C11 with the command

```
RMEAN C1-C10 PUT IN C11
```

The commands

```
DESCRIBE C11
HISTOGRAM C11;
   INCREMENT OF 0.5;
   START WITH MIDPOINT 0.
```

summarize the sample means.

EXHIBIT 7.2   Means and Standard Deviations for Ten Columns Containing
200 Random Integers Each

COLUMN	MEAN	STDEV
C1	4.720	2.902
C2	4.240	2.899
C3	4.460	2.805
C4	4.285	2.764
C5	4.515	2.906
C6	4.495	2.830
C7	4.325	2.844
C8	4.665	2.733
C9	4.575	2.891
C10	4.245	3.015

Exhibit 7.3 presents a comparison of the histograms of the averages and the histogram of the random integers in C1, on the same scale. The solid lines mark frequencies of 20. The dashed lines mark actual frequencies. In the histogram of the averages the classes with midpoints 0 through 1.5 and 7.0 through 9.0 contain no values. The values in the remaining classes are distributed such that a rough bell-shaped figure is the result.

The selection of output from the DESCRIBE command shows that the mean of the averages is 4.4525, very close to the theoretical value of 4.5. The standard deviation of the averages is 0.8896. This number should be close to the theoretical value of $\sigma/\sqrt{n} = 2.87/\sqrt{10} \approx 0.91$, and it is.

NORMAL PROBABILITY PLOTS

Another plot, called a normal probability plot, is a useful supplement to histograms in checking for normality. It plots the sample values versus the values we would get, on the average, if the sample came from a normal population. This plot is approximately a straight line if the sample is from a normal population, but it exhibits curvature if the population is not normal.

Minitab can make a normal probability plot of the sample means in C11. For scaling purposes we standardize the means first. The commands are

```
LET K1 = AVER(C11) #COMPUTE AVERAGE OF MEANS
LET K2 = STAN(C11) #COMPUTE STANDARD DEVIATION OF MEANS
LET C14 = (C11-K1)/K2 #STANDARDIZE THE MEANS
NSCORES OF C14 PUT IN C15 #COMPUTE NORMAL SCORES
PLOT C14 VS C15 #PRODUCE NORMAL PROBABILITY PLOT
CORRELATION C14 C15 #COMPUTE CORRELATION BETWEEN
    MEANS AND NORMAL SCORES
```

EXHIBIT 7.3   Comparison of Histograms of 200 Random Integers and of
200 Averages of Samples of 10 Random Integers

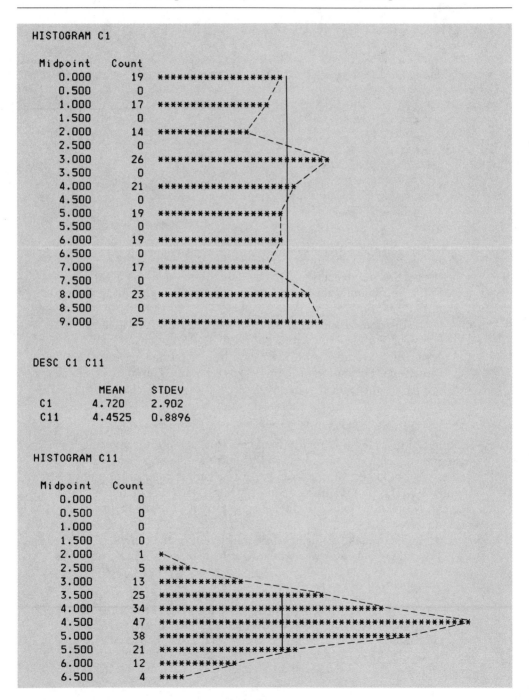

```
HISTOGRAM C1

Midpoint    Count
   0.000      19  ********************
   0.500       0
   1.000      17  *****************
   1.500       0
   2.000      14  **************
   2.500       0
   3.000      26  **************************
   3.500       0
   4.000      21  *********************
   4.500       0
   5.000      19  *******************
   5.500       0
   6.000      19  *******************
   6.500       0
   7.000      17  *****************
   7.500       0
   8.000      23  ***********************
   8.500       0
   9.000      25  *************************


DESC C1 C11

            MEAN    STDEV
   C1      4.720    2.902
   C11     4.4525   0.8896


HISTOGRAM C11

Midpoint    Count
   0.000       0
   0.500       0
   1.000       0
   1.500       0
   2.000       1  *
   2.500       5  *****
   3.000      13  *************
   3.500      25  *************************
   4.000      34  **********************************
   4.500      47  ***********************************************
   5.000      38  **************************************
   5.500      21  *********************
   6.000      12  ************
   6.500       4  ****
```

EXHIBIT 7.4   Normal Probability Plot of Standardized Sample Averages
in Exhibit 7.3

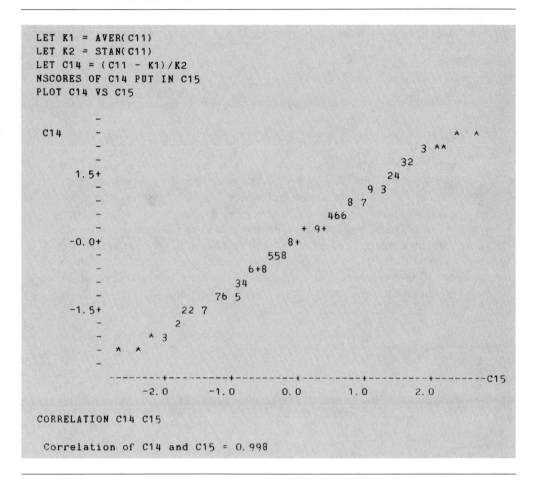

```
LET K1 = AVER( C11 )
LET K2 = STAN( C11 )
LET C14 = ( C11 - K1 )/K2
NSCORES OF C14 PUT IN C15
PLOT C14 VS C15
```

```
          -
  C14     -                                                          *    *
          -                                                3  **
          -                                            32
   1.5+                                               24
          -                                          9 3
          -                                       8 7
          -                                     466
          -                              +  9+
  -0.0+                              8+
          -                        558
          -                     6+8
          -                   34
          -              76  5
  -1.5+           22  7
          -          2
          -      *  3
          -    *    *
          -
          --------+---------+---------+---------+---------+-------C15
               -2.0      -1.0       0.0       1.0       2.0
```

```
CORRELATION C14  C15

Correlation of C14 and C15 = 0.998
```

The output is shown in Exhibit 7.4. The linearity of the plot can be checked
by eye and confirmed by the high correlation coefficient. We have no
reason to doubt the approximate normality of the sample means in
Exhibit 7.4. The sample *means* behave just like numbers generated from a
normal distribution, even though the samples were drawn from a uniform
distribution!

NSCORES of C put in C

Calculates the normal scores of a set of data.

EXAMPLE

```
NSCORES OF C1 PUT IN C2
```

C1	C2
1.1	− .20
1.9	1.28
.8	−1.28
1.3	.64
1.2	.20
.9	− .64

Loosely speaking, the normal scores in the example above can be defined as follows: The number -1.28 in C2 is the smallest value you would get, on the average, if you took samples of size $n = 6$ from a standard normal population (with $\mu = 0$, $\sigma = 1$). This number is placed next to the smallest value in C1. The number $-.64$ in C2 is the second smallest value you would get, on the average, in samples of size 6 from a standard normal. It is placed next to the second smallest value in C1. This is continued for all six values. (More precisely, the ith smallest normal score is found by computing the inverse cdf of $(i - 3/8)/(n + 1/4)$.)

EXERCISES

7–1   Simulate ten random samples of size 46 from a normal distribution with mean 65.478 and standard deviation 2.771 by using the commands

```
RANDOM 46 C1–C10;
    NORMAL 65.478, 2.771.
HIST C1–C10
DESC C1–C10
```

The mean and standard deviation of the heights of the female students in the Class data (pp. 281–283) are 65.478 and 2.771. Compare the histogram of these female heights with the histograms you have generated. Could the female heights have plausibly come from a normal population?

7–2   (a)   Simulate ten random samples of size 10 from a normal population with mean 4.5 and standard deviation 2.87 by using the commands

```
RANDOM 10 C1–C10;
    NORMAL 4.5, 2.87.
HIST C1–C10
DESC C1–C10
```

(b)   Simulate ten random samples of size 10 from a bowl containing chips marked 0, 1, ..., 9 by repeatedly using the commands

```
RANDOM 10 C1-C10;
    INTEGER 0, 9.
HIST C1-C10
DESC C1-C10
```

(c) Cut out the 20 histograms you generated in parts (a) and (b). Put them in a hat or box and mix them up. Now draw one at random and state whether it portrays a sample from a normal population or a population of chips. How do you know? Would you be able to tell the correct population no matter what histogram you drew? Why?

7–3 Use RANDOM to produce a table of random integers containing 200 rows and 5 columns, C1–C5.
(a) Produce histograms of each column.
(b) Use the DESCRIBE command on each column. Compare the means and standard deviations of the columns with the "ideal" values of 4.5 and 2.87. Why are the column statistics not equal to the "ideal" values?
(c) Use the commands

```
RSUM C1-C5, PUT IN C6
LET C7 = C6/5.0
```

to store the sample sums and averages for each of the 200 samples of size 5 in your worksheet. Compare the histograms and descriptive statistics of the sums (C6) and averages (C7). Compute the quantity MEAN/ST. DEV. for both columns (do this by hand). Explain why the values should be equal.

7–4 Repeat Exercise 7–3 but using the command

```
RANDOM 200 C1-C5;
    INTEGER -5, 5.
```

to generate the random integers. (The population mean and standard deviation are 0 and $\sqrt{10}$ for this exercise.)

7–5 Do normal probability plots for each of the following data sets. Comment.
(a) The male heights and weights in the Class data (pp. 281–283).
(b) The female heights and weights in the Class data (pp. 281–283).
(c) The heights of males and females combined in the Class data (pp. 281–283).
(d) The A/S ratios in Exhibit 2.11.
(e) The market values in the Property data (p. 273).

7–6 Use the RANDOM command to generate 100 integers between 0 and 9 into C1. Then do a normal probability plot of these values. How does the plot deviate from a straight line?

7-7   Generate 100 observations from a normal distribution with mean 0 and standard deviation 1 into C1.

(a)   Square these numbers and store the squares in C2. Do a normal probability plot of the numbers in C2. How does the plot deviate from a straight line?

(b)   Now generate a second set of 100 standard normal observations into C3. Divide C1 by C3 and store the result in C4. Do a normal probability plot of the numbers in C4. How does the plot deviate from a straight line?

7.2 / SUMMARY OF DISTRIBUTIONS IN MINITAB

The commands PDF, CDF, INVCDF, and RANDOM all have the same collections of subcommands to specify different distributions. In this section we list these distributions and give the corresponding subcommands.

CONTINUOUS DISTRIBUTIONS

NORMAL mu = K sigma = K

Normal distribution with mean μ and standard deviation σ. The pdf is

$$f(x) = \frac{1}{\sqrt{2\pi}\sigma} e^{-(x-\mu)^2/2\sigma^2} \qquad \sigma > 0$$

UNIFORM a = K b = K

Uniform distribution on a to b. The pdf is

$$f(x) = \frac{1}{b-a} \qquad a < x < b$$

CAUCHY a = K b = K

Cauchy distribution. The pdf is

$$f(x) = \frac{1}{(\pi b)[1 + \{(x-a)/b\}^2]} \qquad b > 0$$

LAPLACE a = K b = K

Laplace or double exponential distribution. The pdf is

$$f(x) = \frac{1}{2b} e^{-|x-a|/b} \qquad b > 0$$

LOGISTIC a = K b = K

Logistic distribution. The pdf is

$$f(x) = \frac{e^{-(x-a)/b}}{b[1 + e^{-(x-a)/b}]^2} \qquad b > 0$$

LOGNORMAL mu = K sigma = K

Log normal distribution. A variable x has a log normal distribution if $\log x$ has a normal distribution with mean μ and standard deviation σ. The pdf of the log normal is

$$f(x) = \frac{1}{x\sqrt{2\pi}\sigma} e^{-\{(\log_e x) - \mu\}^2/2\sigma^2} \qquad x > 0$$

T with v = K

Student's t distribution with v degrees of freedom. The pdf is

$$f(x) = \frac{\Gamma[(v + 1)/2]}{\Gamma[v/2]\sqrt{v\pi}} \frac{1}{(1 + x^2/v)^{(v+1/2)}} \qquad v > 0$$

F with u = K v = K

F distribution with u degrees of freedom for the numerator and v degrees of freedom for the denominator. The pdf is

$$f(x) = \frac{\Gamma[(u + v)/2]}{\Gamma[u/2]\Gamma[v/2]} \left(\frac{u}{v}\right)^{u/2} \frac{x^{(u-2)/2}}{[1 + (u/v)x]^{(u+v)/2}} \qquad x > 0, u > 0, v > 0$$

CHISQUARE v = K

χ^2 distribution with v degrees of freedom. The pdf is

$$f(x) = \frac{x^{(v-2)/2} e^{-x/2}}{2^{v/2} \Gamma(v/2)} \qquad x > 0, v > 0$$

EXPONENTIAL b = K

Exponential distribution. (Caution: Some books use $1/b$ where we have used b.) The pdf is

$$f(x) = \frac{1}{b} e^{-x/b} \qquad x > 0, b > 0$$

GAMMA a = K b = K

Gamma distribution. (Note: Some books use $1/b$ where we have used b.)

The pdf is

$$f(x) = \frac{x^{a-1}e^{-x/b}}{\Gamma(a)b^a} \qquad x > 0,\ a > 0,\ b > 0$$

WEIBULL a = K b = K

Weibull distribution. The pdf is

$$f(x) = \frac{ax^{a-1}e^{-(x/b)^a}}{b^a} \qquad x > 0,\ a > 0,\ b > 0$$

BETA a = K b = K

Beta distribution. The pdf is

$$f(x) = \frac{\Gamma(a + b)x^{a-1}(1 - x)^{b-1}}{\Gamma(a)\Gamma(b)} \qquad 0 \le x \le 1,\ a > 0,\ b > 0$$

DISCRETE DISTRIBUTIONS

INTEGER a = K b = K

Each integer $a, a + 1, \ldots, b$ has equal probability. (Sometimes called "discrete uniform.")

BINOMIAL n = K p = K

Binomial distribution. The probability of x is

$$f(x) = \binom{n}{x}p^x(1 - p)^{n-x} \qquad x = 0, 1, \ldots, n$$

POISSON mu = K

Poisson distribution. The probability of x is

$$f(x) = \frac{e^{-\mu}\mu^x}{x!} \qquad x = 0, 1, 2, 3, \ldots$$

DISCRETE Values in C, Probabilities in C

Arbitrary discrete distribution. You put the values and the corresponding probabilities in two columns beforehand. For example, to simulate 40 observations from a distribution that gives the three values $-1, 0, +1$ with probabilities $1/4, 1/2, 1/4$, respectively, you can use

```
READ C1 C2
  -1 .25
   0 .50
   1 .25
END
RANDOM 40 OBSERVATIONS INTO C6;
   DISCRETE C1, C2.
```

EXERCISES

7–8   *Continuous Uniform Distribution.* The uniform distribution and the *t*
distribution with 2 degrees of freedom are examples of very nonnormal
distributions. Their histograms should look quite different from those for
normal data sets.

   (a)   Simulate 50 observations from a uniform distribution and make a
histogram. Repeat five times. Comment on the general shape of the
histograms.

   (b)   Do part (a) but simulate data from a *t* distribution with 2 degrees of
freedom.

7–9   *Discrete Uniform Distribution.* Suppose there are 30 people at a party. Do
you think it is very likely that at least two of the 30 people have the same
birthday? Try estimating this probability by a simulation. To simplify
things, ignore leap years (thus assume that all years have 365 days) and
assume that all days of the year are equally likely to be birthdays. Use the
following commands to simulate ten sets of 30 birthdays:

```
RANDOM 30 observations into C1–C10;
   INTEGERS 1 to 365.
TALLY C1–C10
```

How many of your ten sets of 30 people had no matching birthdays?

7–10   *Chi-square Distribution.* The mean, standard deviation, and shape of the
chi-square distribution change as the number of degrees of freedom
changes. For a chi-square distribution with n degrees of freedom the mean
is n, and the standard deviation is $\sqrt{2n}$.

   (a)   Simulate 200 observations from a chi-square distribution with 1
degree of freedom into C1. Use DESCRIBE to compute the sample
mean and standard deviation. Are they approximately 1 and $\sqrt{2} =$
1.414, respectively? Now make a histogram and sketch the shape of
the distribution. For all histograms in this exercise, use the subcommands START = .1 and INCREMENT = .2.

   (b)   Repeat part (a) but use 2 degrees of freedom.

   (c)   Repeat part (a) but use 5 degrees of freedom.

   (d)   Repeat part (a) but use 10 degrees of freedom.

7–11   *Chi-square Distribution.* The chi-square distribution arises in several ways
in statistics. Here we will use simulation to illustrate three ways.

   (a)   If X is from a standard normal distribution (with mean 0 and standard
deviation 1), then X^2 has a chi-square distribution with 1 degree of
freedom. Simulate 200 standard normals into a column, then square
them. Then simulate 200 chi-square observations with 1 degree of
freedom. Now make a histogram of the X^2s and a histogram of the
chi-squares. The two histograms should be very similar.

(b)   Another way the chi-square arises is from the variance of samples from a normal distribution. Simulate 200 rows of standard normal observations into C1–C4. Use RSTDEV to compute the standard deviations of the 200 rows. Square the results to get variances. Make a histogram of the variances. Compare this to a histogram of 200 chi-square observations with 3 degrees of freedom.

(c)   Still another source of the chi-square is as follows: Simulate 200 Poisson observations with $\mu = 5$ into C1–C3. Now compute the "chi-square test," discussed in most textbooks, using the following commands:

```
LET  C4  =  (C1+C2+C3)/3
LET  C6  =  (C1-C4)**2+(C2-C4)**2+(C3-C4)**2 **2
LET  C7  =  C6/C4
```

Now make a histogram of C7 and compare it to a histogram of a chi-square with 2 degrees of freedom.

7–12   *The t distribution.* Student's *t* distribution arises most naturally as $(\bar{x} - \mu)/(s/\sqrt{n})$. To illustrate the development of a *t* distribution, simulate 200 rows of normal data into C1–C3. You choose μ and σ. Use RMEAN and RSTDEV to compute $\bar{x}$ and *s* for C1–C3. Use LET to compute $t = (\bar{x} - \mu)/(s/\sqrt{3})$. Make a histogram of *t*. Compare this histogram to one you obtain by using RANDOM to simulate directly 200 observations for a *t* distribution with 2 degrees of freedom. Describe the shapes of the two histograms.

7–13   In this exercise we look at mixtures of normal populations. This means that two normal populations contribute observations to the mixture population. For example, we can create a population such that any observation could have come from a normal population with mean 0 and standard deviation 1, or it could have come from a normal population with mean 0 and standard deviation 3. Suppose we want the chance that an observation comes from the first population to be 0.85 and the chance that it comes from the second to be 0.15. The commands needed are

```
RANDOM 1 C1;
   NORMAL 0,1.
RANDOM 1 C2;
   NORMAL 0,3.
RANDOM 1 C3;
   BERNOULLI 0.85.
LET C4 = C3*C1+(1-C3)*C2
PRINT C1-C4
```

If the Bernoulli trial ends in success (a 1), then the observation in C1 is selected. If the Bernoulli trial ends in failure (a 0), then the observation in C2 is selected. Simulate 30 observations from each of the mixtures listed on the next page.

First Population		Second Population		Probability of Choosing First Population
μ	σ	μ	σ	
0	1	0	3	0.85
0	1	0	3	0.40
65	3	62	4	0.50
100	10	70	10	0.50

DESCRIBE the samples and get histograms.

7.3 / SIMULATION AND STORED COMMANDS

The drawing of a sample from a specified distribution by artificial means, as with a random number generator, is called simulation. The repeated generation of simulated samples to study the effects of random variation is called a Monte Carlo study. The samples and exercises in previous sections are small-scale Monte Carlo studies. We have seen that such studies can give useful insights into the consequences of randomization.

Monte Carlo can require us to implement the same set of commands over and over. This is very tiresome and would be prohibitive if we wanted to include many simulations in a study. Fortunately, Minitab can perform repeated calculations of this nature for us and so takes the drudgery out of Monte Carlo studies. The trick is to store the required commands away in a loop. Minitab does not execute these commands until you ask it to do so with the EXECUTE command. We begin the stored sequence with the STORE command and end it with the END command. The EXECUTE command tells how many times to repeat the stored commands. If no number is given, Minitab executes the stored commands one time.

STORE THE FOLLOWING COMMANDS IN 'filename'

Begins a sequence of stored commands that are not executed until the EXECUTE command is given.

END OF STORING COMMANDS

Ends the sequence of stored commands.

EXECUTE 'filename' [K TIMES]

If K is omitted, it is assumed to be 1.

EXHIBIT 7.5 A Simulation of a Random Sample of Size $n = 9$ from a Normal Population with $\mu = 0$ and $\sigma = 1$

```
DESCRIBE C1

              N      MEAN    MEDIAN    TRMEAN    STDEV    SEMEAN
C1            9    -0.099    -0.391    -0.099    1.078    0.359

            MIN       MAX        Q1        Q3
C1       -1.593     1.296    -1.078     0.917

HISTOGRAM C1

 Histogram of C1   N = 9

Midpoint   Count
   -1.5       2    **
   -1.0       0
   -0.5       3    ***
    0.0       0
    0.5       1    *
    1.0       2    **
    1.5       1    *

NSCORES C1 C2
PLOT C1 C2

C1      -
        -
        -                                                         *
  1.0+                                              *
        -                                        *
        -                                   *
        -
        -
 -0.0+
        -
        -                          *      *
        -                   *
        -
 -1.0+
        -
        -
        -    *          *
        -
 -2.0+
      ---------+---------+---------+---------+---------+-------C2
            -1.20     -0.60     -0.00      0.60      1.20
```

As an example, let's investigate the behavior of several small samples from a standard normal population. Small samples can behave in surprising ways. We will look at commands that generate 20 samples of size 9. The stored commands will generate a sample of size 9 and produce summary statistics, a histogram, and a normal probability plot. The stored commands will be executed 20 times.

```
STORE IN 'SMALLSAM'
PRINT K1
RANDOM 9 C1;
   NORMAL 0, 1.
DESCRIBE C1
HISTOGRAM C1
NSCORES C1 C2
PLOT C1 C2
LET K1 = K1+1
END
LET K1 = 1 #INITIALIZE K1
NAME C1 'SAMPLE' C2 'NSCORES'
EXECUTE 'SMALLSAM' 20 TIMES
```

Notice that we used K1 to index the outputs from this program to help us keep them straight. K1 is updated each time the commands are executed.

These commands produce a lot of output. The results of only one execution are shown in Exhibit 7.5. Small samples are subject to lots of random variation, so we can get plots that do not look very "normal." Studies like this help to sharpen our intuitions and to provide useful frames of reference for analyzing real data.

EXERCISES

7–14 Run the program in this section and comment on the output.

7–15 Redo Exercise 7–14 using stored commands. Generate 30 simulations instead of 20, however.

7–16 So far we have considered the behavior of averages of independent samples of random numbers. Another type of average, called a moving average, comes up in time series analysis. The calculation of some moving averages of a sequence is demonstrated below:

	1st	2nd	3rd			
Sequence	6	6	0	8	4	1	9
Moving average		4	$4\frac{2}{3}$	4	$4\frac{1}{3}$	$4\frac{2}{3}$	

The moving averages are of length 3 in this illustration. We associate the moving average with the middle member of the group of numbers averaged. Note that two of the numbers averaged in the first moving average are also averaged in the second moving average—namely, 6 and 0. The first and third averages have one number in common—namely, 0. But the first and fourth averages have no numbers in common. Now let's develop a computer program that will compute moving averages of length 5 for a sequence of 50 standard normal random numbers.

```
NOTE GENERATE NORMAL RANDOM NUMBERS
RANDOM 50 C1;
    NORMAL 0, 1.
NOTE STORE COMMANDS TO COMPUTE MOVING AVERAGE
STORE
LET C2(K1) = (C1(K1-2)+C1(K1-1)+C1(K1) &
              +C1(K1+1)+C1(K1+2))/5
LET K1 = K1+1
END
NOTE INITIALIZE K1
LET K1 = 3
NOTE EXECUTE STORED INSTRUCTIONS
EXECUTE 46 TIMES
NOTE PRINT ORIGINAL SEQUENCE AND MOVING AVERAGES
PRINT C1 C2
```

Now it will be interesting to plot the sequence that we have created. We will do time series plots of each sequence separately. Then we will do an MTSPLOT of both sequences on the same set of axes. The commands are

```
TSPLOT C1
TSPLOT C2
MTSPLOT C1 C2
```

Connect the Bs in the MTSPLOT. You will see that the moving average sequence is much smoother than the original sequence.

7.4 / SAMPLING FINITE POPULATIONS

So far in this chapter we have talked about random samples from theoretical distributions. But sometimes we are interested in a random sample from an actual finite population.

Sometimes we do this to study the properties of various statistical procedures when we are sampling from a finite population without replacement. In other cases we may have collected a very large set of data and want to do some preliminary analyses on a random subset. If we use a portion of the data, then our work will be faster and cheaper. Once we have some idea about the structure of the data, then we might want to analyze the full set.

> SAMPLE K observations from C, ..., C put into C, ..., C
>
> Takes a random sample of size K from the data in the first group of columns and stores the sample in the second group of columns. The sampling is done without replacement.

EXERCISES

7–17 Stratified sampling is an important sampling design in practice. Let's simulate some samples from a stratified design, using the males and females in the Class data (pp. 281–283) as the two populations. Say we want 20% of the population in our sample, so we want 20% of 137, or 27, people. A useful design here is to select 20% each of the males and females—that is, 18 males and 9 females. Suppose the data for the males are in columns C1–C6 and the data for the females are in C7–C12. The samples will be drawn and printed by the commands

```
SAMPLE 18 ROWS FROM C1-C6, PUT IN C21-C26
PRINT C21-C26
SAMPLE 9 ROWS FROM C7-C12, PUT IN C27-C32
PRINT C27-C32
```

Implement these commands several times and compare the samples you get.

7–18 Suppose the males and females in the Class data on pages 281–283 are combined and the combined data are in C1–C6. Implement the commands

```
SAMPLE 27 C1-C6, PUT IN C11-C16
PRINT C11-C16
```

several times and compare the samples. These are simple random samples from the combined population of males and females.

7.5 / RANDOM WALKS AND THE PARSUM COMMAND

Random walks play a fundamental role in probability, operations research, risk theory, the theory of finance, and sequential decision analysis. In this section we will see how we can use Minitab to simulate some of these important processes. The command that will help us construct random walks efficiently is the PARSUM command.

PARSUM OF C, PUT PARTIAL SUMS INTO C

EXAMPLE

```
PARSUM C1 PUT IN C2
```

C1	C2
1	1
3	4
-2	2
4	6
-8	-2
0	-2

The first number in C2 is the first number in C1, the second number in C2 is the sum of the first two numbers in C1, the third number in C2 is the sum of the first three numbers in C1, the fourth number in C2 is the sum of the first four numbers in C1, and so on.

The simplest example of a random walk is a gambling game in which a player flips a fair coin repeatedly. For each head the player wins $1; for each tail the player loses $1. The random walk is the record of the player's fortune (cumulative winnings) after any specified number of flips. A program to simulate and display 50 flips is

```
READ INTO C1 C2
  1    0.5
 -1    0.5
END
RANDOM 50 C3;
  DISCRETE C1 C2.
PARSUM C3 C4
SET C5
(1:50)
END
NAME C5 '#FLIPS' C4 'FORTUNE'
PRINT C5 C4
TSPLOT C4
```

Exhibit 7.6 shows the output from this program. The player has a positive fortune in only 17 of the 50 plays of the game, but if the game stops after 50 plays, the player has neither a gain nor a loss. What do you think will happen if the game continues? The best way to find out is to run this simulation program many times.

A variation is to let the amount won or lost on any trial be random. For example, we might let the winnings be determined by a standard

EXHIBIT 7.6 The Evolution of a Gambler's Fortune ($1 stake on each play)

ROW	#FLIPS	FORTUNE
1	1	1
2	2	0
3	3	-1
4	4	-2
5	5	-3
6	6	-4
7	7	-3
8	8	-4
9	9	-5
10	10	-4
11	11	-5
12	12	-6
13	13	-7
14	14	-8
15	15	-7
16	16	-8
17	17	-7
18	18	-6
19	19	-5
20	20	-6
21	21	-7
22	22	-6
23	23	-5
24	24	-4
25	25	-3
26	26	-4
27	27	-3
28	28	-2
29	29	-1
30	30	0
31	31	1
32	32	0
33	33	-1
34	34	-2
35	35	-1
36	36	0
37	37	1
38	38	0
39	39	1
40	40	0
41	41	-1
42	42	-2
43	43	-1
44	44	0
45	45	1
46	46	0
47	47	1
48	48	0
49	49	1
50	50	0

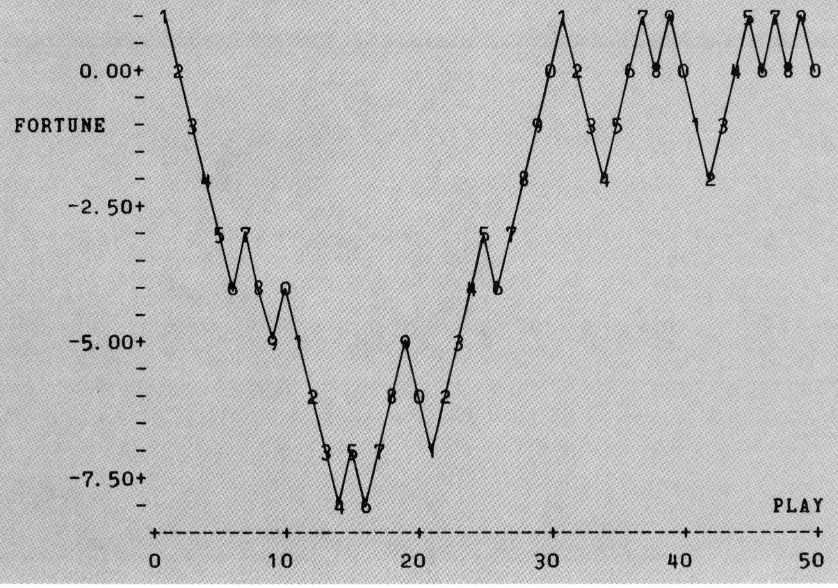
0.00+
FORTUNE
-2.50+
-5.00+
-7.50+
PLAY
0
10
20
30
40
50

normal distribution. A program to simulate this game is

```
RANDOM 69 C1;
   NORMAL 0, 1.
PARSUM C1 C2
NAME C2 'FORTUNE'
TSPLOT C2.
```

The output is shown in Exhibit 7.7. The gambler is ahead by almost $4.00 after 60 plays.

EXHIBIT 7.7   Evolution of a Gambler's Fortune (stakes determined by a standard normal distribution)

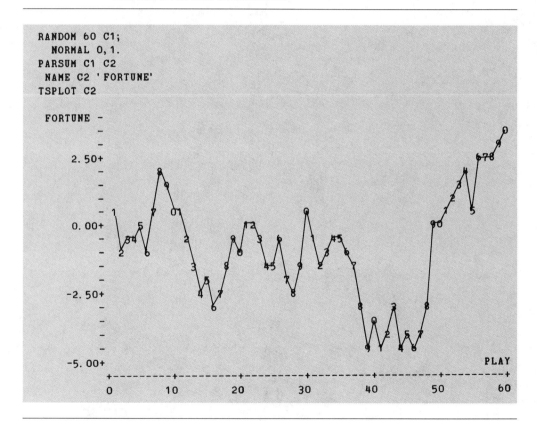

EXERCISES

7–19 *(a)* Using Exhibit 7.6, simulate the game 360 times and plot the evolution of the gambler's fortune. Describe the behavior of the random walk.

(b) Repeat part (a) three times and compare the four random walks.

7–20 Repeat Exercise 7–19 for the game in Exhibit 7.7.

7–21 *(a)* Another type of process that frequently arises can be motivated by considering claims on a group of insurance policies. Here the time at which a claim is made is random, as is the amount of the claim, so this is a doubly stochastic process. Let's let the time between claims have an exponential distribution with parameter $b = 2.0$. (If we pretend that time is measured in weeks, this says that we should receive about two claims per week.) Let's let the amount of claim be lognormal with parameters 7 and 0.03. (This says that the average claim is about $1000.) The commands to simulate 60 claims are

```
RANDOM 60 C2;
   EXPONENTIAL b = 2.
PARSUM C2 C3
RANDOM 60 C4;
   LOGNORMAL 7, 0.03.
PARSUM C4 C5
NAME C3 'TIME' C4 'AMOUNTS' C5 'TOTCLAIM'
PRINT C3 C4 C5 #If you want the results printed.
PLOT C5 VS C3
```

Execute these commands. What was the total amount paid out? What was the last claim payment?

(b) The insurance company will try to offset the claims payments by charging a premium for the insurance. Suppose the premium is $2000 per week, collectable in advance. Then the company is "ahead" if total claims before the end of the first week are less than $2000, total claims before the end of the second week are less than $4000, and so on. Otherwise, the group of policies does not pay its own way. Redo the simulation and print out 'TIME' and 'TOTCLAIM'. For your simulation, for how long do the policies pay their own way, that is, how long before the company "goes in the hole" on the policies? What premium should the company charge to avoid ever going in the hole over the period of the 60 claims?

7–22 Let p_t denote the selling price of a common stock on day t. The daily growth rate of the stock between day $t - 1$ and day t, denoted by r_t, is defined by $p_t = p_{t-1}e^{r_t}$. Thus

$$p_1 = p_0e^{r_1}, \quad p_2 = p_1e^{r_2} = p_0e^{r_1+r_2}, \quad p_3 = p_2e^{r_3}$$
$$= p_0e^{r_1+r_2+r_3}, \quad \ldots, \quad p_t = p_0e^{r_1+r_2+\cdots+r_t}$$

It is generally conceded in the finance literature that the process $r_1 + r_2 + \cdots + r_t$ is approximately a random walk, but the *distribution* of r's has been very controversial. Two theories about the r distribution are that (1) it has mean 0 but the variance is not finite and (2) it is a mixture of normal distributions. (There are many other theories as well.) We can simulate "stock prices" according to both of these theories with Minitab.

We will simulate 365 days, assuming that the stock price on the day preceding the simulation period was $800.

(a) The commands needed to simulate the prices, assuming that the growth rates have a *t* distribution with 2 degrees of freedom, are

```
NOTE GENERATE A T WITH 2DF
RANDOM 365 C4;
  T 2.
NOTE SCALE THE T-DISTRIBUTION TO HAVE A
NOTE REALISTIC RANGE OF VALUES FOR A
NOTE SET OF GROWTH RATES
LET C5 = 0.05*C4
NOTE CONSTRUCT RANDOM WALK
PARSUM C5, PUT IN C1
NOTE CONSTRUCT STOCK PRICES
EXPO C1, PUT IN C2
LET C3 = 800*C2
NAME C3 'PRICES' C1 'RANWALK'
NOTE PLOT PRICES AND RANDOM WALK
TSPLOT C3
TSPLOT C1.
```

Run this program several times and comment on the results.

(b) The commands needed to simulate the prices, assuming that the growth rates have a mixture of normals distribution, are

```
NOTE GENERATE MIXTURE OF NORMALS
RANDOM 365 C1;
  NORMAL 0, .03.
RANDOM 365 C2;
  NORMAL 0, .08.
RANDOM 365 C3;
  BERNOULLI .7.
LET C1 = C3*C1
LET C2 = (1.0-C3)*C2
LET C3 = C1+C2
NOTE CONSTRUCT RANDOM WALK
PARSUM C3 C4
NOTE CONSTRUCT PRICES
EXPO C4 C1
LET C2 = 800*C1
NAME C4 'RANWALK' C2 'PRICES'
NOTE PLOT PRICES AND RANDOM WALK
TSPLOT 'PRICES'
TSPLOT 'RANWALK'
```

Run this program several times and comment on the results.

(c) Collect 365 daily closing prices on IBM common stock. Plot the series of prices and the series of daily growth rates. Compare these to your simulations in parts (a) and (b). Are there any similarities? Explain.

8/INFERENCES BASED ON MEANS AND STANDARD DEVIATIONS

Some of the most common statistical inference procedures use sample means and standard deviations and entail the use of Student's t distribution. Minitab will do all the necessary calculations for you in response to the appropriate commands. In this chapter we will look at commands for the analysis of one or two population means. In Chapter 9 we will see how to handle more populations.

8.1/INFERENCE FOR THE MEAN OF ONE POPULATION

In this section we will look at the commands that yield confidence intervals and hypothesis tests for the mean of a single population. Let's denote the population mean by μ, the sample mean by $\bar{x}$, and the sample standard deviation by s.

CONFIDENCE INTERVALS

The TINTERVAL command computes confidence intervals based on Student's t statistic.

TINTERVAL [K percent confidence] for data in C, ..., C

For each column, TINTERVAL calculates and prints a t confidence interval for the population mean, using the formula

$$\bar{x} - t(s/\sqrt{n}) \quad \text{to} \quad \bar{x} + t(s/\sqrt{n})$$

Here $\bar{x}$ is the sample mean, s is the sample standard deviation, n is the sample size, and t is the value from the t distribution, using $(n - 1)$ degrees of freedom and K percent confidence.

If the confidence level is not specified, 95% is used.

EXAMPLE

The day and night shifts on a certain production line are both full shifts and should be equally productive. Thus on a randomly selected day there should be "even odds" that day shift production exceeds night shift production. The top part of Exhibit 8.1 shows production, in number of units, for the day and night shifts for 15 randomly selected days. The column labeled DIFF shows the difference between day and night shift production. The parameter μ is interpreted as the average difference between day shift production and night shift production over all days. Remember that the 15 days contributing data to the sample were drawn at random. This is fundamental to the validity of the inferences that we draw from the confidence interval. The bottom part of Exhibit 8.1 shows the output from three calls of the TINTERVAL command, one for each of three values of the confidence coefficient, 85%, 90%, and 99%. We see that with 85% confidence we assert that the *average* difference in production between the day and night shifts is somewhere between −0.3 and 9.3 units, whereas with 99% confidence we assert that the average difference is between −4.9 and 13.9 units. In either case we cannot rule out the possibility that night shift production is greater than day shift production, that is, that the average difference is negative. The evidence favors the assumption that the two shifts produce at about the same level, on the average.

HYPOTHESIS TESTS

Hypothesis test calculations are produced by the TTEST command.

TTEST [of mu = K] on data in C, ..., C

For each column, TTEST tests the null hypothesis H_0: μ = K against the alternative hypothesis H_1: $\mu \neq$ K. If μ is not specified on the TTEST command, H_0: μ = 0 is used.

The command calculates Student's t-test statistic

$$t = \frac{\bar{x} - K}{s/\sqrt{n}}$$

Here, $\bar{x}$ is the sample mean, n is the sample size, s is the sample standard deviation, and K is the hypothesized value of the population mean.

If you want to do a one-sided test, use the subcommand

ALTERNATIVE = K

where K = -1 corresponds to H_1: $\mu < $ K and K = $+1$ corresponds to H_1: $\mu > $ K.

There are a couple of things to notice about the TTEST command. First, if no alternative is specified, Minitab assumes that you want a two-sided alternative. A "less than" alternative is coded -1, and a "greater than" alternative is coded $+1$. Second, Minitab computes and

---

EXHIBIT 8.1   Analysis of Production by Day and Night Shifts (in number of units)

```
PRINT C1 C2 C3
  ROW    DAY   NIGHT    DIFF

   1     169    155      14
   2     171    163       8
   3     139    147      -8
   4     151    135      16
   5     175    157      18
   6     147    167     -20
   7     185    179       6
   8     141    117      24
   9     149    141       8
  10     159    169     -10
  11     141    131      10
  12     131    137      -6
  13     159    165      -6
  14     179    177       2
  15     161    149      12

TINT 85 C3

           N      MEAN    STDEV   SE MEAN    85.0 PERCENT C.I.
  DIFF    15      4.53    12.22     3.16   (    -0.27,     9.34)

TINT 90 C3

           N      MEAN    STDEV   SE MEAN    90.0 PERCENT C.I.
  DIFF    15      4.53    12.22     3.16   (    -1.03,    10.09)

TINT 99 C3

           N      MEAN    STDEV   SE MEAN    99.0 PERCENT C.I.
  DIFF    15      4.53    12.22     3.16   (    -4.86,    13.93)
```

prints out the empirical significance level (p value) of the test. If you have specified a significance level ahead of time, you can see whether the test is significant at that level by comparing it to the empirical level. If the empirical significance level is less than the level you specified, then the test is significant at your level. Otherwise, it is not.

As an illustration, let's return once more to the data in Exhibit 8.1. Suppose we had thought that day shift production was higher, on the average, than night shift production. We thus would consider a "greater than" alternative to a null hypothesis of $\mu = 0$. The command to carry out the test is

```
TTEST 0 'DIFF';
   ALT = 1.
```

The output is shown in Exhibit 8.2.

EXHIBIT 8.2   TTEST of Matched Pair Data in Exhibit 8.1

```
TTEST 0 'DIFF';
   ALT = 1.

TEST OF MU = 0.000 VS MU G. T.  0.000

            N        MEAN      STDEV     SE MEAN          T     P VALUE
DIFF       15       4.533     12.223       3.156       1.44       0.086
```

The value of the t statistic is 1.44. The empirical significance level is 0.086, so the null hypothesis cannot be rejected at the 5% significance level because $0.086 > 0.05$. The null hypothesis could be rejected, however, at the 10% significance level because $0.086 < 0.10$.

Textbooks usually discuss the construction of confidence intervals and tests for population means on the assumption that the population standard deviations are known. Minitab has commands to implement these procedures, ZINTERVAL and ZTEST, but they are seldom needed because situations in which σ is known are rare.

ZINTERVAL [K percent confidence] sigma = K, for C, ..., C

For each column, ZINTERVAL calculates and prints a confidence interval for the population mean, μ, using the formula

$$\bar{x} - z(\sigma/\sqrt{n}) \quad \text{to} \quad \bar{x} + z(\sigma/\sqrt{n})$$

Here σ is the known value of the population standard deviation, $\bar{x}$ is the mean of the sample, n is the number of observations in the sample, and z is the value from the standard normal distribution corresponding to K percent confidence.

If the confidence level is not specified, 95% is used.

ZTEST [of mu = K] sigma = K on data in C, ..., C

For each column, ZTEST tests the null hypothesis, H_0: μ = K, against the alternative hypothesis, H_1: $\mu \neq$ K, where μ is the hypothesized population mean. If μ is not specified on the ZTEST command, H_0: μ = 0 is tested. The command calculates the test statistic

$$z = \frac{\bar{x} - K}{\sigma/\sqrt{n}}$$

Here $\bar{x}$ is the sample mean, n is the sample size, σ is the known population standard deviation, and K is the hypothesized value of the population mean.

If you want to do a one-sided test, use the subcommand

ALTERNATIVE = K

where K = -1 corresponds to H_1: $\mu <$ K and K = $+1$ corresponds to H_1: $\mu >$ K.

8.2 / A NOTE ON RANDOMIZATION AND DESIGN OF EXPERIMENTS

All procedures discussed in this chapter for making inferences about populations rest on the assumption that our sample is drawn at random from the population. When we do not have random samples, our inferences must be made with some degree of caution.

The techniques in this chapter require one more condition if they are to be *exactly* valid. They require that the population from which our sample is drawn have a *normal distribution*. This would seem to rule out most applications of these techniques, since no real population is ever *exactly* normal. But, in fact, it does not. Student's t procedures, discussed in this chapter, are very useful even when the population is not normal because they are *robust* to the shape of the population. Loosely speaking, this means that they really do not care much about the shape of the population. If we use these procedures to construct a 95% confidence interval for a population mean when the population is not normal, the real confidence might not be exactly 95%. It might be 94% or 97%. But it will not be very far off. It will not be as far off as, say, 50%. We will be closer than that, no matter what shape the population has. This is what we mean when we say that Student's *t* procedures are *robust* with respect to the shape of the population.

Suppose that our sample is not drawn at *random* from the population. Then our confidence may be way off. It may be only 50%, or even only 10%. Student's *t* procedures, and all the other procedures of basic statistics, are *not robust* to nonrandom sampling. For example, if a haphazard sampling scheme is used, some population units may have no chance at all of entering the sample, thus seriously biasing the statistics used for inference. The moral is: When collecting data, strive for a random sample. And when interpreting results, keep a wary eye out for the effect of nonrandom sampling.

Because data collection can be a very expensive business, it usually pays to think hard about how to design your experiments. You want sufficiently precise information at the lowest possible cost. You can usually hold down costs by (1) striving only for the level of precision that you really need and (2) using what you already know to pinpoint what you really need to find out by experimentation. These issues are treated fully in books on experimental design and on sample surveys; in this handbook you will find them mentioned only briefly.

Of course, randomization is one of the basic tools in experimental design. Another is "blocking." The matched pair data in Exhibit 8.1 are "blocked." The blocks are days, and the production figures for the day and night shifts are matched by the days on which they occurred. An alternative to blocking in this example is to take two random samples of size 15 of days, measure day shift production for one sample of days, and measure night shift production for the other. This is a "completely randomized" design. It requires the sampling of more days and so is probably more costly than the matched pairs design. Moreover, the completely randomized design does not control well for day-to-day variation in working conditions. The matched pair design measures the production of the day and night shift during the same 24-hour period, thus eliminating the effects of day-to-day variation.

These remarks should not lead you to believe that completely randomized designs are not useful. They are quite appropriate for many experiments. The commands presented in Section 8.3 are used to analyze data from completely randomized designs. In Chapter 9, generalizations of both completely randomized and randomized block designs are presented.

EXERCISES

8–1 *(a)* Read the PROPERTY data on page 273 into the Minitab worksheet. Draw a random sample of ten parcels using the SAMPLE command. Using the MARKET values of these ten parcels, construct a 90%

confidence interval for the average market value of all 60 parcels. Now compute the average for all 60 parcels and see whether it is contained in the confidence interval.

(b) Repeat part (a) 19 more times so that you have 20 independently generated confidence intervals. How many of them fail to contain the population mean? If you had repeated the experiment 1000 times, what fraction of the intervals would have failed to contain the population mean? Why?

(c) Compute the average *length* of the confidence intervals obtained in parts (a) and (b).

8–2　Repeat Exercise 8–1, using samples of size 25. Compare the average length of these intervals with that in Exercise 8–1.

8–3　(a) Read the PROPERTY data on page 273 into the Minitab worksheet. Draw a random sample of ten parcels using the SAMPLE command. Store the ASSESSED and MARKET values of the ten sampled parcels in two different columns, subtract the ASSESSED values from the MARKET values, and store the differences in yet another column. Apply the TINTERVAL command to the column of differences to get a 90% confidence interval for the average difference between MARKET and ASSESSED values. Now compute the average difference for all 60 parcels. Is it contained in the confidence interval?

(b) Repeat part (a) 19 more times so that you have 20 independently generated confidence intervals. How many of them fail to contain the difference of the population means? If you had repeated the experiment 1000 times, what fraction of the intervals would have failed to contain the difference of the population means? Why?

(c) Compute the average *length* of the confidence intervals obtained in parts (a) and (b).

8–4　(a) The following commands will generate 50 random samples of size 15 from a normal population with mean 10 and standard deviation 10 and compute 90% confidence intervals for the mean.

```
STORE
RANDOM 15 C1;
    NORMAL 10 10.
TINTERVAL 90 C1
END
NAME   C1 'NORMAL'
EXECUTE 50   TIMES
```

Run this program and count the number of intervals that fail to contain $\mu = 10$.

(b) The following commands perform the same operations as in part (a) except that the data are generated from an exponential population with mean 10 and standard deviation 10.

```
STORE
RANDOM 15 C2;
    EXPO 0.1.
TINTERVAL 90 C2
END
NAME  C2  'EXPO'
EXECUTE 50   TIMES
```

Run this program and count the number of intervals that fail to contain $\mu = 10$. Do your results tend to support the notion that the t interval is robust? Why or why not?

(c) Repeat parts (a) and (b), using samples of size 8 and 25. How are your results affected by sample size?

(d) Repeat parts (b) and (c), substituting a distribution of your choice for the exponential. (The Cauchy would be an inappropriate choice because the mean and variance are not finite!)

8–5 Ten typists were asked to type a passage on two different typewriters (A and B). The order in which each typist used the typewriters was determined by the flip of a coin. The rates in words per minute achieved by the typists are presented below. Use the appropriate t-test to determine whether the performance on one brand is better than that on the other.

Typist	1	2	3	4	5	6	7	8	9	10
Brand A	71	70	65	73	75	69	73	72	70	71
Brand B	59	64	68	60	57	69	73	67	71	60

8–6 Explain the mathematical operation that Minitab must perform to compute the empirical significance level of the t-test. Why can this calculation not be performed using the t tables usually printed in statistics textbooks?

8–7 (a) The following commands generate 50 random samples of size K1 = 4 from a normal population with mean 101 and standard deviation 2 and perform a t-test of the null hypothesis $\mu = 100$ for each sample:

```
STORE
RANDOM K1 C1;
    NORMAL 101 2.
TTEST 100 C1
END
LET  K1 = 4
EXECUTE  50 TIMES
```

Run this program and count the number of times the null hypothesis is rejected at the 10% significance level.

(b) Repeat part (a), letting K1 equal 9, 16, and 25. How is the number of times the null hypothesis is rejected related to sample size?

8–8 Repeat Exercise 8–7, letting the population standard deviation be 3 instead of 2. How is the number of times the null hypothesis is rejected related to population standard deviation?

8.3 / COMPARING MEANS OF TWO POPULATIONS

A completely randomized design for comparing the means of two populations is to draw *independent* random samples from the two populations.
The analysis consists of constructing a confidence interval for the difference in the population means and testing the null hypothesis that the
two means are equal. Minitab has two commands that perform the
analysis: TWOSAMPLE and TWOT. TWOSAMPLE is used for unstacked
data; TWOT for stacked data. If you believe that it is legitimate to assume
that the two populations have approximately equal variances, then you use
the POOLED subcommand. If you believe that the population variances
could be quite different, then you use TWOSAMPLE without the
POOLED subcommand. TWOSAMPLE adjusts the degrees of freedom
of Student's *t* to account for the unequal variances so that inferences about
the means remain valid. When the population variances are unequal, the
POOLED subcommand may not yield reliable inference about the means.
Thus, in a sense, it is safer not to use the POOLED subcommand.
However, you should always ask yourself whether comparing means of
populations with vastly different variances is sensible. It may be more to
the point to rescale the measurements so as to bring about approximately
equal variances than to go forward with the comparison of means.

TWOSAMPLE-T first sample in C, second sample in C

Prints the results of a *t*-test and confidence interval to compare two
independent samples. Suppose there are n_1 observations in the first
sample, with mean $\bar{x}_1$ and standard deviation s_1. Suppose n_2, $\bar{x}$, and s_2 are
the corresponding values for the second sample. Then the confidence
interval goes from

$$(\bar{x}_1 - \bar{x}_2) - t\sqrt{\frac{s_1^2}{n_1} + \frac{s_2^2}{n_2}} \quad \text{to} \quad (\bar{x}_1 - \bar{x}_2) + t\sqrt{\frac{s_1^2}{n_1} + \frac{s_2^2}{n_2}}$$

where *t* is the value from a *t*-table corresponding to 95% confidence
and degrees of freedom defined below. The test statistic is

$$t = \frac{(\bar{x}_1 - \bar{x}_2)}{\sqrt{\frac{s_1^2}{n_1} + \frac{s_2^2}{n_2}}}$$

The degrees of freedom is based on the following approximation:

$$\text{d.f.} = \frac{((s_1^2/n_1) + (s_2^2/n_2))^2}{\frac{(s_1^2/n_1)^2}{(n_1 - 1)} + \frac{(s_2^2/n_2)^2}{(n_2 - 1)}}$$

A confidence level other than 95% can be specified as follows:

```
TWOSAMPLE-T K percent confidence, samples in C, C
```

TWOSAMPLE-T has the two subcommands: POOLED, to do the pooled procedure, and ALTERNATIVE, to do one-sided tests.

POOLED

This subcommand for TWOSAMPLE-T and TWOT tells Minitab to use the pooled procedure. The following pooled estimate of the common variance is calculated:

$$s_p^2 = \frac{(n_1 - 1)s_1^2 + (n_2 - 1)s_2^2}{n_1 + n_2 - 2}$$

The confidence interval goes from

$$(\bar{x}_1 - \bar{x}_2) - ts_p\sqrt{\frac{1}{n_1} + \frac{1}{n_2}} \quad \text{to} \quad (\bar{x}_1 - \bar{x}_2) + ts_p\sqrt{\frac{1}{n_1} + \frac{1}{n_2}}$$

where t is the value from a t-table corresponding to $n_1 - n_2 - 2$ degrees of freedom. The test statistic is

$$t = \frac{(\bar{x}_1 - \bar{x}_2)}{s_p\sqrt{\frac{1}{n_1} + \frac{1}{n_2}}}$$

ALTERNATIVE = K

TWOSAMPLE-T and TWOT both allow one-sided as well as two-sided tests. (The confidence intervals, however, are always two-sided.) The subcommand ALTERNATIVE tells Minitab to do a one-sided test. It uses the following codes:

$K = -1$ means μ_1 is less than μ_2
$K = +1$ means μ_1 is greater than μ_2

EXAMPLE

Here, $H_1: \mu_1 < \mu_2$ and a 90% confidence interval, using the pooled procedure, is requested.

```
TWOT 90 'PULSE' 'SEX';
    POOLED;
    ALTERNATIVE -1.
```

EXAMPLE

A market researcher was trying to determine the effect of questionnaire style on response to a new product. Forty respondents agreed to receive a sample of the product and to fill out and return a questionnaire. Analysis of a questionnaire resulted in a score for the product between 0 and 50. The researcher *randomly* divided the 40 respondents into two groups of 20. One group received one style of questionnaire called "Spartan." The other group received another style called "Athenian." The contents of the questionnaires were the same. Only the styles of presentation varied. It is clear that the market researcher used a completely randomized design.

The responses from the two groups are displayed in both unstacked and stacked form in Exhibit 8.3. The stacked form can be exploited to produce the boxplots also shown in Exhibit 8.3. The data from the two groups are displayed on the same scale. While the two groups of responses overlap considerably, the Athenian responses tend to be a bit higher, on the average, than the Spartan responses.

The TWOSAMPLE command operates on the data in unstacked form. Exhibit 8.4 shows output from TWOSAMPLE both without and with the POOLED subcommand. The TWOSAMPLE analysis uses a Student's *t* with 37.6 degrees of freedom, whereas the POOLED analysis uses a Student's *t* with 38 degrees of freedom. The degrees of freedom adjustment for unequal variance is very slight here. This makes sense because the sample standard deviations are close, 5.7 for Spartan and 5.16 for Athenian. The TWOSAMPLE 95% confidence interval is very slightly wider than the POOLED confidence interval, but the differences do not show up in the first decimal place. Both intervals are to the left of 0, so with 95% confidence we can assert that the average Athenian response is greater than the average Spartan response. The empirical significance level (*p*-value) of the test of the equality of the two population means is 0.022. Thus the test is statistically significant at the 5% level but not at the 1% level. It appears that the average Athenian response would be greater than the average Spartan response by as little as about .6 or by as much as about 7.5. This is a rather wide range. The market researcher probably should consider performing the experiment again with a new set of respondents. The new data could be combined with the data reported here so as to obtain a more precise estimate of the difference in the population means.

The TWOT command operates on the data in stacked form.

TWOT [K percent confidence] data in C, groups in C

Prints the results of a *t*-test and confidence interval to compare two independent samples. The observations from the two samples are in the first column. The second column specifies which sample each observation belongs to. The formulas for the test and confidence interval are the same as those used by TWOSAMPLE-T.

TWOT has two subcommands, POOLED and ALTERNATIVE, described on page 156.

EXHIBIT 8.3 Data in Unstacked and Stacked Form and Boxplots for Questionnaire Data

```
PRINT C1-C4
  ROW   SPARTAN   ATHENIAN   SCORES   STYLE

    1      14         19        14       1
    2      17         19        17       1
    3      17         23        17       1
    4      20         24        20       1
    5      21         28        21       1
    6      23         28        23       1
    7      24         29        24       1
    8      25         29        25       1
    9      25         29        25       1
   10      26         30        26       1
   11      26         30        26       1
   12      27         31        27       1
   13      28         33        28       1
   14      29         33        29       1
   15      29         33        29       1
   16      29         34        29       1
   17      31         34        31       1
   18      32         35        32       1
   19      34         36        34       1
   20      35         37        35       1
   21                           19       2
   22                           19       2
   23                           23       2
   24                           24       2
   25                           28       2
   26                           28       2
   27                           29       2
   28                           29       2
   29                           29       2
   30                           30       2
   31                           30       2
   32                           31       2
   33                           33       2
   34                           33       2
   35                           33       2
   36                           34       2
   37                           34       2
   38                           35       2
   39                           36       2
   40                           37       2
```

EXHIBIT 8.3 *Continued*

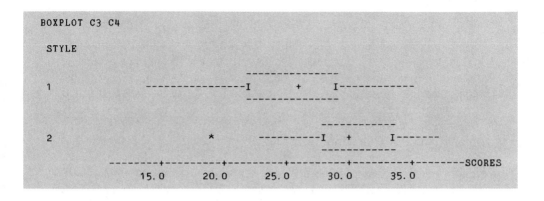

EXHIBIT 8.4   TWOSAMPLE and POOLED Analysis of Questionnaire Data

```
TWOSAMPLE C1 C2

TWOSAMPLE T FOR SPARTAN VS ATHENIAN
                N       MEAN      STDEV    SE MEAN
SPARTAN    20    25.60    5.70      1.3
ATHENIAN   20    29.70    5.16      1.2

95 PCT CI FOR MU SPARTAN - MU ATHENIAN: (-7.6, -0.6)
TTEST MU SPARTAN = MU ATHENIAN ( VS NE): T=-2.38 P=0.022 DF=37.6

TWOSAMPLE C1 C2;
  POOLED.

TWOSAMPLE T FOR SPARTAN VS ATHENIAN
                N       MEAN      STDEV    SE MEAN
SPARTAN    20    25.60    5.70      1.3
ATHENIAN   20    29.70    5.16      1.2

95 PCT CI FOR MU SPARTAN - MU ATHENIAN: (-7.6, -0.6)
TTEST MU SPARTAN = MU ATHENIAN ( VS NE): T=-2.38 P=0.022 DF=38.0
```

To analyze the data in Exhibit 8.3, we could issue the command

TWOT C3 C4

or the command

TWOT C3 C4;
   POOLED.

EXERCISE

8–9   A small study was done to compare how well students with different majors do in an introductory statistics course. Seven majors were found: biology, psychology, sociology, business, education, meteorology, and economics. At the end of the course the students were given a special test to measure their understanding of basic statistics. Then a series of *t*-tests were performed to compare every pair of majors. Thus biology and psychology majors were compared, biology and sociology majors, psychology and sociology majors, and so on, for a total of 21 *t*-tests. Simulate this study, assuming that all majors do about the same. Assume that there are 20 students in each major and that scores on the test have a normal distribution with $\mu = 12$ and $\sigma = 2$. Use RANDOM to get a sample for biology majors and put it in C1, a sample for psychology majors in C2, and so on, for seven samples.

(a)   What is the null hypothesis?

(b)   What are the 21 pairs of majors for the 21 *t*-tests?

(c)   Do the 21 *t*-tests. You will need to issue the TWOSAMPLE command 21 times.

(d)   In how many of the tests did you reject the null hypothesis at $\alpha = 0.10$?

(e)   Since this study was simulated, the true situation is known—there are not any differences. But you probably did find at least one pair of majors for which there was a significant difference. This illustrates the hazards of doing a lot of comparisons. Try to think of some other situations in which one might do a lot of statistical tests. For example, suppose a pharmaceutical firm had 16 possible new drugs that it wanted to try out in hopes that at least one was better than the present best competing brand. What are the consequences of doing a lot of statistical tests?

9/ANALYSIS OF VARIANCE

9.1/ONE-WAY ANALYSIS OF VARIANCE

In Chapter 8 we showed how t-tests could be used to compare the means of two populations. The form of the t-test depended on the way in which subjects were allocated randomly to treatments. What tests are appropriate if we want to compare more than two population means? Let's begin with an example.

A consulting firm wished to purchase some new microcomputer keyboards for its pool of 20 typists. Four brands of roughly comparable keyboards were considered with respect to cost, expected lifetime, and maintenance contract available. Management requested performance data to aid in the decision.

The 20 typists were allocated *randomly* to four brands of keyboard, five typists to each brand. Each typist copied from a selected chapter from a training manual for ten minutes; then the typist's rate (in words per minute) of correct copy was recorded. The data were analyzed to try to answer the question: "On the average, are the rates of correct copy the same for all four brands of keyboard?" If the answer was yes, then performance did not need to be considered further; but if the answer was no, then performance was an important factor in the decision.

The data from the performance experiment are displayed in Exhibit 9.1 and plotted in Exhibit 9.2. The plot tells us a lot. Even on the same keyboard, different typists perform differently, partly because of different abilities and partly because the test conditions were not the same for all typists. This kind of variation can be thought of as simply random error. There are several other names for it: *within-group variation*, *unexplained variation*, *residual variation*, and *variation due to error*. The random allocation of typists to keyboards was done to ensure that the random error would be essentially the same for all four brands of keyboard.

A second source of variation in the data is that due to differences between keyboards. This variation is called *between-group variation*,

---

EXHIBIT 9.1   Performance Data on Four Brands of Typewriter (rates in
               words per minute)

		Brand		
	1	*2*	*3*	*4*
	69	69	71	59
	73	73	70	64
	67	72	65	68
	71	70	73	60
	60	71	75	57
Sample means	68.0	71.0	70.8	61.6

EXHIBIT 9.2   Plot of Performance Measurements for Four Brands
               of Keyboard

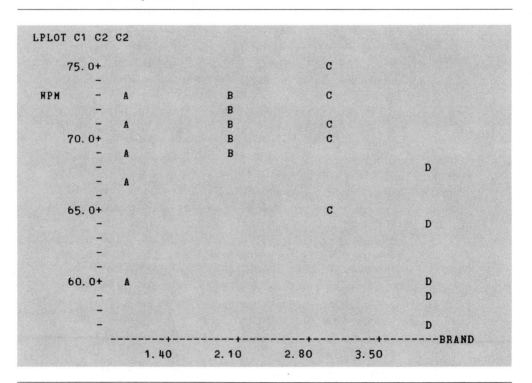

variation due to factor, or *variation explained by the factor*. Here the factor under study is brand of keyboard. Sometimes the word "treatment" is used instead of "factor." If we look at Exhibit 9.2 again, we see some variation among brands. Brand 4, especially, seems to produce lower rates than brands 1, 2, and 3. Instead of using a plot, we could compare the sample means for the four brands. The four sample means do vary from brand to brand, but again some variation is expected. The question is, "Do the four sample means differ any more than we would expect from just random variation?" Put another way, "Is the *between-group variation* significantly greater than the *within-group variation*?" Analysis of variance is a statistical procedure that gives an answer to this question.

THE ONE-WAY ANALYSIS OF VARIANCE PROCEDURE

In one-way analysis of variance we want to compare the means of several populations. We assume that we have a random sample from each population, that each population has a normal distribution, and that all of the populations have the same variance, σ^2. (In practice, the normality assumption is not too important, the equal variances assumption is not important if the sample sizes for the different samples are equal, but the assumption of a random sample is very important.) The main question is, "Do all of the populations have the same mean?" Suppose that we have r populations and that μ_1 is the mean of the first population, μ_2 is the mean of the second population, μ_3 is the mean of the third, and so on. Then the null hypothesis of no differences is

$$H_0: \mu_1 = \mu_2 = \mu_3 = \cdots = \mu_r$$

To test this null hypothesis, we can use Minitab's AOVONEWAY command if the data are unstacked (that is, in separate columns) or the ONEWAY command if the data are stacked. We shall present the analysis with stacked data in detail.

AOVONEWAY C, ..., C

Performs a one-way analysis of variance. The first column contains the sample from the first population (sometimes called first group or level), the second column contains the sample from the second population, the third column from the third population, and so on. The sample sizes need not be equal.

ONEWAY on data in C, levels in C

Does the same analysis and prints the same output as AOVONEWAY. The difference is the form of the input: For ONEWAY, all data for all levels must be put in one column. A second column indicates what level each observation belongs to. Note: The numbers used for levels must be integers. (More in Section 9.4.)

In Exhibit 9.3 the data are presented in stacked form and also in a table, like the one in Exhibit 9.1, that was produced by Minitab's TABLE command. Exhibit 9.4 shows the output from the ONEWAY command.

The first part of the output in Exhibit 9.4 is an analysis of variance table. The total sum of squares is broken down into two sources—the variation due to differences among the four brands and the variation due to random error within a brand. Thus

$$(\text{SS TOTAL}) = (\text{SS FACTOR}) + (\text{SS ERROR})$$

In this example, $532.5 = 288.5 + 244.0$. Each sum of squares has a certain number of degrees of freedom associated with it. These will be used when we do tests. The degrees of freedom also add up:

$$(\text{DF TOTAL}) = (\text{DF FACTOR}) + (\text{DF ERROR})$$

FORMULAS FOR THE THREE SUMS OF SQUARES. In the following table, x_{ij} is the jth observation in the sample from population i, $\bar{x}_i$ and n_i are the sample mean and sample size for sample i, a is the number of populations, n is the total number of observations, and $\bar{x}$ is the mean of all n observations.

Source	DF	SS
Factor	$a - 1$	$\Sigma_i n_i (\bar{x}_i - \bar{x})^2$
Error	$n - a$	$\Sigma_i \Sigma_j (x_{ij} - \bar{x}_i)^2$
Total	$n - 1$	$\Sigma_i \Sigma_j (x_{ij} - \bar{x})^2$

Exhibit 9.4 gives the mean square due to the factor (difference among brands) and the mean square due to error (variation within brands). Each mean square is just the ratio of the corresponding sum of squares and degrees of freedom. The last column gives the quotient of these two mean squares:

$$(\text{F-RATIO}) = (\text{MS FACTOR})/(\text{MS ERROR})$$

This F-RATIO is a useful test statistic. If it is large, then MS FACTOR must be much larger than MS ERROR. That is, the variation between the brands is much greater than the variation due to random error. So we would reject the null hypothesis that the brands all have the same average rate. How large the F-RATIO must be is determined by the critical value from an F-table. To use an F-table, we need the degrees of freedom for the numerator of the F-ratio and the degrees of freedom for the denominator of the F-ratio. Here the numerator has 3 degrees of freedom, and the

EXHIBIT 9.3   Keyboard Performance Data in Stacked and Tabled Form

```
PRINT C1 C2
  ROW   WPM   BRAND

    1    69      1
    2    73      1
    3    67      1
    4    71      1
    5    60      1
    6    69      2
    7    73      2
    8    72      2
    9    70      2
   10    71      2
   11    71      3
   12    70      3
   13    65      3
   14    73      3
   15    75      3
   16    59      4
   17    64      4
   18    68      4
   19    60      4
   20    57      4

TABLE C2;
  DATA C1;
  MEAN C1;
  LAYOUT 0,1.


COLUMNS: BRAND

            1          2          3          4        ALL

        69.000     69.000     71.000     59.000       --
        73.000     73.000     70.000     64.000
        67.000     72.000     65.000     68.000
        71.000     70.000     73.000     60.000
        60.000     71.000     75.000     57.000
        _____

        68.000     71.000     70.800     61.600     67.850

    CELL CONTENTS --
              WPM: DATA
              ____
              MEAN
```

EXHIBIT 9.4   Output from AOVONEWAY Command for Keyboard
Performance Data

```
ONEWAY C1 C2

ANALYSIS OF VARIANCE ON WPM
SOURCE      DF        SS        MS        F
BRAND        3      288.5      96.2     6.31
ERROR       16      244.0      15.2
TOTAL       19      532.5
                                   INDIVIDUAL 95 PCT CI'S
                                   BASED ON POOLED STDEV
LEVEL        N      MEAN      STDEV    ----+---------+---------+-----
  1          5     68.000     5.000                 (-----*------)
  2          5     71.000     1.581                   (-----*------)
  3          5     70.800     3.768                   (-----*-----)
  4          5     61.600     4.393    (------*-----)
                                       ----+---------+---------+-----
POOLED STDEV =       3.905             60.0       66.0       72.0
```

---

denominator has 16. The corresponding value from an F-table, using $\alpha = 0.05$, is 3.24. Since 6.31 is greater than 3.24, we reject the null hypothesis and conclude that we have significant evidence that there is some difference among the four brands. (Note: You can use Minitab's INVCDF command (p. 323) instead of an F-table.)

The next table in Exhibit 9.4 summarizes the results separately for each brand. The sample size, sample mean, sample standard deviation, and a 95% confidence interval are given for each brand. Each confidence interval is calculated by the formula

$$\bar{x}_i - ts_p/\sqrt{n_i} \quad \text{to} \quad \bar{x}_i + ts_p/\sqrt{n_i}$$

Here $\bar{x}_i$ and n_i are the sample mean and sample size for level i, s_p = POOLED STDEV = $\sqrt{\text{MS ERROR}}$ is the pooled estimate of the common standard deviation, σ, and t is the value from a t-table corresponding to 95% confidence and the degrees of freedom associated with MS ERROR. These intervals give us some idea of how the population means differ.

THE AOVONEWAY COMMAND FOR UNSTACKED DATA

To see how to use the AOVONEWAY command, assume that the performance data in Exhibit 9.3 were arranged in four columns, one for each brand. Assume that the columns are C1, C2, C3, and C4. Then the output in Exhibit 9.4 would be achieved by issuing the command AOVONEWAY C1–C4.

9.2 / RANDOMIZED BLOCK DESIGNS

In a randomized block design (abbreviated RBD) the material, people, locations, time periods, or whatever within a block are relatively homogeneous. The treatments that we wish to compare then are assigned at random within each block, each treatment appearing exactly once in each block.

In Section 5.3 we also presented graphically some data that were collected by using a variation on the design used in Section 9.1 to analyze keyboard performance. Here five typists were selected at random from the pool of 20 typists. Each of the five typists typed on each keyboard. The order in which the keyboards were presented to the typists was determined randomly. The purpose of the design is to eliminate the variation between typists from the comparison of the keyboards. (This is so because each typist used each keyboard.) The order of presentation of the keyboards was randomized to allocate the learning effects of repeatedly typing the same passage equally across the keyboards.

In this example the two classifications (or factors) are typists* (also called blocks and corresponding to rows in the table) and keyboards (also called treatments and corresponding to columns in the table). There are five different "levels" of typists and four different "levels" (brands) of keyboard. Thus there are 5 × 4 = 20 cells in the table, and each cell has one observation in it. Notice that we need only five typists in this design instead of the 20 needed in Section 9.1.

The data are presented in Exhibit 5.6. Exhibit 9.5 shows commands to READ the data, to print out the data in a table with row and column means, and to use Minitab's TWOWAY command to do a test.

Exhibit 9.6 contains the output from TABLE. The body of the table contains the original data. The output is in the same form as the data in Exhibit 5.6, so we can easily check for typing errors. The margins of the table give typist and brand means. The typist means allow us to compare typists. On the average, typist 3 had the highest rate, typist 5 the next highest, and so forth. The means of the four keyboards indicate how the different brands fared. For example, brand 3 had an average rate of 71.6 words per minute, whereas brand 4 had an average rate of only 62.8 words per minute.

The plot at the top of Exhibit 5.7 gives a plot of the data. The letters are useful because they show how each keyboard fared with each typist. All the As go with Brand 1, the Bs with Brand 2, the Cs with Brand 3, and the Ds with Brand 4. Here it seems clear that brands B and C are consistently better than brands A and D. Thus part of the variation in the data seems to be due to differences in the brands of keyboard. It also appears that typists make a difference. For example, typist 3 is always faster than typists 1 and 2 and usually faster than typist 4.

---

*Strictly speaking, the typists should be treated as a "random effect," but we ignore this refinement here because emphasis is on comparing typewriters.

```
READ RATES INTO C1, TYPISTS INTO C2, BRANDS INTO C3
70 1 1
68 1 2
68 1 3
60 1 4
57 2 1
67 2 2
68 2 3
65 2 4
72 3 1
75 3 2
72 3 3
70 3 4
63 4 1
68 4 2
72 4 3
52 4 4
62 5 1
72 5 2
78 5 3
67 5 4
END OF DATA
NAME C1 'RATES' C2 'TYPISTS' C3 'BRANDS'
TABLE 'TYPISTS' BY 'BRANDS';
   MEAN 'RATES'.
TWOWAY ANALYSIS OF 'RATES' CLASSIFIED BY 'TYPISTS' AND 'BRANDS'
```

EXHIBIT 9.6   Output from TABLE for Keyboard Data

```
TABLE 'TYPISTS' BY 'BRANDS';
  MEAN 'RATES'.

  ROWS: TYPISTS      COLUMNS: BRANDS

               1         2         3         4        ALL

      1     70.000    68.000    68.000    60.000    66.500
      2     57.000    67.000    68.000    65.000    64.250
      3     72.000    75.000    72.000    70.000    72.250
      4     63.000    68.000    72.000    52.000    63.750
      5     62.000    72.000    78.000    67.000    69.750
    ALL     64.800    70.000    71.600    62.800    67.300

      CELL CONTENTS --
              RATES: MEAN
```

EXHIBIT 9.7   Output from TWOWAY for Keyboard Data

```
TWOWAY 'RATES' 'TYPISTS' 'BRANDS'

ANALYSIS OF VARIANCE   RATES

   SOURCE        DF        SS        MS
   TYPISTS        4     212. 2     53. 0
   BRANDS         3     261. 4     87. 1
   ERROR         12     250. 6     20. 9
   TOTAL         19     724. 2
```

Now, just as we did in one-way analysis of variance, we can express the total variation in the data as the sum of several sources:

Total variation in data = variation due to typists
+ variation due to brands
+ variation due to random error

If the variation due to typists is much greater than the random variation, we will have evidence that there is a significant difference among typists. If the variation due to brands is much greater than random variation, we will have evidence that there is a significant difference among the four brands of keyboard. Of course, the latter type of difference is of most interest to us because we are trying to compare brands.

The TWOWAY output in Exhibit 9.7 gives the breakdown of the total variation. In the table below, a is the number of treatments, b is the number of blocks, x_{ij} is the observation in block i given treatment j, $\bar{x}_{i.}$ is the mean of all a observations in block i, $\bar{x}_{.j}$ is the mean of all b observations given treatment j, and $\bar{x}$ is the mean of all ab observations.

Source	DF	SS
Blocks	$b-1$	$a\Sigma_i(\bar{x}_{i.} - \bar{x})^2$
Treatments	$a-1$	$b\Sigma_j(\bar{x}_{.j} - \bar{x})^2$
Error	$(b-1)(a-1)$	$\Sigma_i\Sigma_j(x_{ij} - \bar{x}_{i.} - \bar{x}_{.j} + \bar{x})^2$
Total	$ba-1$	$\Sigma_i\Sigma_j(x_{ij} - \bar{x})^2$

For the keyboard data the sum of squares due to typists is 212.2 and has 4 degrees of freedom associated with it. The sum of squares due to brands is 261.4 and has 3 degrees of freedom associated with it. The sum of squares due to random error is 250.6 and has 12 degrees of freedom associated with it. So the three respective mean squares are $212.2/4 = 53.0$, $261.4/3 = 87.1$, and $250.6/12 = 20.9$. There are two tests we can do.

To see whether there is a significant difference among the five typists, we form the F-ratio,

$$\frac{\text{MS typist}}{\text{MS error}} = \frac{53.0}{20.9} = 2.54$$

and compare it to a value from an F-table, corresponding to 4 degrees of freedom in the numerator and 12 degrees of freedom in the denominator. Here the F-table value is 2.48 for $\alpha = .10$, whereas it is 3.26 for $\alpha = .05$. Since $2.48 < 2.54 < 3.26$, we have some mild evidence that rates differ among typists, on the average, which agrees with our conclusion from the LPLOT of Exhibit 5.7.

To see whether there is a significant difference between brands, form the F-ratio,

$$\frac{\text{MS brands}}{\text{MS error}} = \frac{87.1}{20.9} = 4.17$$

and compare it to the value from an F-table, corresponding to 3 degrees of freedom in the numerator and 12 degrees of freedom in the denominator. Here the table value is 3.49 for $\alpha = .05$. Since $4.17 > 3.49$, we have fairly strong evidence that the rates differ from brand to brand, on the average. Again this is what we observed in the LPLOT.

TWOWAY analysis, obs in C, blocks in C, treatments in C

Does both a two-way analysis of variance (see Section 9.3) and a randomized block design analysis. In a RBD the first column contains all the observations, the second column denotes which block each observation is in, and the third column denotes which treatment each observation was given. (More in Section 9.4.)

EXERCISES

9–1   As part of a study of the use of statistical methods in property tax management, the Wisconsin Department of Revenue drew a random sample of 49 residential parcels from the village of Palmyra, Wisconsin. The market value of each parcel as of May 1975 was appraised and divided into the assessed value of the parcel as of that date. The resulting assessment/appraisal ratios are reported below. Such ratios are used to determine assessment equity across different statuses of parcels. Each parcel either was vacant (no building) or contained a single-family or a multiple-family dwelling.

Vacant		Single-Family			Multiple-Family
0.320	0.875	0.854	0.868	0.830	0.832
0.472	0.905	0.642	0.897	0.794	0.628
0.472	0.762	0.694	0.937	0.786	0.725
0.750	0.840	0.856	0.863	0.864	0.518
0.596	0.787	0.733	0.925	0.748	
0.644	0.804	0.597	0.761	0.897	
	0.673	0.822	0.887	0.799	
	0.873	0.806	0.887	0.878	
	0.959	0.828	0.941	0.666	
	0.819	0.556	0.808		

(a) Perform a one-way analysis of variance to see whether different parcel statuses are associated with different average ratios.

(b) Comment on the extent to which you think the usual assumption behind the analysis of variance *F*-test is satisfied in this example. How could the sampling have been done if the validation of these assumptions had been a primary goal of the study? (The analysis of variance was not a primary goal of the study, however. To learn more about this, read the article by Miller and Johnson in the References.)

9–2 Reanalyze the typewriter performance in a one-way analysis of variance using brands as groups. What conclusion do you reach? Explain the reason for this result. Comment on the relationship between data analysis and experimental design.

9–3 T. E. Crenshaw (see the References) reported 14 semiannual gains on each of 43 unit trusts in the United Kingdom, adjusted by subtraction of the gain on the *Financial Times* index. The data for the first 15 trusts are reported on page 172.

(a) One purpose of Crenshaw's study was to determine whether the trusts differed in average adjusted gain. Perform a two-way analysis of variance using trusts 8, 11, and 12 as treatments and the 14 semiannual time periods as blocks. (This analysis could arise if these three trusts were especially interesting to an experimenter or if they were selected at random by an experimenter.)

(b) Comment on the kinds of variation that may be controlled for by the blocking suggested in part (a).

(c) Redo part (a) using all 15 trusts. Compare the conclusions in parts (a) and (c).

Year	Semiannual Period	Trust							
		1	*2*	*3*	*4*	*5*	*6*	*7*	*8*
1963	1	4.8	5.8	4.4	5.5	−10.5	5.0	1.6	3.1
	2	−0.2	−1.3	2.9	−2.4	−11.5	−12.7	−1.4	−4.4
1964	1	4.2	1.0	−1.2	1.8	−2.6	5.0	2.8	1.9
	2	1.0	6.2	1.9	1.6	3.5	2.0	2.3	2.7
1965	1	1.6	0.1	2.3	1.6	3.3	4.2	1.1	−1.1
	2	−0.7	−0.2	0.1	−0.1	1.4	2.0	−4.2	−3.8
1966	1	4.6	5.0	2.7	−12.6	−4.5	−1.6	−0.2	4.5
	2	−2.9	−3.4	−0.7	14.1	8.0	8.9	−0.1	1.6
1967	1	−1.1	−2.2	0.4	0.3	−7.6	−8.7	0.2	−0.9
	2	0.9	1.2	−0.0	−1.1	3.0	3.8	−3.6	1.3
1968	1	0.4	−1.1	−2.8	−2.4	−5.2	−7.5	−2.3	2.8
	2	1.2	−1.1	−0.7	0.7	−2.4	−1.6	−3.1	−6.9
1969	1	6.6	3.1	1.6	5.6	−2.0	0.5	2.3	0.7
	2	−8.3	−5.9	−1.1	−4.2	5.4	0.1	−1.6	−4.4

Year	Semiannual Period	*9*	*10*	*11*	*12*	*13*	*14*	*15*
1963	1	3.9	5.6	16.9	3.9	3.1	5.3	−13.1
	2	−0.6	1.4	−9.3	−2.5	−3.2	−2.0	−10.1
1964	1	3.1	−2.3	0.2	2.7	0.4	6.4	−2.9
	2	0.0	6.2	6.0	0.9	1.8	6.0	−8.2
1965	1	2.1	1.4	6.5	1.4	−0.1	−1.2	8.2
	2	−1.2	−2.2	−3.9	1.1	−1.2	−0.9	0.2
1966	1	1.1	2.3	3.7	2.0	2.2	−2.5	−8.5
	2	−2.6	−0.1	−0.2	−0.7	−2.7	7.2	9.9
1967	1	1.6	1.4	0.5	0.8	−0.5	−0.3	−3.3
	2	−11.3	4.0	1.7	−1.9	5.0	13.2	−2.8
1968	1	−3.0	−2.7	−3.3	−3.5	−6.0	0.3	0.0
	2	−2.9	−0.8	3.6	−0.7	4.7	−6.4	−1.8
1969	1	−0.3	3.1	−1.1	−3.3	1.5	0.9	−3.9
	2	−1.2	−6.3	0.4	−2.0	1.1	0.6	11.8

Source: Excerpted from T. E. Crenshaw, "The Evaluation of Investment Performance," *The Journal of Business* 50(4):462–487. © 1977 by The University of Chicago Press. Reprinted by permission.

9.3 / TWO-WAY ANALYSIS OF VARIANCE: TESTING FOR INTERACTION

In a two-way analysis of variance, when there is more than one observation per cell, it is convenient to test whether there is any interaction between the two factors. In this section we will show how this can be done, but first let's take a closer look at the meaning of "interaction" as used in the analysis of variance.

TABLE 9.1   Expected Lifetime Earnings in 1979 for Men and
Women Aged 25 in Thousands of 1981 Dollars
(year of origin: 1979)

	Years of School Completed				
	Less Than 12	*High School 4 Years*	*College 1–3 Years*	*College 4 Years*	*College 5 or More Years*
Men	685	976	1124	1434	1574
Women	227	400	498	573	819
Difference	458	576	626	861	755

Source: Bureau of the Census, *Statistical Abstract of the United States*, Washington, D.C.: U.S. Department of Commerce, 1984, p. 470.

INTERACTION

Let's begin with an example in which it is convenient to suppose that we know the population almost exactly, so that we won't need to worry about random variation for a moment.

In the 1984 *Statistical Abstract of the United States*, the Census Bureau published some projections of expected lifetime earnings of men and women aged 25, making various assumptions about the discount rate (the difference between interest rates and the inflation rate), productivity increases, mortality, the probability of holding a job, and years of school completed. One set of projections is shown in Table 9.1. The table shows expected lifetime earnings to age 64 in thousands of 1981 dollars, assuming a 0 discount rate and 1% per year productivity increases for men and women aged 25. The year of origin of the projections is 1979.

When we plot the male and female salaries as we have in Exhibit 9.8, we see that the amount of difference between men and women depends on the factor "Years of School Completed." For example, among persons with "less than 12" years of school the difference is $458,000, while among persons with four years of college the difference is $861,000. The differences are not constant. They depend on educational level.

This is the meaning of *interaction*. We say that two factors interact whenever the differences between the population means for one factor depend upon the level of the other factor. When random variation is present too, it is usually more difficult to spot interactions. Then the statistical test described below is useful.

EXAMPLE

One step in the marketing of a new soft drink is to determine the combination of ingredients that is most likely to appeal to the target market (usually young adults). The two major ingredients, in addition to water, in a new soft drink called Ms. Bipp were flavored syrup and sugar.

EXHIBIT 9.8   Illustration of Interaction

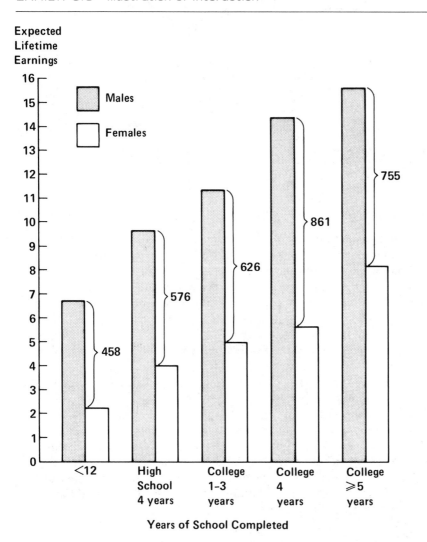

Years of School Completed

These were the two factors. Preliminary chemical analysis and discussion with experts determined the practical levels of these factors. Three specific practical levels of each factor were chosen for taste testing by 36 young adults (subjects). There were $9 = 3 \times 3$ combinations of levels of syrup and sugar, so four subjects were assigned *randomly* to each combination. The responses of the subjects were marks on a scale varying from 0 (extreme dislike) to 10 (extreme like). The data and the program used to analyze the data are in Exhibit 9.9. The output is in Exhibits 9.10, 9.11, and 9.12.

EXHIBIT 9.9   Program for Analyzing Taste Test Data

```
READ C1 C2 C3
 4.0 1 1
 0.5 1 1
 0.0 1 1
 2.1 1 1
 1.1 1 2
 5.6 1 2
 0.0 1 2
 5.1 1 2
 5.3 1 3
 7.5 1 3
 5.2 1 3
 6.4 1 3
 4.4 2 1
 7.5 2 1
 4.8 2 1
 5.1 2 1
 3.2 2 2
 6.3 2 2
 3.6 2 2
 2.4 2 2
 1.6 2 3
10.0 2 3
 7.7 2 3
 7.4 2 3
 9.8 3 1
 5.4 3 1
 4.1 3 1
 3.3 3 1
 7.4 3 2
10.0 3 2
10.0 3 2
 6.9 3 2
 0.1 3 3
 2.0 3 3
 1.9 3 3
 3.9 3 3
END
NAME C1 'RATINGS' C2 'SYRUP' C3 'SUGAR'
TABLE C2 C3;
 DATA C1.
TABLE C2 C3;
 MEANS C1.
READ C11-C14
1 1.65 2.95  6.1
2 5.45 3.875 6.675
3 5.65 8.575 1.975
END
NAME C11 'SYRLEV' C12 'SUG1' C13 'SUG2' C14 'SUG3'
MPLOT C12 C11 C13 C11 C14 C11
TWOWAY C1 C2 C3
```

EXHIBIT 9.10   The Ms. Bipp Data

```
TABLE C2 C3;
 DATA C1.

  ROWS: SYRUP      COLUMNS: SUGAR

            1          2          3

    1    4. 0000    1. 1000    5. 3000
         0. 5000    5. 6000    7. 5000
         0. 0000    0. 0000    5. 2000
         2. 1000    5. 1000    6. 4000

    2    4. 4000    3. 2000    1. 6000
         7. 5000    6. 3000   10. 0000
         4. 8000    3. 6000    7. 7000
         5. 1000    2. 4000    7. 4000

    3    9. 8000    7. 4000    0. 1000
         5. 4000   10. 0000    2. 0000
         4. 1000   10. 0000    1. 9000
         3. 3000    6. 9000    3. 9000

  CELL CONTENTS --
          RATINGS: DATA
```

EXHIBIT 9.11   Table of Means of Ms. Bipp Data and an MPLOT
              Showing Interaction

```
TABLE C2 C3;
 MEANS C1.

  ROWS: SYRUP      COLUMNS: SUGAR

            1          2          3         ALL

    1    1. 6500    2. 9500    6. 1000    3. 5667
    2    5. 4500    3. 8750    6. 6750    5. 3333
    3    5. 6500    8. 5750    1. 9750    5. 4000
  ALL    4. 2500    5. 1333    4. 9167    4. 7667

  CELL CONTENTS --
          RATINGS: MEAN
```

EXHIBIT 9.11 *Continued*

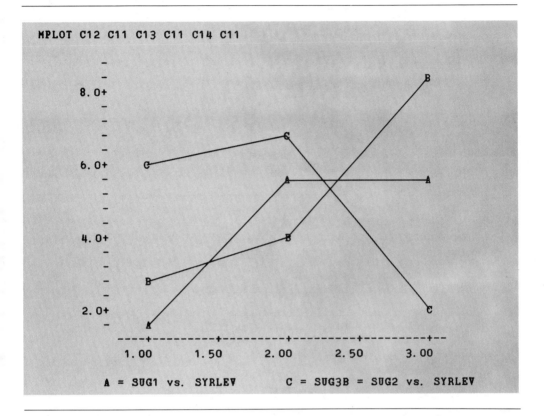

The ratings were all put in one column. A second column was used for the levels of syrup (1, 2 or 3), and a third column for the levels of sugar (1, 2, or 3). The TABLE output in Exhibit 9.10 displays the data in familiar tabular form. Exhibit 9.11 contains a table of means and a plot obtained by reading the cell means into columns C11–C14 and using MPLOT. This exhibit gives us an idea of how syrup and sugar affect the taste of Ms. Bipp. The plot suggests interaction between syrup and sugar. A formal test for interaction is performed by issuing the TWOWAY command. The output is in Exhibit 9.12.

We will use the following notation: a is the number of levels of the first factor (that is, the number of rows in the table of data); b is the number of levels of the second factor (that is, the number of columns in the table of data); n is the number of observations in each cell; x_{ijk} is the kth observation in cell (i, j) (i.e., in the cell in row i and column j); $\bar{x}_{ij.}$ is the mean of the n observations in cell (i, j); $\bar{x}_{i..}$ is the mean of the bn obser-

---

EXHIBIT 9.12   TWOWAY of Ms. Bipp Data

```
THOWAY C1 C2 C3 C4 C5

ANALYSIS OF VARIANCE   RATINGS

SOURCE          DF          SS          MS
SYRUP            2        25. 95      12. 97
SUGAR            2         5. 09       2. 54
INTERACTION      4       140. 06      35. 01
ERROR           27       130. 55       4. 84
TOTAL           35       301. 64
```

---

vations in row i; $\bar{x}_{.j.}$ is the mean of the an observations in column j; and $\bar{x}$ is the mean of all abn observations in the table.

Source	DF	SS
Rows	$a - 1$	$bn\Sigma_i(\bar{x}_{i..} - \bar{x})^2$
Columns	$b - 1$	$an\Sigma_j(\bar{x}_{.j.} - \bar{x})^2$
Interaction	$(a - 1)(b - 1)$	$n\Sigma_i\Sigma_j(\bar{x}_{ij.} - \bar{x}_{i..} - \bar{x}_{.j.} + \bar{x})^2$
Error	$ab(n - 1)$	$\Sigma_i\Sigma_j\Sigma_k(x_{ijk} - \bar{x}_{ij.})$
Total	$abn - 1$	$\Sigma_i\Sigma_j\Sigma_k(x_{ijk} - \bar{x})$

TWOWAY analysis, obs in C, factors levels in C and C

Does a two-way analysis of variance. The design must be balanced; that is, each cell must contain the same number of observations. If each cell contains just one observation, then SS interaction cannot be calculated. Note: The level numbers must be integers. (More in Section 9.4.)

The output in Exhibit 9.12 is similar to the output in Exhibit 9.7, with a few exceptions. The ANALYSIS OF VARIANCE table for the keyboard performance data broke down the total sum of squares into three sources: typists, brands of typewriter, and error. Since the Ms. Bipp data have replicates (more than one observation per cell), we can investigate a fourth possible source of variation—the interaction between the two factors. Thus we have

SS total = SS syrup + SS sugar

            + SS interaction between syrup and sugar + SS error

Here the interaction sum of squares is 140.06, with 4 degrees of freedom. So the mean square for interaction is $140.06/4 = 35.01$. We can do an F-test to see whether this is significant by using

$$F = \frac{(MS\ syrup)(sugar)}{(MS\ ERROR)} = \frac{35.01}{4.84} = 7.23$$

The corresponding value from an F-table, using 4 and 27 degrees of freedom and $\alpha = .05$, is 2.72. Since $7.23 > 2.72$, there is statistically significant evidence that the two factors interact. We can investigate this interaction in the plot in Exhibit 9.11. For the first two levels of sugar, increasing levels of syrup entail increasing average responses. But for the third level of sugar, moving from level 2 to level 3 of syrup entails a drastic drop in average response. The plot also suggests that the most promising combination of ingredients is level 3 of syrup and level 2 of sugar.

INTERACTION WITH ONE OBSERVATION PER CELL

Comparison of the analysis of variance tables obtained in Sections 9.1 and 9.2 is instructive. The one-way analysis yielded an error sum of squares of 244.0, whereas the two-way analysis yielded an error sum of squares of 250.6. This is a surprise, since the randomized block design was supposed to have separated the typist variation from the error variation. The randomized block design did indeed control a fairly substantial amount of between-typist variation (F was significant at the 10% level), but error variation was not reduced from that obtained in the one-way analysis. This result strongly suggests that some typist/keyboard interaction was present in the randomized block experiment. Such interaction is certainly unexpected, but searching for a cause may turn up some useful information either about the typists in the experiment or about miscues in conducting the experiment.

Despite the presence of interaction, the two-way analysis seems to yield essentially the same conclusions about the brands of keyboards as the one-way analysis did. The brand means from the two analyses are shown below.

Analysis	Brand			
	1	2	3	4
One-way	68.0	71.0	70.8	61.6
Two-way	64.8	70.0	71.6	62.8

Clearly, brands 2 and 3 are superior to brands 1 and 4, but brands 2 and 3 are indistinguishable.

In practice we would not usually have two independent experiments to compare. If we conduct a randomized block experiment, then how do we know whether interaction is present? A technique for answering this question is a test due to Tukey.

EXERCISE

9–4   A possible two-way analysis of variance of the trust gain data in Exercise 9.3 uses semiannual periods (1 and 2) and trusts as the two factors.
(a)   Perform the suggested analysis of variance, using firms 8, 11, and 12.
(b)   Redo the suggested analysis, using all 15 trusts.
(c)   Explain the differences between the analyses in parts (a) and (b). (Hint: Use plots.)

9.4 / RESIDUALS AND ADDITIVE MODELS

The commands ONEWAY and TWOWAY have some additional capabilities for more advanced work in statistics. Here we will briefly describe how the commands work.

RESIDUALS AND FITTED VALUES

Analysis of variance can be viewed in terms of fitting a model to the data. This leads to a fitted value and a residual for each observation. A fitted value is our best estimate of the underlying population mean value corresponding to that observation. The residual is how much our observation differs from its fitted value.

In one-way analysis of variance the fitted values are just the group means. A residual is then the difference between an observed value and the corresponding group mean. Consider, for example, the keyboard data. The first few observations, fitted values, and residuals are as follows:

	Brand 1			Brand 2		
Observation	69	73	67 ...	69	73	72 ...
Fitted value	68	68	68 ...	71	71	71 ...
Residual	1	5	−1 ...	−2	2	1 ...

When you use ONEWAY, Minitab will store the fitted values and residuals if you specify two extra columns on the ONEWAY command.

It is good practice to make plots of the residuals to check for unequal variances, nonnormality, dependence on other variables, and so on. We often make the following plots:

Plot of the residuals versus the fitted values.

Histogram of residuals.

Plot of the residuals versus the order in which the data were collected.

Plot of the residuals versus other variables (when data on other variables are available).

The command AOVONEWAY will not compute fitted values and residuals.

In ordinary two-way analysis of variance the fitted values are the cell means. A residual is then the difference between the observed value and the corresponding cell mean. We will use the Ms. Bipp data in Exhibits 9.9 and 9.10 as an example. The observations, fitted values, and residuals from the three cells where syrup is at level 1 are as follows:

		Sugar Level 1				*Sugar Level 2*				*Sugar Level 3*		
Observation	4	.5	0	2.1	1.1	5.6	0	5.1	5.3	7.5	5.2	6.4
Fitted value	1.65	1.65	1.65	1.65	2.95	2.95	2.95	2.95	6.1	6.1	6.1	6.1
Residual	2.35	−1.15	−1.65	0.45	−1.85	2.65	−2.95	2.15	−0.8	1.4	−0.9	0.3

The TWOWAY command, like ONEWAY, will store the fitted values and residuals if you specify two extra columns.

ADDITIVE MODELS

In two-way analysis of variance it sometimes is desirable to try a model in which it is assumed that there is no interaction. This can be done with the ADDITIVE subcommand. In an additive model, the fitted values are no longer the cell means. In the balanced data case treated by the TWOWAY command, the fitted values are computed as follows:

$$\text{Fitted value for cell } (i,j) = \text{mean of data in row } i$$
$$+ \text{ mean of data in column } j$$
$$- \text{ mean of all data}$$

ONEWAY data in C, levels in C, [store fits in C [resids in C]]

Does a one-way analysis of variance and stores both the fitted values and the residuals.

TWOWAY data in C, levels in C, C [store fits in C [resids in C]]

Does either a RBD or a two-way analysis of variance and stores the fitted values and residuals. To fit an additive model (i.e., a model that has no interaction), use the subcommand

ADDITIVE

10/FITTING CURVES TO DATA

In Chapter 3 you saw how Minitab helps to display relationships between variables through graphs called scatterplots. You also saw that the correlation coefficient is a measure of the extent to which a relationship is *linear*. Sometimes discovering an approximate linear relationship is sufficient for your purposes because it helps to confirm the existence of a relationship that you pretty much knew existed. Sometimes, though, you want to make a deeper study of a relationship, to quantify it as fully as possible, to check its descriptive adequacy, and to see how it fits in with other relationships. While straight lines are useful descriptive devices, the implied linearity of relationships hardly ever holds up over wide ranges of the variables. Thus we can be faced with data that must be described by nonlinear curves.

In this chapter we will illustrate the fitting of curves to data by the method of ordinary least squares (OLS), the most popular method of curve fitting.

The REGRESS command is introduced in this chapter. Curve fitting by OLS is often associated with the study of regression analysis, but the formal inferential procedures of regression analysis will not be discussed until Chapter 11. This means that only part of the output from the REGRESS command is explained here. The separation of curve fitting and formal inference is intended to emphasize the usefulness of curve fitting itself as a descriptive tool.

We shall write the equation of a straight line as $\hat{Y} = a + bX$, where Y is the variable whose values appear on the vertical axis, X is the variable whose values appear on the horizontal axis, a is the y intercept, and b is the slope of the line. It is common usage to call Y the dependent variable and X the independent variable.

The equation of a second-degree polynomial (also called a quadratic or a parabolic curve) is written $\hat{Y} = a + b_1X + b_2X^2$.

If there are *two* independent variables, denoted by X_1 and X_2, then a linear relationship between Y and X_1 and X_2 is written

$$\hat{Y} = a + b_1X_1 + b_2X_2$$

182

A full quadratic relationship is written

$$\hat{Y} = a + b_1X_1 + b_2X_2 + b_3X_1X_2 + b_4X_1^2 + b_5X_2^2$$

The symbol n is used to denote the number of rows (sometimes called "cases") in the data set.

10.1/ THE SIMPLEST FORM OF REGRESS

As a first example, let us look at the assets and deposits of the midwestern banks displayed in Exhibit 3.1. We read the data, name the columns, and produce a scatterplot and a correlation coefficient with the following commands:

```
READ INTO C12 AND C13
 14.0  11.4 # Nebraska
 19.6  16.5 # Kansas
 25.5  21.5 # Iowa
 30.0  24.3 # Wisconsin
 36.3  29.8 # Indiana
 36.8  28.0 # Minnesota
 56.6  46.0 # Michigan
 62.4  47.6 # Ohio
130.2  91.8 # Illinois
END
NAME C12 'ASSET.MW' C13 'DEP.MW'
PLOT C13 VS C12
CORRELATION C12 C13
```

The output is in Exhibit 10.1. A correlation coefficient of 0.998 suggests a high degree of linearity in the plot. Because the states are listed in increasing order of bank assets, it is easy to attach the state names to the points. Another way to label the points is to make an LPLOT with the following commands:

```
SET INTO C14
(1:9)         #Numbers from 1 to 9
END
NAME C14 'INDEX'
LPLOT C13 VS C12 LABELS IN C14
```

The output is in Exhibit 10.2. Each state is associated with a letter of the alphabet. This makes identification of plotted points with the states quite easy.

EXHIBIT 10.1   Scatterplot and Correlation Coefficient of Deposits and
                Assets of Midwestern Banks

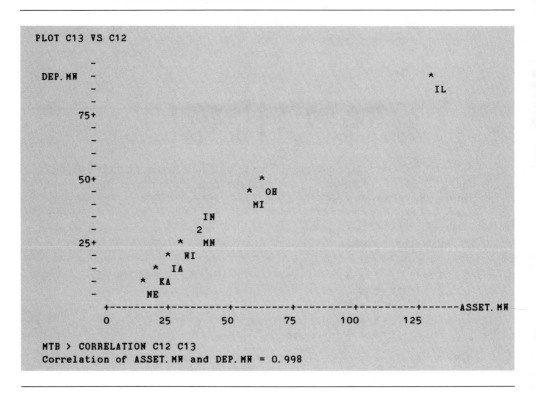

```
PLOT C13 VS C12


         -
DEP.MW   -                                                              *
         -                                                              IL

     75+
         -
         -
         -
         -
     50+                                          *
         -                                    *  OH
         -                                    MI
         -                          IN
         -                          2
     25+                       *    MN
         -                  *  WI
         -               *  IA
         -            *  KA
         -            NE
         +---------+---------+---------+---------+---------+------ASSET.MW
         0        25        50        75       100       125

MTB > CORRELATION C12 C13
Correlation of ASSET.MW and DEP.MW = 0.998
```

The simplest form of the REGRESS command is described below.

REGRESS the y values in C on 1 explanatory variable in C

Computes the regression equation for determining y from x. Output
includes the equation and other information.

More details about REGRESS are given in the remainder of this chapter.

BRIEF output at level K

Controls the amount of output from all REGRESS commands that follow.
K is an integer from 1 to 3; the larger the integer, the more output.

K = 1   The regression line, table of coefficients, line with s, R^2, and
        R^2-adjusted, and the first part of the analysis of variance table
        (regression, error, and total sums of squares) are printed.

K = 2   In addition, the second part of the analysis of variance table (provided that there are two or more predictors) and these "unusual" observations in the table of data, fits, stdev fit, etc. are printed. There are two reasons why an observation is unusual: Its predictors, $x_1, \ldots, x_k$ are unusual (i.e., far away from most other predictors); its standardized residual is large (specifically, over 2). In both cases you should check the observation to make sure it is correct. This is the usual output.

K = 3   In addition, the full table of data, fits, stdev fit, etc. is printed.

The amount of output is controlled by the BRIEF command.

To keep things simple initially, let's use BRIEF 1. We will use deposits as the dependent variable and assets as the independent variable. The commands

```
BRIEF 1
REGRESS C13 VS 1 VARIABLE IN C12
```

yield the output in Exhibit 10.3.

EXHIBIT 10.2   LPLOT of Midwestern Bank Deposits and Assets

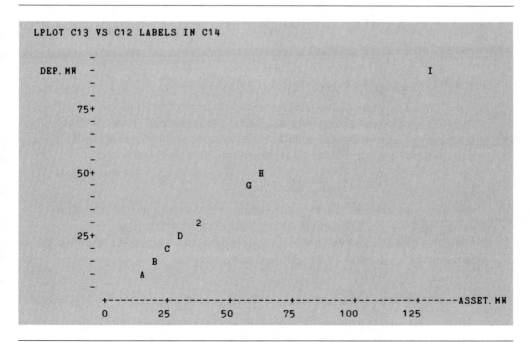

EXHIBIT 10.3   BRIEF 1 Level of Output from the REGRESS Command
              Applied to Midwestern Bank Data

```
BRIEF 1
REGRESS C13 VS 1 VARIABLE IN C12

The regression equation is
DEP.MW = 3.76 + 0.688 ASSET.MW

Predictor         Coef        Stdev       t-ratio
Constant         3.7574       0.9771        3.85
ASSET.MW         0.68810      0.01726      39.87

s = 1.730       R-sq = 99.6%    R-sq(adj) = 99.5%

Analysis of Variance

SOURCE         DF          SS           MS
Regression      1        4756.6       4756.6
Error           7          20.9          3.0
Total           8        4777.6
```

THE EQUATION OF THE LINE

Minitab begins by writing the equation of the fitted line:

    DEP.MW = 3.76+0.688 ASSET.MW.

This means that $\hat{Y}$ = DEP.MW, X = ASSET.MW, a = 3.76, and
b = 0.688. The value of a is rounded to two decimal places and that of b to
three decimal places. The values of a and b are reported to more decimal
places in the table below the equation. The boxed columns labeled "Stdev"
and "t-ratio" will be discussed in Chapter 11.

FITTED VALUES AND RESIDUALS

The next quantity, s = 1.730, can be thought of as the standard deviation
of the differences between the actual deposits and the fitted line. To
compute these differences, we first compute the values on the line
corresponding to each value of the assets.

    LET C15 = 3.7574+0.68810*C12
    NAME C15 'FITTED'

Then we substract the fitted deposits from the actual deposits and print out
and describe the results.

```
LET C16 = C13-C15
NAME C16 'ACT-FIT'
PRINT C12 C14 C15 C16
DESCRIBE C12 C13 C15 C16
```

The output is in Exhibit 10.4. The differences between actual and fitted values are called *residuals*. Column C16 is the column of residuals in Exhibit 10.4. The output from the DESCRIBE command indicates that the mean of the residuals is zero and the standard deviation is 1.62. This standard deviation is different from the *s* in the regression output.

Why are the two standard deviations different? Because they make different assumptions about the curves fitted to the data. The standard deviation in the DESCRIBE command assumes that the *average* is

---

EXHIBIT 10.4 Computation of Fitted Values and Residuals Using Midwestern Bank Data

```
LET C15 = 3.7574 + 0.68810*C12
NAME C15 'FITTED'
LET C16 = C13 - C15
NAME C16 'ACT-FIT'
PRINT C12 C14 C15 C16
  ROW   ASSET.MH   INDEX    FITTED    ACT-FIT
   1       14.0       1    13.3908   -1.99080
   2       19.6       2    17.2442   -0.74416
   3       25.5       3    21.3039    0.19605
   4       30.0       4    24.4004   -0.10040
   5       36.3       5    28.7354    1.06457
   6       36.8       6    29.0795   -1.07948
   7       56.6       7    42.7039    3.29614
   8       62.4       8    46.6948    0.90516
   9      130.2       9    93.3480   -1.54801

DESCRIBE C12 C13 C15 C16
```

	N	MEAN	MEDIAN	TRMEAN	STDEV	SEMEAN
ASSET.MH	9	45.7	36.3	45.7	35.4	11.8
DEP.MH	9	35.21	28.00	35.21	24.44	8.15
FITTED	9	35.21	28.74	35.21	24.38	8.13
ACT-FIT	9	-0.000	-0.100	-0.000	1.618	0.539

	MIN	MAX	Q1	Q3
ASSET.MH	14.0	130.2	22.6	59.5
DEP.MH	11.40	91.80	19.00	46.80
FITTED	13.39	93.35	19.27	44.70
ACT-FIT	-1.991	3.296	-1.314	0.985

subtracted from each observation, that the resulting residuals are squared and summed, and that this sum of squared residuals is divided by $n - 1 = 8$ degrees of freedom. The standard deviation in the REGRESS command assumes that *values on the fitted line* are subtracted from each observation, that the resulting residuals are squared and summed, and that this sum of squared residuals is divided by $n - 2 = 7$ degrees of freedom. Degrees of freedom are the number of observations minus the number of coefficients calculated to produce fitted values. The DESCRIBE command reduces the sample size by 1 because it assumes that $\bar{Y}$ is used to produce fitted values. The REGRESS command reduces the sample size by 2 because a and b are used to produce fitted values. Of course, the assumption made by the REGRESS command is correct, so it computes the correct standard deviation.

It is interesting to compare the two types of residuals and the two types of standard deviations discussed in the previous paragraph. The residuals in column C16 result from subtracting points on the fitted line from the actual deposits. Another set of residuals results from subtracting the average deposit (35.211) from the actual deposits. Let's compute the latter residuals and compare them to the residuals from the line, using the following commands:

```
LET K1 = AVER(C13)
LET C17 = C13-K1
NAME C17 'Y-AVE.Y'
PRINT C16 C17
HISTOGRAM C16 C17
```

The output is in Exhibit 10.5. As explained in the previous paragraph, the residuals in column C16 have 7 degrees of freedom and standard deviation 1.730. The residuals in column C17 have 8 degrees of freedom and standard deviation 24.44. Both sets of residuals have zero means. The residuals in column C16 have a much smaller standard deviation than the residuals in column C17 because the former result from exploiting the strong linear relationship between deposits and assets.

R-SQUARED

Minitab's output in Exhibit 10.3 provides a comparative measure based on the two standard deviations presented in the previous two paragraphs. It is called R-SQUARED, ADJUSTED FOR DEGREES OF FREEDOM and is denoted in the output by the symbol R-sq(adj). The value quoted in the output, 99.5%, is obtained by calculating

$$[1 - (1.730)^2/(24.438)^2] \times 100 = (1 - 0.005) \times 100$$

The multiplication by 100 is to express the value as a percent. The value of the R-sq(adj) is found by subtracting from 1 the ratio of the squared standard deviation of the values in column C16 to the squared standard deviation of the values in column C17. The R-sq(adj) is large (almost

---

EXHIBIT 10.5   Comparison of Two Types of Residuals

```
LET K1 = AVER( C13)
LET C17 = C13 - K1
NAME C17 'Y-AVE.Y'
PRINT C16 C17

  ROW    ACT-FIT    Y-AVE.Y

    1   -1.99080   -23.8111
    2   -0.74416   -18.7111
    3    0.19605   -13.7111
    4   -0.10040   -10.9111
    5    1.06457    -5.4111
    6   -1.07948    -7.2111
    7    3.29614    10.7889
    8    0.90516    12.3889
    9   -1.54801    56.5889

HISTOGRAM C16 C17

 Histogram of ACT-FIT   N = 9

Midpoint    Count
    -2.0        1   *
    -1.5        1   *
    -1.0        1   *
    -0.5        1   *
     0.0        2   **
     0.5        0
     1.0        2   **
     1.5        0
     2.0        0
     2.5        0
     3.0        0
     3.5        1   *


 Histogram of Y-AVE.Y   N = 9

Midpoint    Count
     -20        2   **
     -10        4   ****
       0        0
      10        2   **
      20        0
      30        0
      40        0
      50        0
      60        1   *
```

100%) because the scatter of the deposits about the fitted line is much less than the scatter about the average deposit.

Minitab also prints out another R-SQUARED, which is not adjusted for degrees of freedom. It is simply the square of the correlation coefficient, that is,

$$\text{R-sq} = (0.998)^2 \times 100 \text{ PERCENT} = 99.6\%$$

Another formula that yields R-sq is

$$[1 - 7(1.730)^2/8(24.438)^2] \times 100$$

which resembles the formula for R-sq(adj), with the difference that the squared standard deviations are multiplied by their degrees of freedom.

ANALYSIS OF VARIANCE TABLE

The ANALYSIS OF VARIANCE table conveniently arranges some quantities that are used to compute the standard deviations and R-SQUARED measures discussed above. The abbreviations DF, SS, and MS stand for degrees of freedom, sum of squares, and mean square, respectively. The TOTAL SS is the sum of squared differences between the observed deposits and their mean—in other words, the sum of squares of the numbers in column C17 in Exhibit 10.5. This sum of squares is represented as the sum of two numbers:

$$4777.6 = 4756.6 + 20.9$$

that is, TOTAL SS = REGRESSION SS + RESIDUAL SS. There is not exact numerical equality here because the actual sums of squares have been rounded to one decimal place. The RESIDUAL SS is the sum of the squares of the numbers in column C16 in Exhibit 10.5. The degrees of freedom associated with these sums of squares are

$$8 = 1 + 7$$

that is, TOTAL DF = REGRESSION DF + RESIDUAL DF. We noted the values of the TOTAL DF and RESIDUAL DF in the previous section. The REGRESSION quantities are found by subtracting the RESIDUAL quantities from the TOTAL quantities.

Mean squares are found by dividing sums of squares by degrees of freedom. Thus

$$\text{REGRESSION MS} = \text{REGRESSION SS/REGRESSION DF}$$
$$= 4756.6/1$$

and

$$\text{RESIDUAL MS} = \text{RESIDUAL SS/RESIDUAL DF}$$
$$= 20.9/7 = 2.9857$$

which Minitab rounds to 3.0. The latter number is the square of the residual standard deviation, so $s^2 = 3.0$ and $s = \sqrt{3.0} = 1.73$. Also

$$R\text{-sq} = [1 - \text{RESIDUAL SS/TOTAL SS}] \times 100$$
$$= [1 - 20.9/4777.6] \times 100 = 99.6\%$$

and

$$R\text{-sq(adj)} = [1 - (20.9/7)/(4777.6/8)] \times 100 = 99.5\%$$

EXERCISE

10-1 Repeat the analysis in this section for the Sun Belt states in Exhibit 3.1.

10.2 / HIGHER BRIEF LEVELS AND STORAGE COLUMNS WITH REGRESS

In the previous section we saw the output printed under BRIEF 1. The highest BRIEF level is BRIEF 3. Let us look at the output under this level for the bank data in Exhibit 10.1. The commands

```
BRIEF 3
REGRESS C13 1 C12
```

produce the output in Exhibit 10.6. We see the output that we saw in Exhibit 10.3 plus a table of observed and predicted values, residuals, and standardized residuals for each case in the data set. We will explain all the columns of the table except those that are boxed. The one labeled "Stdev. Fit" will be explained in Chapter 11. The columns labeled "ASSET.MW" and "DEP.MW" contain the values of the independent and dependent variables, the basic data. The next column, labeled "FIT," contains the fitted values. For example, the first fitted value is $3.76 + 0.68810(14) = 13.391$. Each fitted value is found by substituting the value of the independent variable in the equation of the fitted line. The next column that we explain is the residual column. Each residual is found by subtracting each fitted value from the corresponding value of the dependent variable. The first residual is therefore $11.4 - 13.391 = -1.991$. If we write the formula for the residual as

$$\text{RESIDUAL} = \text{ACTUAL Y} - \text{FITTED Y}$$

then we also have the equation

$$\text{ACTUAL Y} = \text{FITTED Y} + \text{RESIDUAL}$$

For the first case in the bank data set,

$$11.4 = 13.391 + (-1.991)$$

EXHIBIT 10.6   BRIEF 3 Level of Output from the REGRESS Command
Applied to Midwestern Bank Data

```
BRIEF 3
REGRESS C13 1 C12

The regression equation is
DEP.MN = 3.76 + 0.688 ASSET.MN

Predictor        Coef        Stdev      t-ratio
Constant        3.7574      0.9771         3.85
ASSET.MN        0.68810     0.01726       39.87

s = 1.730        R-sq = 99.6%      R-sq(adj) = 99.5%

Analysis of Variance

SOURCE          DF          SS           MS
Regression      1         4756.6       4756.6
Error           7           20.9          3.0
Total           8         4777.6
```

Obs.	ASSET.MN	DEP.MN	Fit	Stdev. Fit	Residual	St. Resid
1	14	11.400	13.391	0.795	-1.991	-1.30
2	20	16.500	17.244	0.732	-0.744	-0.47
3	26	21.500	21.304	0.674	0.196	0.12
4	30	24.300	24.400	0.637	-0.100	-0.06
5	36	29.800	28.735	0.599	1.065	0.66
6	37	28.000	29.079	0.597	-1.079	-0.66
7	57	46.000	42.704	0.606	3.296	2.03R
8	62	47.600	46.695	0.645	0.905	0.56
9	130	91.800	93.348	1.568	-1.548	-2.12RX

```
R denotes an obs. with a large st. resid.
X denotes an obs. whose X value gives it large influence.
```

For the second case,

$$16.5 = 17.244 + (-0.744)$$

and so forth.

STANDARDIZED RESIDUALS

The last column in the table reports standardized residuals. We noted earlier that the residuals have a zero mean, and we argued that their standard deviation was $s = 1.730$. Thus you might expect that the standardized residuals are just the residuals divided by their standard deviation. A more complicated argument can be advanced, however, that associates a unique standard deviation with each residual. Minitab does this and divides each residual by its own standard deviation. The method that Minitab uses identifies outliers more readily than the simpler method of dividing each residual by s.

To illustrate, let's compute standardized residuals by the simpler method, using the commands

```
LET C18 = C16/1.730
NAME C18 'STND.RES'
PRINT C18
```

The output is in Exhibit 10.7. Standardized residuals tell how many standard deviations each residual is away from the mean (which is zero). As a rule, residuals that are more than two standard deviations away from zero signal "outlier'" observations that need to be investigated, or at least noted as atypical. In Exhibit 10.7 we see no outliers, but among the standardized residuals printed out in Exhibit 10.6 we see two outliers, the cases in rows 7 and 9, which correspond to Michigan and Illinois. Minitab prints an R by standardized residuals that are greater than 2.0 or less than -2.0, thus flagging the outliers.

EXHIBIT 10.7 Standardizing Residuals by Dividing by s

```
LET C18 = C16/1.730
NAME C18 'STND.RES'
PRINT C18
   STND.RES

  -1.15148  -0.43117   0.11200  -0.05960
   0.61347  -0.62589   1.90234   0.51997
  -0.90158
```

INFLUENTIAL CASES

Minitab also prints an X by row 9, indicating that it is an influential case. This means that if the case were removed from the data set, or if the value of deposits in Illinois were modified substantially, the coefficients of the line fitted to the resulting data set would be substantially different from the coefficients of the line in Exhibit 10.6. We will investigate the implications of this influential case in the next section.

STORING STANDARDIZED RESIDUALS, FITTED VALUES, AND RESIDUALS

Minitab allows us to store the quantities discussed in the preceding sections. This makes it easy to make plots and to perform diagnostic tests that use the quantities. Storage columns for standardized residuals and fitted values are named on the REGRESS command line; a storage column for the raw residuals is named in a subcommand.

Any columns may be chosen as storage columns. The choice is up to you.

To illustrate, let's regress midwestern bank deposits on assets and use all the storage columns. The commands

```
BRIEF 1
REGRESS C13 1 C12 ST.RES IN C20 FITTED IN C21;
   RESIDUALS IN C22.
NAME C20 'ST.RES. C21 'FIT' C22 'RESID'
PLOT C20 VS C12
PLOT C22 VS C12
HISTOGRAM C22 C20
```

produce the output in Exhibit 10.3 plus the output in Exhibit 10.8. The plots and histograms show the effect of standardizing the residuals. The

---

EXHIBIT 10.8   Residual Plots

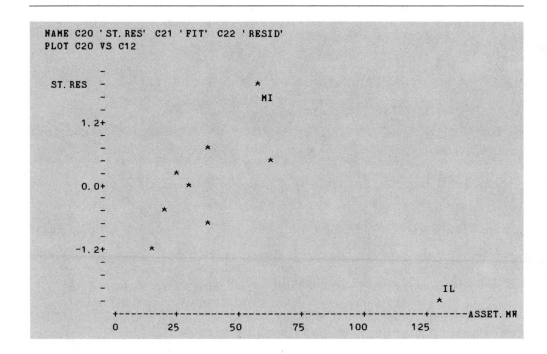

EXHIBIT 10.8   *Continued*

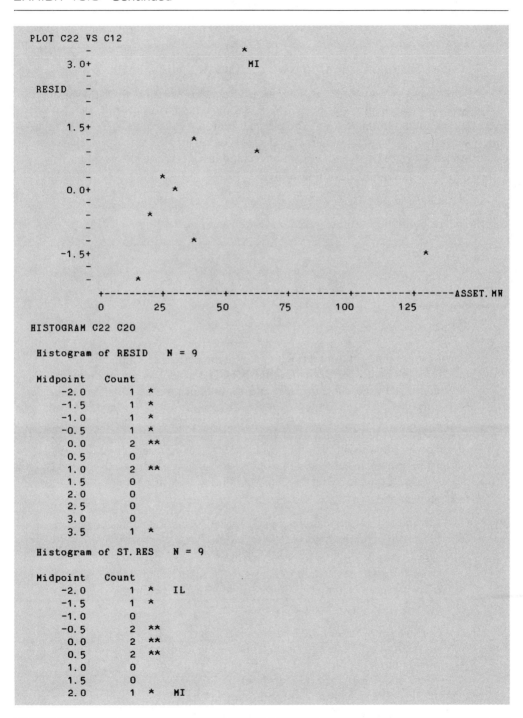

```
PLOT C22 VS C12
         -                         *
     3. 0+                         MI
         -
RESID    -
         -
         -
     1. 5+
         -                  *
         -                          *
         -
         -            *
     0. 0+               *
         -
         -        *
         -
         -               *
    -1. 5+                                          *
         -
         -     *
          +---------+---------+---------+---------+---------+------ASSET. MW
          0        25        50        75       100       125

HISTOGRAM C22 C20

  Histogram of RESID    N = 9

  Midpoint    Count
      -2. 0       1   *
      -1. 5       1   *
      -1. 0       1   *
      -0. 5       1   *
       0. 0       2   **
       0. 5       0
       1. 0       2   **
       1. 5       0
       2. 0       0
       2. 5       0
       3. 0       0
       3. 5       1   *

  Histogram of ST. RES    N = 9

  Midpoint    Count
      -2. 0       1   *    IL
      -1. 5       1   *
      -1. 0       0
      -0. 5       2   **
       0. 0       2   **
       0. 5       2   **
       1. 0       0
       1. 5       0
       2. 0       1   *    MI
```

scale of the standardized residuals makes it easy to look for outliers, that is, values greater than 2 or less than -2.

REGRESS C on 1 in C store st. resid. in C [fits in C]

This allows you to store the standardized residuals and fits by listing just two storage columns on the REGRESS line. Standardized residuals also are printed on the output and are calculated by (residuals)/(standard deviation of residual). The standard deviation is different for each residual and given by the formula (standard deviation of residual) = $\sqrt{MSE - (\text{standard deviation of fit})^2}$

RESIDUALS into C

The residuals are stored in the indicated column.

EXERCISES

10–2 Use the commands in this section to analyze the bank assets and deposits of the Sun Belt states listed in Exhibit 3.1. Describe the similarities and differences between the Sun Belt and midwestern states.

10–3 (a) For the real estate data on page 273, regress market values on assessed values.

(b) Use a table of random numbers to select a random sample of 20 cases from the real estate data. Regress the market values on assessed values. Compare your results with the results in part (a).

(c) Repeat part (b) of this exercise.

10–4 (a) For the real estate data on page 273, regress market values on square feet of living area.

(b) Use a table of random numbers to select a random sample of 20 cases from the real estate data. Regress the market values on square feet of living area. Compare your results with the results in part (a).

(c) Repeat part (b) of this exercise.

10–5 (a) For the stock market data on page 278, regress IBM's rates of return on the market's rate of return. This is an example of the capital asset pricing model of finance. The slope of the fitted line is often called the "beta coefficient." Beta is a Greek B. If you are familiar with this model, give a financial interpretation of b.

(b) Repeat part (b) using Xerox's rates of return.

(c)   In the regressions in parts (a) and (b), what cases were noted as having large residuals, large influence, or both?

10–6 Select any set of regression data that interests you and analyze it. Pay particular attention to outliers and influential cases.

10.3 / FITTING A SECOND-DEGREE POLYNOMIAL USING REGRESS

Look at the plot of standardized residuals versus assets in Exhibit 10.8. Note that the Illinois point is an outlier; if you cover up the Illinois point, you see that the other points exhibit a pronounced upward trend. These two observations together suggest rather strongly that the straight line is an inadequate model for the bank data. In fact, it is easy to visualize a parabolic curve passing through the residual plot, and this contradicts our expectation that the residuals behave randomly. Perhaps a parabolic curve, or second-degree polynomial, would be a better model for the original data. Such a curve makes certain economic sense because it allows for a "law of diminishing returns" of deposits to assets.

To fit an equation of the form $\hat{Y} = a + b_1X + b_2X^2$, we treat X and X^2 as two independent variables and use an expanded form of the REGRESS command.

To illustrate, let's put midwestern bank deposits in column C30, assets in C31, and squared assets in C32. Then we will fit the curve with the REGRESS command.

```
LET C30 = C13        #Deposits
LET C31 = C12        #Assets
LET C32 = C31*C31    #Squared assets
NAME C30 'D' C31 'A' C32 'A.SQ'
BRIEF 3
REGRESS C30 VS 2 VARIABLES C31 AND C32 STORE C35 C36;
  RESIDUALS IN C37.
PLOT C35 VS C31
HISTOGRAM C35
```

The output is in Exhibit 10.9. We see that the fitted curve is

$$\hat{D} = 0.029 + 0.84533A - 0.0010789A^2$$

and that the residual standard deviation is $s = 1.086$. This is less than the standard deviation of 1.730 in Exhibit 10.3, where we fitted the straight line. There is considerably less scatter about the parabolic curve than about the straight line. We see, from the table of observed and fitted values and residuals, that Illinois is an influential case, but it is no longer an outlier. The second-degree polynomial passes acceptably near all the points.

EXHIBIT 10.9   Fitting a Second-Degree Polynomial to Midwestern
               Bank Data

```
LET C30 = C13        # Deposit
LET C31 = C12        # Assets
LET C32 = C31*C31    # Squared assets
NAME C30 'D' C31 'A' C32 'A.SQ'
BRIEF 3
REGRESS C30 VS  2 VARIABLES C31 AND C32 STORE C35 C36;
   RESIDUALS IN C37.


The regression equation is
D = 0.03 + 0.845 A - 0.00108 A.SQ

Predictor        Coef        Stdev      t-ratio
Constant        0.029        1.249        0.02
A             0.84533      0.04713       17.93
A.SQ         -0.0010789    0.0003147     -3.43

s = 1.086        R-sq = 99.9%    R-sq(adj) = 99.8%

Analysis of Variance

SOURCE         DF          SS          MS
Regression      2        4770.5       2385.3
Error           6           7.1          1.2
Total           8        4777.6

SOURCE         DF        SEQ SS
A               1        4756.6
A.SQ            1          13.9

Obs.       A          D       Fit   Stdev.Fit   Residual   St.Resid
  1        14      11.400    11.652    0.712      -0.252      -0.31
  2        20      16.500    16.183    0.554       0.317       0.34
  3        26      21.500    20.883    0.441       0.617       0.62
  4        30      24.300    24.418    0.400      -0.118      -0.12
  5        36      29.800    29.293    0.410       0.507       0.50
  6        37      28.000    29.676    0.413      -1.676      -1.67
  7        57      46.000    44.418    0.629       1.582       1.79
  8        62      47.600    48.576    0.682      -0.976      -1.15
  9       130      91.800    91.802    1.083      -0.002      -0.02 X

X denotes an obs. whose X value gives it large influence.
```

(continues)

REGRESS C on 2 in C and C store st. resid. in C [fits in C]

This allows you to store the standardized residuals and fits by listing just
two storage columns on the REGRESS line. Standardized residuals also

EXHIBIT 10.9 *Continued*

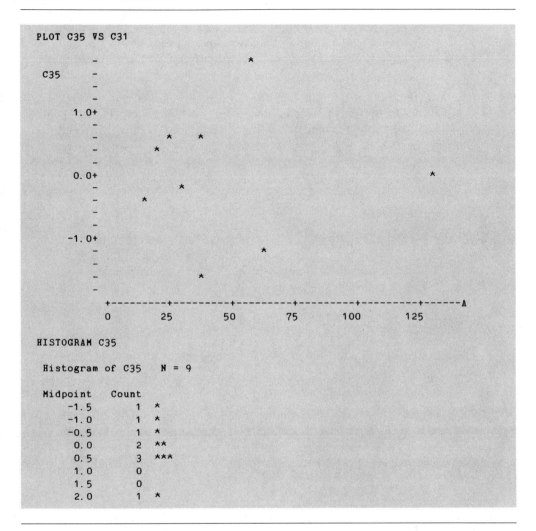

PLOT C35 VS C31

are printed on the output and are calculated by (residual)/(standard deviation of residual). The standard deviation is different for each residual and given by the formula (standard deviation of residual) = $\sqrt{\text{MSE} - (\text{standard deviation of fit})^2}$

RESIDUALS into C

The residuals are stored in the indicated column.

EXERCISES

10–7 Fit a second-degree polynomial to the assets and deposits of the Sun Belt banks in Exhibit 3.1. Compare your analysis with that of the midwestern states.

10–8 *(a)* For the real estate data on page 273, fit market values to a second-degree polynomial in square feet of living area. Does this seem to be a better model than the straight line? Why or why not?

   (b) Use a table of random numbers to draw a random sample of 20 parcels from the real estate data set. Fit the market values to a second-degree polynomial in square feet of living area. Compare your results to those in part (a).

   (c) Repeat part (b).

10–9 For the stock market data on page 278, regress IBM's rates of return on a second-degree polynomial of the market's rates of return. Does this appear to be a better model than the straight line? Why or why not?

10.4 / MULTIPLE REGRESSION

The REGRESS command allows us to fit general regression models of the form

$$\hat{Y} = a + b_1 X_1 + b_2 X_2 + \cdots + b_k X_k$$

where the $X_1, X_2, \ldots, X_k$ are any independent variables we choose to use.

All we have to do is tell Minitab how many independent variables there are and which columns contain them. Notice that the fitted values may be stored via the main command line or via a subcommand.

REGRESS C on K predictors C, ..., C [st. resid. in C [fits in C]]

This is the Minitab command for regression analyses. REGRESS has many subcommands. Here we will describe the more elementary ones. See the *Minitab Reference Manual* or type HELP REGRESS to learn about the others.

RESIDUALS into C

FITS into C

Stores the fitted values in the column.

COEF into C

Stores the coefficients $b_0, b_1, \ldots, b_k$ down the column.

MSE into K

Stores the mean square error, which is the same as s^2, in K.

NOCONSTANT

Fits a model without a constant term, that is, the model

$$\hat{Y} = b_1 X_1 + b_2 X_2 + \cdots + b_k X_k$$

As an illustration, we will use one REGRESS command to fit different second-degree polynomials to the bank assets and deposits for both midwestern and Sun Belt states. The trick is to use the data in stacked form, as in Exhibit 3.1. For this example we will have deposits in column C1, region codes in column C2, and assets in column C3. We need columns for the variables ASSETS.SQUARED, REGION*ASSET, and REGION*ASSET.SQUARED. The model we will use is

DEPOSITS = a + b$_1$REGION + b$_2$ASSET + b$_3$ASSET.SQUARED
$\qquad$ + b$_4$REGION*ASSET + b$_5$REGION*ASSET.SQUARED

The commands to do this are

```
READ DEPOSITS IN C1 REGION IN C2 ASSETS IN C3
       11.5           1      13.6
       11.4           0      14.0
       13.4           1      16.6
       16.5           0      19.6
       16.5           1      20.3
       21.5           0      25.5
       22.9           1      28.1
       24.3           0      30.0
       23.1           1      30.0
       25.9           1      30.8
       29.8           0      36.3
       28.0           0      36.8
       46.0           0      56.6
       49.2           1      59.4
       47.6           0      62.4
       91.8           0     130.2
      120.3           1     152.8
      165.3           1     216.4
END
LET C4 = C3*C3
LET C5 = C2*C3
LET C6 = C2*C4
NAME C1 'DEPOSITS' C2 'REGION' C3 'ASSET'
NAME C4 'ASSET.SQ' C5 'REG*ASS' C6 'R*A.SQ'
NAME C7 'ST.RES' C8 'FITTED'
BRIEF 3
REGRESS C1 ON 5 VARS IN C2-C6 STORE IN C7 C8
```

EXHIBIT 10.10   Fitting Second-Degree Polynomials to Midwestern and
Sun Belt Bank Data

```
BRIEF 3
REGRESS C1 ON 5 VARS C2-C6 STORE IN C7 C8

* NOTE * ASSET.SQ is highly correlated with other  predictor variables
* NOTE * REG*ASS is highly correlated with other  predictor variables
* NOTE * R*A.SQ is highly correlated with other  predictor variables

The regression equation is
DEPOSITS = 0.03 - 0.66 REGION + 0.845 ASSET - 0.00108 ASSET.SQ
           + 0.0080 REG*ASS +0.000678 R*A.SQ
```

Predictor	Coef	Stdev	t-ratio
Constant	0.029	1.073	0.03
REGION	-0.657	1.290	-0.51
ASSET	0.84533	0.04049	20.88
ASSET.SQ	-0.0010789	0.0002704	-3.99
REG*ASS	0.00801	0.04718	0.17
R*A.SQ	0.0006782	0.0002911	2.33

```
s = 0.9332      R-sq = 100.0%    R-sq(adj) = 100.0%

Analysis of Variance
```

SOURCE	DF	SS	MS
Regression	5	29942.8	5988.6
Error	12	10.5	0.9
Total	17	29953.2	

SOURCE	DF	SEQ SS
REGION	1	956.3
ASSET	1	28912.9
ASSET.SQ	1	0.1
REG*ASS	1	68.8
R*A.SQ	1	4.7

The output is in Exhibit 10.10. The boxed material will be explained in Chapter 11. To see that we are fitting the two curves as stated, note that the value of the REGION variable is either 0 or 1. If REGION = 0, the fitted curve is

$$DEPOSITS = 0.03 + 0.845\ ASSETS - 0.00108\ ASSETS.SQ$$

This is the equation of the curve in Exhibit 10.9, as it should be, as REGION = 0 corresponds to the Midwest. If REGION = 1, the fitted curve is

$$DEPOSITS = -0.63 + 0.8530\ ASSETS - 0.000402\ ASSET.SQ$$

and this is the curve obtained in Exercise 10–7. In Exhibit 10.10 we see that $s = 0.9332$, which is smaller than the standard deviation obtained from

EXHIBIT 10.10   *Continued*

Obs.	REGION	DEPOSITS	Fit	Stdev. Fit	Residual	St. Resid
1	1.00	11.500	10.902	0.472	0.598	0.74
2	0.00	11.400	11.652	0.611	-0.252	-0.36
3	1.00	13.400	13.426	0.432	-0.026	-0.03
4	0.00	16.500	16.183	0.476	0.317	0.40
5	1.00	16.500	16.529	0.393	-0.029	-0.03
6	0.00	21.500	20.883	0.379	0.617	0.72
7	1.00	22.900	23.034	0.350	-0.134	-0.15
8	0.00	24.300	24.418	0.344	-0.118	-0.14
9	1.00	23.100	24.611	0.348	-1.511	-1.75
10	1.00	25.900	25.274	0.349	0.626	0.72
11	0.00	29.800	29.293	0.352	0.507	0.59
12	0.00	28.000	29.676	0.355	-1.676	-1.94
13	0.00	46.000	44.418	0.540	1.582	2.08R
14	1.00	49.200	48.646	0.552	0.554	0.74
15	0.00	47.600	48.576	0.586	-0.976	-1.34
16	0.00	91.800	91.802	0.930	-0.002	-0.03 X
17	1.00	120.300	120.407	0.748	-0.107	-0.19
18	1.00	165.300	165.272	0.904	0.028	0.12

```
R denotes an obs. with a large st. resid.
X denotes an obs. whose X value gives it large influence.
```

fitting a second-degree polynomial to the nine midwestern states (the $s = 1.086$ in Exhibit 10.9). Pooling the data from the two geographical regions has lowered the residual standard deviation compared to the model fitted to the midwestern states alone.

We can look at the standardized residuals coded by geographical region using column C2 to generate labels for an LPLOT and a BOXPLOT as follows

```
LPLOT C7 VS C3 LABELS IN C2
BOXPLOT C7 LABELS IN C2
```

The output is in Exhibit 10.11. We see that Michigan is an outlier and that the residuals from the midwestern states are a bit more spread out than the residuals from the Sun Belt states.

We end this section by explaining two portions of the output in Exhibit 10.10 that we have not encountered before: the *NOTE*s printed immediately after the REGRESS command and the additional analysis of variance table.

Minitab checks for high correlation coefficients between independent variables, a condition referred to as "multicollinearity." This condition usually means that the data do not permit precise computation of some of the coefficients of the fitted curve. As a result, seemingly slight changes in the data values may lead to quite substantial changes in the coefficients. When Minitab signals multicollinearity, you should be cautious about interpreting individuals coefficients. Concentrate on the fitted curve instead.

EXHIBIT 10.11　　Residual Plots (Z Denotes Midwest, A Denotes Sun Belt)

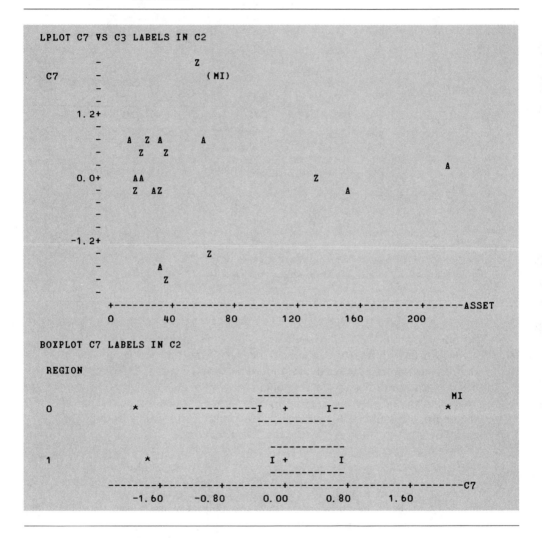

The additional analysis of variance table is displayed below the summary analysis of variance and shows a decomposition of the regression sum of squares into components associated with the independent variables, *in the order in which they appear in the equation of the curve.* In Exhibit 10.10 we have, symbolically,

REGRESSION SS = REGION SS + ASSET SS + ASSET.SQ SS
+ REG*ASS SS + R*A.SQ SS

and, numerically,

$$29942.8 = 956.3 + 28912.9 + 0.1 + 68.8 + 4.7$$

The REGION SS is the regression sum of squares that would result from the regression of deposits on region *alone*, that is, using region as the *only* independent variable. The ASSET SS is an *additional* regression sum of squares that results from adding the asset variable to the model already containing region as an independent variable. Thus the number

$$956.3 + 28912.9 = 29869.2$$

is the regression sum of squares associated with the curve

$$\text{DEPOSITS} = a + b_1 \text{ REGION} + b_2 \text{ ASSET}$$

The other sums of squares in the additional analysis of variance table have similar interpretations. If the variables are listed in a different order in the REGRESS command, the decomposition in the table is different also. Note that each component of the decomposition has one degree of freedom (DF).

EXERCISES

10–10 The data in the table below are the numbers of deaths and number of lives exposed to risk of death ("exposures") among female annuitants in different age groups in the years 1953, 1958, 1963, and 1968. These annuitants were females who retired under group annuity policies on or after normal retirement date. The data originally came from a group of large life insurance companies that issued a high proportion of the group annuity policies in the United States and Canada.

Age Group	1953	1958	1963	1968
51–55	0/ 171	2/ 214	3/ 328	3/ 439
56–60	15/1 371	8/ 1 874	20/ 2 879	28/ 3 597
61–65	63/4 899	87/ 7 939	132/11 230	174/16 530
66–70	111/6 596	235/14 463	430/22 500	529/33 360
71–75	69/2 414	180/ 6 451	407/13 668	611/22 109
76–80	69/ 925	115/ 2 029	340/ 5 387	611/11 689
81–85	35/ 269	59/ 631	158/ 1 448	351/ 3 941
86–90	9/ 62	23/ 130	59/ 363	130/ 802
91–95	2/ 10	7/ 24	13/ 62	48/ 149

Source: Annual reports on mortality and morbidity, *Transactions of the Society of Actuaries*, various issues.

(a) Read the deaths and exposures for 1953 into columns C1 and C2. Actuaries usually work with the ratio of deaths to exposures and call this quantity the "force of mortality." You might call it a death rate. Compute the age-specific forces of mortality by dividing C1 by C2 and storing the result in C3. The purpose of this exercise is to help you study the relationship between age and the force of mortality. Let's read the central ages of each age group into C4 with the commands

```
SET INTO C4
53 58 63 73 78 83 88 93
END
```

Now perform a regression analysis of force of mortality versus age. You will want to consider fitting second- and third-degree polynomials. Carefully examine residuals. Actuaries frequently study the square root of the force of mortality. Create this variable by the command

```
SQRT C3 PUT IN C5
```

and study the regression of C5 on C4. What do you conclude?

(b)   Repeat part (a) for the data from 1958, 1963, and 1968. Do you see any consistency in the relationship between age and force of mortality over the years?

10-11 The data below came from a study conducted by a company that was manufacturing printed electronic circuit boards. The purpose of the study was to develop a technique for predicting completion time for assembly of the boards, to be used for incentive rate calculation and cost estimation. The Y variable is an average time to completion based on actual assembly times of a number of boards (the numbers of boards contributing to each average is not given). The company's goal was to predict the Y variable within 5% of true value. Construct a regression model and comment on the usefulness of your model, given the company's goal. The variables are defined as follows:

Y: mean time to completion (in hours);

X_1:   number of capacitors on the board;

X_2:   number of integrated circuit sockets;

X_3:   number of transistors;

X_4:   number of hand-soldered leads;

X_5:   total number of components on board;

X_6:   number of types of components on board;

X_7:   size of board, where 1 indicates small and 4 indicates large. (The area of the large board is 4 times the area of the small board.)

X_1	X_2	X_3	X_4	X_5	X_6	X_7	Y
87	9	5	0	320	75	4	2.62
36	16	0	0	132	28	4	0.84
43	0	0	0	171	32	4	0.98
43	0	0	0	155	32	4	0.86

(continues)

X_1	X_2	X_3	X_4	X_5	X_6	X_7	Y
39	12	0	0	176	60	4	1.10
72	0	0	0	318	35	4	1.98
72	0	0	0	318	35	4	1.89
75	4	8	0	280	68	4	1.72
70	6	0	0	297	42	4	1.70
37	16	1	0	156	41	4	0.89
53	2	0	0	229	46	4	1.37
57	8	1	0	246	55	4	1.54
76	4	9	0	280	68	4	2.08
0	0	0	10	14	4	1	0.08
0	0	0	12	17	4	1	0.11
9	0	0	73	97	13	1	0.25
0	0	0	24	36	2	1	0.10
0	0	0	14	23	4	1	0.12
0	3	0	0	88	0	1	0.79
0	0	0	0	132	2	1	0.64
0	0	0	0	67	2	1	0.51
16	8	0	0	55	12	1	0.33
14	0	0	0	59	14	1	0.35
0	0	0	0	6	4	1	0.10
22	0	0	0	100	14	1	0.52
8	0	0	0	73	20	1	0.47
14	1	4	0	79	30	1	0.55
12	1	0	0	26	11	1	0.25
27	2	8	0	90	31	1	0.81
2	0	2	0	41	13	1	0.26
10	0	0	0	61	13	1	0.38
2	0	1	0	19	12	1	0.34
14	5	0	0	49	19	1	0.35
12	16	0	0	25	11	1	0.32
10	19	0	0	73	25	1	0.48

10–12 The data on pages 208–211 appeared in the 1984 edition of the *Statistical Abstract of the United States*, an annual publication of the Census Bureau.

    (a) For all establishments, regress receipts on numbers of establishments, where states, including Washington, D.C., are the cases. Is a linear model adequate, or do you need a quadratic model?

    (b) For all establishments, regress receipts on numbers of establishments and population. Does the population variable improve the fit substantially?

    (c) For establishments with payroll, regress receipts on numbers of establishments, numbers of paid employees, and annual payroll. Add population to the model. Does the population variable improve the fit substantially?

Domestic Trade and Services: Selected Service Industries — Summary, by States: 1977 (discrepancies in figures identified after tabulation process was completed have been corrected only at level significantly affected; hence, detail may not add to total)

Division and State	All Establishments		Establishments with Payroll			
	Number (1,000)	Receipts (mil. dol.)	Number (1,000)	Receipts (mil. dol.)	Payroll, Entire Year (mil. dol.)	Paid Employees[1] (1,000)
U.S.	1,834.7	179,515	725.1	164,219	56,055	6,337.3
N.E.	110.9	9,291	42.7	8,348	2,878	334.1
Maine	10.4	527	3.7	456	131	18.2
N.H.	8.9	547	3.2	477	152	20.2
Vt.	5.1	299	1.9	263	81	13.8
Mass.	52.6	5,025	19.5	4,549	1,621	175.9
R.I.	7.5	534	3.2	476	166	20.9
Conn.	26.4	2,359	11.2	2,127	727	85.1
M.A.	307.7	35,976	124.6	33,262	11,541	1,154.7
N.Y.	156.8	21,327	64.5	19,954	6,891	631.8
N.J.	60.2	6,243	26.8	5,711	2,062	218.7
Pa.	90.7	8,406	33.3	7,597	2,588	304.2
E.N.C.	311.1	29,361	119.0	26,727	9,223	1,046.6
Ohio	76.9	7,060	31.4	6,446	2,194	267.8
Ind.	41.3	2,766	14.7	2,447	781	106.3
Ill.	96.9	10,567	34.1	9,644	3,396	347.0
Mich.	60.6	6,389	24.9	5,882	2,059	218.9
Wis.	35.4	2,579	13.9	2,308	793	106.6
W.N.C.	153.2	10,959	54.2	9,762	3,232	417.9
Minn.	34.2	2,785	11.8	2,514	882	109.6
Iowa	27.3	1,560	9.2	1,347	409	60.2
Mo.	43.5	3,748	15.7	3,401	1,157	136.0
N. Dak.	5.4	319	2.0	279	88	12.6
S. Dak.	6.4	309	2.3	263	73	11.5
Nebr.	14.8	976	5.5	863	280	40.1
Kans.	21.6	1,262	7.7	1,095	343	47.9
S.A.	273.5	26,219	116.7	24,145	8,329	1,034.5
Del.	4.4	407	1.9	376	127	16.6
Md.	32.9	3,358	12.6	3,093	1,214	132.0
D.C.	8.6	1,842	4.0	1,760	631	60.4
Va.	36.8	3,613	15.9	3,365	1,220	138.0
W. Va.	11.4	824	4.7	749	231	30.8
N.C.	41.1	2,752	16.6	2,471	790	112.7
S.C.	19.6	1,420	8.5	1,285	415	60.8
Ga.	36.9	3,454	16.0	3,184	1,048	133.6
Fla.	81.8	8,549	36.5	7,862	2,653	349.6

[1] Week including Mar. 12.

Source: U.S. Bureau of the Census, Census of Service Industries, 1977, Geographic Area Series, SC 77-A-1 through 52.

Domestic Trade and Services *Continued*

Business Services		Personal Services		Automotive Repair, Services, and Garages		Resident Population
Establishments	*Receipts (mil. dol.)*	*Establishments*	*Receipts (mil. dol.)*	*Establishments*	*Receipts (mil. dol.)*	*1977 (1,000)*
458,232	**54,500**	**512,140**	**18,433**	**200,153**	**21,576**	**219,760**
29,863	**3,065**	**27,318**	**1,016**	**10,692**	**1,127**	**12,257**
1,668	70	2,943	65	1,346	106	1,105
1,987	102	2,226	65	982	79	872
940	42	1,290	30	579	31	492
15,020	1,830	12,589	504	4,876	532	5,744
1,689	158	2,200	74	824	81	955
8,559	863	6,070	278	2,085	298	3,089
84,859	**12,942**	**81,203**	**3,107**	**30,615**	**3,481**	**37,075**
46,628	8,250	38,096	1,562	12,505	1,629	17,852
18,649	2,257	13,860	626	5,907	746	7,342
19,582	2,435	29,247	919	12,203	1,106	11,882
76,123	**8,982**	**92,328**	**3,598**	**32,683**	**4,007**	**41,353**
17,236	1,895	22,489	936	8,811	1,070	10,771
8,130	651	14,497	450	5,076	493	5,405
28,109	3,844	28,806	1,092	8,650	1,093	11,406
14,268	1,925	17,317	771	6,487	981	9,157
8,380	667	9,219	349	3,659	370	4,613
30,392	**2,951**	**51,132**	**1,416**	**18,463**	**1,649**	**16,950**
6,897	818	10,541	332	3,671	360	3,980
5,315	347	9,838	230	3,429	281	2,914
10,161	1,155	14,224	431	5,290	524	4,845
776	54	1,753	49	645	56	649
787	42	2,137	46	781	49	689
2,506	233	5,034	126	1,914	173	1,554
3,950	302	7,605	202	2,733	206	2,318
63,503	**7,156**	**77,925**	**2,859**	**30,983**	**3,174**	**35,341**
1,062	129	1,245	43	458	55	595
9,441	1,253	8,845	351	2,778	346	4,195
3,114	575	1,757	95	561	107	682
9,139	1,217	10,820	422	3,865	412	5,206
1,668	131	4,069	127	1,391	100	1,906
6,942	601	14,757	458	5,996	464	5,668
3,280	252	6,663	199	2,687	195	2,989
7,824	929	11,544	388	4,826	495	5,212
21,033	2,068	18,225	776	8,421	1,000	8,889

(*continues*)

Domestic Trade and Services *Continued*

Division and State	All Establishments		Establishments with Payroll			
	Number (1,000)	Receipts (mil. dol.)	Number (1,000)	Receipts (mil. dol.)	Payroll, Entire year (mil. dol.)	Paid Employees[1] (1,000)
E.S.C.	**92.7**	**6,910**	**38.1**	**6,211**	**2,022**	**274.6**
Ky.	24.0	1,597	8.8	1,396	435	63.2
Tenn.	32.2	2,729	13.2	2,481	838	106.8
Ala.	21.9	1,696	10.0	1,548	511	68.1
Miss.	14.6	888	6.1	786	238	36.5
W.S.C.	**180.9**	**16,928**	**74.1**	**15,437**	**5,074**	**612.1**
Ark.	16.4	922	6.3	798	233	36.0
La.	27.5	2,941	12.0	2,712	858	108.4
Okla.	25.7	1,661	9.4	1,447	466	61.1
Tex.	111.3	11,404	46.4	10,480	3,517	406.6
Mt.	**100.7**	**10,727**	**40.6**	**9,943**	**3,316**	**391.6**
Mont.	8.0	449	3.0	386	114	17.8
Idaho	8.1	569	2.9	505	209	22.3
Wyo.	4.8	373	2.1	334	92	12.5
Colo.	30.1	2,481	11.7	2,246	757	94.3
N. Mex.	9.7	1,059	4.3	992	351	36.0
Ariz.	20.6	1,853	8.7	1,687	557	75.9
Utah	11.4	838	4.3	756	244	33.5
Nev.	8.0	3,105	3.6	3,037	992	99.3
Pac.	**304.1**	**33,143**	**115.0**	**30,383**	**10,442**	**1,071.2**
Wash.	34.4	2,984	13.2	2,726	892	98.2
Oreg.	23.1	1,752	8.7	1,565	507	65.4
Calif.	234.2	26,617	88.3	24,407	8,484	844.7
Alaska	4.4	514	1.5	469	169	13.5
Hawaii	8.0	1,276	3.3	1,216	390	49.4

[1]Week including Mar. 12.

Source: U.S. Bureau of the Census, *Census of Service Industries, 1977*, Geographic Area Series, SC 77-A-1 through 52.

Domestic Trade and Services *Concluded*

Business Services		Personal Services		Automotive Repair, Services, and Garages		Resident Population
Establishments	Receipts (mil. dol.)	Establishments	Receipts (mil. dol.)	Establishments	Receipts (mil. dol.)	1977 (1,000)
16,207	**1,714**	**31,423**	**1,003**	**12,319**	**1,047**	**14,219**
4,171	323	8,074	265	3,138	217	3,575
5,940	816	10,592	365	4,120	397	4,402
3,851	416	7,516	238	3,096	277	3,783
2,245	160	5,241	135	1,965	156	2,460
40,056	**4,929**	**53,548**	**1,848**	**23,501**	**2,112**	**22,281**
2,461	162	5,635	145	2,610	196	2,207
5,507	899	8,162	255	3,219	295	4,016
5,272	439	8,466	226	3,322	246	2,866
26,816	3,429	31,285	1,222	14,350	1,375	13,192
24,520	**2,454**	**24,622**	**825**	**11,044**	**1,097**	**10,409**
1,413	68	2,067	52	1,035	72	771
1,547	197	2,235	58	997	71	883
847	54	1,097	28	519	45	412
8,007	696	7,567	242	3,036	324	2,696
2,129	496	2,339	77	1,233	99	1,225
5,733	496	4,442	190	2,282	254	2,427
2,817	230	3,203	86	1,251	135	1,316
2,027	217	1,672	92	691	97	678
92,709	**10,308**	**72,641**	**2,763**	**29,853**	**3,881**	**29,874**
8,299	923	9,176	301	3,715	386	3,772
5,532	476	5,999	208	2,670	262	2,439
75,178	8,602	54,695	2,139	22,149	3,015	22,350
1,349	134	844	32	455	54	396
2,351	173	1,927	83	864	164	916

11/REGRESSION MODELING: INFERENCE AND PREDICTION

Regression analysis is a technique for building models of relationships among variables. Once constructed, models may be used for prediction, regulation, or control. The simplest example of regression analysis is the fitting of a straight line to a scatterplot of two variables, as discussed in Chapter 10. We saw there that once a straight line is passed through the scatterplot, the fitted values are subtracted from the observed values of the Y variable to form residuals. The residuals are studied to determine whether or not the straight line is an adequate model and the extent to which the actual values may deviate from the fitted line. If the line is deemed inadequate, then a more complicated curve needs to be fitted to the data. If the deviations from the fitted curve are deemed to be too large, additional X variables may be added to the model in an attempt to increase the precision of prediction. In either case, one is led to the study of multiple regression models. The basic tool for modeling is the REGRESS command, which uses the method of least squares to fit curves to data. The form of the REGRESS command studied in Chapter 10 is described below.

REGRESS C on K predictors C, ..., C

This is the Minitab command for regression analyses. REGRESS has many subcommands. Here we will describe the more elementary ones. See the *Minitab Reference Manual* or type HELP REGRESS to learn about the others.

PREDICT for E, ..., E

This is described on page 220.

RESIDUALS into C

This is described on pages 194–196.

FITS into C

Stores the fitted values in the column.

COEF into C

Stores the coefficients $b_0, b_1, \ldots, b_k$ down the column.

MSE into K

Stores the mean square error, which is the same as s^2, in K.

NOCONSTANT

Fits a model without a constant term, that is, the model

$$Y = b_1X_1 + b_2X_2 + \cdots + b_kX_k$$

The amount of printed output from the REGRESS command is controlled by the BRIEF command.

BRIEF output at level K

Controls the amount of output from all REGRESS commands that follow. K is an integer from 1 to 3; the larger the integer, the more output.

K = 1   The regression line, table of coefficients, line with s, R^2 and R^2-adjusted, and the first part of the analysis of variance table (regression, error, and total sums of squares) are printed.

K = 2   In addition, the second part of the analysis of variance table (provided that there are two or more predictors) and these "unusual" observations in the table of data, fits, stdev fit, etc. are printed. There are two reasons why an observation is unusual: Its predictors, $Y_1, \ldots, Y_k$ are unusual (i.e., far away from most other predictors); its standardized residual is large (specifically, over 2). In both cases you should check the observation to make sure it is correct. This is the usual output.

K = 3   In addition, the full table of data, fits, stdev fit, etc. is printed.

If the data can be interpreted as a random sample from a population, or as part of an ongoing process satisfying certain conditions, then certain inferences about the population can be drawn from the data. The most useful inferential statements will be discussed in this chapter.

11.1/DATA FOR THIS CHAPTER

The examples in this chapter will be based on the property data from an anonymous city on page 273. This data set shows information on 60 residential parcels of real estate. In Sections 11.2 and 11.3 we shall treat this set as a population, draw a random sample (with replacement) of size 10, and make inferences about the population. To draw the sample, we issue the command

```
RANDOM 10 NUMBERS INTO C10;
   INTEGERS UNIFORM ON 1 TO 60.
PRINT C10
```

The output is in Exhibit 11.1. The numbers in C10 are the ten rows that have been chosen randomly from the population to be the cases in the sample. The rows chosen are 9, 16, 20, 21, 23, 28 (twice), 37, 48, and 50. Row 28 is accepted twice, since the sampling is done with replacement. With-replacement sampling ensures the independence of the cases in the sample, an important assumption in inference.

EXHIBIT 11.1   Random Sample of Size 10 from a Population of
               60 Units

```
RANDOM 10 NUMBERS INTO C10;
   INTEGERS UNIFORM ON 1 TO 60.
PRINT C10
C10
    16    48    28    28    37    20    50     9    23    21
```

We now read the chosen cases into the worksheet. We also sort on square feet of living area, name the columns, and print out the sample.

```
READ INTO C10-C15
 9 1.25 10.47 0.90 45.0 65.4
16 1.00  5.77 0.75 33.3 39.3
20 1.25 10.33 0.90 37.8 60.6
21 1.25 10.75 0.90 45.6 64.2
23 1.00 10.60 0.90 36.0 57.0
28 1.00  8.34 0.75 27.0 51.9
28 1.00  8.34 0.75 27.0 51.9
37 1.00  8.90 0.90 30.3 52.5
48 1.00  8.14 0.90 22.2 52.2
50 1.50 10.40 0.90 33.6 60.6
END
```

```
SORT ON C12 CARRY C10 C11 C13-C15 PUT IN C22 C20 C21 &
   C23-C25
NAME C20 'POPROW' C21 'STYLE' C22 'SFLA' C23 'GRADE'
NAME C24 'ASSESSED' C25 'MARKET'
PRINT C20-C25
```

The output is in Exhibit 11.2. Throughout this chapter we will assume that the sample is in column C20–C25, as shown in Exhibit 11.2, and that the population is in columns C1–C5.

EXHIBIT 11.2   Sample of Ten Parcels of Real Property

```
PRINT C20-C25
```

ROW	POPROW	STYLE	SFLA	GRADE	ASSESSED	MARKET
1	16	1. 00	5. 77	0. 75	33. 3	39. 3
2	48	1. 00	8. 14	0. 90	22. 2	52. 2
3	28	1. 00	8. 34	0. 75	27. 0	51. 9
4	28	1. 00	8. 34	0. 75	27. 0	51. 9
5	37	1. 00	8. 90	0. 90	30. 3	52. 5
6	20	1. 25	10. 33	0. 90	37. 8	60. 6
7	50	1. 50	10. 40	0. 90	33. 6	60. 6
8	9	1. 25	10. 47	0. 90	45. 0	65. 4
9	23	1. 00	10. 60	0. 90	36. 0	57. 6
10	21	1. 25	10. 75	0. 90	45. 6	64. 2

EXERCISE

11-1   Verify that the cases in the sample displayed in Exhibit 11.2 correspond to rows 9, 16, 20, 21, 23, 28, 28, 37, 48, and 50 of the data set on page 273.

11.2 / INFERENCES AND PREDICTIONS FOR THE STRAIGHT LINE MODEL

MODEL ASSUMPTIONS

To use the straight line regression model presented here, we assume that the data are generated by the equation

$$Y = A + BX + E$$

where X is the independent variable, A and B are the y intercept and slope of the underlying regressions line, and E is a random error term that accounts for the fact that the observed value Y deviates from the line. From a sample of data consisting of (X, Y) pairs, estimates of A and B may be computed by the method of ordinary least squares (OLS). These estimates are optimal if the data pairs are statistically independent and the error terms all have zero mean and the same standard deviation, which is denoted by σ. Classical inference statements are derived by assuming that the error terms come from a normal distribution. This assumption should be thought of as a convenient working approximation. In practice, nonnormal populations abound, but the inference statements give useful guidance.

INFERENCE ABOUT PARAMETERS

To illustrate inferences using a straight line model, let's consider the regression of MARKET on ASSESSED values. The commands

```
PLOT C25 VS C24
CORRELATION C24 AND C25
BRIEF 3
REGRESS C25 ON 1 VARIABLE IN C24
```

produce the output in Exhibit 11.3. Case 1 is an outlier. The actual market value is almost $16,000 below what is predicted by the model. Perhaps the

---

EXHIBIT 11.3   Regression of MARKET on ASSESSED for Data in
                Exhibit 11.2

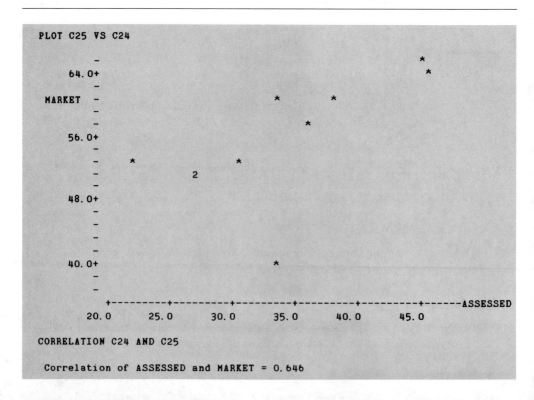

EXHIBIT 11.3 *Continued*

```
BRIEF 3
REGRESS C25 1 VARIABLE IN C24

The regression equation is
MARKET = 33.5 + 0.654 ASSESSED

Predictor        Coef        Stdev       t-ratio
Constant       33.528        9.440         3.55
ASSESSED       0.6540        0.2733        2.39

s = 6.262      R-sq = 41.7%     R-sq(adj) = 34.4%

Analysis of Variance

SOURCE         DF           SS           MS
Regression      1        224.58       224.58
Error           8        313.66        39.21
Total           9        538.24

Obs. ASSESSED    MARKET      Fit  Stdev. Fit   Residual    St. Resid
  1      33.3     39.30     55.31     1.98       -16.01      -2.70R
  2      22.2     52.20     48.05     3.73         4.15       0.83
  3      27.0     51.90     51.19     2.71         0.71       0.13
  4      27.0     51.90     51.19     2.71         0.71       0.13
  5      30.3     52.50     53.34     2.20        -0.84      -0.14
  6      37.8     60.60     58.25     2.26         2.35       0.40
  7      33.6     60.60     55.50     1.98         5.10       0.86
  8      45.0     65.40     62.96     3.65         2.44       0.48
  9      36.0     57.60     57.07     2.07         0.53       0.09
 10      45.6     64.20     63.35     3.79         0.85       0.17

R denotes an obs. with a large st. resid.
```

parcel suffered serious damage between the time it was assessed and the time it was sold. Or perhaps the sale was not "at arm's length." Notice, though, that the parcel has the smallest square feet of living area in the sample and the sixth largest assessed value, so another possibility is that the parcel was badly misassessed. The presence of such a case means that inferences about the population will be subject to rather large errors.

The fitted equation is

$$\text{MARKET} = 33.5 + 0.6540 \text{ ASSESSED}$$

In general terms the equation of the fitted line is written

$$\hat{Y} = a + bX$$

where a and b are the OLS estimates of A and B. Another sample of size 10 from the population would yield different values of a and b.

Measures of the deviation of these sample values from the population values are given by the column labeled "Stdev." In Exhibit 11.3 the standard deviation of the sampling distribution of the y intercept estimate is estimated to be 9.440. The standard deviation of the sampling distribution of the slope estimate is estimated to be 0.2733. Confidence intervals for A and B use these values. The form of the confidence intervals is

(estimate) $\pm$ (value from t-table) $\times$ (estimated stdev of estimate)

The value from the t-table is found by referring to the residual degrees of freedom and the level of confidence desired. The t value corresponding to 8 degrees of freedom and 90% confidence is 1.86. Thus a 90% confidence interval for A is

$$33.528 \pm 1.86(9.440) = 33.5 \pm 17.6$$

and a 90% confidence interval for B is

$$0.6540 \pm 1.86(0.2733) = 0.65 \pm 0.51$$

Tests of hypotheses also use the values printed out by the REGRESS command. The general form of the test statistic is

$$t = \frac{\text{(estimate)} - \text{(hypothesized value)}}{\text{(estimated stdev of estimate)}}$$

To test the hypothesis that $B = 0$, we compute

$$t = \frac{0.6514 - 0}{0.2731} = 2.39$$

If we use a two-tailed test at the 10% significance level, we must compare this value to the tabled t value of 1.86. Since the computed value is bigger than the tabled value, we reject the hypothesis that the slope of the population regression line is zero.

To test the hypothesis that $B = 1$, we compute

$$t = \frac{0.6540 - 1}{0.2733} = -1.3$$

Since $|t| = |-1.3| \leq 1.86$, we cannot reject the hypothesis that $B = 1$ at the 10% significance level.

To test the hypothesis that $A = 0$, we compute

$$t = \frac{33.528 - 0}{9.440} = 3.55$$

Since this value is bigger than 1.86, we reject the hypothesis that $A = 0$ at the 10% significance level.

Notice that the computed t-ratios for the hypotheses $A = 0$ and $B = 0$ are printed out by Minitab in the column labeled "t-ratio."

The statistic $s = 6.262$ is an estimate of the error standard deviation σ. This value is used in the calculation of the standard deviations of the coefficients a and b, of standard deviations of fitted Y values, and of prediction intervals for single Y values.

STANDARD DEVIATIONS OF FITTED Y VALUES

The estimated standard deviations of the fitted Y values are given in the column headed "Stdev.Fit" in Exhibit 11.3. These can be used to get confidence intervals for the population mean of all Y values corresponding to a given value of X. For example, the sixth line shows that the fitted value for $X = 37.8$ is 58.25. The 90% confidence interval for the mean of all Ys corresponding to $X = 37.8$ is given by

$$\text{(fitted } Y) \pm \text{(tabled } t \text{ value)} \times \text{(stdev of fit)}$$

or

$$58.25 \pm 1.86(2.26) = 58.25 \pm 4.2$$

This gives an estimated *average* market value of between $54,050 and $62,450 for parcels whose assessed value is $37,800.

PREDICTION INTERVAL FOR A SINGLE Y VALUE

If we want to predict a single Y value corresponding to an X value that appears in the data set, the procedure is very simple. We use the formula

$$\text{(fitted } Y) \pm \text{(tabled } t \text{ value)} \times \text{sqrt[(estimated stdev of fitted } Y)^2 + s^2]$$

This formula is most often written in textbooks as

$$\text{(fitted } Y) \pm \text{(tabled } t \text{ value)} \times s$$

$$\times \text{sqrt}\left[1 + 1/n + (X - \bar{X})^2 \Big/ \sum_{i=1}^{n} (X_i - \bar{X})^2\right]$$

To illustrate the formula numerically, let's predict a single Y value corresponding to an X value of 37.8 (that is, an assessed value of $37,800). A 90% prediction interval is

$$58.25 \pm 1.86 \times \text{sqrt[}(2.26)^2 + (6.262)^2] = 58.25 \pm 12.4$$

A randomly drawn parcel with assessed value of $37,800 is predicted, with 90% confidence, to have a market value of between $45,850 and $70,650.

If we want to predict a single Y value corresponding to an X value that does not appear in the sample, the calculation is quite complicated. Rather than implement a complicated formula, it is easier to use the PREDICT subcommand of the REGRESS command, as it does the required computation. To use the PREDICT subcommand with $X = 40$ (that is, assessed value of $40,000), issue the commands

```
BRIEF 1
REGRESS C25 ON 1 VARIABLE IN C24;
    PREDICT 40.
```

Minitab will then print the following extra lines.

```
Fit    Stdev.Fit      95% C.I.        95% P.I.
59.69     2.61     (53.67, 65.71)  (44.04, 75.33)
```

The value labeled "Fit" is found by substituting $X = 40$ into the fitted equation, that is, Fit $= 33.528 + 0.6540(40) = 59.69$. The Stdev.Fit is found by using the equation presented earlier. Minitab automatically prints out the 95% confidence interval for the average market value of parcels with assessed value of \$40,000 and the 95% prediction interval for a single parcel with assessed value of \$40,000. The Stdev.Fit is used as illustrated above to get intervals at other levels of confidence.

REGRESS C on 1, C

PREDICT for E

The **PREDICT** subcommand computes estimates for any values of X. It prints out a table of fitted y, standard deviation of fitted Y, standard deviation for predicting a future Y, a 95% confidence interval, and a 95% prediction interval.

E may be a constant such as 68 or K3 or it may be a column containing a list of X values.

EXERCISES

11-2 Redo the example in this section, omitting the first case. Begin with the command

```
COPY C20-C25 INTO C30-C35;
  OMIT ROW 1.
```

How does omission of the outlier affect the results? If you were to use a prediction interval based on these data, what caution would you observe? On the evidence of the sample in Exhibit 11.3, what fraction of the population rows are outliers?

11-3 Using all 60 parcels in the population, REGRESS market values against assessed values. The y intercept and slope of this fitted line are A and B, and s is the population error standard deviation σ. Compare the population parameters to the statistics obtained in Exhibit 11.3 and Exercise 11-2. How many of the population cases are flagged as outliers? What percentage of the population cases is this?

11-4 Draw a random sample of ten rows from the property data set on page 273. REGRESS the market values against the assessed values. Compare your results with those in Exhibit 11.3 and Exercise 11-3. Explain why they are different.

11–5 Draw a random sample of 20 rows from the property data set on page 273. REGRESS the market values against the assessed values. Compare your results with those in Exhibit 11.3 and Exercises 11–3 and 11–4. How does the larger sample size affect the results?

11–6 *(a)* We can simulate data from a regression model as follows. To choose a model, we need to specify three parameters, A, B, and σ. Suppose we take $A = 3$, $B = 5$, and $\sigma = 0.2$. Next, we must specify values for the predictor X. Suppose we take two observations at each integer from 1 to 10. First, put the 20 values of X into a column. Then calculate $A + BX$. Now simulate 20 observations from a normal distribution with $\mu = 0$, $\sigma = 0.2$. Add these to $A + BX$ to get the observed Ys. Get a plot and do a regression for these simulated data.

 (b) Repeat part (a) using $\sigma = 0.05$. Compare the results with those of part (a).

 (c) Repeat part (a) using $\sigma = 1.0$. Compare the results with those of parts (a) and (b).

11–7 Repeat Exercise 11–6 using Student's t distribution with 3 degrees of freedom to generate the errors rather than a normal distribution. Compare your results with those in Exercise 11–6.

11–8 Repeat Exercises 11–6 and 11–7 a number of times. What appears to be the effect of the Student's t error distribution?

11–9 In Exercise 11–6 we simulated data from a regression equation. Repeat those simulations; each time, plot the standardized residuals versus X. This should give you some idea of how a residual plot looks when the correct model is fitted.

11–10 Let us use simulation to look at some residual plots when the wrong model is fitted.

 (a) Use the model $Y = 3X^2 + 10 + E$ with $\sigma = 0.1$. Take one observation at each of the following values of X: 0, .1, .2, .3, .4, .5, .6, .7, .8, .9, .1.0. Now fit the line $Y = a + bX$ and get a residual plot. Is there any pattern?

 (b) Repeat part (a) using $\sigma = 0.5$.

11.3 / INFERENCES AND PREDICTIONS FOR MULTIPLE REGRESSION MODELS

MODEL ASSUMPTIONS

The general multiple regression model has the form

$$Y = B_0 + B_1 X_1 + \cdots + B_k X_k + E$$

where $X_1, \ldots, X_k$ are the independent variables and E is an error term satisfying the conditions outlined under the Model Assumptions subsection of Section 11.2.

INFERENCE ABOUT PARAMETERS

To illustrate, let's use the sample in Exhibit 11.2 and REGRESS the market values on assessed values and a second-degree polynomial in square feet of living area. The justification for the second-degree polynomial is that there is a diminishing return to amount of living area. The following commands accomplish our goal.

```
LET C26 = C22*C22 #Quadratic term in SFLA
NAME C26 'SFLA.SQ'
BRIEF 3
REGRESS C25 3 C24 C22 C26
```

The output is in Exhibit 11.4. The parameters of the population multiple regression curve are B_0, B_1, B_2, and B_3. Their estimates are $b_0 = -44.40$, $b_1 = 0.3799$, $b_2 = 16.872$, and $b_3 -0.7825$. The estimate of σ is $s = 2.134$, which is considerably smaller than the s value in Exhibit 11.3. The use of the columns labeled "Stdev" and "t-ratio" to construct confidence intervals and perform tests follows the discussion presented under *Inference about Parameters* in Section 11.2.

A test can be performed to assess the improvement in fit achieved by adding SFLA and SFLA.SQ to the model containing ASSESSED. Let FULL denote the model in this section, and let REDUCED denote the straight line model in Section 11.2. The test statistic is

$$F = \frac{\dfrac{(\text{RESIDUAL SS(REDUCED)} - \text{RESIDUAL SS(FULL)})}{(\text{DF (REDUCED)} - \text{DF(FULL)})}}{\dfrac{(\text{RESIDUAL SS(FULL)})}{\text{DF(FULL)}}}$$

$$= \frac{(313.66 - 27.33)/(8 - 6)}{27.33/6} = 31.4$$

This statistic is compared to a tabled F-value with 2 and 6 degrees of freedom. At the 1% significance level the tabled number is 10.92. Since 31.4 is greater than 10.92, we *reject* the hypothesis that $B_2 = B_3 = 0$, that is, that the terms involving SFLA do not contribute significantly to the fit.

INFERENCE ABOUT AVERAGE Y VALUES AND PREDICTIONS OF SINGLE Y VALUES

The calculations needed to obtain confidence intervals for average Y values and prediction intervals for single Y values for a set of given values of the independent variables are quite complex. The best way to get these inferential statements is to use the PREDICT subcommand.

EXHIBIT 11.4   Multiple Regression Using Real Property Data in Exhibit 11.2

```
LET C26 = C22*C22
NAME C26 'SFLA.SQ'
BRIEF 3
REGRESS C25 3 C24 C22 C26
 * NOTE *    SFLA is highly correlated with other  predictor variables
 * NOTE *  SFLA.SQ is highly correlated with other  predictor variables
```

The regression equation is
MARKET = - 44.4 + 0.380 ASSESSED + 16.9 SFLA - 0.782 SFLA.SQ

Predictor	Coef	Stdev	t-ratio
Constant	-44.40	34.76	-1.28
ASSESSED	0.3799	0.2036	1.87
SFLA	16.872	7.660	2.20
SFLA.SQ	-0.7825	0.4762	-1.64

s = 2.134   R-sq = 94.9%   R-sq(adj) = 92.4%

Analysis of Variance

SOURCE	DF	SS	MS
Regression	3	510.90	170.30
Error	6	27.33	4.56
Total	9	538.24	

SOURCE	DF	SEQ SS
ASSESSED	1	224.58
SFLA	1	274.02
SFLA.SQ	1	12.30

Obs.	ASSESSED	MARKET	Fit	Stdev.Fit	Residual	St. Resid
1	33.3	39.300	39.548	2.124	-0.248	-1.17 X
2	22.2	52.200	49.521	1.303	2.679	1.58
3	27.0	51.900	52.140	1.097	-0.240	-0.13
4	27.0	51.900	52.140	1.097	-0.240	-0.13
5	30.3	52.500	55.287	1.114	-2.787	-1.53
6	37.8	60.600	60.745	0.850	-0.145	-0.07
7	33.6	60.600	59.195	1.353	1.405	0.85
8	45.0	65.400	63.564	1.473	1.836	1.19
9	36.0	57.600	60.195	1.393	-2.595	-1.60
10	45.6	64.200	63.866	1.306	0.334	0.20

X denotes an obs. whose X value gives it large influence.

REGRESS C on K predictors C, ..., C

PREDICT for E, ..., E

The PREDICT subcommand tells Minitab to compute predicted values, standard deviations, confidence intervals, and prediction intervals. The arguments on PREDICT should be either all columns of the same length or all constants. There should be as many arguments on the PREDICT subcommand as there are predictors on the REGRESS command.

EXAMPLES

```
REGRESS C8 on 4 C1–C4;
    PREDICT 16, 20, 4, 30.
REGRESS C8 on 4 C1–C4;
    PREDICT C11–C14.
```

For example, to get 95% confidence and prediction intervals for the settings (ASSESSED, SFLA) = (25, 8.5) and (40, 10), we issue the following commands:

```
READ INTO C43 C44
25   8.5
40  10.0
END
LET C45 = C44*C44
BRIEF 1
REGRESS C25 3 C24 C22 C26;
    PREDICT C43, C44 C45.
```

Exercise 11–13 asks you to perform these calculations.

EXERCISES

11–11 For the population of 60 parcels in the property data set on page 273, REGRESS the MARKET on ASSESSED, SFLA, and SFLA.SQ. Compare your results with those in Exhibit 11.3. Why are they different?

11–12 Draw a random sample of 20 rows from the property data set on page 273. REGRESS the MARKET on ASSESSED, SFLA, and SFLA.SQ. Compare your results with those in Exhibit 11.3 and Exercise 11–11. Why are they different?

11–13 Read the sample data in Exhibit 11.2 into Minitab's worksheet and issue the commands listed at the end of this section to get confidence and prediction intervals. Interpret carefully the intervals that are thus calculated.

11.4 / STEPWISE REGRESSION

Stepwise regression is an aid in regression model building. It is a semiautomatic screening device that attempts to choose an optimal set of predictors from a large set of candidate variables. The hope is that a model with a small number of predictors will give acceptably precise predictions and fewer management problems than a large model. Minitab's STEPWISE command is described below.

STEPWISE regression y in C, predictors in C, ..., C

Summary of subcommands

FENTER = K	default is 4
FREMOVE = K	default is 4
FORCE C, ..., C	
ENTER C, ..., C	
REMOVE C, ..., C	
BEST K alternative predictors	default is 0
STEPS = K	default depends on output width

The STEPWISE regression command provides several methods for selecting a useful subset from a large collection of predictors. Three commonly used automatic procedures are provided: forward selection, backwards elimination, and conventional stepwise. In addition (if you are using Minitab in interactive mode), you can intervene at selected points in the analysis.

For details on use of the subcommands, see the *Minitab Reference Manual*. To illustrate, we shall apply the STEPWISE command to all 60 cases and all the variables in the property data set on page 273, including SFLASQ. Remember that columns, C1–C5 contain the variables STYLE, SFLA, GRADE, ASSESSED, and MARKET. We shall put SFLASQ in C6. The commands

```
LET C6 = C2*C2
NAME C6 'SFLASQ'
STEPWISE C5 ON VARIABLES C1 C2 C3 C4 C6
```

produce the output in Exhibit 11.5. The STEPWISE command with default settings has picked the model with independent variables SFLA, GRADE, SFLASQ, and ASSESSED. This model could now be explored in detail by using the REGRESS command. Other models could be constructed with the STEPWISE command by changing the settings of the defaults or by adding other candidate independent variables. This could be

---

EXHIBIT 11.5   Stepwise Regression Using Real Property Data
(60 cases)

```
LET C6=C2*C2
NAME C6 'SFLASQ'
STEPWISE C5 ON VARIABLES C1 C2 C3 C4 C6

 STEPWISE REGRESSION OF  MARKET  ON  5 PREDICTORS, WITH N =    60
```

STEP	1	2	3	4
CONSTANT	30.76	-12.15	-28.90	-26.61
SFLA	2.75	1.90	6.82	6.89
T-RATIO	8.60	6.13	5.25	5.73
GRADE		58	49	37
T-RATIO		5.30	4.82	3.73
SFLASQ			-0.227	-0.235
T-RATIO			-3.87	-4.35
ASSESSED				0.226
T-RATIO				3.26
S	5.97	4.93	4.42	4.08
R-SQ	56.07	70.56	76.79	80.55

---

done, for example, by creating interactions such as GRADE*SFLA, GRADE*ASSESSED, and so on.

EXERCISES

11-14 For the data discussed in this section, REGRESS the MARKET on GRADE, ASSESSED, SFLA, and SFLASQ. Comment on the quality of the fit by doing a detailed analysis of the residuals. In particular, do a plot of the standardized residuals versus their NSCORES.

11-15 Repeat Exercise 11-14 after removing rows 17 and 52 from the data set (these are the extreme outliers). Compare your results with those of Exercise 11-14.

11-16 Draw a random sample of size 20 from the data set discussed in this section. Do the STEPWISE analysis and compare the results with those of Exercises 11-14 and 11-15.

11.5 / TRANSFORMATIONS

In analyzing data we are always on the lookout for *simple* relationships between variables. Simple relationships are the easiest to grasp visually, and it is easier to spot exceptions when the rule is simple. A linear relationship is the simplest we can think of, but the pattern of the data may be clearly nonlinear or rather ambiguous. In many cases, however, adjustments of the data, called transformations, will bring them into approximately linear relationship. Besides providing simplification, transformations can give us real insight into our data. The most commonly applied transformations are logarithms and powers. Let Y denote a dependent variable, and let X denote an independent variable. The transformation may be applied to Y alone, to X alone, or to both Y and X. For example, we could fit sqrt(Y) to X, Y to sqrt(X), or sqrt(Y) to sqrt(X).

As another example, suppose we have a dependent variable Y and two independent variables X_1 and X_2. We have decided to regress $1/Y$ on X_1 and $\log_e(X_2)$. Suppose Y, X_1, and X_2 are stored in columns C1, C2, and C3. We could use the following commands to accomplish our goal:

```
LET C11 = 1/C1
LET C12 = C2
LET C13 = LOGE(C3)
NAME C11 '1/Y' C12 'X.ONE' C13 'LNX.TWO'
REGRESS C11 ON 2 VARIABLES IN C12 AND C13
```

EXERCISES

11–17 For the property data on page 273, fit MARKET to sqrt (SFLA). Does a straight line model appear to be adequate? Examine the residuals carefully. Now fit $\log_e$(MARKET) to SFLA. Does this model seem sensible?

11–18 If the dependent variable is a proportion, the logistic transformation $\log_e(Y/(1 - Y))$ is often applied. Suppose that the independent variable is age and the dependent variable is the proportion of women who use a certain brand of hairspray. Suppose the data for Y and X are in columns C1 and C2. Write the commands that create the logistically transformed Ys and regress them on X.

11–19 The data in the NEWSPRINT data set on page 279 are excerpted from a larger data set reported in the text by Miller and Wichern listed in the references. They are observations on a number of U.S. cities in the year 1960. The variables are defined as follows:

Y: newsprint consumption;

X_1:   number of newspapers in the city;

X_2:   proportion of the city population under age 18 (multiplied by 1000);

X_3: median school years completed (city residents);

X_4: proportion of the city population employed in white collar occupations (multiplied by 1000);

X_5: number of families in the city;

X_6: total retail sales in the city in 1960.

(a) Use the data from the first 45 cities to construct a model for predicting newsprint consumption from the other variables. You may wish to consider transformations of the variables (including Y). After you have obtained a model, substitute the X values of the *other* 45 cities and predict newsprint consumption for each of them. Subtract your predicted values from the actual values and analyze these prediction errors.

(b) Repeat part (a) but use the second 45 cities to build the model and predict the first 45 cities.

(c) Miller and Wichern recommend the following model. Let LX5 denote the natural logarithm of X_5 and let LX5C denote this variable centered. Let TY denote $1/\mathrm{SQRT}(Y)$. The predicted values of Y are found by first predicting TY from the equation.

$$\hat{\mathrm{TY}} = a + b_1\mathrm{LX5C} + b_2(\mathrm{LX5C})^2$$

and then forming $\hat{Y} = 1/(\hat{\mathrm{TY}})^2$. Redo parts (a) and (b) using this predictive model. What do you conclude?

11.6 / OTHER SUBCOMMANDS OF REGRESS

The full REGRESS command is described below.

```
REGRESS C on K pred. C, ..., C st. res. in C [fits in C]
NOCONSTANT                in equation
WEIGHTS are in C
MSE put into K
COEFFICIENTS put into C
PREDICT for E, ..., E
XPXINV put into M
RMATRIX put into M
HI put into C              leverage
RESIDUALS put into C
TRESIDUALS put into C      studentized residuals
```

COOKD put into C	Cook's distance
DFITS put into C	
VIF	variance inflation factor
DW	Durbin-Watson statistic
PURE	pure error lack-of-fit test
XLOF	experimental lack-of-fit test

We briefly discuss those subcommands that were not previously discussed. Some details may be found in the *Minitab Reference Manual*. The quantities presented briefly here are discussed in detail in the references by Weisberg and by Belsley, Kuh, and Welsch.

Function	Subcommand	Brief Description
Computation	RMATRIX	Stores the R matrix of the QR decomposition
Diagnostics	XPXINV	Stores $(X'X)^{-1}$
	HI	Stores the leverages, that is the diagonal elements of $H = X(X'X)^{-1}X$
	TRESIDUALS	Stores the Studentized residuals
	COOKD	Stores Cook's distance for each case
	DFITS	Stores DFITS for each case
	VIF	Prints variance inflation factors in the output
	DW	Prints the Durbin-Watson statistic in the output
Lack of fit	PURE	Prints the usual pure error test for lack of fit (uses replicates)
	XLOF	A lack-of-fit test that does not require replicates
Weighted least squares	WEIGHTS	A weighted regression is done. Each case is weighted by the corresponding values in the designated column

12/TIME SERIES ANALYSIS

In Section 3.3 a time series was defined as a collection of observations whose values are associated with epochs of time. In that section you learned how to plot time series, using annual GNP as an example. In Section 4.4 you learned how to display time series in tables. In this chapter we will go beyond displaying time series data to analyzing time series. Analysis means discovering something of the process that generated the data. The better our understanding of the underlying process, the better our ability to quantify our uncertainty about the future and to plan for it.

Pure time series analysis uses only the past history of a single time series to model and forecast values of that series. In business and economics, time series and regression techniques are usually combined to establish relationships between variables that are useful for policy making and prediction. Section 12.6 hints at some regression considerations, but the bulk of this chapter is devoted to pure time series analysis. Consult the text by Granger and Newbold in the References for a survey of time series regression methods.

12.1/ TREND

WHAT IS TREND?

Business and economics time series almost always have trends. A trend may be a rather steady upward or downward movement of the observations, or it may be a wavelike movement that locally displays ups followed by downs. Many other patterns are possible. A time series analysis always begins with a plot to give a visual impression of trend. Exhibit 12.1 lists two time series: annual iron and steel exports from the United States (excluding scrap) in millions of tons, for the years 1937–1980; and annual numbers of births per 1000 women aged 20–24 in the United States, for the years 1948–1980. Both series are DESCRIBEd in the exhibit.

EXHIBIT 12.1   Data and Descriptive Statistics for Two Time Series

```
PRINT 'METAL. EX'
METAL. EX
    3.89    2.41    2.80    8.72    7.12    7.24    7.15    6.05
    5.21    5.03    6.88    4.70    5.06    3.16    3.62    4.55
    2.43    3.16    4.55    5.17    6.95    3.46    2.13    3.47
    2.79    2.52    2.80    4.04    3.08    2.26    2.17    2.78
    5.94    8.14    3.55    3.61    5.06    7.13    4.15    3.86
    3.22    3.50    3.76    5.11


PRINT 'BIRTH. RT'
BIRTH. RT
  192.4   194.1   192.8   207.1   213.5   220.5   231.7
  236.3   248.5   257.0   252.0   252.7   246.1   253.0
  243.2   227.6   215.4   190.0   178.9   170.2   163.6
  162.8   163.1   149.1   128.8   119.4   117.7   113.6
  112.1   115.2   112.3   115.7   115.1   111.8   111.3


DESCRIBE 'METAL. EX'  'BIRTH. RT'

                 N     MEAN    MEDIAN   TRMEAN    STDEV   SEMEAN
METAL. EX       44    4.418    3.875    4.331    1.754    0.264
BIRTH. RT       35   180.99   190.00   180.69    53.09     8.97


                MIN      MAX       Q1        Q3
METAL. EX      2.130    8.720    3.100     5.200
BIRTH. RT    111.30   257.00   117.70    231.70
```

Exhibit 12.2 shows plots of the metal export and the birth rate time series. The plotting symbols have been connected and the means sketched in to facilitate inspection of the plots. The birth rates are clearly decreasing over time, whereas the metal exports, while exhibiting a great deal of variability, do not clearly exhibit a trend. For example, for the metal export series the interval $\bar{x} \pm 2s = 4.4 \pm 2(1.75) = 4.4 \pm 3.9 = (0.9, 7.9)$. If this interval's endpoints were sketched on the plot, they would contain all but two of the series values. It appears plausible, therefore, that most future values of the series will fall somewhere in this interval, barring dramatic shifts in the mean level of exports. For the births the interval $\bar{x} \pm 2s = (74.8, 287.2)$. The relationship between this interval and future values of the series is problematic. It certainly contains all the observed series values, but we judge from the past behavior of the series

EXHIBIT 12.2   Plots of Time Series in Exhibit 12.1

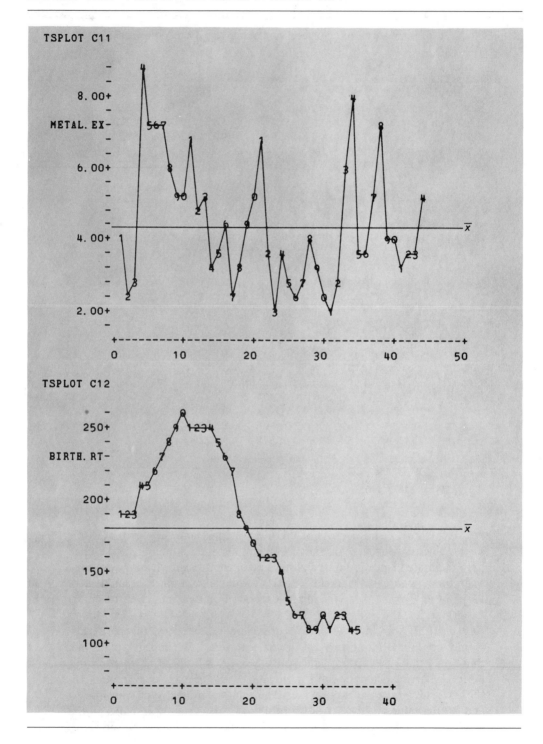

that future values probably will not differ much from the most recent value of 111.3. Most of the values in the $\bar{x} \pm 2s$ interval are implausible guesses at the future values. A more natural forecast interval would be an interval of values centered on the most recent observation, 111.3.

TREND LINES

An approach to modeling trend that is advanced in many textbooks is to fit functions of time to the data. The simplest function to fit is the straight line. Exhibit 12.3 shows the least squares fit of a straight line to the birth rates in Exhibit 12.1. The commands used are

```
SET 'BIRTH.DAT' INTO C1
SET INTO C2
  (1:35)
END
NAME C1 'BIRTH.RT' C2 'TIME' C3 'RESIDUAL' C4 'FIT'
BRIEF 1
REGRESS C1 1 C2 C50 C4;
  RESIDUALS INTO C3.
TSPLOT C3
```

If the line properly desribes the trend, then the residuals should behave like random observations, but the nonrandomness of the residuals is quite evident in the plot. The trend line fails to capture the essence of the trend in the birth rates. Moreover, extrapolation of the trend line into future time periods could be interpreted as a forecast of a completely unbelievable decline in the birth rate. Exhibit 12.4 shows the birth rates, the fitted trend line, and part of its extrapolation. If birth rates follow the trend line, there will be no births to women aged 20–24 in 2007 and negative births thereafter.

DIFFERENCES

An alternative to fitting trend lines is studying the behavior of *changes* in the series from one time period to the next. Such changes are called *differences* by time series analysts. Differences were used in Section 3.4, where percentage changes in GNP were computed. For the birth rate series in Exhibit 12.1 the difference between the 1949 rate and the 1948 rate is $194.1 - 192.4 = 1.7$, the difference between the 1950 and 1949 rates is $192.8 - 194.1 = -1.3$, and so forth. To make the concept of differencing easy to follow, let's just work with the first five birth rates. We set them up in C12 with the commands

```
COPY C1 INTO C12;
  USE ROWS 1:5.
NAME C12 'BR.SHRT'
```

EXHIBIT 12.3   Fit of a Trend Line to the Birth Rate Data

```
NAME C2 'TIME' C3 'RESIDUAL' C4 'FIT'
BRIEF 1
REGRESS C1 1 C2 C50 C4;
   RESIDUALS INTO C3.

The regression equation is
BIRTH.RT = 258 - 4.25 TIME

Predictor        Coef         Stdev      t-ratio
Constant        257.58        10.62       24.26
TIME            -4.2550        0.5145      -8.27

s = 30.74       R-sq = 67.5%    R-sq(adj) = 66.5%
Analysis of Variance

SOURCE        DF          SS            MS
Regression     1         64635         64635
Error         33         31186           945
Total         34         95820


TSPLOT C3

RESIDUAL-                   4
      -              2  5
      -            01 3
 35.0+                   6
      -          9         7
      -
      -       8
      -       7           8
  0.0+                  90 23         345
      -                   1  4        2
      -       6                      01
      -      5                  5   9
      -                        678
-35.0+     4
      -
      -   3
      - 2
      - 1
-70.0+
         +---------+---------+---------+---------+
         0        10        20        30        40
```

EXHIBIT 12.4   Birth Rates and Fitted Trend Line

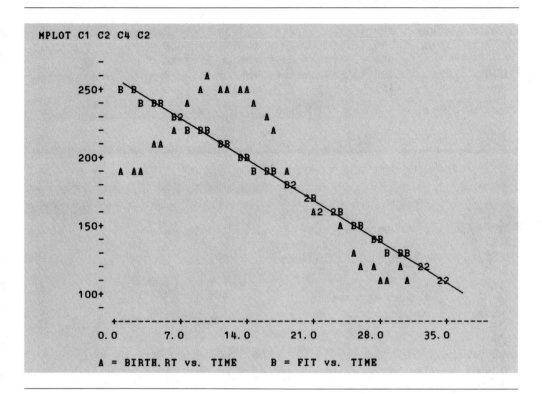

```
MPLOT C1 C2 C4 C2
```

A = BIRTH.RT vs. TIME   B = FIT vs. TIME

Let's also put years in C11:

```
SET INTO C11
  (1948:1952)
END
NAME C11 'YEAR'
```

Now we compute the differences in two ways:

1. using LAG and LET, and
2. using DIFF.

(Recall the LAG command from Section 3.4.) The commands that we need are

```
LAG C12 PUT IN C13
LET C14 = C12-C13
DIFF C12 PUT IN C15
NAME C13 'LAGBR' C14 'DLAGLET' C15 'DIFF'
PRINT C11-C15
```

EXHIBIT 12.5   Differences of Birth Rates Computed in Two Ways

```
PRINT C11-C15
  ROW    YEAR   BR.SHRT    LAGBR   DLAGLET      DIFF

   1     1948    192.4        *        *          *
   2     1949    194.1     192.4    1.7000     1.7000
   3     1950    192.8     194.1   -1.3000    -1.3000
   4     1951    207.1     192.8   14.3000    14.3000
   5     1952    213.5     207.1    6.4000     6.4000
```

EXHIBIT 12.6   Behavior of Differences of Birth Rates

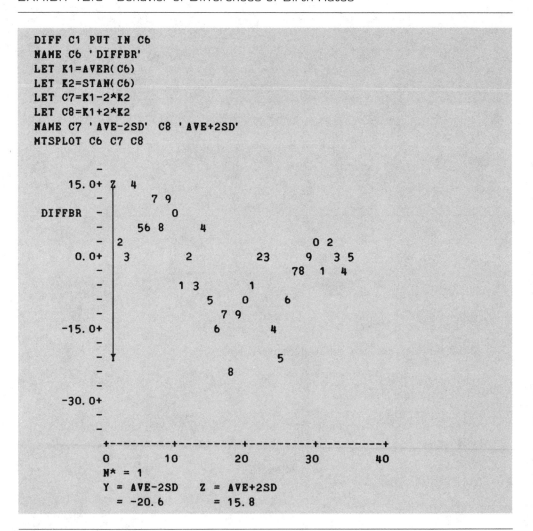

Exhibit 12.5 shows the results. Columns C14 and C15 are identical. The single DIFF command can be used in place of the two commands LAG and LET. The asterisks in row 1 of the output are missing data symbols. They are needed because without data from 1947 the differences and lags for 1948 cannot be computed.

Now let's look at the result of differencing the birth rates in Exhibit 12.1. We use the commands

```
DIFF Cl PUT IN C6
NAME C6 'DIFFBR'
LET Kl = AVER(C6)
LET K2 = STAN(C6)
LET C7 = Kl−2*K2
LET C8 = Kl+2*K2
NAME C7 'AVE−2SD' C8 'AVE+2SD'
MTSPLOT C6   C7 C8
```

Exhibit 12.6 shows the output. The $\bar{x} \pm 2s$ limits are joined for clarity. The series of differences of the birth rates behaves somewhat like the metal export series. At least it is plausible that future values of changes in the birth rates will fall in the $\bar{x} \pm 2s$ interval.

We can put this notion to use. Suppose we believe that the next change in the birth rate will be between -20.6 and 15.8. This means that we believe that the next birth rate will be between $111.3 - 20.6 = 90.7$ and $111.3 + 15.8 = 127.1$. This defines a prediction interval that is symmetric about 111.3, the sort of interval that we found intuitively plausible on page 233! The study of differences has yielded a useful and appealing result.

DIFFERENCES [of lag K] for data in C, put in C

EXAMPLE

```
DIFFERENCE 2 FOR Cl, STORE IN C2
Cl                 C2
  1                 *
  3                 *
  8        →        7
 12                 9
  7                −1
```

Note that row 3 of C2 contains $8 - 1$, row 4 contains $12 - 3$, and row 5 contains $7 - 8$.

In general, if C1 contains $Z(1), Z(2), \ldots, Z(n)$, then DIFF K C1, C2 puts $*$ into rows 1 through K of C2, and puts $Z(i) - Z(i - K)$ into row i, $K + 1 < i < n$. If K is omitted, $K = 1$ is used. $K > 1$ is often a seasonal difference.

EXERCISES

12-1 Make a time series plot of rates of return on Xerox common stock on page 278. Does the series exhibit trend? Compute the $\bar{x} \pm 2s$ interval and discuss its relevance to forecasting "future" rates of return.

12-2 Fit a trend line to the annual constant dollar GNP series in Exhibit 3.6 and make a time series plot of the residuals. Would you feel confident about extrapolating this trend line to future years?

12-3 Fit a trend line to the *logarithms* of the current dollar GNP series in Exhibit 3.6 and make a time series plot of the residuals. Would you feel confident about extrapolating this trend line to future years?

12-4 Make a time series plot of the annual differences of the constant dollar GNP series in Exhibit 3.6. Compute the $\bar{x} \pm 2s$ interval and discuss its relevance to future values of GNP.

12-5 Make a time series plot of the annual percentage changes of the constant dollar GNP series in Exhibit 3.6. Compute the $\bar{x} \pm 2s$ interval and discuss its relevance to future values of GNP.

12-6 Fit a trend line to the seasonally adjusted quarterly M1 series on page 274, and make a time series plot of the residuals. Would you feel confident about extrapolating this trend line to future quarters?

12-7 Compute the percentage changes of the seasonally adjusted quarterly M1 series on page 274, and make a time series plot of the resulting series. Compute the $\bar{x} \pm 2s$ interval and discuss its relevance to future values of M1.

12-8 For the annual constant dollar GNP series in Exhibit 3.6, compute
   (a)   the annual percentage changes;
   (b)   100 times the differences of the natural logarithms of GNP.
   Compare these two series. Why are they so similar?

12.2 / STATIONARITY, AUTOCORRELATION, AND PARTIAL AUTOCORRELATION

STATIONARITY

Series that lack trend will be referred to as *stationary*. A stationary series tends to vary about a fixed mean level with a fixed standard deviation. (These are informal remarks on stationarity. For formal definitions, consult the references.)

AUTOCORRELATION

For stationary series, autocorrelation is a measure of linear relationship between current and past values of the series. To illustrate, let's look at the metal export series in Exhibit 12.1 and its first two lags. Assume that the series is in C22 and issue the following commands:

```
NAME C22 'METAL.EX' C23 'LAG1.MET' C24 'LAG2.MET'
LAG C22 PUT IN C23
LAG C23 PUT IN C24
PRINT C22-C24
PLOT C22 VS C23
PLOT C22 VS C24
```

The output is in Exhibit 12.7. The asterisks in rows 1 and 2 of C24 denote the missing data that result from the double lag. The scatterplot of 'METAL.EX' versus 'LAG1.MET' suggests some positive correlation between exports in the current year and in the previous year. (The "N* = 1" at the bottom of the plot reminds us of the one missing observation in column C23.) The scatterplot of 'METAL.EX' versus 'LAG2.MET' suggests no substantial correlation between exports in the current year and year before last. (The "N* = 2" of the bottom of the plot reminds us of the two missing observations in column C24.)

We obtain quantitative measures of these relationships by using the ACF command. (ACF stands for autocorrelation function.) To get the correlation between metal exports at lags 1 through 10, we issue

```
ACF 10 LAGS OF C2
```

The output is in Exhibit 12.8. The lag 1 autocorrelation coefficient is 0.472, the lag 2 coefficient is 0.105, and so on. Only the autocorrelation coefficient at lag 1 is substantial.

PARTIAL AUTOCORRELATION

Another measure of linear relation is partial autocorrelation. The partial autocorrelation function (PACF) is used to help analysts pinpoint the nature of the process underlying a set of data. You may consult the references for material on how to use the PACF. Here we simply note that Minitab can calculate it.

ACF [with up to K lags] for series in C [put in C]

Computes autocorrelations of the time series stored in the column and prints a graph. If the number of lags is not specified, sqrt(n) + 10 are computed, where n = length of the series.

EXHIBIT 12.7   Metal Exports and Two Lags

```
NAME C23 'LAG1.MET' C24 'LAG2.MET'
LAG C22 PUT IN C23
LAG C23 PUT IN C24
PRINT C22-C24
 ROW    METAL.EX   LAG1.MET   LAG2.MET

   1      3.89         *          *
   2      2.41       3.89         *
   3      2.80       2.41       3.89
   4      8.72       2.80       2.41
   5      7.12       8.72       2.80
   6      7.24       7.12       8.72
   7      7.15       7.24       7.12
   8      6.05       7.15       7.24
   9      5.21       6.05       7.15
  10      5.03       5.21       6.05
  11      6.88       5.03       5.21
  12      4.70       6.88       5.03
  13      5.06       4.70       6.88
  14      3.16       5.06       4.70
  15      3.62       3.16       5.06
  16      4.55       3.62       3.16
  17      2.43       4.55       3.62
  18      3.16       2.43       4.55
  19      4.55       3.16       2.43
  20      5.17       4.55       3.16
  21      6.95       5.17       4.55
  22      3.46       6.95       5.17
  23      2.13       3.46       6.95
  24      3.47       2.13       3.46
  25      2.79       3.47       2.13
  26      2.52       2.79       3.47
  27      2.80       2.52       2.79
  28      4.04       2.80       2.52
  29      3.08       4.04       2.80
  30      2.26       3.08       4.04
  31      2.17       2.26       3.08
  32      2.78       2.17       2.26
  33      5.94       2.78       2.17
  34      8.14       5.94       2.78
  35      3.55       8.14       5.94
  36      3.61       3.55       8.14
  37      5.06       3.61       3.55
  38      7.13       5.06       3.61
  39      4.15       7.13       5.06
  40      3.86       4.15       7.13
  41      3.22       3.86       4.15
  42      3.50       3.22       3.86
  43      3.76       3.50       3.22
  44      5.11       3.76       3.50
```

EXHIBIT 12.7 *Continued*

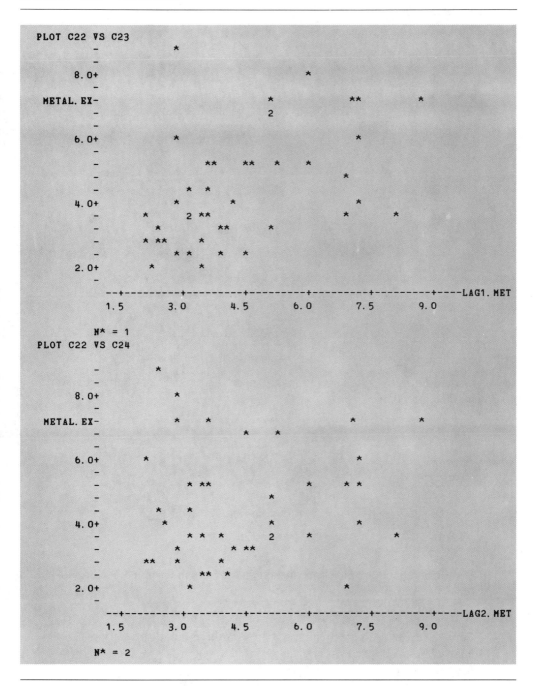

EXHIBIT 12.8   Output from ACF Applied to Metal Exports

```
ACF 10 LAGS OF C22

 ACF of METAL. EX

                  -1.0 -0.8 -0.6 -0.4 -0.2  0.0  0.2  0.4  0.6  0.8  1.0
                  +----+----+----+----+----+----+----+----+----+----+
   1     0.472                             XXXXXXXXXXXX
   2     0.105                             XXXX
   3     0.045                             XX
   4     0.103                             XXXX
   5     0.099                             XXX
   6     0.008                             X
   7    -0.053                           XX
   8    -0.100                          XXX
   9    -0.083                          XXX
  10    -0.085                          XXX
```

PACF [up to K lags] for series in C [put in C]

Computes partial autocorrelations and prints a graph. The output is similar to that for ACF.

EXERCISES

12–9 For the rates of return on Xerox common stock on page 278, compute
  (a)   the ACF;
  (b)   the PACF.

12–10 For the percentage changes in constant dollar GNP in Exhibit 3.6, compute
  (a)   the ACF;
  (b)   the PACF.

12–11 For the series of quarterly interest rates on three-month treasury bills on page 278, and the first differences series, compute
  (a)   the ACF;
  (b)   the PACF.

12–12 For the metal export series in this section, compute the PACF.

12.3 / IDENTIFYING, FITTING, AND CHECKING NONSEASONAL ARIMA MODELS

This section presupposes a knowledge of ARIMA models and the modeling and forecasting framework due to Box and Jenkins. If you are not familiar with them, you will need to consult the references for the necessary background information. In this section we will develop ARIMA models for the metal export and birth rate series and compute some forecasts.

IDENTIFICATION

The first step in model selection is to match sample ACFs and PACFs with the known theoretical patterns in order to limit the number of models that need to be fitted to the data. We will discuss ACFs here. If you compute PACFs, then you can take those into account, too. We have suggested that the metal export series is stationary and needs no differencing. The ACF in Exhibit 12.8 signals an MA(1) model. This model will be estimated in a moment.

We have suggested that the first difference of the birth rate series is stationary. The ACFs of the birth rates and their first differences are shown in Exhibit 12.9. The ACF of the birth rates fails to die out exponentially, and the ACF of the first differences could be signaling an AR(1) model. This model will be estimated in a moment.

ESTIMATION

The suggested model for metal exports is MA(1) or ARIMA with $p = 0$, $d = 0$, and $q = 1$. We will encode this as ARIMA(0, 0, 1). The general code is ARIMA(p, d, q). The model is estimated with the ARIMA command.

ARIMA   p = K, d = K, q = K, data in C [put residuals
        in C [put predicted values in C]]

The ARIMA command fits models to a time series. The input to the command consists of a time series stored in a column and information about the model to be fitted. In addition to the printed output, results may be stored in the worksheet for further analysis.

Assuming that the metal exports series is in C22, we issue the commands

```
ARIMA 0 0 1 C22 C23 C24
NAME C23 'RESIDUAL' C24 'FIT'
```

EXHIBIT 12.9   ACFs of Birth Rates and Their First Differences

```
ACF C1

  ACF BIRTH.RT

             -1.0 -0.8 -0.6 -0.4 -0.2  0.0  0.2  0.4  0.6  0.8  1.0
             +----+----+----+----+----+----+----+----+----+----+
    1   0.959                          XXXXXXXXXXXXXXXXXXXXXXXXX
    2   0.899                          XXXXXXXXXXXXXXXXXXXXXXXX
    3   0.826                          XXXXXXXXXXXXXXXXXXXXXX
    4   0.739                          XXXXXXXXXXXXXXXXXXX
    5   0.641                          XXXXXXXXXXXXXXXX
    6   0.535                          XXXXXXXXXXXXX
    7   0.419                          XXXXXXXXXX
    8   0.298                          XXXXXXXX
    9   0.174                          XXXX
   10   0.051                          XX
   11  -0.064                        XXX
   12  -0.157                       XXXX
   13  -0.233                     XXXXXX
   14  -0.306                    XXXXXXXX
   15  -0.371                   XXXXXXXXX

  ACF C6

  ACF of DIFFBR

             -1.0 -0.8 -0.6 -0.4 -0.2  0.0  0.2  0.4  0.6  0.8  1.0
             +----+----+----+----+----+----+----+----+----+----+
    1   0.591                          XXXXXXXXXXXXXXX
    2   0.475                          XXXXXXXXXXXXX
    3   0.360                          XXXXXXXXXX
    4   0.166                          XXXXX
    5   0.233                          XXXXXX
    6   0.102                          XXXX
    7   0.094                          XXX
    8  -0.007                         X
    9  -0.133                        XXXX
   10  -0.151                       XXXX
   11  -0.372                   XXXXXXXXX
   12  -0.325                    XXXXXXXX
   13  -0.235                     XXXXXX
   14  -0.344                   XXXXXXXXX
   15  -0.268                    XXXXXXX
```

EXHIBIT 12.10   Output from the ARIMA(0, 0, 1) Command Applied to
Metal Exports

```
ARIMA 0 0 1 C22 C23 C24


Final Estimates of Parameters
Type        Estimate     St. Dev.    t-ratio
MA    1      -0.5008      0.1348      -3.71
Constant     4.4244      0.3506      12.62
Mean         4.4244      0.3506

No. of obs.:   44
Residuals:     SS = 101.291   (backforecasts excluded)
               MS =   2.412  DF = 42

Modified Box-Pierce chisquare statistic
Lag                12              24              36              48
Chisquare    3.2(DF=11)    14.0(DF=23)    27.9(DF=35)    * (DF= *)
```

The output is in Exhibit 12.10. The parameters of time series models are estimated by an iterative nonlinear least squares estimation routine. The method of backforecasting is used to avoid the inefficient estimates produced by the so-called conditional least squares estimation method. Minitab prints only the final estimates—that is, the ones that are produced after the estimation procedure converges. They are printed as -0.05008 and 4.4244, yielding a residual sum of squares (SS) of 101.291 and a residual mean square of 2.412. These estimates, along with approximate standard errors and t-ratios, are also printed. For moving average models the "CONSTANT" and "MEAN" are equal. Both the moving average parameter and the mean have significant t-ratios.

The degrees of freedom (DF) of 42 are 2 less than the number of observations, 44, because two parameters were estimated: the MA parameter and the mean. The residual mean square is $MS = SS/DF = 101.291/42 = 2.412$. The square root of this number, $\sqrt{2.412} = 1.553$, is an estimate of the error standard deviation.

The last part of the output is a table showing several values of the "Modified Box-Pierce chi-square statistic" (sometimes referred to as the Box-Ljung statistic). This statistic is a function of the residual autocorrelations and is designed to test the hypothesis that the theoretical autocorrelation function of the *noise* of the fitted model is equal to zero at all lags except lag zero. In Exhibit 12.10 the value of the statistic is reported for three lags: 12, 24, and 36. (For longer time series, Minitab also reports a statistic for lag 48, but the metal exports series is not long enough.) Notice that the degrees of freedom (DF) are always one less that the number of lags. The number of degrees of freedom depends on the number of lags and the number of parameters in the model. In this example, one degree of freedom is subtracted from the number of lags to account for the estimation of the moving average parameter.

The modified Box-Pierce statistic for lag 12 is a function of the residual autocorrelations at lags 1 through 12. The value of the statistic is compared to an appropriate critical value of the chi-square statistic with 11 degrees of freedom. For example, if the null hypothesis is tested at the 1% level, the critical chi-square value obtained from a chi-square table, or from Minitab's CDF command, is 24.72. Since the value of the statistic in the output, 3.2, is less than 24.72, the test does not reject the hypothesis of uncorrelated errors at the 1% significance level. For lags 24 and 36 the values of the statistic are likewise less than the tabled critical values at the usual significance levels, so we have no evidence against the null hypothesis of uncorrelated errors in the fitted model.

Now let's fit the tentatively identified model to the birth rates. The model form is ARIMA(1, 1, 0). Assuming that the birth rates are in C1, we issue the commands

```
ARIMA 1 1 0 C1 C3 C4
NAME C3 'RESIDUAL' C4 'FIT'
```

Note that the command operates on the original series. The differencing is done by specifying $d = 1$. The output is in Exhibit 12.11. No mean is estimated in Exhibit 12.11 because differencing removes the mean. The order of differencing is reported above the residual sum of squares. All other items of output were discussed in connection with Exhibit 12.10. Note that one degree of freedom is deducted from 35 because of differencing and one because of estimating the autoregressive parameter.

CHECKING RESIDUALS

Residuals are checked for signs that some key model assumption or set of assumptions might be violated by the data. If such signs are present, then either the model must be modified to account for the observed behavior or the data must be modified to cause it to behave according to the model assumptions. In time series analysis, one is most concerned to discover evidence of variability in the series mean or the error variance and of residual autocorrelation. Variability in the mean or error variance can be modeled by additional differencing, by regression, or by modeling a transformation of the data such as the logarithm or square root. Residual autocorrelation can frequently be accounted for by adding autoregressive or moving average terms to the model, but this must be done with care. Mean and variance variability can cause significant autocorrelations to appear. For example, if a series needs differencing, its autocorrelation

EXHIBIT 12.11   Output from the ARIMA(1, 1, 0) Command Applied to
Birth Rates

```
ARIMA 1 1 0 C1 C3 C4


Final Estimates of Parameters
Type        Estimate      St. Dev.   t-ratio
AR   1        0.6219       0.1363      4.56

Differencing: 1 regular difference
No. of obs.:  Original series 35, after differencing 34
Residuals:    SS = 1790.99  (backforecasts excluded)
              MS =   54.27  DF = 33


Modified Box-Pierce chisquare statistic
Lag               12             24             36             48
Chisquare   16.3(DF=11)   25.3(DF=23)   * (DF= *)   * (DF= *)
```

function will have many "significant" lags, and outliers can also cause "significant" autocorrelations. Such autocorrelations are not well modeled by autoregressive and moving average parameters. Standard residual checks include time series plots, histograms, autocorrelation functions, and functions of autocorrelations such as the modified Box-Pierce statistic.

Exhibit 12.12 shows a listing, a histogram, and an autocorrelation function of the residuals from the model fit in Exhibit 12.10 (the time series plot is left as an exercise). The standardized residuals were formed by the command

```
LET C4 = C2/SQRT(2.412)
```

where 2.412 is the estimate of the error variance read from Exhibit 12.10. The output suggests that the observation at time period 4 is an outlier. The residual autocorrelation function displays no significant spikes, so it does not suggest fitting a more elaborate model. In Exercise 12–14 you are asked to examine the residuals from the model fitted in Exhibit 12.11 to the birth rates.

FORECASTING

In this subsection we treat the models fitted above as adequate and show how to produce point and interval forecasts. Forecasts are computed with a subcommand of ARIMA. Refer to page 249.

EXHIBIT 12.12   Residual Analysis of Model Fit in Exhibit 12.10

```
LET C25=C23/SQRT( 2. 412)
NAME C25 'ST. RES'
PRINT C22 C23 C24 C25
  ROW  METAL. EX  RESIDUAL       FIT   ST. RES

    1     3.89   -0. 44488   4. 33488  -0. 28646
    2     2.41   -1. 79163   4. 20163  -1. 15361
    3     2.80   -0. 72720   3. 52720  -0. 46824
    4     8.72    4. 65975   4. 06025   3. 00036
    5     7.12    0. 36205   6. 75795   0. 23312
    6     7.24    2. 63427   4. 60573   1. 69618
    7     7.15    1. 40638   5. 74362   0. 90555
    8     6.05    0. 92129   5. 12871   0. 59321
    9     5.21    0. 32421   4. 88579   0. 20876
   10     5.03    0. 44322   4. 58678   0. 28538
   11     6.88    2. 23362   4. 64638   1. 43821
   12     4.70   -0. 84298   5. 54298  -0. 54279
   13     5.06    1. 05773   4. 00227   0. 68106
   14     3.16   -1. 79412   4. 95412  -1. 15521
   15     3.62    0. 09404   3. 52596   0. 06055
   16     4.55    0. 07848   4. 47152   0. 05053
   17     2.43   -2. 03372   4. 46373  -1. 30949
   18     3.16   -0. 24597   3. 40597  -0. 15837
   19     4.55    0. 24875   4. 30125   0. 16017
   20     5.17    0. 62101   4. 54899   0. 39986
   21     6.95    2. 21459   4. 73541   1. 42595
   22     3.46   -2. 07345   5. 53345  -1. 33507
   23     2.13   -1. 25607   3. 38607  -0. 80877
   24     3.47   -0. 32540   3. 79540  -0. 20952
   25     2.79   -1. 47147   4. 26147  -0. 94746
   26     2.52   -1. 16754   3. 68754  -0. 75176
   27     2.80   -1. 03974   3. 83974  -0. 66948
   28     4.04    0. 13626   3. 90374   0. 08774
   29     3.08   -1. 41266   4. 49266  -0. 90960
   30     2.26   -1. 45698   3. 71698  -0. 93814
   31     2.17   -1. 52479   3. 69479  -0. 98179
   32     2.78   -0. 88083   3. 66083  -0. 56716
   33     5.94    1. 95669   3. 98331   1. 25989
   34     8.14    2. 73570   5. 40430   1. 76149
   35     3.55   -2. 24442   5. 79442  -1. 44516
   36     3.61    0. 30955   3. 30045   0. 19931
   37     5.06    0. 48056   4. 57944   0. 30943
   38     7.13    2. 46492   4. 66508   1. 58714
   39     4.15   -1. 50881   5. 65881  -0. 97151
   40     3.86    0. 19117   3. 66883   0. 12309
   41     3.22   -1. 30016   4. 52015  -0. 83716
   42     3.50   -0. 27333   3. 77333  -0. 17599
   43     3.76   -0. 52754   4. 28754  -0. 33968
   44     5.11    0. 94976   4. 16024   0. 61154
```

EXHIBIT 12.12   *Continued*

```
HIST C23

Histogram of RESIDUAL    N = 44

Midpoint    Count
    -2         7    *******
    -1        11    ***********
     0        14    **************
     1         5    *****
     2         4    ****
     3         2    **
     4         0
     5         1    *

ACF 10 C23

ACF of RESIDUAL

             -1.0 -0.8 -0.6 -0.4 -0.2  0.0  0.2  0.4  0.6  0.8  1.0
             +----+----+----+----+----+----+----+----+----+----+
    1    0.057                             XX
    2    0.093                             XXX
    3   -0.025                             XX
    4    0.084                             XXX
    5    0.078                             XXX
    6   -0.019                             X
    7   -0.004                             X
    8   -0.078                             XXX
    9   -0.053                             XX
   10   -0.010                             X
```

ARIMA   p = K, d = K, q = K, data in C [put residuals
        in C [put predicted values in C]]

FORECASTS [forecast origin = K] up to K leads ahead
        [store forecasts in C [confidence limits in C and C]]

Minitab prints out minimum mean squared error point forecasts and 95% prediction error limits. These quantities can be stored for plotting and other manipulations.

To illustrate, suppose that the metal export series in Exhibit 12.1 is in C22 and the following command is issued.

```
ARIMA 0 0 1 C22;
   FORECAST 8 OBSERVATIONS.
```

EXHIBIT 12.13   Forecasts of Metal Exports

```
ARIMA O O 1 C22;
  FORECAST 8 OBSERVATIONS.


Final Estimates of Parameters
Type        Estimate    St. Dev.    t-ratio
MA    1      -0.5008      0.1348      -3.71
Constant      4.4244      0.3506      12.62
Mean          4.4244      0.3506

No. of obs.:   44
Residuals:    SS = 101.291  (backforecasts excluded)
              MS =   2.412   DF = 42

Modified Box-Pierce chisquare statistic
Lag                  12           24           36              48
Chisquare    3.2(DF=11)   14.0(DF=23)   27.9(DF=35)    *(DF= *)


Forecasts from period 44
                           95 Percent Limits
Period      Forecast      Lower       Upper       Actual
  45         4.90005      1.85563     7.94446
  46         4.42442      1.01959     7.82925
  47         4.42442      1.01959     7.82925
  48         4.42442      1.01959     7.82925
  49         4.42442      1.01959     7.82925
  50         4.42442      1.01959     7.82925
  51         4.42442      1.01959     7.82925
  52         4.42442      1.01959     7.82925
```

Part of the resulting output is shown in Exhibit 12.13. The forecast origin is time period 44, the last for which data are available. For each period in the future a point forecast and 95% forecast limits are reported. Thus the model predicts that in 1981 there is a 95% chance that iron and steel exports weigh between 1.37 and 7.47 million tons, in 1982 there is a 95% chance that iron and steel exports weigh between 1.02 and 7.83 million tons, and so forth. If a forecast origin prior to time period 44 had been specified in the FORECAST subcommand, the ACTUAL column would have contained the observed values through period 44.

Notice that for periods 46 through 52, the point forecasts are essentially the series mean 4.42, and the forecast limits are only slightly narrower than $\bar{x} \pm 2s$ limits, which are 0.9 and 7.9. Only the one-year-ahead forecast interval is a substantial improvement over $\bar{x} \pm 2s$. This is typical behavior for stationary models.

Let's turn to the birth rate series listed in Exhibit 12.1. Assuming that the birth rates are in C1, we compute and store ten forecasts with the commands

```
ARIMA 1 1 0 C1 C3 C4;
   FORE 10 PUT IN C15 C16 C17.
NAME C15 'FORECAST' C1 'BIRTH.RT'
```

The output is in Exhibit 12.14. Also shown is a plot of the series and the forecasts. This plot was created with the following commands:

```
LET K2 = 2*SQRT(54.27)
LET C31 = C1-K2
LET C32 = C1+K2
STACK (C31 C1 C32) ON (C16 C15 C17) PUT IN (C31 C1 C32)
MTSPLOT C1 C31 C32
```

EXHIBIT 12.14   Forecasts of Birth Rates

```
ARIMA 1 1 0 C1 C3 C4;
   FORE 10 PUT IN C15 C16 C17.


Final Estimates of Parameters
Type        Estimate       St. Dev.    t-ratio
AR    1       0.6219        0.1363        4.56

Differencing: 1 regular difference
No. of obs.:  Original series 35, after differencing 34
Residuals:    SS = 1790.99  (backforecasts excluded)
              MS =   54.27  DF = 33

Modified Box-Pierce chisquare statistic
Lag                 12              24            36            48
Chisquare   16.3(DF=11)   25.3(DF=23)    *(DF= *)      *(DF= *)

Forecasts from period 35
                            95 Percent Limits
Period        Forecast        Lower         Upper       Actual
  36          110.989        96.547       125.431
  37          110.796        83.278       138.313
  38          110.675        70.692       150.659
  39          110.601        59.087       162.115
  40          110.554        48.476       172.632
  41          110.525        38.773       182.278
  42          110.507        29.859       191.155
  43          110.496        21.624       199.368
  44          110.489        13.967       207.011
  45          110.485         6.802       214.167
```

(continues)

EXHIBIT 12.14   *Continued*

```
NAME C15 'FORECAST'
LET K2=2*SQRT(54.27)
LET C31=C1-K2
LET C32=C1+K2
STACK (C31 C1 C32) ON (C16 C15 C17) PUT IN (C31 C1 C32)
NAME C31 'LO' C32 'HI'
MTSPLOT C1 C31 C32


 BIRTH. RT-
         -              ZZZ Z
         -             Z+012Z4Z
     240+          ZZ8YYYY3Y5Z
         -       ZZ6+Y     Y Y6Z
         - ZZZ45Y             Y+Z                           ZZ
         - 123YY              8ZZ                      ZZ
         - YYY                Y90ZZZ                 ZZ
     160+                     YY123Z              Z
         -                    YYY4Z            ZZ
         -                   Y5ZZZZZZZZZZZZ
         -                   Y+78901234567890123456789012345
         -                   YYYYYYYYYY
      80+                            Y
         -                           YY
         -                            Y
         -                             YY
         -                              YY
       0+                              Y
         +---------+---------+---------+---------+---------+
         0        10        20        30        40        50
         Y = LO           Z = HI
```

The first command stores twice the estimated error standard deviation in K2. The next two commands place two standard error limits around each observation into C31 and C32. (The intervals so formed are reminders of the "noise" present in each observation.) The next command stacks the actual observations and their error limits on top of the point forecasts and the 95% forecast limits. The last command produces the plot. The forecast intervals expand rapidly as the forecast lead time increases. This is typical of nonstationary models.

The one-year-ahead 95% forecast interval is (96.5, 125.4). Compare this with the interval (90.7, 127.1) quoted at the end of Section 12.1. The interval in Section 12.1 was created without taking the autocorrelation in the differenced birth rates into account. The interval in Exhibit 12.14 is narrower because it flows from a model that takes the autocorrelation into account.

Another version of the plot in Exhibit 12.14 does not put the one-step-ahead error bounds around the observed values. After the ARIMA and NAME commands on page 251 are issued, the command

```
MTSPLOT C1 C15 C16 C17;
   ORIGIN 1981 FOR C15-C17.
```

produces the plot.

EXERCISES

12–13 Make a time series plot of the residuals from the fit in Exhibit 12.10.

12–14 Analyze the residuals from the fit in Exhibit 12.11.

12–15 Use the command at the end of this section to produce the suggested time series plot.

12–16 Model and forecast the logarithms of the constant dollar GNP series in Exhibit 3.6. Convert your forecasts to forecasts of GNP.

12.4 / SEASONALITY

Seasonality means roughly periodic behavior in a time series. For example, each year the numbers of housing starts in the spring and early summer months are relatively high, whereas the numbers are relatively low in the fall and winter months. Because such a pattern is predictable, it can be modeled and forecasted.

In Section 4.4, Exhibit 4.9, we noted a seasonal pattern in the money supply measure M1. The money supply tends to be lowest in February and highest in December; and it tends to rise steadily from February to December except for downturns in May and August.

We also see from the yearly averages in Exhibit 4.9 that M1 has a strong upward trend. As we noted in Section 12.1, it is useful to look at the *changes* in trending series. Of course, seasonality in the series will be converted to seasonality in the changes. To see this, let's compute and tabulate the monthly changes in M1. The M1 values are in C3, year designations in C4, and month designations in C5. The commands

```
DIFF C3   C13 #Compute Changes
NAME C13 'DM1.NSA'
OUTPUTWIDTH 132
TABLE C4 C5;
   MEAN C13.
```

produce the table in Exhibit 12.15. The command OUTPUTWIDTH 132 was used to display the complete table in one panel. The row labeled "ALL" at the bottom of the table contains the average monthly changes.

EXHIBIT 12.15   Changes in the U.S. Money Supply by Month and by Year, with Monthly and
Yearly Averages, 1970 –1984

TABLE C4 C5;
MEAN C13.

ROWS: YEAR   COLUMNS: MONTH

	1	2	3	4	5	6	7	8	9	10	11	12	ALL
70	--	-8.9000	1.5000	4.6000	-3.9000	2.7000	1.2000	-0.1000	2.8000	1.6000	2.3000	5.5000	0.8455
71	0.4000	-6.0000	2.0000	5.1000	-2.6000	4.1000	2.3000	-1.6000	1.8000	1.4000	2.1000	5.7000	1.2250
72	0.6000	-6.1000	2.8000	5.3000	-4.8000	4.1000	3.0000	-0.5000	3.2000	2.5000	3.5000	8.4000	1.8333
73	0.5000	-8.2000	0.4000	5.4000	-3.4000	5.7000	1.9000	-2.6000	0.9000	1.9000	4.3000	7.6000	1.2000
74	-1.5000	-7.7000	2.4000	5.1000	-5.3000	5.2000	2.0000	-2.5000	1.6000	2.2000	4.0000	6.4000	0.9917
75	-3.4000	-8.5000	3.1000	5.0000	-3.3000	7.9000	2.0000	-1.7000	1.5000	0.7000	5.0000	5.5000	1.1500
76	-2.2000	-7.8000	2.4000	8.5000	-4.8000	4.3000	2.9000	-1.3000	1.5000	4.5000	2.7000	8.9000	1.6333
77	-0.9000	-8.7000	3.2000	10.5000	-7.1000	6.1000	4.6000	-2.0000	3.4000	4.3000	3.4000	8.7000	2.1250
78	-0.7000	-11.4000	2.9000	12.6000	-5.1000	7.0000	4.5000	-2.2000	5.3000	2.4000	3.5000	9.6000	2.3667
79	-4.7000	-11.4000	4.4000	15.4000	-9.1000	9.6000	6.6000	-1.4000	3.7000	2.1000	2.1000	8.8000	2.1750
80	-2.5000	-9.8000	1.5000	4.8000	-9.3000	9.8000	7.4000	3.8000	6.8000	6.2000	4.0000	3.5000	2.1833
81	-3.0000	-11.2000	6.7000	19.0000	-12.8000	4.3000	5.0000	-1.9000	1.4000	2.8000	5.3000	11.8000	2.2833
82	2.1000	-16.4000	3.0000	15.4000	-10.2000	5.2000	3.5000	0.1000	6.5000	9.9000	8.6000	11.9000	3.3000
83	-2.2000	-9.1000	8.7000	16.1000	-4.6000	9.3000	7.4000	-2.7000	3.1000	6.2000	4.5000	11.2000	3.9917
84	-2.9000	-12.9000	6.5000	15.2000	-8.3000	10.6000	2.0000	-4.9000	3.5000	-0.3000	7.7000	14.5000	2.5583
ALL	-1.4571	-9.6067	3.4333	9.8667	-6.3067	6.3933	3.7533	-1.4333	3.1333	3.2267	4.2000	8.5333	1.9972

CELL CONTENTS —
DM1.NSA:MEAN

EXHIBIT 12.16 Time Series Plot of Monthly Changes in Money Supply
Series M1, 1970 –1984

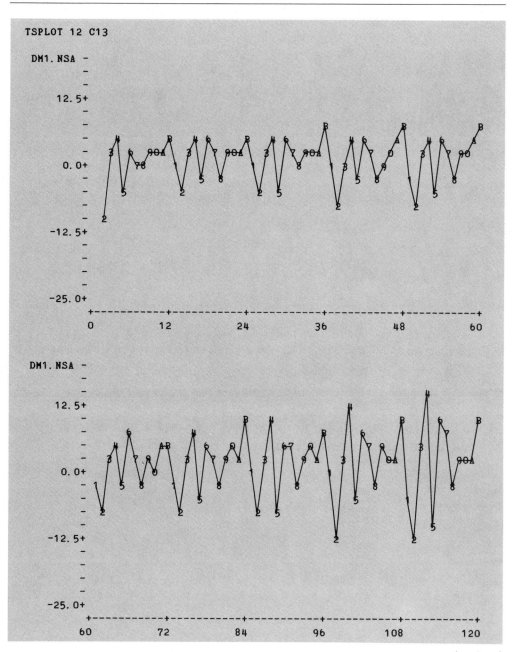

(continues)

EXHIBIT 12.16 *Continued*

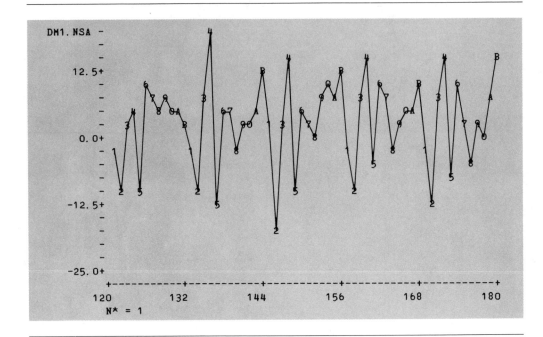

We see the downward movement from December to January and from January to February. Then the changes are positive except for May and August. The seasonal pattern can also be seen graphically by issuing the command

```
TSPLOT 12 C13
```

The output is in Exhibit 12.16. The 4s and Bs symbolize April and December, the 2s and 5s February and May. These months account for the extremes in every year except a couple in which June exhibits a large positive change.

EXERCISES

12–17 Continue the example in this section by issuing the commands

```
DIFF 12 C13 C14
NAME C14 'DD12M1'
TABLE C4 C5;
   MEAN C14.
TSPLOT 12 C14
```

C14 contains the annual changes in the monthly changes. Do you see any evidence of seasonality in this series?

12–18 The plot in Exhibit 12.16 suggests that the variability in M1 has increased over time. The column labeled "ALL" in Exhibit 12.15 suggests that the average monthly change in M1 has also tended to increase over time. The increasing variability with increasing level signals the need for a transformation to stabilize the variability. Economists usually use the logarithmic transformation in their analyses. Create a column of natural logarithms of M1 and analyze these values for trend, seasonality, and stable variance.

12–19 Analyze the quarterly M1 data on page 274 for trend, seasonality, and variance stability.

12–20 Analyze the quarterly GNP data on page 274 for trend, seasonality, and variance stability. Note that these data are seasonally adjusted.

12–21 Analyze the quarterly three-month treasury bill rates on page 274 for trend, seasonality, and variance stability. Note that these data are not seasonally adjusted.

12.5 / IDENTIFYING, FITTING, CHECKING, AND FORECASTING SEASONAL ARIMA MODELS

The only new item introduced in this section is the seasonal form of the ARIMA command, so the presentation is quite brief.

```
ARIMA   p = K, d = K, q = K, [P = K, D = K, Q = K]
        data in C [put residuals in C [put predicted
        values in C [put estimated parameters in C]]]

FORECASTS [forecast origin = K] up to K leads ahead
        [store forecasts in C [confidence limits in C and C]]
```

Continuing the analysis of monthly M1 begun in Section 12.4, we look at the ACF of the first differences in C13:

```
ACF 36 LAGS OF C13
```

The output is in Exhibit 12.17. The big spikes at lags 12, 24, and 36 indicate a need for seasonal differencing. This is accomplished with the commands

```
DIFF 12 C13 PUT IN C14
NAME C14 'DD12M1'
ACF 36 LAGS OF C14
```

The output is in Exhibit 12.18.

EXHIBIT 12.17   Sample Autocorrelation Function of Changes in Monthly
                    Money Supply

```
ACF 36 LAGS OF C13

 ACF of DM1.NSA

              -1.0 -0.8 -0.6 -0.4 -0.2  0.0  0.2  0.4  0.6  0.8  1.0
              +----+----+----+----+----+----+----+----+----+----+
    1  -0.144                          XXXX
    2  -0.400                    XXXXXXXXXX
    3   0.271                              XXXXXXX
    4  -0.102                          XXXX
    5  -0.115                          XXXX
    6   0.274                              XXXXXXX
    7  -0.134                          XXXX
    8  -0.019                          X
    9   0.260                              XXXXXX
   10  -0.417                   XXXXXXXXXXX
   11  -0.159                         XXXX
   12   0.814                              XXXXXXXXXXXXXXXXXXXXX
   13  -0.168                         XXXX
   14  -0.343                    XXXXXXXXXX
   15   0.255                              XXXXXX
   16  -0.076                          XXX
   17  -0.106                         XXXX
   18   0.249                              XXXXXX
   19  -0.113                          XXXX
   20  -0.040                          XX
   21   0.215                              XXXXX
   22  -0.376                    XXXXXXXXXX
   23  -0.142                         XXXX
   24   0.764                              XXXXXXXXXXXXXXXXXXX
   25  -0.152                         XXXX
   26  -0.317                    XXXXXXXXX
   27   0.255                              XXXXXX
   28  -0.053                          XX
   29  -0.103                         XXXX
   30   0.204                              XXXXX
   31  -0.125                         XXXX
   32  -0.041                          XX
   33   0.202                              XXXXX
   34  -0.335                    XXXXXXXXX
   35  -0.138                         XXXX
   36   0.676                              XXXXXXXXXXXXXXXXX
```

EXHIBIT 12.18   Sample Autocorrelation Function of Annual Changes in Monthly Changes of Money Supply

```
DIFF 12 C13 PUT IN C14
NAME C14 'DD12M1'
ACF 36 LAGS OF C14

 ACF of DD12M1

            -1.0 -0.8 -0.6 -0.4 -0.2  0.0  0.2  0.4  0.6  0.8  1.0
            +----+----+----+----+----+----+----+----+----+----+
   1   0.261                             XXXXXXX
   2  -0.074                          XXX
   3  -0.067                          XXX
   4  -0.183                        XXXXX
   5   0.009                             X
   6  -0.007                             X
   7  -0.017                             X
   8   0.225                             XXXXXX
   9   0.191                             XXXXX
  10  -0.025                            XX
  11  -0.153                         XXXXX
  12  -0.485              XXXXXXXXXXXXX
  13  -0.195                        XXXXX
  14   0.080                             XXX
  15   0.007                             X
  16  -0.016                             X
  17   0.009                             X
  18   0.084                             XXX
  19   0.013                             X
  20  -0.175                         XXXXX
  21  -0.180                         XXXXX
  22  -0.039                            XX
  23   0.030                             XX
  24   0.098                             XXX
  25   0.114                             XXXX
  26   0.046                             XX
  27   0.047                             XX
  28   0.069                             XXX
  29  -0.032                            XX
  30  -0.031                            XX
  31  -0.050                            XX
  32   0.051                             XX
  33   0.088                             XXX
  34  -0.031                            XX
  35  -0.007                             X
  36  -0.044                            XX
```

The ACF pattern suggests a multiplicative seasonal model with a lag 1 moving average and a lag 12 moving average. Thus the identified model is ARIMA$(0, 1, 1) \times (0, 1, 1)$12. The model is fitted and the residual ACF computed with the commands

```
ARIMA 0 1 1 0 1 1 12 C3 C6
NAME C6 'RESIDUAL'
ACF 24 C6
```

The output is in Exhibit 12.19. The modified Box-Pierce statistic at lag 12 has a value of 24.3. Note that we are to compare this value to a critical value of a chi-square with 10 degrees of freedom. We get $10 = 12 - 1 - 1$ because we deduct one degree of freedom from the lag for each moving average parameter. The 1% critical value of a chi-square with 10 degrees of freedom is 23.21. Since 24.3 is greater than this critical value, we reject the hypothesis that the noise of the fitted model is not autocorrelated.

In the residual autocorrelation function in Exhibit 12.19 there is a hint of residual autocorrelation at lag 4. Thus we might wish to fit a model of the form ARIMA$(0, 1, 1) \times (0, 0, 1)4 \times (0, 1, 1)$12 to M1. Minitab does not permit more than one multiplicative factor, but we can approximate this model with an ARIMA$(0, 1, 4) \times (0, 1, 1)$12:

```
ARIMA 0 1 4 0 1 1 4 C3 C6;
  FORE 24 C8 C9 C10.
ACF 12 C6
SET C11
  (1:24)
END
NAME C8 'FORECAST' C11 'LEADTIME'
MPLOT C8 C11 C9 C11 C10 C11
```

The output is in Exhibit 12.20. The residual ACF shows no inadequacy, and the forecasts show an appropriate trend and seasonal pattern. For practical purposes this model is quite acceptable, even though the *t*-ratios on the second, third, and fourth MA parameters are somewhat low.

EXERCISES

12–22 Model the natural logarithms of the money supply values analyzed in this section. Don't forget to transform the forecasts from log scale back to the original scale of M1.

12–23 Model the labor force figures given on page 285 for the period 1970–1979. Forecast values for 1980 and 1981 and compare the forecasted and actual values.

12–24 Model the quarterly three-month treasury bill rates on page 285.

EXHIBIT 12.19   Fit of an ARIMA(0, 1, 1) × (0, 1, 1)12 Model to
Monthly Money Supply, 1970 –1984

```
ARIMA 0 1 1 0 1 1 12 C3 C6


Final Estimates of Parameters
Type        Estimate      St. Dev.   t-ratio
MA    1      -0.3014       0.0742     -4.06
SMA  12       0.5803       0.0683      8.50

Differencing: 1 regular, 1 seasonal of order 12
No. of obs.:  Original series 180, after differencing 167
Residuals:    SS = 952.509  (backforecasts excluded)
              MS =   5.773  DF = 165

Modified Box-Pierce chisquare statistic
Lag              12            24            36            48
Chisquare   24.3(DF=10)   35.3(DF=22)   41.4(DF=34)   51.9(DF=46)

NAME C6 'RESIDUAL'
ACF 24 C6


ACF of RESIDUAL

             -1.0 -0.8 -0.6 -0.4 -0.2  0.0  0.2  0.4  0.6  0.8  1.0
             +----+----+----+----+----+----+----+----+----+----+
   1  -0.054                              XX
   2  -0.102                             XXXX
   3   0.075                              XXX
   4  -0.203                           XXXXXX
   5   0.024                              XX
   6   0.056                              XX
   7  -0.075                             XXX
   8   0.108                              XXXX
   9   0.154                              XXXXX
  10  -0.162                          XXXXX
  11  -0.029                             XX
  12  -0.077                            XXX
  13  -0.108                           XXXX
  14   0.103                              XXXX
  15  -0.010                             X
  16  -0.039                            XX
  17  -0.039                            XX
  18   0.092                              XXX
  19  -0.014                             X
  20  -0.089                            XXX
  21  -0.059                             XX
  22  -0.099                            XXX
  23  -0.024                             XX
  24   0.046                              XX
```

EXHIBIT 12.20   Fit of ARIMA(0, 1, 4) × (0, 1, 1)12 Model to Money Supply

```
NAME C6 'RESIDUAL'
ARIMA 0 1 4 0 1 1 12 C3 C6;
FORE 24 C8 C9 C10.

Final Estimates of Parameters
Type        Estimate      St. Dev.   t-ratio
MA    1      -0.2893       0.0783     -3.70
MA    2       0.1023       0.0820      1.25
MA    3      -0.0390       0.0822     -0.47
MA    4       0.1488       0.0812      1.83
SMA  12       0.5627       0.0711      7.91


Differencing: 1 regular, 1 seasonal of order 12
No. of obs.:  Original series 180, after differencing 167
Residuals:    SS = 903.646  (backforecasts excluded)
              MS =   5.578  DF = 162

Modified Box-Pierce chisquare statistic
Lag                   12            24            36            48
Chisquare    11.4(DF= 7)   23.6(DF=19)   33.1(DF=31)   42.6(DF=43)


Forecasts from period 180
                               95 Percent Limits
Period      Forecast        Lower         Upper        Actual
  181        568.546       563.916       573.176
  182        557.292       549.737       564.846
  183        563.074       553.731       572.416
  184        577.895       566.964       588.827
  185        569.923       557.907       581.938
  186        578.767       565.757       591.776
  187        582.946       569.013       596.879
  188        580.075       565.276       594.873
  189        583.883       568.266       599.499
  190        587.285       570.891       603.678
  191        593.701       576.566       610.837
  192        606.012       588.165       623.858
  193        604.067       584.892       623.242
  194        592.371       571.745       612.996
  195        598.379       576.469       620.289
  196        613.377       590.229       636.525
  197        605.404       581.171       629.637
  198        614.248       588.977       639.519
  199        618.428       592.160       644.696
  200        615.556       588.328       642.785
  201        619.364       591.208       647.521
  202        622.766       593.712       651.821
  203        629.183       599.257       659.109
  204        641.493       610.721       672.266
```

EXHIBIT 12.20   *Continued*

```
ACF 12 C6

 ACF of RESIDUAL

             -1.0 -0.8 -0.6 -0.4 -0.2  0.0  0.2  0.4  0.6  0.8  1.0
             +----+----+----+----+----+----+----+----+----+----+
   1  -0.018                            X
   2  -0.024                            XX
   3  -0.002                            X
   4  -0.040                            XX
   5  -0.003                            X
   6   0.043                            XX
   7  -0.067                           XXX
   8   0.106                            XXXX
   9   0.125                            XXXX
  10  -0.125                        XXXX
  11  -0.061                          XXX
  12  -0.092                          XXX

 NAME C8 'FORECAST' C11 'LEADTIME' C9 'LOWLIM' C10 'UPLIM'
 MPLOT C8 C11 C9 C11 C10 C11
```

```
         -                                                     C
   665+                                                      C
         -                                                  e
         -                                               e-e
         -                                            e-e
         -                                         e-e          A
   630+                                          e              A
         -                                    e-e              A
         -                              e-e  e       A  A A A A
         -                            e-e    A       A
         -                          e  A      A      A
   595+                          e-e-e      A     A A         B-B
         -                     e-C A     B-B      B-B    B  B
         -                 e-C A A A A A   B      B-B  B-B
         -              C-C-C       A B-B       B-B
         -           e-C     R-A B-B-B-B        B-B
   560+          G-C   A A   B
         -          B-B
         -
         +---------+---------+---------+---------+---------+------
          0.0       5.0      10.0      15.0      20.0      25.0
         A = FORECAST vs. LEADTIME    B = LOWLIM vs. LEADTIME
                    C = UPLIM vs. LEADTIME
```

12.6 / MULTIPLE SERIES AND CROSS-CORRELATION

We study relationships among series in hopes that a series or group of series may form a "leading indicator" of the behavior of a series of special interest. The cross-correlation function (CCF) is a tool that helps us infer relationships between two time series. To illustrate, consider the three series listed in Exhibit 12.21: seasonally adjusted quarterly M1, quarterly interest rates on three-month treasury bills, and seasonally adjusted

---

EXHIBIT 12.21 Quarterly Values of Seasonally Adjusted M1, Three-Month Treasury Bill Interest Rates, and Seasonally Adjusted GNP, with Marginal Averages

ROWS: YR	COLUMNS: QUARTER				
	1	2	3	4	ALL
70	207.00	208.53	210.57	214.90	210.25
	7.599	6.742	6.541	5.820	6.675
	972.0	986.3	1003.6	1009.0	992.7
71	218.03	222.60	227.07	229.60	224.33
	4.376	3.747	5.061	4.449	4.408
	1049.3	1068.9	1086.6	1105.8	1077.7
72	232.73	237.77	241.37	247.53	239.85
	3.535	3.698	3.982	4.715	3.983
	1142.4	1171.7	1196.1	1233.5	1185.9
73	253.83	255.87	260.30	262.30	258.08
	5.309	6.230	7.958	7.833	6.833
	1283.5	1307.6	1337.7	1376.7	1326.4
74	267.10	270.17	272.47	275.40	271.28
	7.393	8.215	8.214	7.731	7.888
	1387.7	1423.8	1451.6	1473.8	1434.2
75	277.63	280.77	287.13	289.73	283.82
	6.418	5.518	5.940	5.977	5.963
	1479.8	1516.7	1578.5	1621.8	1549.2
76	292.70	297.87	301.10	305.93	299.40
	5.106	5.037	5.291	4.938	5.093
	1672.0	1698.6	1729.0	1772.5	1718.0
77	313.00	319.30	324.33	330.97	321.90
	4.538	4.698	5.217	6.039	5.123
	1834.8	1895.1	1954.4	1988.9	1918.3

EXHIBIT 12.21 *Continued*

78	337.80	344.23	351.87	358.87	348.19
	6.323	6.352	6.939	8.252	6.966
	2031.7	2139.5	2202.5	2281.6	2163.8
79	363.53	370.60	380.80	386.90	375.46
	9.246	9.510	9.252	11.174	9.795
	2335.5	2377.9	2454.8	2502.9	2417.8
80	391.80	390.33	399.50	415.93	399.39
	12.307	12.893	8.127	11.930	11.314
	2572.9	2578.8	2639.1	2736.0	2631.7
81	417.13	427.90	430.83	435.60	427.87
	15.097	14.469	14.956	13.364	14.472
	2875.8	2918.0	3009.3	3027.9	2957.7
82	446.07	449.73	453.90	470.83	455.13
	12.373	12.487	11.009	7.996	10.966
	3026.0	3061.2	3080.1	3109.6	3069.2
83	485.10	500.27	514.37	523.57	505.83
	7.984	8.247	9.110	8.823	8.541
	3173.8	3267.0	3346.6	3431.7	3304.8
84	531.20	539.67	547.70	551.20	542.44
	8.973	9.677	10.187	9.723	9.640
	3553.3	3644.7	3694.6	3758.7	3662.8
ALL	335.64	341.04	346.89	353.28	344.21
	7.772	7.835	7.852	7.918	7.844
	2026.0	2070.4	2117.6	2162.0	2094.0

```
CELL CONTENTS --
          SA.M1:MEAN
      3MO.TBIL:MEAN
         SA.GNP:MEAN
```

quarterly GNP. These series are stored in the worksheet in C6, C7, and C9. The following commands compute the changes in the interest rates and GNP and cross-correlate the changes:

```
DIFF C7 PUT IN C17
DIFF C9 PUT IN C19
NAME C17 'DIFFTBIL' C19 'DIFFGNP'
CCF 10 LAGS OF C17 AND C19
```

The output is in Exhibit 12.22. The value of K ranges from -10 to $+10$. For negative values of K the CCF measures the correlation between

EXHIBIT 12.22   Cross-Correlation Function of Changes in Interest Rates and GNP

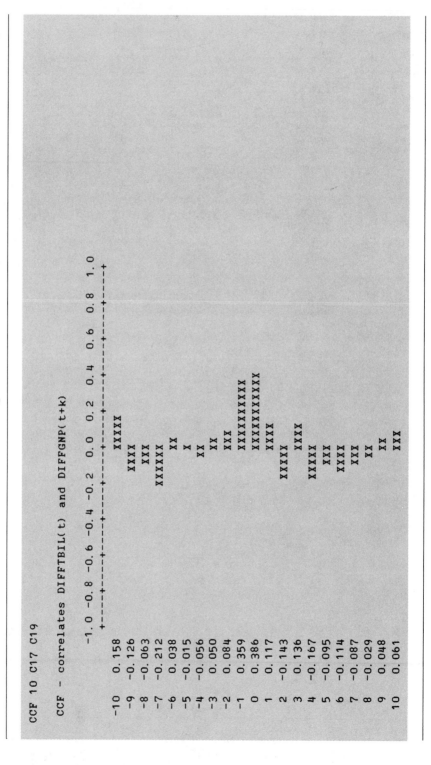

```
CCF 10 C17 C19

CCF - correlates DIFFTBIL(t) and DIFFGNP(t+k)

       -1.0 -0.8 -0.6 -0.4 -0.2  0.0  0.2  0.4  0.6  0.8  1.0
        +----+----+----+----+----+----+----+----+----+----+
-10   0.158                                XXXXX
 -9  -0.126                           XXXX
 -8  -0.063                            XXX
 -7  -0.212                         XXXXXX
 -6   0.038                                XX
 -5  -0.015                               X
 -4  -0.056                             XX
 -3   0.050                                XX
 -2   0.084                                XXX
 -1   0.359                                XXXXXXXXXX
  0   0.386                                XXXXXXXXXXX
  1   0.117                           XXXX XXXX
  2  -0.143                          XXXXX
  3   0.136                                XXXX
  4  -0.167                          XXXXX
  5  -0.095                            XXX
  6  -0.114                           XXXX
  7  -0.087                            XXX
  8  -0.029                              XX
  9   0.048                                XX
 10   0.061                                XXX
```

current interest rates and past GNP. For positive values of K the CCF measures the correlation between current GNP and past values of interest rates. For K equal to zero the CCF value measures the correlation between contemporaneous values of the two series. The largest correlations in Exhibit 12.21 are lags 0 and -1, indicating some relationship of current interest rates with current and past GNP.

EXERCISES

12–25 Cross-correlate the changes of M1 with the changes of GNP.

12–26 Cross-correlate the changes of M1 with the changes of the interest rates on three-month treasury bills.

12–27 Redo the analysis in this section after making logarithmic transformations of the series.

12.7 / OTHER FEATURES OF ARIMA

The full ARIMA command is described below.

ARIMA $p = K, d = K, q = K, [P = K, D = K, Q = K]$
 data in C [put residuals in C [put predicted
 values in C [put estimated parameters in C]]]

CONSTANT

NOCONSTANT

STARTING values in K

FORECASTS [forecast origin = K] up to K leads ahead
 [store forecasts in C [confidence limits in C and C]]

Optional storage is as follows: If one column is specified, the residuals are stored; if two storage columns are specified, the predicted values are stored as well. A third column can be specified for storage of estimated parameters.

CONSTANT Tells Minitab to include the constant term $\theta(0)$ in the model. If $d = 0$ (and D = 0), this is the default.

NOCONSTANT Tells Minitab not to include the constant term $\theta(0)$ in the model. If $d > 0$ (or D > 0), this is the default.

STARTING values in C Tells Minitab initial values for the parameters. Starting values (initial values) for the parameters must be entered into the column before using ARIMA; they are entered in the same order as they appear on the output: AR, seasonal AR, MA, seasonal MA, constant. The starting value for the constant is optional.

If you do not use START, Minitab uses 0.1 for all ϕs and θs (except $\theta(0)$); this usually works well.

BRIEF K

The BRIEF command controls the amount of output produced by the ARIMA command as follows:

BRIEF 1   The output contains the table of final estimates, differencing information, residual sum of squares, and number of observations.

BRIEF 2   Above plus table of estimates at each iteration. In addition, if the backforecasts are not dying out rapidly, the backforecasts are printed.

BRIEF 3   Above plus correlation matrix of the estimated parameters.

BRIEF 4   Above plus the backforecasts are always printed out.

APPENDIXES

A/DATA SETS USED IN THIS HANDBOOK

BANK DATA

Data on assets, total deposits (demand and time), and number of banks in selected Midwest and Sun Belt states are given. Assets and deposits are in billions of dollars. These data are also reported in Table 3.1 in the text.

Column	Description
1	State name
2	Region (1 denotes Sun Belt, 0 denotes Midwest)
3	Assets
4	Deposits
5	Number of banks

1	2	3	4	5
Alabama	1	20.3	16.5	294
Arizona	1	16.6	13.4	30
California	1	216.4	165.3	361
Florida	1	59.4	49.2	477
Georgia	1	30.0	23.1	416
Illinois	0	130.2	91.8	1250
Indiana	0	36.3	29.8	400
Iowa	0	25.5	21.5	643
Kansas	0	19.6	16.5	620
Louisiana	1	30.8	25.9	278
Michigan	0	56.6	46.0	374
Minnesota	0	36.8	28.0	759
Mississippi	1	13.6	11.5	167
Nebraska	0	14.0	11.4	461
Ohio	0	62.4	47.6	355
Tennessee	1	28.1	22.9	346
Texas	1	152.8	120.3	1598
Wisconsin	0	30.0	24.3	624

Source: U.S. Department of Commerce, *Statistical Abstract of the United States*, Washington, D.C., 1982, p. 511.

WOODRUFF SALES DATA

During 1975, 61 parcels of residential property were sold on the open market in Woodruff, Wisconsin. The ratio of the assessed value of a parcel to its selling price (the A/S ratio) is used in analyzing the property valuation process. The 61 ratios for Woodruff are listed below.

0. 03030	0. 32500	0. 20000	0. 22857	0. 20000
0. 24390	0. 24444	0. 39286	0. 27500	0. 48000
0. 30000	0. 48000	0. 48980	0. 54737	0. 43333
0. 51853	0. 31638	0. 33333	0. 35714	0. 66667
0. 21053	0. 66790	0. 66667	0. 44444	0. 66667
0. 36667	0. 41379	0. 31579	0. 65217	0. 28966
0. 45685	0. 31875	0. 46957	0. 39286	0. 29474
0. 28095	1. 28000	0. 36667	0. 34091	0. 54676
0. 54667	0. 76522	0. 40455	0. 33571	0. 55882
0. 88034	0. 64375	0. 47083	0. 50222	0. 48163
0. 41667	0. 52941	0. 53200	0. 46154	0. 82218
0. 67500	0. 60938	0. 74444	0. 50000	0. 85172
0. 84267				

Source: The Wisconsin Department of Revenue, Madison, Wisconsin, 1976.

WOODRUFF STUDY DATA

The data set presented below was part of a study done for the Wisconsin Department of Revenue, Bureau of Property and Utility Tax. Reported are four characteristics of 50 residential parcels selected at random from Woodruff, Wisconsin, in 1977. The 1975 assessed values of *all* the residential parcels in Woodruff were known. The second column of data lists the proportion of these parcels that had assessed values less than or equal to the assessed value of the parcel in the data set. Thus we see that rows 1–4 of the data set report four parcels having the same assessed value in 1975, and about 8% of the assessed values in Woodruff were less than or equal to that assessed value. (Actual assessed values are not reported for reasons of confidentiality.) Detailed appraisals of the 1975 market values of the 50 sample parcels were done by expert appraisers, and the ratios of the assessed values to these appraised values were computed. These ratios are reported in the first column. The third column reports a 1 if the parcel was improved (contained a structure) and a 0 otherwise (vacant parcel). The fourth column reports a 1 if the parcel had water frontage and a 0 otherwise.

Column	Description
1	Ratio of assessed to appraised value
2	Proportion of parcels having assessed value less than or equal to parcel in data set
3	1 means improved, 0 means vacant parcel
4	1 means water frontage, 0 means no water frontage

1	2	3	4	1	2	3	4
0. 2500	0. 0795	0	0	0. 5682	0. 5836	1	0
0. 2000	0. 0795	0	0	0. 3269	0. 5861	1	0
0. 1667	0. 0795	0	0	0. 3041	0. 5899	1	1
0. 1428	0. 0795	0	0	0. 7887	0. 6000	1	0
0. 3000	0. 1344	0	0	0. 3081	0. 6013	1	0
0. 3500	0. 1464	0	0	0. 6226	0. 6315	1	0
0. 2000	0. 2132	0	0	0. 4177	0. 6315	1	0
0. 2000	0. 2132	0	0	0. 4054	0. 6625	1	1
0. 3333	0. 2132	0	0	0. 6847	0. 6637	1	0
0. 2286	0. 2132	0	0	0. 5389	0. 7009	1	1
0. 2500	0. 3268	0	0	0. 7869	0. 7224	1	1
0. 4000	0. 3268	0	0	0. 7500	0. 7508	1	1
0. 2222	0. 3268	0	0	0. 4826	0. 7596	1	1
0. 2222	0. 3268	0	0	0. 5257	0. 8044	1	1
0. 2444	0. 3785	0	0	0. 5361	0. 8221	1	1
0. 3000	0. 4013	0	0	0. 6326	0. 8524	1	0
0. 0691	0. 4107	1	0	0. 7468	0. 8808	1	0
0. 7500	0. 4397	0	0	0. 6545	0. 8921	1	0
0. 4000	0. 4486	1	0	0. 7414	0. 9104	1	0
0. 1978	0. 4612	0	0	0. 6536	0. 9161	1	1
0. 3158	0. 5281	0	1	0. 6990	0. 9274	1	1
0. 4000	0. 5319	0	0	0. 5757	0. 9338	1	1
0. 3306	0. 5552	1	0	0. 6808	0. 9697	1	1
0. 3083	0. 5565	1	0	0. 6667	0. 9716	1	1
0. 2938	0. 5722	1	0	0. 8873	0. 9830	1	0

Source: R. B. Miller and Scott Johnson, "Some Statistical Aspects of Real Property Tax Equalization," *Assessors Journal*, 13:153–180, September 1978.

REAL ESTATE MARKET DATA

Data routinely become available on residential parcels that sell on the open market. The data set below shows five pieces of information on 60 residential parcels that sold during a calendar year in an anonymous U.S. city. The columns are described below.

Column	Description
1	A "style" code assigned by the assessors
2	Square feet of living area (in hundreds)
3	A "grade" code assigned by the assessors
4	Assessed value of the parcel at time of sale
5	Market value of the parcel

1	2	3	4	5	1	2	3	4	5
1. 25	10. 11	0. 90	39. 00	57. 6	1. 25	10. 11	0. 90	42. 00	65. 4
1. 00	7. 21	0. 90	32. 40	49. 2	1. 25	10. 24	0. 90	40. 50	63. 3
1. 00	7. 60	0. 90	39. 90	53. 7	1. 00	6. 91	0. 75	33. 90	49. 5
1. 00	6. 62	0. 90	29. 40	51. 9	1. 00	9. 66	0. 90	45. 30	66. 0
1. 25	9. 31	0. 90	36. 90	57. 0	1. 25	11. 06	0. 90	47. 40	64. 2
1. 00	7. 22	0. 75	11. 10	38. 4	1. 00	11. 00	0. 90	45. 00	62. 4
1. 75	16. 02	1. 00	46. 50	71. 1	1. 00	8. 90	0. 90	30. 30	52. 5
1. 00	6. 77	0. 90	34. 20	54. 6	1. 00	9. 20	0. 75	31. 20	46. 8
1. 25	10. 47	0. 90	45. 00	65. 4	2. 00	18. 04	0. 90	45. 90	68. 1
1. 00	8. 38	0. 90	38. 40	53. 4	1. 12	9. 65	0. 90	21. 90	55. 8
1. 25	9. 18	0. 90	48. 30	61. 8	1. 25	6. 61	0. 75	35. 70	46. 5
1. 00	7. 87	0. 90	33. 60	58. 8	1. 75	11. 64	1. 00	44. 10	62. 7
1. 75	8. 58	0. 75	33. 60	53. 7	1. 25	10. 79	0. 90	36. 30	60. 9
1. 25	11. 71	0. 90	48. 30	72. 6	1. 00	8. 15	0. 90	21. 60	51. 6
1. 00	8. 99	0. 90	34. 80	56. 4	1. 75	10. 60	1. 00	43. 80	67. 2
1. 00	5. 77	0. 75	33. 30	39. 3	2. 00	12. 98	1. 00	35. 40	67. 8
1. 00	5. 38	0. 75	42. 30	29. 1	2. 00	12. 49	0. 90	33. 00	70. 8
1. 25	10. 56	0. 90	38. 70	62. 7	1. 00	8. 14	0. 90	22. 20	52. 2
1. 25	8. 83	0. 90	38. 70	59. 4	1. 00	5. 21	0. 75	11. 70	39. 0
1. 25	10. 33	0. 90	37. 80	60. 6	1. 50	10. 40	0. 90	33. 60	60. 6
1. 25	10. 75	0. 90	45. 60	64. 2	1. 25	10. 51	0. 90	39. 60	62. 1
1. 25	10. 70	0. 90	34. 20	65. 4	1. 00	7. 12	0. 90	31. 80	63. 6
1. 00	10. 60	0. 90	36. 00	57. 6	1. 00	6. 94	0. 90	42. 00	56. 1
1. 25	11. 38	0. 90	38. 40	58. 5	1. 50	10. 52	0. 90	30. 30	59. 4
1. 00	5. 44	0. 90	34. 80	37. 8	1. 00	9. 23	0. 75	6. 90	45. 0
1. 00	8. 25	0. 90	42. 30	57. 0	1. 00	9. 67	0. 90	39. 00	66. 3
2. 00	14. 35	0. 90	32. 10	58. 2	1. 00	7. 43	0. 90	39. 30	52. 2
1. 00	8. 34	0. 75	27. 00	51. 9	1. 50	12. 37	0. 90	25. 50	59. 7
1. 00	7. 80	0. 75	33. 90	46. 5	1. 00	9. 26	0. 90	27. 33	56. 1
1. 00	7. 67	0. 75	33. 30	50. 4	1. 00	8. 02	0. 90	38. 10	54. 0

QUARTERLY MACROECONOMIC DATA, 1970–1984

Seven columns of data are listed below. The data in these columns are defined as follows. All data are for the United States.

Column	Definition
1	Year designation
2	Quarter designation
3	Money supply (seasonally adjusted)
4	Interest rate on three-month treasury bills
5	Inflation rate (GNP implicit price deflator)
6	GNP in current dollars (seasonally adjusted)
7	GNP in 1972 "constant" dollars (seasonally adjusted)

1	2	3	4	5	6	7
70	1	207.000	7.5993	89.89	972.0	1081.4
70	2	208.533	6.7417	91.07	986.3	1083.0
70	3	210.567	6.5407	91.79	1003.6	1093.3
70	4	214.900	5.8197	93.03	1009.0	1084.7
71	1	218.033	4.3757	94.40	1049.3	1111.5
71	2	222.600	3.7473	95.70	1068.9	1116.9
71	3	227.067	5.0607	96.52	1086.6	1125.7
71	4	229.600	4.4493	97.39	1105.8	1135.4
72	1	232.733	3.5353	98.72	1142.4	1157.2
72	2	237.767	3.6980	99.42	1171.7	1178.5
72	3	241.367	3.9823	100.25	1196.1	1193.1
72	4	247.533	4.7147	101.54	1233.5	1214.8
73	1	253.833	5.3087	102.95	1283.5	1246.8
73	2	255.867	6.2303	104.75	1307.6	1248.3
73	3	260.300	7.9583	106.53	1337.7	1255.8
73	4	262.300	7.8330	108.74	1376.7	1266.1
74	1	267.100	7.3930	110.72	1387.7	1253.3
74	2	270.167	8.2150	113.48	1423.8	1254.7
74	3	272.467	8.2137	116.42	1451.6	1246.8
74	4	275.400	7.7307	119.79	1473.8	1230.3
75	1	277.633	6.4183	122.88	1479.8	1204.3
75	2	280.767	5.5177	124.44	1516.7	1218.9
75	3	287.133	5.9400	126.68	1578.5	1246.1
75	4	289.733	5.9773	128.99	1621.8	1257.3
76	1	292.700	5.1057	130.12	1672.0	1285.0
76	2	297.867	5.0367	131.30	1698.6	1293.7
76	3	301.100	5.2913	132.89	1729.0	1301.1
76	4	305.933	4.9383	134.99	1772.5	1313.1
77	1	313.000	4.5380	136.80	1834.8	1341.3
77	2	319.300	4.6983	139.01	1895.1	1363.3
77	3	324.333	5.2167	141.03	1954.4	1385.8

1	2	3	4	5	6	7
77	4	330. 967	6. 0393	143. 24	1988. 9	1388. 4
78	1	337. 800	6. 3227	145. 12	2031. 7	1400. 0
78	2	344. 233	6. 3517	148. 89	2139. 5	1437. 0
78	3	351. 867	6. 9390	152. 02	2202. 5	1448. 8
78	4	358. 867	8. 2517	155. 38	2281. 6	1468. 4
79	1	363. 533	9. 2460	158. 60	2335. 5	1472. 6
79	2	370. 600	9. 5097	161. 85	2377. 9	1469. 2
79	3	380. 800	9. 2523	165. 12	2454. 8	1486. 6
79	4	386. 900	11. 1740	168. 05	2502. 9	1489. 3
80	1	391. 800	12. 3070	171. 94	2572. 9	1496. 4
80	2	390. 333	12. 8930	176. 46	2578. 8	1461. 4
80	3	399. 500	8. 1267	180. 24	2639. 1	1464. 2
80	4	415. 933	11. 9297	185. 13	2736. 0	1477. 9
81	1	417. 133	15. 0967	190. 01	2875. 8	1513. 5
81	2	427. 900	14. 4693	193. 03	2918. 0	1511. 7
81	3	430. 833	14. 9560	197. 70	3009. 3	1522. 1
81	4	435. 600	13. 3643	201. 69	3027. 9	1501. 3
82	1	446. 067	12. 3727	203. 98	3026. 0	1483. 5
82	2	449. 733	12. 4873	206. 77	3061. 2	1480. 5
82	3	453. 900	11. 0093	208. 53	3080. 1	1477. 1
82	4	470. 833	7. 9960	210. 27	3109. 6	1478. 8
83	1	485. 100	7. 9843	212. 87	3173. 8	1491. 0
83	2	500. 267	8. 2470	214. 25	3267. 0	1524. 8
83	3	514. 367	9. 1100	215. 89	3346. 6	1550. 2
83	4	523. 567	8. 8233	218. 21	3431. 7	1572. 7
84	1	531. 200	8. 9733	220. 58	3553. 3	1610. 9
84	2	539. 667	9. 6767	222. 40	3644. 7	1638. 8
84	3	547. 700	10. 1867	224. 57	3694. 6	1645. 2
84	4	551. 200	9. 7233	226. 10	3758. 7	1662. 4

Source: U.S. Department of Commerce, *The Survey of Current Business*, various issues.

MONTHLY MONEY SUPPLY AND THREE-MONTH TREASURY BILL INTEREST RATES, JANUARY 1970 THROUGH DECEMBER 1984

Money isn't everything, but it is way ahead of whatever is in second place. It lets us efficiently trade a day's work for a warm place to live and a good meal. And it gives economists a topic of endless conversation. Various measures of the amount of money in the economy are published by the Federal Reserve Board. The best known of these is called M1. The value of M1 is published monthly in both seasonally adjusted and raw form. Some of these values are given on pages 276–277. Money, properly invested, makes money. Also given below are the monthly interest rates earned by investments in three-month treasury bills.

Column	Description
1	Money supply (M1), seasonally adjusted
2	Interest rates (%) on three-month treasury bills, not seasonally adjusted
3	Money supply (M1), not seasonally adjusted

1	2	3	1	2	3
208. 200	7. 914	212. 900	260. 400	8. 015	261. 200
207. 000	7. 164	204. 000	260. 800	8. 672	258. 600
207. 700	6. 710	205. 500	260. 900	8. 478	259. 500
208. 700	6. 480	210. 100	262. 000	7. 155	261. 400
209. 200	7. 035	206. 200	264. 000	7. 866	265. 700
209. 600	6. 742	208. 900	265. 900	7. 364	273. 300
210. 100	6. 468	210. 100	267. 100	7. 755	271. 800
212. 000	6. 412	210. 000	268. 300	7. 060	264. 100
213. 900	6. 244	212. 800	269. 800	7. 986	266. 500
215. 000	5. 927	214. 400	270. 100	8. 229	271. 600
215. 800	5. 288	216. 700	270. 600	8. 430	266. 300
216. 600	4. 860	222. 200	271. 800	8. 145	271. 500
217. 800	4. 494	222. 600	272. 500	7. 752	273. 500
219. 700	3. 773	216. 600	273. 100	8. 744	271. 000
221. 100	3. 323	218. 600	274. 100	8. 363	272. 600
222. 300	3. 780	223. 700	275. 300	7. 244	274. 800
224. 400	4. 139	221. 100	276. 800	7. 585	278. 800
225. 900	4. 699	225. 200	277. 500	7. 179	285. 200
227. 300	5. 405	227. 500	277. 300	6. 493	281. 800
228. 000	5. 078	225. 900	278. 100	5. 583	273. 300
228. 900	4. 668	227. 700	280. 100	5. 544	276. 400
229. 600	4. 489	229. 100	279. 700	5. 694	281. 400
230. 300	4. 191	231. 200	282. 500	5. 315	278. 100
230. 800	4. 023	236. 900	286. 300	5. 193	286. 000
232. 600	3. 403	237. 500	286. 800	6. 164	288. 000
234. 800	3. 180	231. 400	288. 300	6. 463	286. 300
236. 800	3. 723	234. 200	289. 100	6. 383	287. 800
238. 100	3. 723	239. 500	288. 700	6. 081	288. 500
238. 400	3. 648	234. 700	291. 400	5. 468	293. 500
239. 300	3. 874	238. 800	291. 100	5. 504	299. 000
241. 300	4. 059	241. 800	292. 400	4. 961	296. 800
243. 500	4. 014	241. 300	294. 600	4. 852	289. 000
245. 800	4. 651	244. 500	295. 900	5. 047	291. 400
247. 700	4. 719	247. 000	297. 900	4. 878	299. 900
249. 100	4. 774	250. 500	299. 800	5. 185	295. 100
252. 000	5. 061	258. 900	299. 700	5. 443	299. 400
254. 500	5. 307	259. 400	300. 800	5. 278	302. 300
255. 000	5. 558	251. 200	302. 800	5. 153	301. 000
254. 400	6. 054	251. 600	303. 400	5. 075	302. 500
255. 500	6. 289	257. 000	306. 900	4. 930	307. 000
257. 700	6. 348	253. 600	307. 500	4. 810	309. 700
259. 700	7. 188	259. 300	310. 300	4. 355	318. 600

1	2	3	1	2	3
313.200	4.597	317.700	417.100	14.724	421.800
315.500	4.662	309.000	419.500	14.905	410.600
317.400	4.613	312.200	423.900	13.478	417.300
320.000	4.540	322.700	431.100	13.635	436.300
320.500	4.942	315.600	428.700	16.295	423.500
322.200	5.004	321.700	428.400	14.557	427.800
324.600	5.146	326.300	430.600	14.699	432.800
326.200	5.500	324.300	433.500	15.612	430.900
328.400	5.770	327.700	433.900	14.951	432.300
331.400	6.188	332.000	434.800	13.873	435.100
333.100	6.160	335.400	438.100	11.269	440.400
335.300	6.063	344.100	441.800	10.926	452.200
338.800	6.448	343.400	449.400	12.412	454.300
339.300	6.457	332.000	447.000	13.780	437.900
340.800	6.319	334.900	447.300	12.493	440.900
344.300	6.306	347.500	450.900	12.821	456.300
347.600	6.430	342.400	451.000	12.148	446.100
350.000	6.707	349.400	451.600	12.108	451.300
352.000	7.074	353.900	452.400	11.914	454.800
353.600	7.036	351.700	457.700	9.006	454.900
357.600	7.836	357.000	463.600	8.196	461.400
358.600	8.132	359.400	471.200	7.750	471.300
360.400	8.787	362.900	477.700	8.042	479.900
363.000	9.122	372.500	480.800	8.013	491.800
363.100	9.351	367.800	484.400	7.810	489.600
364.500	9.265	356.400	490.100	8.130	480.500
367.300	9.457	360.800	495.800	8.304	489.200
372.100	9.493	376.200	499.200	8.252	505.300
372.400	9.579	367.100	505.800	8.185	500.700
377.400	9.045	376.700	509.900	8.820	510.000
381.200	9.262	383.300	514.800	9.120	517.400
383.800	9.450	381.900	518.400	9.390	514.700
386.200	10.182	385.600	520.500	9.050	517.800
387.000	11.472	387.700	524.000	8.710	524.000
387.500	11.868	389.800	526.200	8.710	528.500
389.000	12.071	398.600	528.000	8.960	539.700
391.400	12.036	396.100	531.400	8.930	536.800
395.000	12.814	386.300	534.200	9.030	523.900
394.500	15.526	387.800	537.300	9.440	530.400
388.100	14.003	392.600	539.200	9.690	545.600
388.400	9.150	383.300	542.500	9.900	537.300
393.800	6.995	393.100	547.300	9.940	547.900
398.300	8.126	400.500	546.900	10.130	549.900
406.400	9.259	404.300	548.900	10.490	545.000
412.100	10.321	411.100	551.500	10.410	548.500
416.700	11.580	417.300	548.300	9.970	548.200
419.000	13.888	421.300	553.800	8.790	555.900
414.800	15.661	424.800	558.500	8.160	570.400

Source: U.S. Department of Commerce, *Survey of Current Business*, Washington, D.C., various issues.

STOCK MARKET DATA, 1963–1968

The theory of finance has provided a number of hypotheses that are amenable to empirical testing. E. F. Fama, of the University of Chicago, discusses a number of these hypotheses in his book *Foundations of Finance*. Four columns of data are listed below. They are described as follows.

Column	Description
1	Month/year designation; the years 1963–1968 are designated 63, 64,..., 68, and the months January–December are designated 1, 2,..., 12
2	Monthly rate of return on a share of IBM common stock
3	Monthly rate of return on a share of Xerox common stock
4	Monthly rate of return on a portfolio consisting of equal shares of each stock on the New York Stock Exchange

These rates of return include capital gains, such as stock splits and stock dividends, as well as cash dividends, that is,

$$\text{Rate of return} = \frac{\begin{array}{c}(\text{Price at end of month } t) + (\text{Dividend in month } t) \\ + (\text{Capital gain in month } t) - (\text{Price at end of month } t - 1)\end{array}}{(\text{Price at end of month } t - 1)}$$

1	2	3	4	1	2	3	4
763.	-0.0040	0.2470	-0.0095	465.	0.0677	0.1250	0.0359
863.	0.0259	0.1650	0.0506	565.	-0.0113	0.0791	-0.0079
963.	0.0163	-0.0070	-0.0184	665.	-0.0418	-0.0360	-0.0743
1063.	0.0929	0.2950	0.0163	765.	0.0459	0.0947	0.0291
1163.	-0.0152	0.0270	-0.0068	865.	0.0449	0.1020	0.0451
1263.	0.0448	0.1390	0.0075	965.	0.0271	-0.0090	0.0308
164.	0.0690	-0.0770	0.0201	1065.	0.0400	0.0360	0.0474
264.	0.0521	0.0090	0.0270	1165.	-0.0122	0.1220	0.0300
364.	0.0444	0.0780	0.0314	1265.	-0.0495	0.0310	0.0327
464.	-0.0404	0.1140	-0.0031	166.	-0.0060	0.0750	0.0435
564.	0.0549	0.2230	0.0116	266.	0.0413	0.0830	0.0109
664.	-0.0063	-0.0010	0.0154	366.	0.0019	0.0450	-0.0219
764.	-0.0314	-0.0940	0.0277	466.	0.0804	0.0270	0.0337
864.	-0.0438	-0.0420	-0.0090	566.	-0.0220	-0.0410	-0.0724
964.	-0.0091	0.2210	0.0370	666.	-0.0296	0.0150	-0.0048
1064.	-0.0378	-0.1220	0.0170	766.	-0.0278	-0.0740	-0.0127
1164.	-0.0149	-0.1170	0.0007	866.	-0.0562	-0.2190	-0.0931
1264.	-0.0073	0.0450	-0.0069	966.	-0.0094	-0.0150	-0.0143
165.	0.0952	0.1255	0.0587	1066.	0.0457	-0.0740	0.0127
265.	0.0195	0.1240	0.0278	1166.	0.1358	0.2670	0.0382
365.	-0.0033	-0.0310	0.0053	1266.	-0.0120	-0.0370	0.0162

1	2	3	4	1	2	3	4
167.	0.0754	0.1700	0.1428	1067.	0.0825	0.0530	-0.0359
267.	0.0791	0.0780	0.0209	1167.	0.0330	-0.0020	0.0067
367.	0.0488	0.1250	0.0320	1267.	0.0245	0.0400	0.0554
467.	0.1009	0.0230	0.0365	168.	-0.0518	-0.1650	-0.0035
567.	-0.0352	-0.0510	-0.0179	268.	-0.0222	-0.0250	-0.0416
667.	0.0670	0.0050	0.0516	368.	0.0560	-0.0810	-0.0045
767.	0.0206	-0.0180	0.0709	468.	0.1061	0.1490	0.1164
867.	-0.0136	-0.0170	0.0028	568.	0.0558	0.0900	0.0586
967.	0.0970	0.0550	0.0378	668.	-0.0091	-0.0180	0.0192

Source: Center for Research in Security Prices, University of Chicago. Discussed in E. F. Fama, *Foundations of Finance*, New York: Basic Books, 1976, Chapter 4.

NEWSPRINT CONSUMPTION DATA

The data set listed below is part of a large study of newsprint consumption in the United States in the year 1960. Each row corresponds to a U.S. city. The variables listed are described as follows.

Column	Description
1	Number of newspapers in the city
2	Proportion of the city population under age 18 (multiplied by 1000)
3	Median school years completed by city residents (multipled by 10)
4	Proportion of the city population employed in white collar occupations
5	Number of families in the city
6	Total retail sales in the city
7	Newsprint consumption

1	2	3	4	5	6	7
2.	437.	124.	531.	8070.	82897.	1097.
1.	382.	122.	491.	7061.	59506.	613.
1.	340.	102.	388.	11374.	71118.	1940.
1.	341.	112.	434.	16348.	122028.	2293.
1.	320.	98.	498.	10104.	77745.	1260.
1.	313.	114.	514.	9437.	86450.	2557.
2.	285.	125.	594.	17052.	137543.	4275.
4.	311.	100.	417.	909204.	5630939.	373616.
1.	343.	98.	442.	11095.	95031.	2127.
2.	336.	111.	474.	20802.	161250.	4376.
1.	373.	87.	348.	20281.	120688.	1885.
1.	275.	105.	431.	11635.	94032.	1287.
1.	326.	110.	447.	7052.	44329.	761.
1.	312.	117.	448.	9429.	67757.	1218.
1.	330.	109.	457.	16898.	150626.	2571.
1.	350.	100.	375.	7114.	82687.	1683.

(continued)

1	2	3	4	5	6	7
1.	325.	114.	462.	11601.	105009.	1925.
1.	353.	106.	397.	7825.	46282.	702.
2.	318.	105.	441.	26315.	220128.	8182.
1.	317.	102.	445.	11512.	81530.	1983.
2.	345.	110.	455.	33569.	262212.	7525.
1.	327.	114.	448.	13723.	71882.	1694.
2.	306.	111.	550.	22138.	177692.	5739.
1.	358.	117.	453.	14371.	128507.	2617.
1.	343.	101.	322.	12909.	106541.	2000.
1.	238.	126.	555.	6792.	62979.	696.
1.	352.	113.	436.	10470.	79043.	1211.
2.	344.	102.	429.	36840.	219556.	8367.
2.	354.	116.	479.	41354.	314611.	13989.
1.	392.	101.	316.	43435.	258525.	6458.
1.	367.	108.	350.	29433.	177403.	6064.
2.	340.	108.	441.	120624.	916535.	59666.
1.	370.	106.	346.	12376.	88303.	1252.
1.	356.	118.	464.	10921.	96389.	2870.
2.	347.	106.	376.	9367.	80653.	1390.
1.	346.	100.	394.	8906.	61866.	656.
2.	342.	105.	387.	17339.	122103.	2881.
1.	353.	99.	423.	10021.	57421.	291.
1.	341.	108.	403.	11616.	89526.	1304.
1.	353.	114.	466.	34507.	229514.	13593.
2.	311.	107.	433.	19264.	176910.	3828.
1.	273.	133.	609.	5888.	42342.	215.
1.	377.	96.	379.	8551.	70269.	916.
2.	354.	101.	421.	86029.	567165.	30171.
1.	369.	110.	489.	7823.	54982.	580.
1.	390.	102.	428.	7987.	64661.	1007.
1.	369.	109.	449.	8163.	56723.	569.
1.	375.	98.	378.	15029.	78490.	1119.
1.	387.	118.	541.	18783.	178005.	837.
1.	399.	112.	477.	48981.	283197.	10540.
1.	380.	119.	493.	32921.	204371.	6959.
1.	399.	102.	408.	6652.	43413.	308.
1.	323.	107.	455.	13379.	84086.	981.
2.	390.	124.	594.	11022.	115023.	1235.
1.	412.	120.	431.	8373.	97623.	260.
1.	379.	118.	483.	110878.	804942.	32987.
2.	371.	121.	488.	53076.	368955.	8818.
1.	360.	120.	445.	6843.	43087.	470.
1.	353.	112.	492.	14337.	117209.	1975.
1.	283.	98.	453.	7725.	68966.	630.
2.	312.	121.	515.	28007.	233105.	15297.
1.	365.	105.	431.	11048.	73166.	1514.
1.	300.	121.	503.	14950.	57806.	586.
1.	253.	121.	568.	15972.	123481.	1382.
1.	412.	123.	519.	26461.	289389.	1367.

1	2	3	4	5	6	7
1.	369.	120.	513.	14534.	212523.	3924.
1.	249.	129.	613.	26761.	174763.	3000.
1.	188.	127.	719.	8544.	215501.	1159.
1.	303.	122.	508.	25862.	180968.	467.
1.	448.	123.	501.	8847.	79823.	525.
1.	375.	121.	439.	9803.	84532.	780.
1.	346.	122.	504.	8790.	127643.	897.
1.	339.	116.	458.	7448.	74034.	1877.
1.	351.	117.	514.	34026.	374227.	13715.
1.	402.	125.	552.	14255.	112821.	953.
1.	451.	123.	487.	20537.	146707.	2500.
1.	251.	123.	578.	34550.	236305.	1986.
1.	444.	121.	446.	17911.	176649.	4045.
1.	193.	111.	460.	8824.	102845.	2208.
1.	253.	122.	571.	18880.	181612.	1100.
1.	273.	121.	508.	90928.	558118.	18258.
4.	305.	121.	503.	636522.	4463965.	310512.
1.	340.	120.	547.	9807.	142382.	2090.
1.	311.	121.	486.	7423.	59757.	494.
1.	291.	114.	453.	97193.	694345.	36246.
1.	376.	119.	421.	12239.	85477.	1455.
1.	353.	122.	510.	6907.	58838.	230.
1.	406.	110.	373.	9009.	91740.	637.
1.	359.	133.	691.	13217.	153157.	2720.
1.	256.	124.	530.	30200.	340361.	5652.

Source: Professor Gilbert Churchill, University of Wisconsin, Madison, Wisconsin.

CLASS DATA

In the spring semester of 1981 a class of 137 business statistics students was surveyed. The students were asked to write on a card their sex, age, academic classification, height, weight, and a guess at the perimeter of the first edition of the *Minitab Handbook* by Ryan, Joiner, and Ryan. The table below describes the variables in more detail.

Column	Description
1	Sex: 2 = female, 1 = male
2	Age: 1 = age < 18, 2 = 18 ≤ age < 21, 3 = 21 ≤ age < 24, 4 = 24 ≤ age < 26, 5 = age ≥ 26
3	Class: 1 = prebusiness, 2 = business undergraduate, 3 = business graduate, 4 = nonbusiness student
4	Height: height in inches
5	Weight: weight in pounds
6	Guess: guess at perimeter in inches

1	2	3	4	5	6	1	2	3	4	5	6
1.	5.	4.	66.00	120.	28.	2.	2.	1.	70.00	165.	34.
2.	2.	1.	74.00	172.	29.	2.	2.	1.	71.00	190.	32.
2.	2.	1.	73.00	240.	26.	1.	2.	1.	67.00	130.	24.
1.	3.	1.	63.00	100.	23.	1.	5.	3.	63.50	115.	32.
2.	2.	1.	73.00	155.	40.	2.	2.	1.	71.00	167.	24.
1.	4.	3.	65.00	145.	28.	2.	2.	1.	71.00	154.	30.
2.	2.	1.	71.00	150.	24.	2.	2.	4.	71.00	155.	28.
2.	2.	1.	76.00	180.	28.	2.	2.	1.	66.00	140.	32.
1.	2.	1.	64.00	112.	28.	2.	2.	1.	75.00	200.	26.
1.	2.	1.	67.00	135.	24.	2.	2.	1.	72.00	142.	32.
2.	2.	1.	72.00	145.	32.	1.	5.	4.	65.00	114.	20.
2.	3.	1.	68.00	158.	35.	2.	2.	2.	71.00	170.	32.
1.	3.	1.	67.00	120.	22.	2.	2.	1.	71.00	150.	38.
2.	2.	1.	72.00	150.	29.	2.	2.	1.	70.00	155.	32.
1.	2.	2.	64.00	107.	32.	2.	2.	1.	71.00	145.	34.
1.	2.	1.	64.50	130.	30.	2.	2.	1.	72.00	155.	32.
2.	4.	3.	73.00	188.	34.	2.	2.	2.	69.00	168.	34.
1.	2.	2.	68.00	132.	28.	2.	2.	1.	70.00	180.	36.
1.	2.	1.	65.00	125.	28.	2.	2.	1.	71.00	165.	26.
2.	2.	1.	69.00	155.	28.	2.	2.	1.	73.00	170.	29.
1.	3.	2.	66.50	123.	36.	2.	2.	1.	71.00	155.	38.
2.	4.	4.	70.00	185.	32.	2.	4.	2.	74.50	195.	29.
2.	2.	1.	71.00	135.	36.	2.	2.	1.	71.00	175.	34.
2.	2.	1.	69.00	165.	26.	2.	2.	1.	69.00	143.	30.
1.	2.	1.	63.00	130.	30.	2.	2.	2.	68.75	154.	28.
1.	2.	1.	69.00	135.	26.	2.	3.	2.	71.00	160.	22.
2.	2.	1.	71.00	157.	34.	2.	5.	4.	70.00	145.	30.
1.	2.	1.	60.50	105.	24.	2.	5.	1.	71.00	175.	28.
1.	2.	1.	62.00	145.	28.	2.	3.	1.	73.00	150.	29.
1.	3.	4.	65.00	123.	36.	1.	2.	1.	69.00	157.	39.
1.	2.	1.	69.00	107.	26.	2.	3.	3.	69.00	175.	30.
1.	2.	1.	68.00	140.	40.	2.	5.	4.	68.00	135.	30.
2.	2.	1.	78.00	185.	27.	2.	5.	3.	73.00	160.	26.
2.	1.	1.	70.00	150.	29.	2.	2.	4.	70.00	167.	30.
1.	2.	1.	66.00	120.	32.	2.	2.	4.	75.00	190.	28.
2.	2.	1.	68.00	135.	30.	1.	4.	3.	67.00	110.	26.
2.	3.	4.	68.00	155.	20.	1.	2.	1.	62.00	110.	30.
2.	4.	4.	70.00	150.	28.	2.	2.	2.	69.00	150.	20.
1.	2.	1.	68.00	130.	24.	1.	5.	3.	66.00	123.	26.
1.	4.	1.	60.00	100.	30.	1.	3.	4.	72.00	147.	28.
2.	2.	1.	71.50	170.	26.	1.	2.	1.	63.00	118.	40.
2.	3.	2.	70.00	165.	36.	2.	4.	4.	72.00	185.	33.
2.	2.	1.	76.00	170.	30.	2.	4.	4.	72.00	172.	30.
2.	2.	1.	74.00	180.	30.	1.	5.	3.	65.00	135.	28.
2.	2.	1.	71.00	160.	24.	2.	2.	1.	69.00	145.	30.
2.	2.	1.	68.00	145.	28.	1.	2.	1.	66.00	130.	38.

1	2	3	4	5	6		1	2	3	4	5	6
2.	2.	1.	73.00	155.	28.		2.	2.	1.	71.00	160.	28.
1.	2.	1.	68.00	115.	16.		2.	3.	4.	68.00	160.	36.
2.	3.	2.	71.00	240.	36.		2.	2.	1.	70.00	125.	32.
1.	2.	2.	62.00	115.	28.		1.	2.	1.	62.00	130.	26.
2.	3.	4.	73.00	190.	26.		1.	5.	3.	69.00	123.	40.
2.	2.	2.	71.00	155.	30. 2377		1.	5.	2.	62.00	127.	28.
2.	4.	4.	70.00	135.	36.		1.	3.	4.	61.00	119.	32.
2.	2.	1.	71.00	165.	30.		1.	5.	3.	68.00	137.	36.
2.	4.	2.	67.50	157.	19.		1.	3.	3.	70.00	150.	32.
1.	5.	4.	64.00	125.	28.		1.	5.	2.	62.00	128.	28.
2.	2.	1.	71.00	193.	32.		2.	4.	3.	74.00	170.	32.
2.	2.	1.	73.00	160.	26.		2.	3.	2.	69.00	155.	26.
2.	2.	1.	71.00	195.	30.		2.	2.	1.	69.00	117.	29.
1.	2.	1.	66.00	115.	32.		2.	2.	1.	71.00	170.	30.
1.	2.	1.	67.00	120.	26.		2.	2.	4.	70.00	185.	32.
1.	2.	1.	68.00	135.	22.		2.	2.	1.	72.00	200.	22.
2.	2.	1.	71.00	165.	28.		2.	2.	1.	68.00	148.	36.
2.	2.	1.	70.00	135.	28.		2.	2.	1.	70.00	139.	26.
2.	2.	4.	69.00	140.	26.		2.	3.	4.	74.00	190.	28.
1.	5.	2.	67.00	120.	32.		2.	2.	4.	70.00	140.	35.
2.	3.	4.	77.00	186.	26.		2.	2.	1.	68.00	150.	38.
2.	3.	1.	73.50	180.	36.		2.	2.	2.	74.00	180.	28.
2.	3.	4.	71.50	178.	36.							

EMPLOYMENT DATA

Gainful employment concerns everyone, and measures of employment and unemployment are among our most intensely studied social and economic indicators. Three panels of data are listed below. Each contains monthly values for the years 1950–1982. As you read across rows, you pass from month to month. The first value in a row corresponds to a January value, the second a February value, and so on. Each row corresponds to a year. The first row lists data for 1950, the second row data for 1951, and so on.

The first panel of data lists seasonally adjusted unemployment rates. The second panel lists the number of unemployed persons (in millions). The third panel lists the number of persons in the labor force (in millions). The labor force consists of unemployed and employed persons. Note that the ratio of unemployed persons to labor force (multiplied by 100) is the unemployment rate *not seasonally adjusted*.

Seasonally Adjusted Unemployment Rates

1	2	3	4	5	6	7	8	9	10	11	12
3.40	3.80	4.00	3.90	3.50	3.60	3.60	3.90	3.80	3.70	3.80	4.00
4.30	4.70	5.00	5.30	6.10	6.20	6.70	6.80	6.60	7.90	6.40	6.60
6.50	6.50	6.30	5.80	5.50	5.40	5.00	4.50	4.40	4.20	4.20	4.30
3.70	3.40	3.40	3.10	3.00	3.20	3.10	3.10	3.30	3.50	3.50	3.10
3.20	3.10	2.90	2.90	3.00	3.00	3.20	3.40	3.10	3.00	2.80	2.70
2.90	2.60	2.60	2.70	2.50	2.50	2.60	2.70	2.90	3.10	3.50	4.50
4.90	5.20	5.70	5.90	5.90	5.60	5.80	6.00	6.10	5.70	5.30	5.00
4.90	4.70	4.60	4.70	4.30	4.20	4.00	4.20	4.10	4.30	4.20	4.20
4.00	3.90	4.20	4.00	4.30	4.30	4.40	4.10	3.90	3.90	4.30	4.20
4.20	3.90	3.70	3.90	4.10	4.30	4.20	4.10	4.40	4.50	5.10	5.20
5.80	6.40	6.70	7.40	7.40	7.30	7.50	7.40	7.10	6.70	6.20	6.20
6.00	5.90	5.60	5.20	5.10	5.00	5.10	5.20	5.50	5.70	5.80	5.30
5.20	4.80	5.40	5.20	5.10	5.10	5.40	5.50	5.60	6.10	6.10	6.60
6.60	6.90	6.90	7.00	7.10	6.90	7.00	6.60	6.70	6.50	6.10	6.00
5.80	5.50	5.60	5.60	5.50	5.50	5.40	5.70	5.60	5.40	5.70	5.50
5.70	5.90	5.70	5.70	5.90	5.60	5.60	5.40	5.50	5.50	5.70	5.50
5.60	5.40	5.40	5.30	5.10	5.20	4.90	5.00	5.10	5.10	4.80	5.00
4.90	5.10	4.70	4.80	4.60	4.60	4.40	4.40	4.30	4.20	4.10	4.00
4.00	3.80	3.80	3.80	3.90	3.80	3.80	3.80	3.70	3.70	3.60	3.80
3.90	3.80	3.80	3.80	3.80	3.90	3.80	3.80	3.80	4.00	3.90	3.90
3.70	3.80	3.70	3.50	3.50	3.70	3.70	3.50	3.40	3.40	3.40	3.40
3.40	3.40	3.40	3.40	3.40	3.50	3.50	3.50	3.70	3.70	3.50	3.50
3.90	4.20	4.40	4.60	4.70	4.90	5.00	5.10	5.40	5.60	5.90	6.10
5.90	5.90	5.90	5.90	5.90	5.90	6.00	6.10	6.00	5.90	6.00	6.00
5.80	5.70	5.80	5.70	5.60	5.60	5.60	5.60	5.60	5.70	5.20	5.10
4.90	5.00	4.90	5.00	4.80	4.80	4.80	4.80	4.90	4.70	4.80	4.90
5.00	5.10	5.00	5.00	5.10	5.30	5.50	5.50	4.90	6.10	6.70	7.20
7.90	8.00	8.50	8.60	9.00	8.70	8.70	8.50	8.60	8.60	8.40	8.30
7.80	7.60	7.50	7.50	7.30	7.60	7.80	7.90	7.80	7.90	8.00	7.80
7.40	7.60	7.40	7.10	7.10	7.10	6.90	7.00	6.80	6.80	6.70	6 40
6.30	6.10	6.20	6.00	6.10	5.70	6.20	5.90	6.00	5.80	5.80	5.90
5.80	5.70	5.70	5.80	5.80	5.70	5.70	5.90	5.80	5.90	5.80	5.90
6.20	6.00	6.20	7.00	7.80	7.70	7.80					

Number of Unemployed

1	2	3	4	5	6	7	8	9	10	11	12
2.40	2.80	2.60	2.40	2.00	2.40	2.40	2.20	2.10	1.70	2.00	2.20
3.00	3.50	3.40	3.30	3.50	4.00	4.40	4.00	3.60	3.80	3.60	3.70
4.60	4.80	4.30	3.70	3.30	3.60	3.30	2.60	2.50	2.00	2.40	2.40
2.60	2.50	2.30	1.90	1.80	2.10	2.10	1.80	1.90	1.80	2.00	1.80
2.20	2.30	2.00	1.80	1.80	2.00	2.10	1.90	1.70	1.50	1.60	1.50
2.10	2.00	1.80	1.80	1.50	1.70	1.70	1.50	1.60	1.60	2.00	2.60
3.60	4.00	4.00	3.80	3.60	3.70	3.70	3.50	3.40	2.90	3.10	3.00
3.70	3.60	3.30	3.20	2.70	2.90	2.70	2.50	2.30	2.30	2.50	2.60
3.10	3.10	3.10	2.70	2.80	3.20	3.00	2.50	2.30	2.10	2.60	2.70
3.20	3.10	2.80	2.60	2.60	3.10	2.80	2.50	2.50	2.50	3.10	3.30
4.50	5.10	5.20	5.10	4.80	5.20	5.10	4.60	4.00	3.80	3.80	4.10
4.70	4.70	4.30	3.60	3.30	3.80	3.60	3.30	3.20	3.20	3.60	3.50
4.10	3.90	4.20	3.60	3.40	4.20	3.90	3.70	3.30	3.50	4.00	4.50
5.30	5.60	5.40	4.90	4.80	5.30	5.00	4.40	4.00	3.90	3.90	4.00
4.60	4.50	4.30	3.90	3.90	4.20	3.80	3.80	3.40	3.20	3.70	3.80
4.60	4.90	4.40	4.00	3.90	4.60	4.10	3.80	3.50	3.40	3.80	3.80
4.50	4.50	4.20	3.80	3.50	4.40	3.70	3.60	3.30	3.20	3.30	3.40

1	2	3	4	5	6	7	8	9	10	11	12
3.90	4.20	3.70	3.50	3.20	4.00	3.40	3.20	2.80	2.70	2.90	2.80
3.20	3.10	3.00	2.70	2.80	3.60	3.00	2.80	2.50	2.50	2.60	2.60
3.20	3.20	3.00	2.70	2.40	3.60	3.20	2.90	2.90	3.00	2.90	2.70
3.10	3.30	2.90	2.50	2.30	3.60	3.20	2.80	2.60	2.50	2.60	2.40
2.90	2.90	2.70	2.50	2.30	3.40	3.20	2.90	3.00	2.80	2.70	2.60
3.40	3.80	3.70	3.60	3.40	4.70	4.50	4.20	4.30	4.30	4.60	4.60
5.40	5.40	5.20	4.70	4.40	5.50	5.30	5.10	4.80	4.60	4.80	4.70
5.40	5.40	5.20	4.70	4.30	5.40	5.20	4.80	4.60	4.50	4.30	4.10
4.70	4.80	4.50	4.20	3.80	4.80	4.60	4.20	4.20	3.80	4.00	4.00
5.00	5.10	4.80	4.30	4.10	5.40	5.30	4.90	5.20	5.00	5.70	6.10
8.20	8.30	8.40	7.80	7.60	8.60	8.20	7.70	7.50	7.20	7.20	7.20
8.20	8.00	7.50	6.90	6.30	7.60	7.60	7.30	7.00	6.80	7.10	7.00
7.80	8.10	7.60	6.60	6.20	7.40	6.90	6.80	6.40	6.20	6.30	5.90
6.90	6.70	6.50	5.70	5.40	6.30	6.40	5.90	5.80	5.50	5.60	5.70
6.40	6.50	6.20	5.60	5.20	6.20	6.10	6.10	5.80	5.80	5.80	5.80
7.00	7.00	6.80	6.80	7.30	8.30	8.40					

Monthly Labor Force

1	2	3	4	5	6	7	8	9	10	11	12
58.70	59.20	59.20	59.90	59.80	62.10	62.40	61.90	61.40	61.00	61.00	60.80
59.50	59.80	60.20	60.20	61.20	62.20	62.60	62.50	62.00	61.80	62.20	61.40
60.80	61.00	61.00	61.50	62.00	63.50	63.20	63.60	62.70	62.80	62.70	61.80
60.80	60.60	61.70	61.10	62.00	62.50	63.00	62.90	62.30	62.70	62.40	62.00
61.10	61.20	60.90	61.10	62.00	63.00	62.90	62.80	62.90	62.50	63.00	62.30
62.30	62.20	62.70	62.50	62.60	63.90	63.90	63.80	63.10	63.40	63.30	62.40
62.20	63.00	63.20	63.40	63.70	64.20	64.20	64.30	64.40	64.10	64.00	63.00
63.00	62.90	63.10	64.00	64.50	65.50	66.10	66.40	66.00	66.40	66.40	65.90
65.10	64.90	65.30	65.70	66.80	67.90	67.90	67.60	67.10	67.20	66.90	66.30
65.10	65.60	66.00	66.10	66.80	68.20	68.60	67.50	67.30	67.60	67.20	66.90
66.00	66.40	66.70	67.20	67.90	68.90	68.90	68.60	67.80	68.20	67.70	67.30
66.70	66.70	67.40	67.80	68.40	69.70	69.80	69.20	68.60	69.10	68.50	68.40
67.50	67.80	67.80	69.00	69.70	71.50	71.10	70.70	70.20	70.10	70.40	69.80
69.10	69.50	70.10	69.80	70.50	72.50	71.90	71.50	70.10	70.60	70.30	69.60
68.80	69.40	69.70	69.80	70.60	72.10	71.70	71.90	71.10	71.10	70.80	70.30
69.80	70.40	70.80	71.20	71.90	73.40	73.40	72.80	72.00	72.40	72.30	71.60
71.00	71.60	71.90	72.80	73.50	74.90	74.50	74.20	73.10	73.30	73.20	73.00
72.20	72.90	73.00	73.70	74.50	76.30	76.50	75.90	74.20	74.80	74.70	74.60
73.60	73.80	74.10	74.80	75.40	77.60	77.70	77.50	75.60	76.20	76.60	76.20
75.30	75.70	75.50	76.10	76.10	79.00	79.50	79.10	77.50	78.10	78.10	78.00
76.30	77.40	77.40	77.60	78.20	80.90	81.00	80.20	78.50	78.90	79.10	79.10
78.20	79.10	79.30	79.60	79.60	82.40	82.80	82.50	81.00	81.50	81.40	81.40
80.70	81.30	81.70	82.00	81.70	84.00	84.80	84.10	82.50	83.20	83.30	83.20
82.60	82.70	82.70	82.90	83.10	85.00	86.00	86.70	84.10	84.60	85.00	84.90
84.60	84.80	85.40	85.30	85.60	88.00	88.60	88.60	86.40	86.70	87.20	87.00
85.10	86.70	87.30	87.50	87.60	90.40	90.90	90.10	89.00	89.80	89.90	89.70
89.10	89.40	89.60	89.50	89.90	92.50	93.30	92.40	91.90	91.60	91.60	91.30
91.10	91.90	91.40	91.40	91.80	94.00	94.80	94.30	92.80	93.30	92.80	92.70
92.70	92.80	93.10	93.50	93.60	96.10	97.20	96.70	95.00	95.50	95.60	95.50
94.70	95.30	95.80	95.80	96.20	99.10	99.30	99.10	97.70	98.40	98.80	98.50
98.00	97.90	98.40	98.90	99.30	102.20	102.60	102.00	100.80	101.60	101.60	101.60
100.90	101.20	101.70	101.20	104.20	104.20	105.00	104.40	103.40	103.90	103.70	103.90
103.20	103.20	103.40	104.00	106.10	107.00	106.10					

Source: U.S. Department of Commerce, *Survey of Current Business*, various issues.

RESTAURANT (SAVED WORKSHEET IS CALLED RESTRNT)

The survey is described in Chapter 4.

	Column	Description
1	OUTLOOK	Values 1, 2, 3, 4, 5, 6, denoting from very unfavorable to very favorable
2	SALES	Gross 1979 sales in thousands of dollars
3	NEWCAP	New capital invested in 1979, in thousands of dollars
4	VALUE	Estimated market value of the business, in thousands of dollars
5	COSTGOOD	Cost of goods sold as a percentage of sales
6	WAGES	Wages as a percentage of sales
7	ADS	Advertising as a percentage of sales
8	TYPEFOOD	1 = fast food, 2 = supper club, 3 = other
9	SEATS	Number of seats in dining area
10	OWNER	1 = sole proprietorship, 2 = partnership, 3 = corportion
11	FT.EMPL	Number of full-time employees
12	PT.EMPL	Number of part-time employees
13	SIZE	Size of restaurant: 1 = 1 to 9.5 full-time equivalent employees, 2 = 10 to 20 full-time equivalent employees, 3 = over 20 full-time equivalent employees, where full-time equivalent employees equals (number of full time) + ($\frac{1}{2}$)(number of part time)

ID	1	2	3	4	5	6	7	8	9	10	11	12	13
1	2	480	0	600	35	25	2	2	200	3	8	30	3
2	4	507	22	375	59	20	5	2	150	1	6	25	2
3	5	210	25	275	40	24	3	1	46	1	0	17	1
4	5	246	*	80	43	30	1	1	28	3	2	13	1
5	2	148	*	85	45	35	1	3	44	1	*	*	*
6	3	50	*	135	40	30	10	2	50	3	2	*	*
7	2	72	0	125	85	10	5	2	50	1	0	5	1
8	3	99	7	150	43	25	1	2	130	1	1	8	1
9	4	160	5	85	*	*	*	*	*	2	2	10	1
10	4	243	7	150	38	15	2	2	50	2	2	19	2
11	4	200	3	225	42	22	2	1	64	1	3	12	1
12	4	1000	20	1500	20	20	10	1	240	3	30	40	3
13	4	350	*	*	31	35	*	1	111	3	10	19	2
14	3	550	0	410	50	26	2	2	125	3	6	16	2
15	3	500	10	1000	50	40	10	2	120	1	4	28	2
16	4	1100	8	900	*	*	*	*	*	3	13	47	3
17	3	416	0	400	40	21	4	1	92	3	7	15	2
18	2	650	*	*	63	32	5	1	90	3	20	25	3
19	5	292	0	425	42	13	1	2	150	3	1	16	1

ID	1	2	3	4	5	6	7	8	9	10	11	12	13
20	3	400	10	350	30	25	5	2	90	1	15	10	2
21	3	42	0	15	64	35	1	3	15	2	0	0	1
22	2	100	15	185	50	15	1	2	80	3	0	7	1
23	4	75	0	160	*	*	*	2	76	1	0	10	1
24	3	180	0	180	50	20	2	2	65	1	1	14	1
25	4	201	0	250	70	27	3	2	178	1	0	20	2
26	6	273	60	300	32	28	10	3	110	3	7	13	2
27	4	150	0	150	*	*	*	2	60	*	51	80	3
28	5	60	4	100	*	*	*	1	0	1	0	0	1
29	4	1200	50	800	35	32	3	3	150	3	35	45	3
30	3	247	4	*	38	*	2	1	60	3	4	8	1
31	2	290	3	200	39	29	1	1	85	3	16	14	3
32	2	58	2	75	45	28	5	2	25	3	2	2	1
33	4	400	0	100	40	35	1	3	85	3	18	15	3
34	3	75	*	26	40	40	5	3	20	2	4	4	1
35	5	*	*	*	32	40	4	2	200	*	*	*	*
36	4	144	0	25	45	25	0	3	0	1	6	3	1
37	4	65	0	25	48	20	1	1	0	1	2	2	1
38	3	*	*	*	*	*	*	1	210	*	*	*	*
39	4	465	0	75	38	28	7	1	111	3	6	32	3
40	5	*	*	*	50	40	10	3	0	3	10	5	2
41	5	510	3	750	35	29	4	1	152	3	30	25	3
42	3	440	0	*	38	20	5	1	62	3	9	16	2
43	4	608	30	395	31	28	2	3	165	3	30	12	3
44	3	200	3	350	43	21	4	1	68	2	3	18	2
45	1	90	5	40	60	30	10	1	60	1	3	3	1
46	5	45	3	40	40	20	3	3	0	1	0	7	1
47	6	36	1	*	65	25	5	1	0	2	3	0	1
48	4	249	6	275	65	30	5	1	52	1	8	10	2
49	5	200	5	60	35	20	2	3	24	3	4	20	2
50	2	80	0	150	60	30	5	2	70	1	1	4	1
51	1	500	5	350	40	30	3	1	72	3	20	6	3
52	2	125	10	140	50	20	5	2	68	3	0	8	1
53	2	101	0	140	54	13	1	2	58	1	2	3	1
54	4	110	2	160	60	20	1	2	46	1	0	6	1
55	3	1200	0	2500	37	29	3	1	200	3	80	45	3
56	1	*	*	*	33	25	25	3	120	3	25	5	3
57	4	4700	20	1500	50	20	4	1	200	3	15	50	3
58	3	48	0	45	45	25	2	3	10	3	0	12	1
59	2	150	20	150	45	25	5	3	0	3	10	20	2
60	1	185	40	*	40	40	4	1	62	3	2	18	2
61	4	157	2	250	*	*	*	1	99	1	3	8	1
62	6	621	9	0	36	23	3	1	120	3	5	45	3
63	2	257	10	365	40	22	0	1	100	1	14	3	2
64	2	137	0	75	55	30	3	1	0	3	1	3	1
65	1	190	0	400	60	40	0	1	125	1	2	11	1
66	1	*	*	*	*	*	*	*	0	*	*	*	*

(*continued*)

ID	1	2	3	4	5	6	7	8	9	10	11	12	13
67	2	320	6	350	50	20	3	2	96	1	10	10	2
68	5	650	*	*	50	30	1	2	140	3	20	15	3
69	5	610	61	*	38	19	5	1	100	3	10	30	3
70	2	385	4	150	36	29	4	3	48	3	20	28	3
71	5	360	75	325	29	23	3	1	120	3	4	15	2
72	1	276	*	200	65	30	5	1	0	3	20	3	3
73	6	600	20	500	38	22	2	2	125	3	28	5	3
74	2	330	0	100	45	25	2	1	0	1	2	14	1
75	3	215	10	125	45	30	2	1	15	1	11	0	2
76	3	425	15	1750	39	27	12	3	250	1	2	70	3
77	4	250	10	10	40	40	10	2	80	3	10	4	2
78	2	120	0	80	*	*	*	3	30	1	1	2	1
79	3	60	30	45	60	30	10	1	16	2	0	4	1
80	3	141	6	80	85	10	5	1	34	2	0	4	1
81	5	800	50	500	50	25	5	3	120	2	35	13	3
82	3	207	4	200	48	20	1	1	0	*	*	*	*
83	5	1016	16	1000	40	36	1	3	200	3	20	40	3
84	3	60	0	40	50	30	20	3	80	3	2	4	1
85	3	309	10	500	52	18	2	2	80	1	6	14	2
86	2	960	20	400	54	22	2	3	0	3	7	40	3
87	3	150	*	650	70	20	10	2	220	3	3	18	2
88	4	56	5	125	40	20	10	2	44	1	0	2	1
89	6	250	5	100	33	30	2	1	55	3	10	15	2
90	4	275	10	295	50	25	5	2	85	3	10	3	2
91	5	150	50	300	30	30	0	1	77	3	4	13	2
92	4	325	2	175	45	25	5	3	125	3	20	6	3
93	5	110	5	235	50	30	20	2	65	2	2	10	1
94	3	250	5	230	50	30	4	2	90	3	4	12	2
95	3	550	0	500	48	22	2	2	100	3	13	6	2
96	1	100	3	200	35	25	0	1	50	3	0	6	1
97	3	32	1	42	35	10	2	1	30	1	3	0	1
98	7	366	10	300	42	25	1	2	150	3	12	40	3
99	5	70	3	150	50	7	2	2	50	3	3	2	1
100	3	531	2	450	46	30	1	3	72	3	1	39	3
101	4	225	0	300	50	40	0	1	43	1	10	4	2
102	3	108	5	110	*	*	*	*	*	2	0	8	1
103	3	100	*	*	86	14	0	3	0	1	3	2	1
104	4	40	4	75	30	1	1	3	20	1	*	2	*
105	4	750	0	1000	40	22	5	2	140	2	15	25	3
106	2	312	*	250	40	34	2	3	110	3	6	20	2
107	2	50	5	75	40	20	5	3	56	1	0	5	1
108	5	163	3	115	50	28	5	2	75	3	5	4	1
109	1	75	1	55	*	*	*	3	32	1	0	0	1
110	6	550	6	600	48	24	1	2	76	2	3	30	2
111	1	3450	8	100	*	*	*	2	80	3	3	9	1
112	3	50	4	305	45	9	4	2	60	1	4	6	1
113	5	80	0	50	43	18	2	3	0	1	0	6	1
114	3	435	10	250	30	14	5	3	36	1	1	11	1
115	1	70	2	75	30	35	0	1	0	1	1	2	1

ID	1	2	3	4	5	6	7	8	9	10	11	12	13
116	1	78	0	125	90	0	10	3	62	1	5	0	1
117	5	210	20	225	80	18	2	1	28	1	0	5	1
118	4	280	*	300	40	16	8	1	50	3	2	18	2
119	4	192	*	300	35	85	5	2	82	3	8	4	2
120	4	116	15	135	50	*	*	1	28	1	2	7	1
121	5	245	0	450	36	24	2	2	100	3	7	20	2
122	1	110	*	160	*	*	*	2	80	1	0	0	1
123	3	229	*	150	35	25	5	1	72	3	7	8	2
124	4	275	*	1100	60	40	0	1	96	3	4	7	1
125	1	100	*	75	50	20	2	3	46	1	4	4	1
126	4	647	10	350	50	30	5	1	90	3	5	12	2
127	4	300	1	100	*	*	*	*	*	3	*	*	*
128	7	54	0	*	35	20	15	3	70	*	0	0	1
129	5	400	*	300	*	*	*	3	78	3	3	25	2
130	2	120	2	100	84	15	1	2	55	1	1	5	1
131	5	*	*	*	30	15	9	1	40	3	10	15	2
132	1	179	6	70	43	23	2	1	27	1	1	15	1
133	4	300	3	175	35	30	1	1	30	3	7	8	2
134	3	500	125	300	45	78	5	1	125	3	10	22	3
135	2	150	12	210	45	15	2	2	60	1	0	10	1
136	3	135	2	90	60	18	2	1	42	1	3	4	1
137	5	400	4	250	42	35	1	1	36	3	13	3	2
138	1	480	*	450	57	38	0	2	200	2	30	8	3
139	3	530	40	200	40	30	8	2	180	3	25	12	3
140	5	*	*	*	*	*	*	3	20	1	0	2	1
141	5	600	12	90	35	30	5	1	30	3	36	4	3
142	4	*	4	150	42	0	2	3	50	1	7	3	1
143	2	125	1	*	55	20	2	1	35	3	3	8	1
144	1	382	0	190	*	*	*	1	51	3	4	0	1
145	5	*	*	400	30	13	4	1	100	3	2	7	1
146	3	200	10	200	30	30	5	3	50	3	4	12	2
147	5	800	21	750	38	25	3	3	144	3	20	21	3
148	4	144	*	200	40	20	1	2	50	1	2	5	1
149	4	130	1	150	0	40	1	2	60	3	3	9	1
150	2	1010	50	*	50	25	3	2	127	3	25	35	3
151	5	60	5	150	*	*	*	3	25	1	0	2	1
152	4	292	20	100	49	30	8	2	75	2	6	24	2
153	3	100	56	*	45	25	5	2	75	3	6	14	2
154	3	98	0	70	70	28	2	1	32	1	0	7	1
155	2	250	6	250	50	25	1	2	90	3	7	7	2
156	4	172	1	200	35	14	3	1	0	1	0	20	2
157	3	145	12	155	*	*	*	2	74	1	1	9	1
158	4	*	*	*	*	*	*	2	0	3	*	0	*
159	1	*	*	*	*	*	*	*	*	*	*	*	*
160	4	*	*	*	*	*	*	1	0	3	3	1	1
161	3	37	1	20	45	10	1	3	12	1	1	1	1
162	3	*	*	*	*	*	3	1	82	2	5	22	2
163	4	77	0	150	*	*	*	1	35	2	4	1	1

(*continued*)

ID	1	2	3	4	5	6	7	8	9	10	11	12	13
164	3	400	*	400	*	*	*	3	44	3	6	8	2
165	4	1000	20	*	40	34	2	2	*	2	*	*	*
166	2	250	15	750	40	20	5	2	95	3	26	13	3
167	4	50	*	90	*	*	*	3	24	1	0	0	1
168	1	120	6	*	80	15	5	1	70	1	1	6	1
169	4	750	78	0	30	32	3	3	94	2	40	6	3
170	5	190	8	75	42	31	1	3	60	3	6	3	1
171	1	140	5	180	40	5	5	2	87	1	3	3	1
172	4	80	52	60	36	23	1	2	100	1	0	8	1
173	5	55	0	50	50	20	10	3	40	3	0	6	1
174	5	690	0	250	45	21	3	3	196	3	8	35	3
175	4	200	1	175	49	19	2	1	100	1	0	18	1
176	4	28	2	55	33	0	1	3	34	3	0	0	1
177	5	40	1	0	*	*	*	3	24	3	1	3	1
178	4	2	0	2	30	5	0	1	10	3	0	2	1
179	2	217	0	750	51	29	4	2	95	3	3	25	2
180	4	250	0	300	40	30	10	1	20	3	10	10	2
181	3	990	*	1500	40	29	5	1	175	3	12	43	3
182	4	2	2	*	90	10	0	1	0	2	0	4	1
183	3	50	20	325	50	30	20	2	75	3	2	3	1
184	7	290	150	450	51	59	3	2	110	1	5	14	2
185	1	75	10	140	*	*	*	1	0	1	0	0	1
186	1	*	*	*	*	*	*	*	*	1	0	0	1
187	5	400	10	300	20	25	5	2	85	3	10	10	2
188	3	30	0	60	49	30	1	1	0	2	2	4	1
189	2	70	0	32	40	30	1	3	65	1	2	3	1
190	2	250	0	0	37	14	4	1	16	3	3	13	1
191	5	1600	20	1000	34	32	4	1	52	3	20	55	3
192	2	290	0	125	60	35	5	1	70	3	6	2	1
193	4	203	2	40	39	31	4	1	0	1	8	4	2
194	5	*	*	*	60	30	0	1	16	1	0	3	1
195	2	100	5	300	60	0	1	2	50	2	0	0	1
196	3	551	0	1500	*	*	*	1	100	3	10	25	3
197	3	220	10	70	42	40	4	1	85	3	6	7	1
198	3	225	10	550	50	15	5	1	200	3	1	15	1
199	3	140	14	175	33	10	5	1	0	1	0	4	1
200	1	154	0	20	45	28	0	*	80	3	6	5	1
201	4	39	0	65	42	42	0	1	75	1	0	30	2
202	4	565	0	500	*	*	*	2	85	3	15	35	3
203	3	0	2	0	43	15	2	2	75	1	1	4	1
204	2	1096	73	2000	34	29	1	1	142	3	42	30	3
205	4	35	1	0	90	10	0	1	60	1	4	0	1
206	5	53	20	125	40	20	5	1	30	3	5	7	1
207	2	390	8	450	*	*	*	*	*	3	30	16	3
208	3	*	*	*	32	34	2	1	104	3	2	16	2
209	4	*	*	80	*	*	*	3	45	1	1	9	1
210	5	500	25	450	45	35	1	2	132	3	18	20	3
211	4	180	5	300	58	40	2	3	30	3	8	3	1
212	6	89	4	120	45	15	2	1	0	1	1	2	1

ID	1	2	3	4	5	6	7	8	9	10	11	12	13
213	1	77	10	175	35	10	1	3	0	1	0	5	1
214	1	460	3	75	40	23	6	1	94	3	2	35	2
215	3	440	35	1000	38	39	3	3	110	3	40	30	3
216	5	56	8	125	40	33	2	3	0	1	12	0	2
217	4	15	23	30	52	46	2	1	0	1	0	0	1
218	5	150	*	150	*	*	*	*	*	2	0	7	1
219	5	8064	300	12000	37	31	3	1	550	3	250	60	3
220	3	200	*	*	20	20	*	1	20	3	1	8	1
221	3	30	*	350	50	20	5	1	80	3	0	4	1
222	5	71	0	185	40	8	0	3	0	1	0	3	1
223	4	11	0	0	99	0	0	1	4	1	0	0	1
224	1	267	2	125	40	25	5	1	44	3	2	13	1
225	7	325	10	400	46	25	3	2	70	1	3	9	1
226	1	155	0	85	35	35	5	3	70	1	10	3	2
227	4	1000	100	5000	35	20	7	1	180	3	30	20	3
228	3	85	30	45	45	25	2	1	54	1	1	6	1
229	3	250	50	1000	35	35	0	3	150	3	25	30	3
230	2	30	5	40	30	30	3	3	55	1	1	4	1
231	2	20	1	0	45	20	2	3	0	3	0	3	1
232	*	*	*	*	40	10	5	1	40	*	*	*	*
233	2	125	5	125	50	30	10	1	65	1	0	6	1
234	4	720	13	650	37	24	6	1	150	3	6	25	2
235	4	*	*	*	40	30	5	3	150	3	25	100	3
236	1	240	3	225	50	20	2	2	30	1	5	6	1
237	4	10	*	10	50	38	2	3	35	2	3	10	1
238	5	240	0	125	45	25	1	1	0	1	7	3	1
239	6	59	*	*	*	*	*	3	0	2	2	4	1
240	3	1080	20	1000	32	30	5	3	170	3	40	50	3
241	1	225	1	150	34	22	4	3	120	3	18	5	3
242	3	*	*	*	*	*	*	*	*	3	4	20	2
243	2	70	7	225	25	35	10	3	43	1	4	2	1
244	1	430	35	500	42	26	2	2	0	3	6	30	3
245	4	198	*	130	45	21	1	1	62	1	5	8	1
246	5	65	12	150	35	30	2	1	35	1	10	4	2
247	2	69	3	18	44	26	1	3	43	1	0	9	1
248	4	230	0	0	35	36	3	3	150	3	20	12	3
249	4	250	25	850	40	15	1	1	40	3	0	*	*
250	5	140	80	140	*	*	*	*	*	1	2	12	1
251	5	180	5	150	40	25	5	1	130	3	2	6	1
252	3	60	7	*	40	10	2	1	18	1	1	0	1
253	1	80	0	150	51	18	0	1	0	1	1	2	1
254	1	42	0	75	65	25	10	1	36	1	0	3	1
255	4	8	0	14	25	15	0	3	0	1	*	2	*
256	3	210	*	350	*	*	*	2	100	1	0	16	1
257	3	95	0	70	45	25	2	3	42	1	4	1	1
258	4	55	50	89	65	30	5	3	32	3	0	2	1
259	5	121	1	160	55	30	5	1	30	1	3	2	1

(*continued*)

ID	1	2	3	4	5	6	7	8	9	10	11	12	13
260	3	75	10	80	40	26	5	3	26	1	2	2	1
261	1	*	*	*	45	21	4	3	205	3	8	32	3
262	6	250	10	300	38	29	4	1	50	3	5	20	2
263	4	220	10	350	55	25	10	2	70	1	0	15	1
264	4	120	10	80	35	60	2	1	80	1	2	22	2
265	2	25	1	40	40	10	6	1	0	*	*	*	*
266	1	500	0	175	75	20	5	2	200	3	32	1	3
267	3	*	*	475	45	20	10	2	80	1	2	15	1
268	3	200	10	70	45	20	25	1	70	3	0	10	1
269	4	250	3	5	35	50	0	3	15	2	1	3	1
270	5	215	1	100	36	33	2	3	98	3	5	17	2
271	4	*	*	*	*	*	*	2	36	2	7	6	2
272	3	733	35	500	53	21	0	1	0	1	6	40	3
273	1	*	*	*	*	*	*	3	0	1	0	0	1
274	1	200	1	210	50	20	5	2	70	*	*	*	*
275	5	305	0	450	58	27	2	2	85	3	3	25	2
276	1	110	5	175	*	*	*	2	99	1	0	7	1
277	2	*	*	100	*	*	*	3	45	1	3	6	1
278	3	100	20	250	24	30	10	3	100	3	0	7	1
279	4	355	*	95	40	20	5	1	130	3	8	12	2

Source: Professor William E. Strang, University of Wisconsin, Madison.

B/ADDITIONAL FEATURES IN MINITAB

This Appendix gives additional information on some commands that have already been described. It also introduces a few new commands.

B.1/INPUT AND OUTPUT OF DATA IN COMPUTER FILES

READ AND SET

On pages 6–11, we showed how READ and SET can be used when data are typed as part of a Minitab program. READ and SET can also input data that previously have been stored in a computer file. As an example, suppose the data in Exhibit B.1 had been stored in a file named PLANT. The following commands input the data and assign names.

```
READ 'PLANT' INTO C10, C1-C5
NAME C1 = 'MON' C2 = 'TUES' C3 = 'WED' &
     C4 = 'THURS' C5 = 'FRI' C10 = 'LINE'
```

EXHIBIT B.1   Example to Illustrate Input and Output Commands

Production Line	Yield for Each Day				
	Monday	Tuesday	Wednesday	Thursday	Friday
1	25	29	30	26	22
2	32	36	35	33	28
3	21	24	23	21	20
4	17	18	16	17	17

READ data from 'FILENAME' into C, ..., C

This form of READ inputs data from a computer file. The name of the file must be enclosed in single quotes (apostrophes). The computer file that

READ inputs could have been created by your computer's editor, by Minitab's WRITE command, or by another program that outputs standard data files. The file must be in a form suitable for READ (see p. 10). *Note*: You should not give a column of your worksheet the same name as a file you plan to use.

SET data from 'FILENAME' into C

This form of SET inputs data from a computer file. The file name must be enclosed in single quotes. The computer file that SET inputs could have been created by your computer's editor or by Minitab's WRITE command. The file must be in a form suitable for a SET command (see p. 11). *Note*: You should not give a column of your worksheet the same name as a file you plan to use.

WRITE TO A FILE

In some cases you may want to put data from the worksheet into a computer file for later use with Minitab or some other program. This can be done with WRITE. For example,

```
WRITE 'YIELD' C1-C5
```

puts the data that are in C1–C5 into a computer file named YIELD. If we used this instruction after the commands on page 293, the file YIELD would look like this:

25	29	30	26	22
32	36	36	33	28
21	24	24	21	20
17	18	18	17	17

Note: The column headers that occur with PRINT are not used with WRITE. You can use READ to input this file. You also can use your computer's editor to print or modify the file.

WRITE data into 'FILENAME' from C, ..., C

WRITE creates a computer file from columns of the worksheet. The columns must all be the same length. The file name must be enclosed in single quotes.

Usually one line is put in the data file for each row of the worksheet. The numbers on a line are separated by blanks. If you WRITE many columns, they may not all fit on one line. Minitab then uses two or more lines per row and the continuation symbol, & (see p. 9). If you WRITE just one column, as many numbers as will fit are put on each line.

If you WRITE one column, you can use SET to input the resulting file. If you WRITE more than one column, you can use READ to input the resulting file. You may use your computer's editor or other computer programs to read, print, or modify files created by WRITE.

B.2 / ENTERING PATTERNED DATA WITH SET AND INSERT

The SET command has a feature that makes it easy to input certain kinds of patterned data. For example, you can put the integers from 1 to 12 into C2 by typing.

```
SET C2
  1:12
END
```

In general, any list of consecutive integers can be abbreviated with a colon. For example,

```
SET C1
37:40,   6:4,  −3:2
END
```

puts 37, 38, 39, 40, 6, 5, 4, −3, −2, −1, 0, 1, 2, into C1.

A slash allows you to abbreviate other types of patterns. For example,

```
SET C2
10:20/2
END
```

puts 10, 12, 14, 16, 18, 20 into C2 and

```
SET C3
2:1.4/.1
END
```

puts 2, 1.9, 1.8, 1.7, 1.6, 1.5, 1.4 into C3. In general, you put the distance between consecutive numbers after the slash.

Parentheses can be used to repeat a list of numbers. For example, suppose C1 contains the blood pressure for 27 people. Suppose the first 15 are women and the last 12 are men. You could enter the sex of each person, coded 1 for men and 2 for women, by typing

```
SET C2
15(2)  12(1)
END
```

The number in front of the open parenthesis is a repeat factor. The 15 says to repeat the number inside the parentheses 15 times. *Note*: There must not be any blanks (or other symbols) between the repeat factor and the parenthesis. Thus the 15 must be next to the open parenthesis. You may, however, put blanks and commas inside the parentheses.

In general, any list of numbers may be repeated. Just enclose the list in parentheses and put the repeat factor in front. For example,

```
SET C1
2(0:2, 10)
END
```

puts 0, 1, 2, 10, 0, 1, 2, 10 into C1.

If you put the repeat factor after the parentheses, each number is repeated individually. For example,

```
SET C1
(0, 1)4
END
```

puts 0, 0, 0, 0, 1, 1, 1, 1, into C1. Again, do not leave any blanks between the right parenthesis and the repeat factor.

You can use a repeat factor both before and after the parentheses. For example,

```
SET C1
2(0, 1)3
END
```

Here, each number inside the parentheses is repeated three times to give the list 0, 0, 0, 1, 1, 1. Then this list is repeated twice. Thus C1 will contain 0, 0, 0, 1, 1, 1, 0, 0, 0, 1, 1, 1.

If you use INSERT to enter data into just one column, you can use all the patterned data features of SET.

B.3 / CALCULATIONS WITH LET

The LET command makes it easy to perform relatively complicated calculations. In most data analysis, however, you will need just a few of the simpler forms of this command.

Unlike most other Minitab commands, no extra text may be used on a LET line (unless you use the line terminator, #; see p. 306).

ARITHMETIC

The simplest form of LET is

```
LET C = arithmetic expression
```

or

```
LET K = arithmetic expression
```

The arithmetic expression uses the symbols + for add, − for subtract, * for multiply, / for divide, and ** for raise to a power (exponentiation). Parentheses may be used for grouping. (This was discussed in Section 1.3). In addition, you can use column statistics, such as MEAN and MAX in LET. (This was described in Section 2.5.)

You can access an individual number in a column by using a subscript. For example, suppose C2 contains the five numbers 13, 12, 10, 14, 12. Then

```
LET K2 = C2(2)
```

takes the second number, 12, from C2 and puts it into K2. You can also store a number in one spot in a column. For example,

```
LET C2(3) = 17
```

puts 17 into the third row of C2. In Section 1.3, we showed how this form of LET could be used to correct numbers in the worksheet.

Any expression which evaluates to an integer may be used as a subscript. For example, (COUNT (C2) − 1) is 5 − 1, or 4, so

```
LET C2(COUNT(C2) - 1) = 15
```

puts the value 15 into row 4 of C2.

Subscripted columns can be part of a more complicated expression. For example,

```
LET C7 = (C2-MIN(C2))*C2(1)/C2(COUNT(C2)-3)
```

subtracts 10 from each number in C2, then multiplies by 13, and divides by 2.

FUNCTIONS

LET can use the functions described below. In all cases the input is either a single column or a constant.

ABSOLUTE	Computes the absolute value
SIGNS	Returns -1, 0, or 1 for negative, zero, or positive values, respectively
SQRT	Computes the square root
ROUND	Rounds to the nearest integer
LOGE	Computes the logarithm to base e
LOGTEN	Computes the logarithm to base 10
EXPONENTIAL	Computes the value of e^x
ANTILOG	Computes the value of 10^x
SIN	Computes the sine of the angle given in radians
COS, TAN	Cosine or tangent, angle in radians

ASIN	Inverse sine or arcsine; the answer is in radians
ACOS, ATAN	Inverse cosine and inverse tangent
RANKS	Assigns 1 to the smallest number in the column, 2 to the second smallest, 3 to the third smallest, etc; the average rank is assigned when there are ties
SORT	Orders the numbers in a column, putting the smallest on top
NSCORES	Calculates normal scores (see p. 129)
PARSUMS	Calculates partial sums; for example, if C1 contains 2, 4, 1, 9, then LET C2 = PARSUMS(C1) puts $2, 2 + 4 = 6, 2 + 4 + 1 = 7, 2 + 4 + 1 + 9 = 16$ into C2
PARPRODUCTS	Calculates partial products
LAG	Moves all numbers down one now, puts $*$ (the missing data code, see p. 304) in the first row, and omits the number in the last row; for example, if C1 contains 2, 4, 1, 9, then LET C2 = LAG(C1) puts $*$, 2, 4, 1 into C2

Here are some examples using these functions. Suppose C1 contains the five numbers 4, -3.6, 0, -8, 4.2. Then after

```
LET C2 = ABSO(C1)
LET C3 = SIGNS(C1)
LET C4 = ROUND(C1)
LET C5 = SORT (C1)
LET K1 = SQRT(9)
```

the worksheet is

C1	C2	C3	C4	C5	K1
4	4	1	4	-8	3
-3.6	3.6	-1	-4	-3.6	
0	0	0	0	0	
-8	8	-1	-8	4	
4.2	4.2	1	4	4.2	

B.4 / THE COPY COMMAND

The COPY command has two functions: It allows you to copy data from one place in the worksheet to another, and it allows you to select a subset of data. For example, it can be used to select the data for just the women in a study.

> COPY C, ..., C into C, ..., C
> COPY K, ..., K into K, ..., K
> COPY C into K, ..., K
> COPY K, ..., K into C
>
> The copy command allows you to make a second copy of data and to move data from columns to constants, and vice versa.

SELECTING SUBSETS OF DATA

COPY has two subcommands, USE and OMIT. We will explain these with a simple example. Suppose we've entered sex (coded 1 = male, 2 = female), height, and weight for seven people into C1–C3, which we have named SEX, HT, WT. Then the following commands put the data for women into C12–C13.

```
COPY C2 C3 INTO C12 C13;
   USE 'SEX' = 2.
NAME C12 = 'HT.F', C13 = 'WT.F'
```

All rows where SEX = 2 are copied into C12 and C13. Now the worksheet contains the following data:

| C1 | C2 | C3 | C12 | C13 |
SEX	HT	WT	HT.F	WT.F
2	66	130	66	130
1	70	155	64	125
2	64	125	65	115
2	65	115	63	108
2	63	108		
1	66	145		
1	69	160		

In general, you may specify any list of values or range of values for the variable on USE. For example,

```
COPY C2 C3 INTO C22 C33;
   USE 'HT' = 64, 65, 66.
```

copies all rows that have any of the values 64, 65, or 66 for HT. You can use a colon to indicate a range of values. For example,

```
COPY C2 C3 INTO C22 C33;
   USE 'HT' = 0:64.
```

copies the data for all people who are 64 inches or shorter.

You also can subset by giving row numbers. For example,

```
COPY C2 C3 INTO C22 C23;
  USE 1, 3:5.
```

copies rows 1, 3, 4, 5.

The OMIT subcommand is the opposite of USE. USE says which rows to copy, OMIT says which rows not to copy. For example,

```
COPY C2 C3 INTO C22 C23;
  OMIT 'SEX' = 1.
```

again copies just the women. You also can use row numbers with OMIT. For example, to copy all but rows 2, 6, and 7, type

```
COPY C2 C3 INTO C22 C23;
  OMIT 2, 6, 7.
```

COPY C, ..., C into C, ..., C

USE ROWS
USE C = VALS
OMIT ROWS
OMIT C = VALS

These subcommands copy selected rows. The USE subcommand says which rows to copy; OMIT says which rows not to copy. These rows can be specified by their row numbers or by the values in a column.

ROWS can be any list of row numbers. Consecutive numbers can be abbreviated with a colon. Thus, USE 2, 5:8 is the same subcommand as USE 2, 5, 6, 7, 8.

VALS can be any list of values. An interval can be abbreviated with a colon. Thus USE C1 = 5: 8, 20 says to copy all rows where C1 is a value in the range of 5 through 8, or equal to 20.

B.5 / HOW TO STACK AND UNSTACK DATA

In Section 5.1 (p. 88) we introduced the concept of stacked versus unstacked data. Here we will show how to change from one form to the other.

Suppose we have height and weight for two groups of people, men and women. In Exhibit B.2(a) the data for men are in one pair of columns and the data for women are in a second pair. In Exhibit B.2(b) the data for men and women are all stacked together. The column SEX is used to indicate which rows are for males (SEX = 1) and which rows are for females (SEX = 2).

EXHIBIT B.2   Illustrations of Stacked and Unstacked Data

(a) Unstacked Data   (b) Stacked Data

C1	C2	C3	C4		C5	C6	SEX
----	----	----	----		----	----	-----
66	130	70	155		70	155	1
64	125	66	145		66	145	1
65	115	69	160		69	160	1
63	108				66	130	2
					64	125	2
					65	115	2
					63	108	2

Sometimes we need to change data from one format to the other. The STACK and UNSTACK commands make this relatively easy. For example, to stack the data in Exhibit B.2(a) so that they look like the data in part (b), use the command

```
STACK (C3, C4) (C1, C2) into C5, C6;
    SUBSCRIPTS 'SEX'.
```

Similarly, to unstack the data in Exhibit B.2(b) so that they look like the data in part (a), use the command

```
UNSTACK (C5, C6) into (C3, C4) (C1, C2);
    SUBSCRIPTS 'SEX'.
```

STACK also can be used with numbers and stored constants. For example,

```
STACK C1, 61, 64, C3, 66 into C20
```

creates one column that contains 10 numbers, 66, 64, 65, 63, 61, 64, 70, 66, 69, 66. Note that we omitted the parentheses in this command. We can omit the parentheses if everything is stacked into one column.

STACK (E, ..., E), ..., (E, ..., E) store in (C, ..., C)

This command stacks blocks of columns and constants on top of each other. In general, each block must be enclosed in parentheses. However, if each block contains just one argument, the parentheses may be omitted. If you want to create a column of subscripts, use the subcommand

SUBSCRIPTS into C

In this case, all rows in the first block will be given subscripts of 1, all rows in the second block subscripts of 2, and so on.

UNSTACK (C, ..., C) into (E, ..., E), ..., (E, ..., E)

SUBSCRIPTS are into C

This command separates one block of columns into several blocks of columns and/or stored constants. In general, each block must be enclosed in parentheses. However, if each block contains just one argument, the parentheses may be omitted.

For most applications, the subcommand SUBSCRIPTS will be needed. The rows with the smallest subscript are stored in the first block, the rows with the second smallest subscript stored in the second block, and so on. If you do not use SUBSCRIPTS, each row is stored in a separate block. The numbers in the subscript column must be integers between −10000 and 10000. They need not be in order; nor do they need to be consecutive integers.

B.6 / CHANGING VALUES WITH CODE

The CODE command changes values in columns. For example,

        CODE (−2, −1) to 0 in C1 C2, put in C11 C12

changes the worksheets as follows:

C1	C2	C11	C12
8	16	8	16
−2	13	0	13
6	−2	6	0
0	−2	0	0
−1	14	0	14

Every −2 and −1 in C1 and C2 is changed into 0. All other values are kept the same.

You can make many changes at once, and you can specify a range with a colon. For example,

        CODE (30:55)1 (56:80)2 (81:120)3 C1−C5, C11−C15

changes all values from 30 up through 55 into 1, values from 56 up through

80 into 2, and values from 81 up through 120 into 3. These changes are made on columns C1–C5 and the results are stored in C11–C15. The original columns, C1–C5, are not changed.

CODE (VALS) to K, ..., (VALS) to K for C ... C put in C ... C

This command changes the specified values. All other values in the columns are left as is. VALS can be any list of values. In addition, an interval can be abbreviated with a colon. For example, CODE (1:1.5, 2)0 changes all values in the range 1 through 1.5, and the value 2 into zeros. VALS must be enclosed in parentheses.

If two instances of VALS overlap, the last one is used. For example, CODE (10:20)1 (20:30)2 changes the value 20 into a 2.

CODE can change values into the missing value code, ∗. For example, to change all occurrences of −99 to missing values, use

```
CODE (-99) '*' C1-C10, put in C1-C10
```

B.7 / HOW TO SORT AND RANK DATA

THE SORT COMMAND

Here is a simple example.

```
SORT C1, carry along C2-C4, put into C11-C14
```

changes the worksheet as follows:

C1	C2	C3	C4	C11	C12	C13	C14
10	0.2	31	131	10	0.2	31	131
10	0.1	35	210	10	0.1	35	210
12	0.1	37	176	10	0.4	31	140
12	0.1	36	190	11	0.2	29	180
10	0.4	31	140	11	0.1	33	182
12	0.1	30	110	12	0.1	37	176
11	0.2	29	180	12	0.1	36	190
11	0.1	33	182	12	0.1	30	110

The first column listed, C1, determined the order. C2–C4 were carried along as the ordering was done. The smallest value in C1 is 10. So, all rows where C1 = 10 were put first. The second smallest value in C1 is 11. So the two rows where C1 = 11 were stored next, and so on.

THE RANK COMMAND

The RANK command does not reorder the data. It creates a new column containing the rank of each value in the original column. The smallest value is given rank 1, the second smallest rank 2, the third smallest rank 3, and so on. For example,

```
RANK C1 into C11
```

changes the worksheet as follows:

C1	C11
1.4	3
1.1	1
2.0	4.5
3.1	6
2.0	4.5
1.3	2

Ranks for C1 were put into C11. The smallest number in C1 is 1.1, so a 1 was put into C11. The second smallest number in C1 is 1.3, and so a 2 was put into C11, and so on. If there are ties, the average rank is assigned to each value. For example, the fourth and fifth values in C1 are both 2.0. They both were given the rank of $(4 + 5)/2 = 4.5$.

SORT C, carry along C, ..., C store in C, ..., C

Sorts the first column into increasing order. The next group of columns are just carried along as the sorting is done.

RANK C into C

Ranks are determined as follows: The number 1 is put next to the smallest value in the column, the number 2 next to the second smallest, and so on. If several entries in a column are equal, they are all given the average rank.

B.8 / MISSING DATA

Section 1.5 introduced Minitab's missing data code, *. Here we will give some additional information.

THE MISSING DATA CODE ON A COMMAND LINE

In general, an * may be used on a command or subcommand line in place of a number whenever it makes sense. On command and subcommand lines, the * must be enclosed in single quotes (apostrophes). For example,

```
COPY C2 INTO C12;
   OMIT C2 = '*'.
```

copies all rows that do not have an * in C2. The statement

```
LET C1(5) = '*'
```

changes the value in row 5 of C1 to *.

Another use of * is to code values that already have been entered with some other missing data code. For example, if missing data have been coded as −99, then the CODE command (see p 303) can be used to change −99 to *:

```
CODE (-99) TO '*' IN C1-C10, PUT BACK IN C1-C10
```

CALCULATIONS THAT RESULT IN MISSING VALUES

Suppose C1 contains the three values 2, 0, 3 and we use

```
LET C2 = 12/C1
```

Then C2 will contain 6, *, 4. The * was put in row two, since 12/0 is undefined and the answer therefore is missing. There are a number of algebraic calculations that are undefined and result in *, for example, $\sqrt{-5}$ and $\log(-3)$.

HOW MINITAB COMMANDS TREAT MISSING DATA

The arithmetic operations (+, −, *, /, and **) and functions, such as SQRT and LOGE, set the answer to missing if any input value is missing. The column summaries such as SUM and MEAN, and the row summaries such as RSUM and RMEAN, just omit all missing values from the calculations. For example, the commands

```
LET C4 = C1 + C2
LET C5 = C1 + C2 + C3
LET C6 = SQRT(C2)
RSUM C1-C3 PUT INTO C7
RMEAN C1-C3 PUT INTO C8
LET K1 = SUM(C3)
LET K2 = MEAN(C3)
```

change the worksheet as follows;

C1	C2	C3	C1	C2	C3	C4	C5	C6	C7	C8	K1	K2
2	4	3	2	4	3	6	9	2	9	3	10	5
5	*	7	5	*	7	*	*	*	12	6		
5	9	*	5	9	*	14	*	3	14	7		

Most other commands simply omit missing values from all calculations the way SUM and RSUM do. For example, suppose C1 and C2 both contain 50 observations but C2 has *s in rows 2 and 34. Then HISTO-GRAM C1 C2 would produce one histogram of the 50 values in C1 and one histogram of the 48 nonmissing values in C2. PLOT C1 C2 would plot the 48 pairs in which both values are nonmissing.

The command SORT (see p 304) involves ordering data. This command treats * as if it were the largest number in the column.

B.9 / SOME MISCELLANEOUS FEATURES

HOW TO ANNOTATE A PROGRAM

There are two ways to annotate a Minitab program: with the NOTE command and with the symbol #. If you type NOTE as the first word on a line, then everything after it is ignored by Minitab. You can type any words or symbols you wish. The symbol # may be typed anywhere on a line. All text after the # is ignored by Minitab. For example,

```
#Now we will analyze the data for men.
LET C4 = C1-MEAN(C1) #centered data
```

There is one difference between a NOTE command and a line beginning with #. In a stored command file, the NOECHO command (see p 312) tells Minitab not to print any commands except NOTE commands. Thus in this case, # lines are not printed, but the text following the word NOTE is printed.

SIZE OF INPUT AND OUTPUT

IW = K spaces

IW specifies the input width. The first K spaces on each line are read by Minitab. The rest of the line is ignored. The value of K can be from 10 to 160. The default value depends on the brand of computer, but is at least 80 on most computers.

OW = K spaces
OH = K lines

OW specifies the output width from the commands PRINT, TABLE, CORRELATION, AOVONEWAY, and ONEWAY. Output from all other commands is always 65 or fewer spaces. The value of K may be from 65 to 132 spaces. The default value of K is 79 (120 in batch mode).

OH specifies the output height, that is, the number of lines on a page or a screen. When you use Minitab interactively, Minitab prints a page of output, then asks CONTINUE? If you type YES or Y or push RETURN, the next page is printed. If you type NO or N, no more output from this command is printed. All storage, however, is done.

When you use Minitab in batch mode or put output into a file with the OUTFILE command, the output is divided into pages of K lines each. If you do not want Minitab to divide your output into pages, use OH = 0. The default value of K is 24 on most computers using terminals with screens. (It is 60 in batch mode or when output is to PAPER or a file.)

PUTTING OUTPUT IN A COMPUTER FILE

The OUTFILE command puts all Minitab output that follows into a computer file. You may then print the file or use your editor to edit it.

```
READ 'STUDY1' into C1-C4
LET C5 = C1/C2
PLOT C5 versus C3
OUTFILE 'REPORT'
PLOT C2 versus C1
DESCRIBE C1-C3
HISTOGRAM C1-C3
NOOUTFILE
ONEWAY C2 C4
OUTFILE 'REPORT'
ONEWAY C2 C4
```

Output from the first three commands is printed on your terminal. OUTFILE says to print the output from the next three commands on your terminal and also put it into the file REPORT. The next command, NOOUTFILE, tells Minitab to stop putting output into the file REPORT. Therefore the output from ONEWAY is printed only on the screen. Now suppose you decide you want the ONEWAY output added to REPORT. The last two commands do this.

Notice that, unlike the commands SAVE and WRITE, OUTFILE does not erase the previous contents of a file; it appends the new output to the old output.

B.10 / MATRIX CALCULATIONS

In addition to columns and stored constants, Minitab has matrices, denoted M1, M2, M3, and so forth. The total number of matrices available to you depends on your computer. In addition, columns can be used as column matrices.

There are two ways to enter data with a matrix. You can use READ, as in the following example:

```
READ  3 BY 4  MATRIX M3
    1    4  6  3
    2    8  1  8
   16   12 14 10
END
```

and you can COPY columns into a matrix as in the following example:

```
COPY C2-C4 into M2
```

C2	C3	C4			M2	
16	2	40		16	2	40
18	4	35	→	18	4	35
20	3	42		20	3	42

Commands to do matrix calculations are described in boxes. Here is a simple example using them.

```
COPY C1-C3 into M1
MULTIPLY M1 by C5 put in M2
TRANSPOSE C4 into M3
MULTIPLY M3 by M1 put in M4
MULTIPLY M3 by M2 put in K1
ADD 2 to M1 put in M5
```

C1	C2	C3	C4	C5	K1
1	4	2	10	5	334
1	0	3	12	0	
				4	

$$
M1 = \begin{bmatrix} 1 & 4 & 2 \\ 1 & 0 & 3 \end{bmatrix} \quad
M2 = \begin{bmatrix} 13 \\ 17 \end{bmatrix} \quad
M3 = \begin{bmatrix} 10 & 12 \end{bmatrix} \quad
M4 = \begin{bmatrix} 22 & 40 & 56 \end{bmatrix} \quad
M5 = \begin{bmatrix} 3 & 6 & 4 \\ 3 & 2 & 5 \end{bmatrix}
$$

READ into K by K matrix M

Data follow, one line for each row of the matrix.

PRINT M, ..., M

Prints out the matrices.

COPY C, ..., C into M
COPY M into C, ..., C

The first version of COPY forms a matrix M out of columns. The second version puts a matrix into columns.

ADD M to M put into M
SUBTRACT M from M put into M
MULTIPLY M by M put into M
TRANSPOSE M put into M
INVERT M put into M

These five commands do the usual matrix arithmetic calculations. You can also do scalar addition, subtraction, and multiplication with ADD, SUBTRACT, and MULTIPLY. For example:

```
ADD K to M put in M
SUBTRACT M from K put in M
MULTIPLY M by K put in M
```

You can use a column as a column matrix and a constant as a 1 by 1 matrix when doing matrix arithmetic. For example, suppose M1 is a 4 by 3 matrix, and C2 contains three numbers.

```
MULTIPLY M1 C2 put in M2
TRANSPOSE C2 into M3
MULTIPLY M3 by C2, put in K1
TRANSPOSE M1 into M4
MULTIPLY M4 by M2, put in C1
```

DIAGONAL is in C put into M
DIAGONAL of M put into C

In the first form of DIAGONAL, the matrix M will have the entries in C on its diagonal and zeros elsewhere. The second form puts the entries on the diagonal of M into the column C.

EIGEN for M, put values in C [vectors in M]

EIGEN calculates eigenvalues (also called characteristic values and latent roots) and eigenvectors for a symmetric matrix. The eigenvalues are stored in decreasing order of magnitude down the column. The eigenvectors are stored as columns of the matrix; the first column corresponds to the first eigenvalue (largest magnitude), the second column to the second eigenvalue, etc.

B.11/STORED COMMAND FILES AND SIMPLE LOOPS

You can store a block of Minitab commands in a computer file. Anytime you want to use this block, you type one command, EXECUTE. An instructor may store commands to do a complicated exercise; his students then would not have to type them. A researcher may have an analysis that she does each week, when she gets a new data set. If she stores the commands to do the analysis, she will not have to retype them each week.

As an example, we will use the commands in an exercise, which simulate fifty 90% confidence intervals.

```
STORE 'INTERVAL'
RANDOM 50 C1-C5;
   NORMAL 30 2.
RMEAN C1-C5 C10
LET K1 = 1.645*2/SQRT(5)
LET C21 = C10-K1
LET C22 = C10+K1
SET C23
   1:50
   END
MPLOT C21 C23, C22 C23
END
```

STORE says to put all the Minitab commands that follow into a computer file called INTERVAL. When you have typed all commands to be stored, then type END to tell Minitab you are finished typing stored commands. Now if sometime in the same session or in another session, you type

```
EXECUTE 'INTERVAL'
```

Minitab will execute the commands in the file. (If a command file is very long, this may take a few moments.) When Minitab is done, C1–C5, C21–C23, and K1 will contain the calculated results and an MPLOT will be printed.

You can EXECUTE a file several times just by specifying the number of times you wish to do so. For example,

```
EXECUTE 'INTERVAL' 3
```

would do the simulation three times, with different random data each time, and print three MPLOTS. C1–C5, C21–C23, and K1 would contain the calculations from the last simulation.

As another example of using EXECUTE to loop through a block of commands several times, we will calculate a moving average of length 2 for data in C1. Here are the commands.

```
STORE 'MOVEAVG'
NOECHO
LET C2(K1) = (C1(K1)+C1(K1+1))/2
LET K1 = K1+1
ECHO
END
LET K1 = 1
LET K2 = COUNT(C1)-1
EXECUTE 'MOVEAVG' K2
```

There are two new commands in the stored file: NOECHO says do not (echo) print the commands that follow, just do the calculations and print output. ECHO returns to the usual state, where commands in a STORE file are printed when the file is executed. Without NOECHO the two LET commands would be printed every time through the file. But we do not need to see them.

After EXECUTE, the worksheet is

C1	C2	K1	K2
4	3	6	5
2	2.5		
3	4.5		
6	5.5		
5	4.5		
4			

The calculations that we did are very simple, although the Minitab commands may at first look somewhat complicated. C1 contains the original data. C2 contains the moving average of C1. The first entry in C2 is the average of the first and second entries in C1, the second entry in C2 is the average of the second and third entries in C1, and so on. Notice that, since C1 contains six numbers, C2 contains $6 - 1 = 5$ numbers. Before we used EXECUTE, we set K1 = 1 and K2 = 5. We EXECUTED the file K2 = 5 times, once to calculate each value in C2. The first time K1 = 1, and we calculated

```
C2(1) = (C1(1)+C1(2))/2
```

and increased K1 to 2. The second time, we calculated

```
C2(2) = (C1(2)+C1(3))/2
```

and increased K1 to 3. This continued until we looped five times.

If you use STORE to create a command file and make a typing error, there is, unfortunately, no way to correct the file in Minitab. You must start over. Thus STORE is most useful for short command files, when you are not likely to make an error. If you want to store a long file, then it is best to create the file outside of Minitab, using your computer's editor. You also can create the file in Minitab using STORE, then leave Minitab and use your editor to make corrections.

A Minitab file of stored commands must have an appropriate extension to its file name. Exactly how this is done varies with computer brand. Usually the extension is MTB. If you use STORE, Minitab automatically adds the appropriate extension. If you use your computer's editor (or operating system) to list the names of your files, you will see what extension Minitab uses on your computer. If you create a file of Minitab commands with your editor, make sure the name of the file contains the appropriate extension.

LOOPING THROUGH COLUMNS

There is a little device, called the CK capability, that allows you to loop through columns. As a simple example, suppose we want to plot each of C1 through C25 against C30. This would require 25 separate PLOT commands. With the CK capability, we do the following:

```
STORE 'PLOTS'
PLOT CK1 C50
LET K1 = K1+1
END
LET K1 = 1
EXECUTE 'PLOTS' 25
```

The file PLOTS is EXECUTED 25 times, once to produce each plot. The first time, K1 = 1, so Minitab susbtitutes a 1 for the K1 in the PLOT command and does PLOT C1 C50. Then K1 is increased to 2. The second time through the file, Minitab substitutes a 2 for K1 and does PLOT C2 C50, and so on.

Anytime a column appears in a command, you may use CK1 (or CK2 or CK3, ...) for the column. When Minitab executes the command, it substitutes the correct value for K1.

NOECHO
ECHO

These commands are used mostly in a STORED file; NOECHO is the first command in the file, right after STORE, and ECHO is the last, just before END. When the file is EXECUTED, no commands are printed out, only output is printed. This is what you usually want.

There is one time when you may not want to use NOECHO. When you first create a file, especially one that is a little complicated, you should EXECUTE it to check for errors. Having the commands printed out will help you interpret any error messages. Once you are sure the commands in your file are correct, you can add NOECHO and ECHO to it.

B.12 / FORMATTED INPUT AND OUTPUT OF DATA

Minitab has five commands that allow FORTRAN formats: READ, SET, INSERT, PRINT, and WRITE. In this section we will give just a brief introduction to the use of formats. You may need to consult a FORTRAN manual for more details.

Minitab can use all format specifications except I (for integers). These include F (for real numbers), E (for numbers using exponential notation), A (for alphabetic data), X (to skip over numbers), and / (to go to the next line).

FORMATTED INPUT WITH READ, SET, AND INSERT

Suppose you have data that were typed without any blanks or commas between the numbers. READ by itself cannot enter these, but it can if you use a FORMAT subcommand. For example, suppose we have the data

$$231615.411821143 \quad 9$$
$$55431.8911941138128$$

and we want these numbers read into C1–C6 as follows:

C1	C2	C3	C4	C5	C6
231	61	5.4	1182	1143	9
554	31	.89	1194	1138	128

First we determine how wide each number is. In this case, the first number on each line uses three spaces, the second number uses two spaces, the third uses three spaces, the fourth and fifth both use four spaces, and the last uses three spaces. We use a FORMAT subcommand with READ as follows:

```
READ C1-C6;
   FORMAT (F3.0,F2.0,F3.0,2F4.0,F3.0).
```

This FORMAT describes one row of data. In F3.0, the 3 says that the number to be read uses three spaces; F2.0 says that the second number uses two spaces; and F3.0 says that the third number uses three spaces.

Notice that in this instance, one of the spaces holds the decimal point. The next two numbers both use four spaces. To save typing, we can write 2F4.0 instead of F4.0, F4.0.

The last F3.0 says the last number uses three spaces. Notice that the number on the first line, 9, is just one space wide. The remaining two spaces are blank. When the field a number uses is wider than the number, the number must be right justified; that is, all blanks must appear before the number.

You can skip over numbers with formats. For example, suppose we wanted the data read into the worksheet as follows:

C1	C2	C3	C4	C5	C6
231			1182		
554			1194		

We could use the command

```
READ C1 C4;
  FORMAT (F3.0,5X,F4.0).
```

The 5X says to skip over five spaces. Thus we read a number from the first three spaces, skip five spaces, then read a number from the next four spaces. The rest of the line is ignored since there are no more format specifications in the FORMAT subcommand.

Formats must be typed according to strict rules. You must use the parentheses and you must put a comma between format specifications.

You can enter several data lines into one row of the worksheet by using a slash. For example, suppose a file continues data for 200 people, three lines for each person. Here are the data for the first two people:

```
2431442012
1421431422
02011
0531340013
0531021421
11120
```

Suppose we want to enter these data into C1–C25, one digit per column. The following format does this:

```
READ C1-C25;
  FORMAT(10F1.0/10F1.0/5F1.0).
```

The first 10F1.0 reads ten numbers from the first line. The slash says go to the next line. The second 10F1.0 says to read ten numbers from this line. The second slash says to go to another new line. The 5F1.0 says to read five numbers from this line. This procedure is repeated for each person, always using three lines of data. Notice that FORMAT describes one row of the worksheet.

You also can use slashes to skip over data lines. For example, suppose we use the following format on the data for 200 people:

```
READ C1-C3;
  FORMAT (3F1.0//).
```

This would take three numbers from the first line for each person and skip over the other two lines.

FORMATTED OUTPUT WITH PRINT AND WRITE

Formats also can be used to output data. This is done if you want to control the spacing of the numbers or if you want to print the numbers to a different (usually larger) number of decimal places than Minitab would choose.

If you use FORMAT with PRINT you must use a carriage control (see a FORTRAN manual for a complete discussion of carriage controls) at the beginning of the format statement. The most common is 1X, which gives single-spaced output.

As an example, consider the data that we read into C1–C6 in the first example of this section. The command

```
PRINT C1-C6;
  FORMAT (1X,F5.0,F4.0,F5.2,2F6.0,F5.0).
```

would print out the data as follows:

```
231.  61.  5.40  1182.  1143.    9.
554.  31.  0.89  1194.  1138.  128.
```

The first specification, F5.0, describes the first five spaces: The 5 says to use five spaces, and the 0 says to print no digits after the decimal point. The decimal is printed, however. The number, 231., is then right justified in the field of five spaces. Similarly, the second number, 61., is right justified in a field of four spaces. The next specification, F5.2, says to use five spaces and put two digits after the decimal point.

You may use the X format to skip spaces on the printed page. For example,

```
PRINT C1-C6;
  FORMAT (1X,F5.0,F4.0,12X,F5.2,2F6.0,F5.0).
```

would print two numbers, then skip 12 spaces, then print the last four numbers.

You may use slashes to print one row of the worksheet on several lines of output. You must put a carriage control at the beginning of each line. For example,

```
PRINT C1-C6;
  FORMAT (1X,F5.0,F4.0,F5.2/1X,2F6.0,F5.0).
```

puts three numbers on the first line and three on the second.

C/A LIST OF MINITAB COMMANDS

This appendix summarizes all Minitab commands in Releases 5 through 7. Features that are in Release 6 but not in Release 5 are marked with an *. Release 7 features are marked with **. In Minitab, type HELP COMMANDS for full documentation.

Notation:

K denotes a constant such as 8.3 or K14

C denotes a column, such as C12 or 'Height'

E denotes either a constant or colum~

M denotes a matrix, such as M5

[] encloses an optional argument

Subcommands are shown indented under the main command.

1. General Information

```
HELP    explains Minitab commands, can be a
        command or a subcommand
INFO    [C...C] gives the status of worksheet
STOP    ends the current session
```

2. Input and Output of Data

```
READ    the following data      into C...C
READ    data [from 'filename'] into C...C
SET     the following data      into C
SET     data [from 'filename'] into C
INSERT  data [from 'filename'] between rows
        K and K of C...C
INSERT  data [from 'filename'] at the end
        of C...C
  READ, SET and INSERT have the
          subcommands:
    FORMAT (Fortran format)
    NOBS = K
END     of data (optional)
NAME    for C is 'name', for C is 'name'...
        for C is 'name'
PRINT   the data in E...E
```

```
WRITE     [to 'filename'] the data in C...C
   PRINT and WRITE have the subcommand:
      FORMAT (Fortran format)
SAVE      [in 'filename'] a copy of the
          worksheet
*     PORTABLE
RETRIEVE the Minitab saved worksheet [in
          'filename']
*     PORTABLE
```

3. Editing and Manipulating Data

```
LET       C(K) = K # changes the number in
          row K of C
DELETE    rows K...K of C...C
ERASE     E...E
INSERT    (see Section 2)
COPY      C...C into C...C
COPY      C into K...K
     USE  rows K...K
     USE  rows where C = K...K
     OMIT rows K...K
     OMIT rows where C = K...K
COPY      K...K into C
CODE      (K...K) to K ... (K...K) to K for
          C...C, store in C...C
STACK     (E...E) ... on (E...E), store in
          (C...C)
        SUBSCRIPTS into C
UNSTACK (C...C) into (E...E) ... (E...E)
        SUBSCRIPTS are in C
CONVERT using table in C C, the data in C,
        and store in C
*CONCATENATE C...C put in C
*ALPHA C...C
```

4. Arithmetic

```
LET = expression
```

Expressions may use arithmetic operators $+$ $-$ $*$ / $**$ (exponentiation),
**Comparison operators $=$ $\sim=$ $<$ $>$ $<=$ $>=$
**Logical operators   & | $\sim$
and any of the following: ABSOLUTE, SQRT, LOGTEN, LOGE, EXPO,

ANTILOG, ROUND, SIN, COS, TAN, ASIN, ACOS, ATAN, SIGNS,
NSCORE, PARSUMS, PARPRODUCTS, COUNT, N, NMISS, SUM,
MEAN, STDEV, MEDIAN, MIN, MAX, SSQ, SORT, RANK, LAG,
**EQ, NE, LT, GT, LE, GE, AND, OR, NOT.

Examples: `LET C2 = SQRT(C1 - MIN(C1))`
`LET C3(5) = 4.5`

Simple Arithmetic Operations

```
ADD        E to E ...     to E, put into E
SUBTRACT E from           E, put into E
MULTIPLY E by E ...    by E, put into E
DIVIDE     E by           E, put into E
RAISE      E to the power E, put into E
```

Columnwise Functions

```
ABSOLUTE value         of E, put into E
SQRT                   of E, put into E
LOGE                   of E, put into E
LOGTEN                 of E, put into E
EXPONENTIATE              E, put into E
ANTILOG                of E, put into E
ROUND to integer          E, put into E
SIN                    of E, put into E
COS                    of E, put into E
TAN                    of E, put into E
ASIN                   of E, put into E
ACOS                   of E, put into E
ATAN                   of E, put into E
SIGNS                  of E, put into E
PARSUMS                of C, put into C
PARPRODUCTS            of C, put into C
```

Normal Scores

```
NSCORES                of C, put into C
```

Columnwise Statistics

```
COUNT the number of values in        C [put into K]
N (number of nonmissing values in)   C [put into K]
NMISS (number of missing values in)  C [put into K]
SUM       of the values in           C [put into K]
MEAN      of the values in           C [put into K]
STDEV     of the values in           C [put into K]
```

```
MEDIAN    of the values in        C [put into K]
MINIMUM   of the values in        C [put into K]
MAXIMUM   of the values in        C [put into K]
SSQ (uncorrected sum of sq.) for  C [put into K]
```

Rowwise Statistics

```
RCOUNT              of E...E put into C
RN                  of E...E put into C
RNMISS              of E...E put into C
RSUM                of E...E put into C
RMEAN               of E...E put into C
RSTDEV              of E...E put into C
RMEDIAN             of E...E put into C
RMINIMUM            of E...E put into C
RMAXIMUM            of E...E put into C
RSSQ                of E...E put into C
```

Indicator Variables

```
INDICATOR variables for subscripts in C, put
          into C...C
```

5. Plotting Data

```
HISTOGRAM  C...C
DOTPLOT    C...C
   HISTOGRAM and DOTPLOT have the subcommands:
      INCREMENT = K
      START at K [end at K]
      BY C
      SAME scales for all columns
PLOT      C vs C
   SYMBOL = 'symbol'
MPLOT     C vs C, and C vs C, and ... C vs C
LPLOT     C vs C using tags in C
TPLOT     C vs C vs C
   PLOT, MPLOT, LPLOT and TPLOT have the
                     subcommands:
**      TITLE      = 'text'
**      FOOTNOTE   = 'text'
**      YLABEL     = 'text'
**    XLABEL      = 'text'
      YINCREMENT = K
```

```
       YSTART      at K [end at K]
       XINCREMENT = K
       XSTART      at K [end at K]
  TSPLOT [period K] of C
       ORIGIN = K
  MTSPLOT [period K] of C...C
       ORIGIN = K for C...C [... origin K for
                  C...C]
     TSPLOT and MTSPLOT have the subcommands:
       INCREMENT = K
       START at K [end at K]
       TSTART at K [end at K]
  GRID     C [K to K] C [K to K]
  CONTOUR C vs C and C
       BLANK bands between letters
       YSTART = K [up to K]
       YINCREMENT = K
  WIDTH  of all plots that follow is K spaces
  HEIGHT of all plots that follow is K lines
```

High Resolution Graphics

```
  GOPTIONS
     +DEVICE = 'device'
      HEIGHT = K inches
      WIDTH  = K inches
  GHISTOGRAM C...C
       INCREMENT = K
       START at K [end at K]
       BY C
       SAME scales for all columns
  GPLOT     C vs C
       SYMBOL = 'symbol'
  GMPLOT    C vs C, and C vs C, and ... C vs C
  GLPLOT    C vs C using tags in C
  GTPLOT    C vs C vs C
     GPLOT, GMPLOT, GLPLOT and GTPLOT have the
                            subcommands:
**     TITLE      = 'text'
**     FOOTNOTE   = 'text'
**     YLABEL     = 'text'
**     XLABEL     = 'text'
```

+   Not implemented in the microcomputer version

```
YINCREMENT = K
YSTART      at K [end at K]
XINCREMENT = K
XSTART      at K [end at K]
LINES [style K [color K]] connecting
      points in C C
COLOR C
```

All high resolution graphics commands have the subcommand:

```
FILE 'filename' to store graphics output
```


6. Basic Statistics

```
DESCRIBE C...C
    BY C
ZINTERVAL [K% confidence] assuming sigma = K
              for C...C
ZTEST [of mu = K] assuming sigma = K for
    C...C
    ALTERNATIVE = K
TINTERVAL [K% confidence] for data in C...C
TTEST [of mu = K] on data in C...C
    ALTERNATIVE = K
TWOSAMPLE test and c.i. [K% confidence]
         samples in C C
    ALTERNATIVE = K
    POOLED procedure
TWOT test and c.i. [K% confidence] data in
    C, groups in C
    ALTERNATIVE = K
    POOLED procedure
CORRELATION between C...C [put into M]
COVARIANCE  between C...C [put into M]
CENTER the data in C...C put into C...C
    LOCATION [subtracting K...K]
    SCALE    [dividing by K...K]
    MINMAX   [with K as min and K as max]
```


7. Regression

```
REGRESS C on K predictors C...C [store st.
       resids in C [fits in C]]
    NOCONSTANT    in equation
```

```
      WEIGHTS            are in C
      MSE                put into K
      COEFFICIENTS       put into C
      XPXINV             put into M
      RMATRIX            put into M
      HI                 put into C (leverage)
      RESIDUALS          put into C (observed –
                         fit)
      TRESIDUALS         put into C (deleted
                         studentized)
      COOKD              put into C (Cook's
                         distance)
      DFITS              put into C
      PREDICT            for E...E
      VIF                (variance inflation
                         factors)
      DW                 (Durbin-Watson statistic)
      PURE               (pure error lack-of-fit
                         test)
      XLOF               (experimental lack-of-fit
                         test)
      TOLERANCE          K [K]
STEPWISE regression of C on the predictors
         C...C
      FENTER             = K (default is four)
      FREMOVE            = K (default is four)
      FORCE              C...C
      ENTER              C...C
      REMOVE             C...C
      BEST               K alternative predictors
                           (default is zero)
      STEPS              = K (default depends on
                             output width)
*BREG C on predictors C...C
    INCLUDE predictors C...C
    BEST K models
    NVARS K [K]
    NOCONSTANT in equation
NOCONSTANT in REGRESS, STEPWISE and BREG
          commands that follow
  CONSTANT    fit a constant in REGRESS,
              STEPWISE and BREG
  BRIEF       K
```

8. Analysis of Variance

```
AOVONEWAY aov for samples in C...C
ONEWAY     aov, data in C, subscripts in C
           [store resids in C [fits in C]]
TWOWAY     aov, data in C, subscripts in C C
           [store resids in C [fits in C]]
       ADDITIVE model
*      MEANS for the factors C [C]
*ANOVA model
       RANDOM      factorlist
       EMS
       FITS        put into C...C
       RESIDUALS put into C...C
       MEANS       for termlist
       TEST        for termlist/errorterm
       RESTRICT
*ANCOVA model
       COVARIATES are in C...C
       FITS        put into C...C
       RESIDUALS put into C...C
       MEANS       for termlist
       TEST        for termlist/errorterm
**GLM model
       COVARIATES   are in C...C
       WEIGHTS      are in C
       FITS         put into C...C
       RESIDUALS    put into C...C
       SRESIDS      put into C...C
       TRESIDS      put into C...C
       HI           put into C
       COOKD        put into C...C
       DFITS        put into C...C
       XMATRIX      put into M
       COEFFICIENTS put into C...C
       MEANS        for termlist
       TEST         for termlist/errorterm
       BRIEF        K
       TOLERANCE    K [K]
```

9. Multivariate Analysis

```
*PCA principal component analysis of C...C
     COVARIANCE matrix
     NCOMP      = K (number of components)
     COEF       put into C...C
     SCORES     put into C...C
*DISCRIMINANT groups in C, predictors in
                 C...C
     QUADRATIC discrimination
     PRIORS     are in K...K
     LDF        coef put in C...C
     FITS       put in C [C]
     XVAL       cross-validation
     PREDICT    for E...E
     BRIEF      K
```

10. Nonparametrics

```
RUNS   test [above and below K] for C
STEST  sign test [median = K] for C...C
     ALTERNATIVE = K
SINTERVAL sign c.i. [K% confidence] for
          C...C
WTEST  Wilcoxon one-sample rank test
          [median = K] for C...C
     ALTERNATIVE = K
WINTERVAL Wilcoxon c.i. [K% confidence] for
          C...C
MANN-WHITNEY test and c.i. [K% confidence]
          on C C
**     ALTERNATIVE = K
  KRUSKAL-WALLIS test for data in C,
          subscripts in C
**MOOD median test, data in C, subscripts in C
          [put res. in C [fits in C]]
**FRIEDMAN data in C, treatment in C, blocks
          in C [put res. in C [fits in C]]
  WALSH averages for C, put into C [indices
          into C C]
 *WDIFF for C and C, put into C [indices into
          C C]
 *WSLOPE y in C, x in C, put into C [indices
          into C C]
```

11. Tables

```
TALLY the data in C...C
     COUNTS
     PERCENTS
     CUMCOUNTS    cumulative counts
     CUMPERCENTS  cumulative percents
     ALL          four statistics above
CHISQUARE test on table stored in C...C
TABLE the data classified by C...C
     MEANS        for C...C
     MEDIANS      for C...C
     SUMS         for C...C
     MINIMUMS     for C...C
     MAXIMUMS     for C...C
     STDEV        for C...C
     STATS        for C...C
     DATA         for C...C
     N            for C...C
     NMISS        for C...C
     PROPORTION of cases = K [through K] in
                 C...C
     COUNTS
     ROWPERCENTS
     COLPERCENTS
     TOTPERCENTS
     CHISQUARE analysis [output code = K]
     MISSING level for classification
             variable C...C
     NOALL in margins
     ALL for C...C
     FREQUENCIES are in C
     LAYOUT K rows by K columns
```

12. Time Series

```
ACF    [with up to K lags] for series in C
       [put into C]
PACF   [with up to K lags] for series in C
       [put into C]
CCF    [with up to K lags] between series in
       C and C
```

```
DIFFERENCES [of lag K] for data in C, put
     into C
LAG [by K] for data in C, put into C
ARIMA p = K, d = K, q = K, data in C [put
     resids in C [preds in C [coefs in C]]]
ARIMA p = K, d = K, q = K, P = K, D = K,
     Q = K, S = K, data in C [put resids
     in C [preds in C [coefs in C]]]
     CONSTANT    term in model
     NOCONSTANT  term in model
     STARTING    values are in C
     FORECAST    [origin = K] up to K leads
                 [put in C [limits in C C]]
```

**13. Statistical Process Control

**High resolution commands begin with the letter G.

```
**XBARCHART   for C...C, subgroups are in E
**GXBARCHART for C...C, subgroups are in E
     MU = K
     SIGMA = K
     RSPAN = K
     TEST K...K
     SUBGROUP size is E
     See additional subcommands listed below
**RCHART   for C...C, subgroups are in E
**GRCHART for C...C, subgroups are in E
     SIGMA = K
     SUBGROUP size is E
     See additional subcommands listed below
**SCHART   for C...C, subgroups are in E
**GSCHART for C...C, subgroups are in E
     SIGMA = K
     SUBGROUP size is E
     See additional subcommands listed below
**ICHART   for C...C
**GICHART for C...C
     MU = K
     SIGMA = K
     RSPAN = K
     TEST K...K
     See additional subcommands listed below
```

```
**MACHART  for C...C, subgroups are in E
**GMACHART for C...C, subgroups are in E
      MU = K
      SIGMA = K
      SPAN = K
      RSPAN = K
      SUBGROUP size is E
      See additional subcommands listed below
**EWMACHART  for C...C, subgroups are in E
**GEWMACHART for C...C, subgroups are in E
      MU = K
      SIGMA = K
      WEIGHT = K
      RSPAN = K
      SUBGROUP size is E
      See additional subcommands listed below
**MRCHART  for C...C
**GMRCHART for C...C
      SIGMA = K
      RSPAN = K
      See additional subcommands listed below
**PCHART  number of nonconformities are in
          C...C, sample size = E
**GPCHART number of nonconformities are in
          C...C, sample size = E
      P = K
      TEST K...K
      SUBGROUP size is E
      See additional subcommands listed below
**NPCHART  number of nonconformities are in
          C...C, sample size = E
**GNPCHART number of nonconformities are in
          C...C, sample size = E
      P = K
      TEST K...K
      SUBGROUP size is E
      See additional subcommands listed below
**CCHART  number of nonconformities are in
          C...C
**GCCHART number of nonconformities are in
          C...C
      MU = K
      TEST K...K
      See additional subcommands listed below
```

```
**UCHART   number of nonconformities are in
          C...C, sample size = E
**GUCHART number of nonconformities are in
          C...C, sample size = E
       MU = K
       TEST K...K
       SUBGROUP size is E
       See additional subcommands listed below
```
**All statistical process control charts have the subcommands:
```
       SLIMITS are K...K
       HLINES at E...E
       ESTIMATE using just samples K...K
       TITLE = 'text'
       FOOTNOTE = 'text'
       YLABEL = 'text'
       XLABEL = 'text'
       YINCREMENT = K
       YSTART at K [end at K]
       XSTART at K [end at K]
```
**All high resolution charts have the subcommand:
```
       FILE 'filename'
```

14. Exploratory Data Analysis

```
STEM-AND-LEAF display of C...C
     TRIM outliers
     INCREMENT = K
     BY C
BOXPLOT  for C
GBOXPLOT for C (high resolution version)
   BOXPLOT and GBOXPLOT have the subcommands:
     INCREMENT = K
     START at K [end at K]
     BY C
     LINES = K
     NOTCH [K% confidence] sign c.i.
     LEVELS K...K
     FILE 'filename' to store GBOXPLOT output
LVALS of C [put lvals in C
       [mids in C [spreads in C]]]
MPOLISH C, levels in C C [put residuals in C
       [fits in C]]
       COLUMNS    (start iteration with column
                   medians)
```

```
      ITERATIONS = K
      EFFECTS  put common into K, rows into C,
               cols into C
      COMPARISON values, put into C
 RLINE y in C, x in C [put resids in C [fits
       in C [coefs in C]]]
      MAXITER = K (max. number of iterations)
 RSMOOTH C, put rough into C, smooth into C
      SMOOTH by 3RSSH, twice
 CPLOT (condensed plot) C vs C
      LINES = K
      CHARACTERS = K
      XBOUNDS = from K to K
      YBOUNDS = from K to K
 CTABLE (coded table) data in C, row C,
        column C
      MAXIMUM value in each cell should be
              coded
      MINIMUM value in each cell should be
              coded
 ROOTOGRAM data in C [use bin boundaries in C]
      BOUNDARIES store them in C
      DRRS store them in C
      FITTED values store them in C
      COUNTS store them in C
      FREQUENCIES are in C [bin boundaries are
                 in C]
      MEAN = K
      STDEV = K
```

15. Distributions and Random Data

```
 RANDOM K observations into C...C
      BERNOULLI trials p = K
 PDF     for values in E [store results in E]
 CDF     for values in E [store results in E]
 INVCDF for values in E [store results in E]
    RANDOM, PDF, CDF, INVCDF have the
    subcommands:
    BINOMIAL  n = K, p = K
    POISSON   mu = K
    INTEGER   discrete uniform on integers K
              to K
```

```
         DISCRETE   dist. with values in C and
                    probabilities in C
         NORMAL     [mu = K [sigma = K]]
         UNIFORM    [continuous on the interval K
                    to K]
         T          degrees of freedom = K
         F          df numerator = K,
                    df denominator = K
         Additional subcommands are BETA, CAUCHY,
         LAPLACE, LOGISTIC, LOGNORMAL, CHISQUARE,
         EXPONENTIAL, GAMMA, WEIBULL
      SAMPLE  K rows from C...C put into C...C
 **      REPLACE (sample with replacement)
      BASE     for random number generator = K
```

16. Sorting

```
      SORT   C [carry along C...C] put into C [and
          C...C]
 **      BY C...C
 **      DESCENDING C...C
      RANK   the values in C, put ranks into C
```

17. Matrices

```
      READ     [from 'filename'] into a K by K
             matrix M
      PRINT        M...M
      TRANSPOSE M into M
      INVERT       M into M
      DEFINE       K into K by K matrix M
      DIAGONAL  is C, form into M
      DIAGONAL  of M, put into C
      COPY         C...C into M
      COPY         M into C...C
      COPY         M into M
         USE     rows K...K
         OMIT    rows K...K
      EIGEN       for M put values into C [vectors
                  into M]
```

In the following commands E can be either C, K or M

```
      ADD         E to E,    put into E
      SUBTRACT  E from E,  put into E
      MULTIPLY  E by E,    put into E
```

18. Miscellaneous

```
ERASE      E...E
OUTFILE    'filename' put all output in file
    OW     = K output width of file
    OH     = K output height of file
    NOTERM no output to terminal
NOOUTFILE  output to terminal only
PAPER      output to printer
    OW     = K output width of printer
    OH     = K output height of printer
    NOTERM no output to terminal
NOPAPER    output to terminal only
JOURNAL    ['filename'] record Minitab
           commands in this file
NOJOURNAL  cancels JOURNAL
NOTE       comments may be put here
NEWPAGE    start next output on a new page
UC         use only upper case letters on
           output
LC         use mixed case letters on output
OW         = K number of spaces for width of
           output
OH         = K number of lines for height of
           one page (or screen) of output
IW         = K number of spaces for width of
           input
BRIEF      = K controls amount of output from
           REGRESS, GLM, DISCRIM, ARIMA,
           RLINE
RESTART    begin fresh Minitab session
SYSTEM     provides access to operating
           system commands
TSHARE     interactive or timesharing mode
BATCH      batch mode
```

19. Stored Commands and Loops

The commands STORE and EXECUTE provide the capability for simple macros (stored command files) and loops.

```
EXECUTE  'filename' [K times]
STORE    [in 'filename'] the following
         commands (Minitab commands go here)
END      of storing commands
```

```
 NOECHO   the commands that follow
  ECHO    the commands that follow
**YESNO   K
```

The CK capability. The integer part of a column number may be replaced by a stored constant.

Example: `LET K1 = 5`
            `PRINT C1 - CK1`

Since K1 = 5, this PRINTS C1 through C5.

20. Symbols

* Missing Value Symbol. An * can be used as data in READ, SET and INSERT and in data files. Enclose the * in single quotes in commands and subcommands.

   Example: `CODE (-99) to '*' in C1, put into C3`
   Example: `COPY C6 INTO C7;`
               `OMIT C6 = '*'.`

\# Comment Symbol. The symbol # anywhere on a line tells Minitab to ignore the rest of the line.

& Continuation Symbol. To continue a command onto another line, end the first line with the symbol &. You can use + + as a synonym for &.

21. Worksheet and Commands

Minitab consists of a worksheet for data and over 200 commands. The worksheet contains columns of data denoted by C1, C2, C3 . . . , stored constants denoted by K1, K2, K3 . . . , and matrices denoted by M1, M2, M3, ...

A column may be given a name with the command NAME (Section 2). A name may be up to eight characters long, with any characters except apostrophes and #. Names may be used in place of column numbers. When a name is used, it must be enclosed in apostrophes (single quotes).

Example: `PLOT 'INCOME' vs 'AGE'`

Each command starts with a command word and is usually followed by a list of arguments. An argument is a number, a column, a stored constant, a matrix or a file name. Only the command word and arguments are needed. All other text is for the readers' information.

22. Subcommands

Some Minitab commands have subcommands. To use a subcommand, put a semicolon at the end of the main command line. Then type the subcommands. Start each on a new line, then end it with a semicolon. When you are done, end the last subcommand with a period.

The subcommand ABORT cancels the whole command.

APPENDIX D
Changes in Release 6 and Release 7

Most of the major changes in Release 6 and Release 7 are additions of capabilities beyond the scope of this *Handbook*. For a more comprehensive description of new Minitab features, mini/mainframe users can type NEWS at the MTB > prompt. PC users can PRINT or TYPE the README file which is included with the Minitab package.

The new commands (all listed in Appendix C) for Release 6 are ANOVA/ANCOVA (general balanced analysis of variance and analysis of covariance), DISCRIM (linear and quadratic discriminant analysis), PCA (principal component analysis), BREG (best subset of variables for regression), WDIFF and WSLOPES (for computing certain robust estimates) and several commands for dealing with alphanumeric data. High resolution graphics were in some versions of Release 5 and in more versions of Release 6 (including the standard PC version); these commands have been added to Appendix C. Subcommands have been added to TWOWAY, SAVE, RETRIEVE, and the high resolution graphics commands. All commands listed in Appendix C of previous printings continue to work.

Many Release 6 commands have changes in output format (such as number of decimal digits printed for numbers), changes in spacing, and changes from all upper case to mixed upper and lower case for text. These should not cause any difficulties for users. Other changes that may affect users are listed below by chapter.

Additional capabilities in Release 7 (also listed in Appendix C) include the GLM command to fit the general linear model (analysis of variance and of covariance for unbalanced designs), eleven commands to produce statistical process control charts, and two new nonparametric commands, MOOD (performs the mood median test) and FRIEDMAN. Release 7 also allows the use of comparison operators (EQ, NE, LT, GT, LE, GE) and logical operators (AND, OR, NOT) in the LET command. The new subcommands TITLE, FOOTNOTE, YLABEL, and XLABEL are used with graphics commands to label plots. The SORT command has two new subcommands BY (allows sorting by multiple columns) and DESCENDING (allows sorting columns in descending order). In addition, the YESNO command allows interruption of a macro to input a YES or NO value. Release 7 also improves Minitab's alpha data handling capabilities. Other changes that may affect users are listed below by chapter.

Chapter 1.

In Release 7, the INFO command identifies alpha data columns.

Chapter 6.

In Release 7, the SAMPLE command has a subcommand REPLACE which allows sampling with replacement.

Chapter 9.

In Release 6, the AOVONEWAY and ONEWAY commands print the p-value (significance level) for the F-test.

TWOWAY has a new subcommand, MEANS, which prints marginal means and individual 95% confidence intervals for the factors.

A three factor model (as in Exercise 9-11, p. 214) can be fit with the new ANOVA command. See HELP ANOVA for details.

Chapter 10.

In Release 6, the output from the REGRESS command now contains, for each coefficient, the p-value for the test whether the true coefficient is zero. This is computed from the t for each coefficient, as explained on pages 232 and 239. In addition, the F-statistic for overall significance of regression is printed in the analysis of variance table, along with the associated p-value.

In Release 7, BRIEF 3 controls the amount of output for the GLM command and also prints the p-value for unequal spreads in the MOOD command output.

Chapter 12.

In Release 6, the SINTERVAL output now contains an additional line. In addition to the intervals with confidence levels below and above, there is a "middle" line with (approximately) the desired confidence. This is found using a "nonlinear interpolation" procedure, abbreviated NLI, developed by Thomas P. Hettmansperger and Simon J. Sheather (Confidence Intervals Based on Interpolated Order Statistics, Statistics and Probability Letters, Volume 4, Number 2, 1986, pp. 75–79). The NLI procedure is complicated, and explaining how to calculate it is beyond the scope of this *Handbook,* but it can be used easily. More assumptions are needed than for the other two lines, it is nearly exact if the distribution being sampled from is symmetric.

The example shown in Exhibit 12.4 was redone using Release 6, with the results shown below.

```
MTB > SINT 'SALES'
SIGN CONFIDENCE INTERVAL FOR MEDIAN
```

```
                                 ACHIEVED
              N   N*   MEDIAN  CONFIDENCE   CONFIDENCE    INTERVAL   POSITION
SALES    29   1    144.0     0.9386     (    110.0;      210.0)         10
                                        0.9500     (    108.5;      211.7)        NLI
                                        0.9759     (    101.0;      220.0)          9
```

In Release 7, the MANN-WHITNEY command has a subcommand ALTERNATIVE (similar to STEST and WTEST) and the test statistic adjusted for ties is also output.

REFERENCES

CHAPTER 9

Crenshaw, T. E., "The Evaluation of Investment Performance." *The Journal of Business* 50(4):462–485, 1977.

CHAPTER 11

Four books on regression are:

Belsley, D. E., Kuh, E., and Welsch, R. E. *Regression Diagnostics: Identifying Influential Data and Sources of Collinearity.* New York: Wiley, 1980.

Draper, N. R., and Smith, H. *Applied Regression Analysis.* 2nd ed. New York: Wiley, 1981.

Miller, R. B., and Wichern, D. W. *Intermediate Business Statistics: Analysis of Variance, Regression, and Time Series.* New York: Holt, Rinehart, and Winston, 1977.

Weisberg, S. *Applied Linear Regression.* New York: John Wiley and Sons, 1985.

CHAPTER 12

Three good references on time series analysis are:

Abraham, B., and Ledolter, J. *Statistical Methods for Forecasting,* New York: Wiley, 1983.

Cryer, J. D. *Time Series Analysis.* Boston: Duxbury Press, 1986.

Granger, C. W. J., and Newbold, P. *Forecasting Economic Time Series.* New York: Academic Press, 1987.

INDEX